Horse Racing the Chicago Way

Sports and Entertainment

For a full list of titles in this series,
visit https://press.syr.edu/supressbook-series
/sports-and-entertainment/.

Horse Racing
the
Chicago Way

Gambling, Politics, and Organized Crime, 1837–1911

Steven A. Riess

SYRACUSE UNIVERSITY PRESS

First Edition 2022

22 23 24 25 26 27   6 5 4 3 2 1

∞ The paper used in this publication meets the minimum requirements
of the American National Standard for Information Sciences—Permanence
of Paper for Printed Library Materials, ANSI Z39.48-1992.

For a listing of books published and distributed by Syracuse University Press,
visit https://press.syr.edu.

ISBN: 978-0-8156-3741-7 (hardcover)
       978-0-8156-3727-1 (paperback)
       978-0-8156-5528-2 (e-book)

Library of Congress Cataloging-in-Publication Data
Names: Riess, Steven A., author.
Title: Horse racing the Chicago way : gambling, politics, and organized crime,
    1837–1911 / Steven A. Riess.
Description: First edition. | Syracuse, New York : Syracuse University Press, 2022. |
    Series: Sports and entertainment | Includes bibliographical references and index. |
    Summary: ""Horse Racing the Chicago Way" contextualizes the history of horse
    racing in Chicago, analyzing the role of political influence and class in the rise and fall
    of thoroughbred racing; the business of racing; the cultural and social significance
    of racing; and the impact widespread opposition to gambling in Illinois had on the
    sport. It also examines the nexus that existed between horse racing, politics,
    and syndicate crime"— Provided by publisher.
Identifiers: LCCN 2021011011 (print) | LCCN 2021011012 (ebook) |
    ISBN 9780815637417 (hardcover) | ISBN 9780815637271 (paperback) |
    ISBN 9780815655282 (ebook)
Subjects: LCSH: Horse racing—Illinois—Chicago—History—19th century. |
    Horse racing—Illinois—Chicago—History—20th century. | Horse racing—
    Social aspects—Illinois—Chicago. | Horse racing—Betting—Illinois—Chicago.
Classification: LCC SF335.U6 I37 2022 (print) | LCC SF335.U6 (ebook) |
    DDC 798.4009773/11—dc23
LC record available at https://lccn.loc.gov/2021011011
LC ebook record available at https://lccn.loc.gov/2021011012

Manufactured in the United States of America

I am pleased to dedicate this book to my youngest grandchildren, six and under: Emily, Jordyn, and Carly Bright as well as Lucas and Henry Broton. I can't wait to see them flicking through the pages.

Contents

Illustrations

Tables

Preface

Scholars and other serious writers have been examining in depth the history of American sports for nearly fifty years, but they have given the turf sport history limited attention, rarely recognizing its historic significance as a social institution, a source of recreation, a legal business, and often an illicit commercial enterprise. In 1971 crime historian Mark Haller called for social historians to examine the social history of racing and gambling, but few have heeded his call. Recently, scholars have become aware of the importance of the turf industry in American history, reflected by books about southern racing and racing at Saratoga Park, metropolitan New York, and Churchill Downs that analyze the sport's connection to politics, gambling, and crime; the cultural significance of racing; and its involvement with slavery and racism.[1]

The absence of extensive attention to gambling's history is surprising, since the United States was built in large part by "people of chance." Voluntary newcomers, going back to the early colonists, and then followed by later immigrants willing to gamble on their futures, left loved ones behind and traveled thousands of miles on hazardous ocean voyages in hopes of a better life. Their descendants and subsequent newcomers often continued westward in risky journeys to better themselves. People who avoided perilous resettlement, dangerous choices in their private lives, or hazardous decisions in their work might still become gamblers to add some excitement to their humdrum lives. On the other hand, people who were not risk aversive in their jobs or personal behavior might still enjoy perilous amusements that reflected their lifestyles, like colonial plantation owners who raced and bet on horse racing, the first organized sport in America. Such men also enjoyed other forms of wagering when they played card games at friends' homes, competed in board games at taverns, or bought lottery tickets. Many founding fathers attended thoroughbred races and bet on the outcomes. When the Republic was established, the states and the national government enacted laws against thoroughbred racing, less because of religious opposition to gambling but mainly because the sport's aristocratic nature seemed out of character for a democratic nation. Nonetheless, by the antebellum era, thoroughbred races and trotting contests were widely attended to test the breed, usually accompanied by on-course betting among spectators.[2]

This book examines equine sports in Chicago, the United States' "shock city," with an emphasis on the relationship between the turf, politics, gambling, and organized crime. Chicago in just sixty years grew from a speck on the edges of the frontier to become the second-largest city in the nation, undergoing astonishing, troubling, and marvelous changes in economic, cultural, and social life. Chicago's earliest male settlers were people of chance who migrated into a desolate but promising location. They were people of modest origins who arrived from the East, intending to survive by the sweat of their brows or taking a risk as entrepreneurs. A small minority of Chicagoans, blessed with capital, intelligence, astute judgment, pluck, luck, and the good fortune to get in on the ground floor, became small businessmen, and maybe even bankers, merchants, manufacturers, or property owners. A few men were enriched in the bloody Civil War (1861–65), supplying the Union army with war matériel, like food, clothing, and armaments. But then came the devastating Great Fire of 1871, a debacle that should have been enough to wear down even the most optimistic Chicagoan, but men of vision, undeterred by their apparent bad luck, stayed in town to rebuild the city. These risk takers took advantage of opportunities in real estate, banking, commerce, and industry to help create a great city. Unfortunately, such opportunities were beyond the reach of most Chicagoans. By 1900 Chicago had 1,698,575 residents, but few of them could afford a middle-class home that cost $3,500. The vast majority of people were blue-collar workers with no expectations of advancement. In the Packingtown slum, for example, more than 90 percent of heads of households were blue-collar employees. Thousands of Chicagoans turned to gambling on horse racing as a means to demonstrate their manliness, prove their skill as handicappers, and maybe make a lot of money very fast. Chicago by the 1880s and 1890s was the nation's second-leading thoroughbred racing center and second-leading locus of illegal offtrack gambling, surpassed in both categories by only Greater New York.[3]

My analysis of horse racing in Chicago begins in the early 1830s, when a young bachelor subculture dominated a social life that included gambling on equestrian events. The finest racing steeds were "blooded" horses, or thoroughbreds, either Arabians or descendants of Arabians mixed with English horses. They were renowned for their speed, agility, and high-strung natures. Thoroughbreds were expensive and not very practical, useful only for racing, fox hunting, and breeding. Most Chicago horses were the more democratic, more useful, and less expensive trotting horse, mainly employed to pull two- or four-wheeled wagons to transport people and ship freight. They were also used for the middle-class sport of harness racing that dominated road racing and racing at several modest local courses. Their ascendency continued until the early 1880s, when Chicago's extremely wealthy men got into the more prestigious sport of thoroughbred racing. They joined the elite new Washington Park Club, formed in 1883 to promote sociability, social status, and a place to gamble. The WPC opened the Washington Park Racetrack (WPR) one year later, a not-for-profit elite facility that almost immediately became one of the most prestigious racecourses in the United States. The state legislature in 1887 passed a law that legalized gambling only on racecourses. The access to legal gambling helped thoroughbred racing become Chicago's most popular spectator sport. Opportunities to attend races were enhanced by the establishment of several proprietary racecourses, owned by middle-class men with considerable political connections, intent on making money. The boom in thoroughbred racing pretty much killed off harness racing.[4]

By the end of the century, Chicago was the second-leading American city in thoroughbred racing behind only New York. It was also second to New York in the valuable offtrack gambling business. This illegal enterprise was controlled in Chicago by a criminal syndicate formed in the 1870s by politician and gambler Mike McDonald, whose organization used its political influence to secure speedy information on races and protect their poolrooms and handbooks from interlopers and police interference.

I argue that the gambling on racing events, and the risks that it entailed, was essential for racing's success because without betting, there would be no spectators, and without spectators paying admission fees and gambling, racecourses could not make money, or at least break even. People would quickly find it very boring to watch horses run around an oval unless there was money involved. But when a few dollars are on the line, the sport becomes exciting and a lot of fun. Thoroughbred racing outdrew baseball, the "national pastime," even though the city's White Stockings were one of the top teams in the National League, with six pennants, including five between 1880 and 1886.

My second main point is that the sport needed financial support to succeed. Thoroughbred racing was known even then as "the sport of kings." The Washington Park Club was organized as a nonprofit organization, but it did not want to lose money. It required a lot of money to build a first-class racecourse with a luxurious club, maintain the facility, and offer valuable purses to attract the finest American stables. The city's other tracks were proprietary enterprises, set up with the intention of making money. Their facilities were more modest, their horses less esteemed, but they provided the gambling to bring in the crowds.

My third point is that the track managers needed political connections to survive and thrive. Thoroughbred racing in Illinois did not have any legal standing in 1884. The sport needed clout to get the sport legalized, which it did in 1887, and keep it legalized. The owners of Washington Park were not politically powerful, though some of the owners of proprietary tracks had considerable political clout to help protect their investment and compete with competitors. Chicago track owners did not work well together to promote their mutual interests and were far less powerful than their counterparts in New

York City, whose owners included leaders in the powerful Tammany Hall political machine. The New York racing crowd was just as effective as Chicagoans in getting the sport legalized, but far more successful in sustaining their sport's legitimacy.

Despite racing's huge fandom, it struggled to survive because of the very gambling that made it popular. Unlike in Europe and the rest of the world, horse racing got banned nearly everywhere in the United States. I argue this prohibition resulted from the strong opposition to gambling among white Anglo-Saxon evangelical Protestants (WASPs) for moral reasons and by urban social reformers who believed that gambling on racing harmed families, increased criminality, and corrupted public officials. In the United States, unlike most countries, the lawfulness of gambling was not a national issue, but a state matter. Racing's opponents in Illinois employed their influence with gerrymandered state legislatures and with friendly judges to fight the sport tooth and nail and succeeded in 1905 in banning pari-mutuel racing and closing the racecourses. Thoroughbred racing was soon shuttered in nearly every state.

Yet despite the success of reformers in closing tracks, they had limited success in halting offtrack gambling. Offtrack gambling (except among friends) was banned everywhere. However, this "victimless crime" thrived in Chicago and other metropolises. Clients enjoyed the opportunity to test their expertise with poolroom operators organized into gambling syndicates or with neighborhood handbooks that were also connected to the underworld. The illegal enterprise was protected by the political clout of Mike McDonald and his associates who ran poolrooms for the convenience of their downtown clients, employed handbook operators for their neighborhood customers, secured the necessary racing news for their clients from the racing wire, and were heavily involved in local politics, which provided them with protection against reformers, competitors, and government interference. The business flourished in Chicago, even after the end of local racing.

This book is a follow-up to my previous analysis of thoroughbred racing in New York, the national capital of racing. *The Sport of Kings and the Kings of Crime: Horse Racing, Politics, and Organized Crime in*

New York, 1865–1913 demonstrates how and why New York became the national center of horse racing after the Civil War, when the state barred on-track betting. Horse racing thrived in New York City and Saratoga Springs after the Civil War because of the sponsorship of elite New Yorkers who raced and bred horses and established prestigious jockey clubs to "promote the breed," facilitate gambling, and certify or enhance their social status. Racing became so popular in the metropolitan area that in the 1880s, entrepreneurs in the adjacent city of Brooklyn established proprietary tracks to attract a broader audience, including the less well-to-do, drawn by the thrill of the betting, the excitement of the races, and the rituals of the sport.[5]

Horse Racing the Chicago Way: Gambling, Politics, and Organized Crime, 1837–1911 consists of seven substantive chapters and a conclusion. The first chapter examines the rise in Chicago of middle-class harness racing, the origins of local thoroughbred racing, and the emergence of the underworld in racing. The second and fourth chapters describe the rise and fall of the elite Washington Park Racetrack, the most important track west of New York in the late nineteenth century. The third chapter explores the development of the major proprietary racetracks in the early 1890s, focusing on the importance of owners' political connections in facilitating success, with an in-depth study of the huge profits generated by the gambler-owned Garfield Park racetrack. The fifth chapter examines the years following the panic of 1893, when Chicago's tracks were temporarily closed after the courts ruled that on-track gambling was illegal. The tracks resumed operations in 1897 and 1898, bolstered by the success of racing in nearby Joliet and the election of Mayor Carter Harrison II, who opposed the imposition of social control over his constituents.

Next, the book examines the brief golden age of Chicago racing at the turn of the twentieth century, when Washington Park regained its stature as one of the outstanding upper-class American recreational sites. However, the glory days were short-lived. Chapter 6 analyzes the demise of Chicago racing, which reflected the strong national opposition to the sport and its gambling. I attribute the fall of the WPR to the long-standing opposition of religious and progressive reformers and the reversal by Mayor Carter Harrison II, once one of racing's biggest supporters. He surprisingly became a foe of racing to enhance his aspirations for higher office. This about-face led one year later to the state's attorney forcing the closure of Chicagoland's three other tracks. Chapter 7 examines the huge boom in offtrack betting in the early 1900s when a handful of syndicates controlled the illegal enterprise, secured by their access to cash, racing news, political protection, and violence. The rival organizations were united by Jacob "Mont" Tennes, who used the power of persuasion, political clout, strong-arm tactics, and his takeover of the national racing wire to control Chicago poolrooms and handbook operators. Ultimately, Tennes used the wire to control the distribution of racing news throughout the United States. This chapter is followed by a conclusion that emphasizes the importance of politics in the operation of horse-racing tracks and illegal offtrack gambling.

Acknowledgments

I have several institutions and people to thank for their assistance in completing this book. I first have to thank the National Endowment for the Humanities, which all the way back in 1992 gave me a summer grant to work on this project. Yes, it took a long time to complete. I want to thank Northeastern Illinois University for sabbaticals in 1993, 2000, and 2007 to work on my books on the history of thoroughbred racing. I also want to thank the NEIU Committee on Organized Research funds in 1995 to purchase one hundred reels of microfilm of the *New York Morning Telegraph*, in 2001 to purchase sixty reels of microfilm on the *Chicago Examiner*, and for a travel grant in 2007. I want to thank Roda Ferraro of the Keeneland Library, Lexington, Kentucky, for copying materials from *Goodwin's Annual Turf Guide* for the years 1882–1908. I appreciate the assistance I received at the Abraham Lincoln Library for unpublished materials on the early history of horse racing in Illinois.

I greatly appreciate readers of the manuscript for Syracuse University Press, whose comments and criticisms were particularly astute and also helped prevent several factual errors, as well as correcting some pretty flawed prose. I want to thank by name Timothy Mennell and Melvin Adelman for their very useful commentary on an earlier draft and several anonymous readers of earlier drafts. David Hochfelder, author of an outstanding history of the American telegraph, was kind enough to share with me his copy of the Western Union revenues from 1895 through 1908, published in an internal company document. I want to deeply express my gratitude to Annette Wenda, who did an awesome job of copyediting my manuscript.

I am very grateful to the outstanding staff at the Ronald Williams Library, NEIU, especially senior library specialist Deborah Siegel, who is in charge of the interlibrary loan office. At NEIU we benefited from our membership in the awesome I-Share Library system, which did a wonderful job fulfilling virtually all my research needs for published sources, ranging from secondary sources to microfilm, state publications, and maps. Many institutions and individuals helped me in my quest for photographs, including the Library of Congress Prints and Photographs Division, the Chicago History Museum, librarian Sarah C. Biel at the University of Illinois at Urbana-Champaign, director Robert O'Shaughnessy of the Worth (Illinois) Parks and Recreation System, Erica Libhart of the National Sporting Library & Museum, Alexandra Lane of the White House Historical Association, Neil Gale, John Hmurovic, R. P. Sierz, and Stephen Sullivan.

I am grateful to the University of Illinois Press for permission to employ material from my essays "The Demise of Horse Racing and Boxing in Chicago in 1905," in *Sports in Chicago*, edited by Elliot J. Gorn, 43–61 (2008); and "Horse Racing in Chicago, 1883–1894: The Interplay of Class, Politics, and Organized Crime," in *The Chicago Sports Reader: 100 Years of Sports in the Windy City*, edited by Steven A. Riess and Gerald Gems, 59–80 (2009).

Finally, I want to thank my daughters, Jennifer, for helping me cope with my computer ignorance, and Jamie, for producing the graphic materials for this book, and my wonderful wife, Tobi, for bearing with me during the decades it took to complete this project, which ranged from reading some of my materials, discussing my ideas, and calming me down when I displaced some documents or struggled with an uncooperating computer.

Horse Racing the Chicago Way

1

Harness Racing, Politics, Gambling, and the Origins of Syndicate Crime in Chicago, 1837–1883

Two decades before Chicago became the midwestern center of thoroughbred racing with the opening of the fabled Washington Park Racetrack in 1884, equine sports were already taken seriously in the growing city. Chicago was the center of western harness racing and since the 1840s was the epicenter of midwestern gambling, having surpassed Cincinnati and St. Louis. This attribute was hardly something to brag about. Devout Protestants considered gambling sinful, and merchants saw gamblers as dishonest, untrustworthy, and poor credit risks. Gambling by the 1860s was centered downtown at "Gamblers' Alley" (bounded by Clark, Madison, LaSalle, and Washington), because of the many poolrooms (betting parlors) located there.[1]

On Saturday, September 22, 1866, the Chicago Driving Park, located on the South Side, adjacent to the Union Stockyards, hosted the biggest trotting event in the West, a $5,000 match race between Hiram Hasting's gelding Cooley, driven by William Riley, and William McKeaver's General Butler, brought in from New York for the race. The latter had recently defeated Dexter, the premier trotter in the world. The event consisted of separate one-mile races, known as heats. The winner of the event was the first to win three heats. After Cooley won the first two heats, McKeaver took over General Butler's driver reins and won the next two heats. Afterward, the *Chicago Tribune* reported, "A bedlamite wrangle . . . started between the drivers and blacklegs who had staked their money on the race, growing out of an alleged 'foul'" by McKeaver during the fourth race. When the tiebreaker went off, "it was so dark that the horses could not be seen more than half a dozen lengths from the judges' stand." Two and a half minutes later, General Butler ran by without his driver. Rescuers found McKeaver at the head of the stretch, close to the fence, with his skull crushed. An unknown person had mortally wounded him with a piece of the fence railing, presumably a Cooley bettor. The *Tribune* berated the sport as "altogether demoralizing and disgraceful . . . of one-part gambling, and one-part cruelty to animals." The murder was never solved. The heinous crime hurt the status of the city's turf industry and almost killed the local trotting scene.[2]

When Chicago became a city in 1837, horseback racing was America's most popular spectator sport, just as it had been since the late seventeenth century, when the leading breeders and racers were Chesapeake tobacco planters, usually heavily involved in local politics. The planters, who rode their own working horses, used the sport to demonstrate their manliness, earn respect from their peers, and promote a sense of shared values among them. Wealthy planters wagered on these contests to demonstrate self-confidence in their horses' breeding and their own horsemanship, expertise in judging horseflesh, and social status (the common folk were not allowed to bet with them), thereby reinforcing traditional patterns of respect and deference. The early elite raced horses that were usually short cross-breeds. These contests were quarter-mile races on a straightaway, usually near a tavern, church, or courthouse.[3]

By the 1730s and 1740s, major movers and shakers would often get together during "Race Week" at colonial capitals such as Annapolis, Jamestown, Charles Town, and New York, which typically coincided with meetings of local courts and legislatures. The horses raced were increasingly thoroughbred descendants of Bull Rock, the first Arabian imported from England in 1730, and a few others. These mounts were strong, agile, hot-tempered ("spirited"), and speedy. Thoroughbreds were expensive to buy, costly to maintain, finicky, prone to health problems and accidents from overexertion, and likely to experience low fertility rates. They were mainly used for breeding and racing long distances at urban jockey clubs.[4]

Prior to the American Revolution, many of the founding fathers, including George Washington, were well-known racing fans. The coming of the Revolution and the accompanying upheaval contributed to halting the sport everywhere except in Loyalist New York. In addition, the Continental Congress on September 5, 1774, passed a resolution discouraging racing because of the sport's aristocratic pretensions. Such views were reflected in a petition drawn up in 1802 by Philadelphia mechanics and manufacturers and presented to the Pennsylvania legislature, asking to halt horse racing as a sport more appropriate to the lifestyle of the English gentry than hardworking Americans.[5]

By the early nineteenth century, there was little racing in the North, curtailed by antiracing state laws. New York barred racing in 1802, but nineteen years later elite New Yorkers successfully campaigned to legalize racing in Queens County, which led to the revitalization of northern racing. The sport flourished at this time in the South and the West, where gambling was firmly established in local culture. Racing especially thrived in wide-open New Orleans, which joined the United States in 1803 as part of the Louisiana Purchase. Life in New Orleans was dominated by its Continental culture, Roman Catholic moral belief system, a polyglot population, and the presence of slavery. When Louisiana became a state in 1812, the federal government banned gambling there except for in the old colonial capital, where gambling was a big part of its male culture. The state did not ban betting there until 1835, by which time the habit was well entrenched.[6]

American racing in the 1830s and 1840s received considerable attention in the emerging daily press and the first sporting weekly, the *Spirit of the Times*, established in 1831. The growing popularity of thoroughbred racing was embodied by the five "Great Intersectional Races" (1823–45). These were four-mile match races, staged in heats, that attracted top steeds from the North and South and reportedly drew well over fifty thousand spectators. The victor of each contest symbolized the winning region's superior social, economic, and cultural systems.[7]

During these two decades, prominent urbanites from New York to New Orleans and southern plantation owners bred, owned, and raced outstanding thoroughbreds and bet heavily among themselves. The ability of racing men to judge bloodlines and racing flesh, and their readiness to bet on that expertise, reflected their self-confidence, financial success, wisdom, vision, and leadership. Owners of blooded racehorses belonged to prestigious jockey clubs, which certified their social status and honor and helped build social networks that contributed to their economic and political success. In 1832 two of the most prominent American horsemen, National Republican senator Henry Clay of Kentucky and incumbent Democratic president Andrew Jackson, vied for the White House. They were both men of the South who owned slaves, plantations, and blooded horses, and men of honor who engaged in duels.[8]

This chapter examines the development of equine sports in mid-nineteenth-century Chicago. There were impromptu races in the 1830s, before the first formal organized race meetings began in 1840 under the management of the city's early economic and political leaders. Harness racing, by the end of that decade, became the more popular form of equine sports in the Midwest. It was a newer and more innovative version of racing, more democratic, and relatively inexpensive to maintain. The horses were usually shorter, lighter, more docile, placid, easier to train, and more useful than thoroughbreds. They were typically employed in such practical purposes as hauling freight and transporting people. Riders sometimes raced trotters and pacers astride but mainly raced them on city streets and rural roads under a harness that bound them to a cart or wagon. These horses used one of two gaits, trotting or pacing. Trotters moved their front left leg and rear right leg nearly together, and then followed with the front right leg and rear left leg. Pacers moved their legs on the same side in unison. They were usually faster and less likely to break stride, which would disqualify them in a race. The first harness racers pulled a four-wheeled wagon that weighed seventy-five to a hundred pounds for up to five miles on improved local roads. But in the 1840s, these vehicles were supplanted by high two-wheeled buggies, later known as sulkies, that weighed as little as forty pounds.[9]

It was only after the Chicago Fire of 1871, when wealth exploded through opportunities provided by the city's physical regeneration and industrial boom, that Chicago's richest men got involved in thoroughbred racing to conspicuously display their wealth and facilitate connecting with their peers in an elite jockey club. The increased interest in the turf led to expanding opportunities for gambling, which facilitated the rise of syndicate crime (organized gangs protected by intimidation, bribery, and political connections that operate illegal enterprises) in Chicago.[10]

Chicago in 1830 was a frontier village of 50 people, mostly men. The end of the Black Hawk War of 1832 made the area safe for settlement. One year later, Chicago became a town with 200 residents, and in 1837 Chicago was chartered as a city with 4,170 inhabitants. It is considered an "instant city" because it transformed itself from a wilderness into a city in less than a generation. The instant city flourished as a trading center because of its location on Lake Michigan, abetted in 1848 by establishing a direct connection to the Mississippi River via the Illinois and Michigan Canal. In addition, the Galena and Chicago Union Railroad opened in 1848, and the Board of Trade was established to rationalize agrarian businesses. These developments quickly made the "City by the Lake" the focal point for the regional trade in wheat, corn, livestock, and lumber, leading to industrialization.[11]

Chicago's population reached 29,963 at midcentury, more than tripled a decade later to 109,260, and then nearly tripled again by 1870 to 298,977. Chicago was the fastest-growing city in the world. This remarkable growth was briefly halted by the Chicago Fire that devastated the city, causing 300 deaths and destroying 3.3 square miles. More than 100,000 people were left homeless, and property losses amounted to $200 million. But the residents refused to surrender to the catastrophe, and they rebuilt Chicago, which rose like a phoenix from the ashes with shocking speed. The city's redevelopers emphasized the creation of a new central business district (CBD), whose property-value appreciation created fabulous wealth for real-estate investors like Potter Palmer. Chicago extended its role in national commerce through its transportation and communication networks and became an awesome commercial, financial, and industrial center. Its three steel mills in 1880 produced 30 percent of America's steel rails. Chicago was also the "hog butcher for the world." Local packinghouses in 1900 employed 25,000 cheaply paid immigrant laborers. The growing economy created great fortunes for the likes of Marshall Field, Philip D. Armour, and George Pullman.[12]

GAMBLING AND EQUINE SPORT IN EARLY CHICAGO

Hunting was the most popular sport in frontier Chicago, but the first organized sport was horseback riding. The state drew up antiwagering laws in 1819 to prevent vice and immorality, stating that betting losses from horse racing or games of chance "need not be paid" and that "any bond, note, contract, judgment, etc.," given for the same is voided. However, these laws were disregarded by young men, who gambled to demonstrate their manliness and self-confidence and participated in a lively bachelor subculture. They enjoyed manly pastimes at local brothels and saloons such as drinking, gambling, and whoring. They also watched sports such as animal baiting and boxing at taverns and horse racing at nearby courses.[13]

The first reported harness races, known as "brushes," were mainly impromptu races in New York City on improved local streets between owners and drivers. The sport was organized by middle-class horsemen and was considered a democratic American sport, unlike thoroughbred racing, with its British and elitist connotations. The first step in modernizing the sport was the formation of the New York Trotting Club in late 1824, which subsequently built a racecourse in Centerville, Long Island. By the 1830s and 1840s, it had become a popular spectator sport at racecourses run by entrepreneurs. Matches required speed and endurance for contests of one mile, raced in the best of three races.[14]

Chicago's initial racing promoter was Mark Beaubien, a French Indian trader, who shortly after his arrival in 1826 established the Eagle Exchange Tavern and soon began racing his horses against all comers. Five years later, he opened the fabled Sauganash Hotel in 1831. Beaubien arranged horse races to promote his guesthouse and its related businesses, especially gambling, which frontiersmen loved. The racing matches were held at Wolf Point, where the three main branches of the Chicago River converged, or across a nearby rickety toll bridge in front of the Sauganash. By the mid-1830s, purses reached as high as $1,500. Beaubien was the first of several hotel owners to get involved in promoting harness racing by entering their own horses in the races, donating trophies and purses, and helping to lay out courses.[15]

Historian Christopher Thale points out that many residents in the new city felt that gambling was closely connected to vice and idleness and unfitting to a commercial society that emphasized hard work and self-discipline. The leading members of the community worried about the commercialization of gambling with the arrival of dishonest professional gamblers. Their customers were mainly eastern newcomers or poor immigrants who were attracted to betting at horse races and boxing matches or simply playing card games. These leisure pastimes provided them an opportunity to express the independence unavailable at work and promote a sense of manliness through risk taking. Gambling was vilified by Protestant clerics in the 1830s, which led to public suppression of gambling-house owners. However, the reformers were apparently not very successful cleaning up the city because there were hundreds of Chicago gambling houses by midcentury, usually directly connected to saloons.[16]

In 1837 New Yorker Willard F. Myrick opened a tavern on Cottage Grove Avenue, near Twenty-Ninth Street. He also bought an additional ninety acres for $1,800 and built a one-mile racetrack (Twenty-Sixth to Thirty-First Streets, Lake Michigan to Calumet Avenue). While a noteworthy moment for Chicago racing, it took place at an inauspicious moment in American racing history. The sport was then hindered nationally by the economic impact of the panic of 1837, caused by the Specie Circular of 1836, rising interest rates, dropping cotton prices, and the demise of the Bank of the United States, as well as by growing moral opposition to racing because of its connection to gambling.[17]

The antigambling movement was a product of the "Second Great Awakening" that peaked in the 1830s and 1840s that began in the "Burned-Over District" of western New York, led by Protestant evangelicals, mainly Baptists and Methodists, in preparation for the imminent Second Coming of Christ. Evangelical Christians considered gambling a sin because the Tenth Commandment forbids coveting a neighbor's property and the Bible identifies the love of money as the root of all evil (1 Tim. 6:101) that encourages people to get rich quick (Prov. 13:11; Eccles. 5:10) by wagering, instead of by hard work.[18]

Despite the decline of northern racing, thoroughbred racing continued to thrive in the South, where it had been firmly established in the local culture since colonial times among the great planters. It remained a popular pastime, providing an opportunity for well-to-do businessmen, attorneys, and politicians to demonstrate their manliness through gambling, especially in wide-open New Orleans.[19]

Organized racing in Chicago began in the fall of 1840 behind Myrick's tavern under the auspices of the Chicago Sporting Club (CSC). The one-mile course staged one- and two-mile races for purses up to $200. The first Chicago racing clubs were owned and operated by prominent business and political leaders. The CSC was led by respected horseman William Ogden, the city's first mayor in 1837 at just thirty-two. He was Chicago's leading businessman and booster, promoter of the Illinois and Michigan Canal, and first president of both the highly profitable Chicago and Galena Union Railroad (1848) and the renowned Union and Pacific Railroad (1862). In 1844 Myrick built a more formal four-mile course at the Cottage Grove location. His racetrack held three-day meets, with one event each day that required the victorious horse to win two heats. One day was set aside for saddle races and the other two for harness events. Bets were handled by professional gamblers.[20]

One year later, the Chicago Sporting Club was reorganized as the Chicago Jockey Club (CJC). Its presidents, besides Ogden, included Chicago Board of Trade founders and future mayors, John P. Chapin (1846–47), a wholesaler and retailer, and Walter S. Gurnee (1851–53), who made his fortune in his tannery and saddlery and leather businesses. He was also president of the Milwaukee & Chicago Railroad. There were eight days of racing, including a few days for "racking" horses. They were calm, beautiful horses with a lot of stamina, bred on southern plantations. Their pace was smooth and natural, described as a single-foot gait because only one foot touched the ground at a time.[21]

At the end of 1845, the course was leased for ten years to Dr. William Tichnor of Kentucky, who built a grandstand and a fence around the course to keep out nonpaying spectators. The meets were held in summer and autumn and until 1848 were almost exclusively for running horses, with purses of up to $600. Two years later, the Chicago Trotting Club was organized there.[22]

The Harness Horses Take Over

Harness racing became in the 1840s the dominant form of horse racing in the Midwest. Harness racing utilized docile, inexpensive working horses that were easier to train than the larger, hot-tempered thoroughbreds, who were bred for speed and racing. In 1879 high-quality trotting horses became known as "standardbred," not because of their bloodline, but because of their ability to complete a mile in 2:35. These horses were descendants of English horses, especially Messenger (b. 1780), a thoroughbred imported to the United States in 1788. His great-grandson Hambletonian 10 (b. 1849) is regarded as the foundational sire of the breed. A prime example of their humble origins was Lady Suffolk, the first great American trotter, born in Long Island and purchased as a four-year-old when employed pulling an oyster cart. She went on to race in saddle and in harness during her fifteen-year career (1838–52). Lady Suffolk made her reputation by setting the world record for trotting a mile in 2:29.5 under saddle at the Beacon Course in Hoboken, New Jersey, in 1845, the first to break 2:30 for that distance.[23]

1. Ulysses S. Grant in a carriage pulled by Dexter. Dexter won forty-six of fifty races. Owner Robert Bonner invited presidential candidate Ulysses S. Grant to drive the horse in this illustration. Color lithograph by Currier & Ives, 1868. Library of Congress Prints and Photographs Division, Washington, DC, LC-DIG-pga-01612.

Nearly all standardbred owners, drivers, and spectators enjoyed betting on races, but a few owners participated simply for the competition. Robert Bonner, the wealthy publisher of the *New York Ledger* and one of the nation's most prominent midcentury harness owners, spent nearly $500,000 on horses, including $35,000 in 1867 for Dexter, "king of the trotters." Bonner, a Presbyterian, never wagered on racing, which he considered a sin. He used his animals as "road-horses," driving them on local roads and racing them in private time trials.[24]

By 1870, when the National Trotting Association (NTA) was formed, harness racing was, according to historian Melvin Adelman, a modern sport. He claims that harness racing was the first successful commercialized sport and among the most popular spectator sports of the 1850s. It was highly organized, with standardized rules across the country, considerable press coverage, extensive records of statistics (such as records for mile races and other events), and the first exclusively harness stud book, which appeared in 1871. Illinois tracks belonged to the NTA's Western District, whose office was in Chicago.[25]

In 1854 the managers of the third-rate Garden City Hotel opened the Garden City track with Ogden as president. The track was located three miles south of Myrick's facility on the Near South Side (Thirty-Sixth Street and Indiana Avenue), accessible by special Illinois Central trains for twenty-five cents. One of their partners was Henry Graves, who first came to Chicago in 1831 with his parents. He eventually became the longest-living pioneer in the city, residing there until his death in 1907. Graves became a wealthy man and a very successful breeder and racer. His best horse was Ike Cook, the first Illinois harness horse to race a mile in under 2:30. Years later, Graves planned to build a life-size statue of his horse at the drinking fountain at the Fifty-Fifth Street entrance to Washington Park. The statue was never built, but an *Inter Ocean* editorial did not scoff at the plan, pointing out that "such feelings of men toward their horses are not unusual," and there were many monuments to racehorses.[26]

One year after the Garden City track opened, "Long John" Went-worth, editor of the *Chicago Democrat*, a prominent landowner, six-term congressman, and future Republican mayor (1857–58, 1860–61), opened the Brighton Driving Park (Thirty-Eighth Street and Indiana Avenue) in cooperation with the prominent Brighton House in the village of Brighton (annexed to Chicago in 1889), five and a half miles southwest of central Chicago. The facility, named for a renowned English track, offered purses of $100–$1,125 for one-mile races. Both Garden City and Brighton Park were well patronized before the Civil War and engaged in a friendly rivalry, drawing up to three thousand fans to bet on prominent horses. In 1861 the Illinois State Fair was staged in September at Brighton Park, and the harness races drew large crowds. Then in September 1862, the World's Horse Fair was held in Chicago, and the afternoon races were its biggest attraction.[27]

American Racing during the Civil War

The coming of the Civil War quickly killed off the turf in southern cities like New Orleans, Charleston, and Memphis, where the sport had been popular through the 1850s, with weeklong meets. This speedy decline resulted from many of the battles being fought on southern soil, economic problems at the home front, the negative regard given to people enjoying their leisure time while Confederate soldiers were dying for their nation, concerns about the course of the war, and the cavalry's need for quality steeds.[28]

The national racing scene in the North was not markedly better, but for other reasons. Many of the best horses and some of the top tracks were controlled by professional gamblers. In New York, for instance, many Tammanyites were involved in local tracks as gamblers who bought concessions to run betting pools, roulette, keno, and faro. Faro was a simple and extremely popular card game with better odds than most card games. The cards were dealt out of a tightly sealed box (the "shoe") to lessen cheating. The gambling regularly attracted infamous swindlers, pickpockets, and thieves. A writer to *Vanity Fair* in 1860 described an exclusively male crowd on the Long Island Railroad bound for the well-known Union Course on Long Island: "Mostly sporting men with dyed mustaches, kid gloves, concealed weapons and pearl-colored pantaloons. Some fighters. Short stocky fellows with small round heads, close cropped hair, and very little shirt collar visible. Not nice persons to invite to teas in the bosom of your family." New York–based *Turf, Field, and Farm* reported in 1866 that few women attended the Fashion Race Course and never the Union or Centreville courses (all located in Queens County), "looked upon as resorts for the roughest characters that haunt the Babel City of New York and rowdyism seems to be the order of the day."[29]

The big exception was the opening of the Saratoga Racetrack in a resort community in upstate New York in 1863, shortly after the Battle of Gettysburg. The main person behind it was John Morrissey, a former American boxing champion, who had become a prominent gambler, a leading member of Tammany Hall, and a future congressman.

The four-day event was so successful that right after the meet he organized the Saratoga Jockey Club, to make racing there a permanent
summer pastime. In the meantime, racing at Union and Confederate camps became a popular way to temporarily escape the misery of
camp life and thoughts of war, and also to test bloodlines to produce
faster horses.[30]

The Chicago Racing Scene during the Civil War

According to popular historian Herbert Asbury, Chicago in the 1860s
"richly deserved its reputation of being the wickedest and toughest
place in the United States." It was the Midwest's gambling center, with
about 30 high-quality betting houses, with little interference from the
authorities. Considerable wagering went on at some of Chicago's best-
known hotels, like the Richmond House, a fashionable 60-room guesthouse, which hosted the Prince of Wales in 1860. Travelers found it
an excellent site for passengers making train connections at the nearby
Illinois Central Depot, as well as its reasonable $1.50 a night rate. The
Richmond became a leading hangout for Chicago's gamblers, bookmakers, and confidence men intent on swindling hotel guests. In late
1861 the inn's bar was purchased by professional gambler Calvin Page,
along with his young partner, Michael C. McDonald, a newcomer
from Buffalo. Mike was responsible for taking bets on harness racing
and developing close ties to local politicians. Several hotels backed
betting on races, including the famed Tremont Hotel, owned by noted
hotelier John B. Drake. He permitted pool selling there, believing
it promoted business In 1867, several hotels would sponsor trotting
sweepstakes and other races at the new Dexter Park, located next to
the Union Stockyards.[31]

On August 25, 1863, the $10,000 Chicago Driving Park Associa-
tion (CDPA) was established under President Daniel Thompson, an
elevator and packing businessman and future head of the Chicago
City Railway. Thompson was a noted horseman and owner of a gor-
geous $100,000 home on Prairie Avenue, which after the Chicago Fire
became one of the most fashionable streets in the city. The CDPA was

immediately considered the best course in local history. The directors included Myrick and horseman David A. Gage, a partner in the Tremont Hotel and the Sherman House, president of the Chicago City Railway (a horse-drawn rail line), city treasurer (1863–64 and 1870–73), and president of the city's first professional baseball team, the White Stockings, in 1870. He was supplanted as president when the club started poorly, and the team went on to defeat the renowned Cincinnati Red Stockings, thereby gaining recognition as one of the finest pro teams in the land. Three years later, city treasurer Gage was indicted for misappropriating $507,703, for which he and his bondsmen were held responsible.[32]

The CDPA owners believed that men who got rich supplying the Union army with war matériel, like food, clothing, and armaments, and manufactured the rolling stock and rails needed to transport military goods would be interested in establishing racing stables of harness horses to raise their social status and that the masses were eager for excitement and entertainment during the depressing days of the Civil War. Driving Park was about three and a half miles from the center of town (Thirty-First Street and State Avenue), on the site of the 1862 World's Horse Fair, just blocks from the notorious Camp Douglas Prison, close enough for inmates to hear the races. It was one of the biggest prisoner camps in the North during the war.[33]

Fans were warned that at the four-day meet, "as hitherto been the case, no malt or spirituous liquors would be permitted to be introduced or sold on the grounds. No profane or boisterous language will be permitted. No female will be admitted without an escort. No improper character known to be such will be admitted; and if found on the grounds will be removed."[34]

The track opened at 3:00, and the first race was at 3:30 with a thousand in attendance. The entrance fee was 30 cents. The four-day meet's $400 purse went to the first horse to win three heats. The horse Silas Rich won in five heats. A brief fall meet was held in October. The feature event for a $2,000 purse was a three-out-of-five-heat race by traders under saddle. Admission was raised to $1 for the special event.[35]

In March 1864, the new track president, James Van Etta, announced the track had expenses of $10,885, just slightly higher than the receipts of $10,746. However, the association also had another $2,383 in debts. The track had an eleven-day trotting meet in the summer of 1864 with purses and stakes amounting to $25,000. Crowds were large, but business fell off for the fall meet, though *Wilkes Spirit of the Times* thought it started out well. Driving Park was the primary site of major Chicago racing through 1866 and included such unusual events as a ladies' riding match and such stunt promotions as Native American runners against racehorses. In 1864 management discouraged professional gambling and proclaimed an intent to bar them from the course, but did not.[36]

The CDPA in 1865 tried to coordinate its business with other American track associations and jockey clubs, which may have never been done in the past. The purpose was not to coordinate racing schedules, but, according to historian Danael Suttle, "to prevent thieves, including rebel guerrillas, from profiting from stolen horses." It was not unusual then for stolen racehorses to be raced elsewhere where they were not known.

One year later, the supervisors forced pool sellers off the grounds, but they simply moved into a nearby building. Despite the owners' best intentions, Driving Park, along with the entire local racing scene, ended up with a poor reputation, even before McKeaver's murder on the track. By then, professional gamblers owned the best horses in Chicago and played a big role in running the courses. According to the *Chicago Tribune*, "Honest horse-racing is now the exception."[37]

The George Trussell Era

In the early 1860s, George Trussell was the city's most influential bookmaker and gambler and the leading figure in local racing. George came to Chicago in 1839 from Caledonia, Virginia, and worked as a bookkeeper, but soon became enchanted with the "fast life." He was discharged for gambling at faro. Trussell became well known on the

"Hairtrigger Block" of Randolph Street, between State and Dearborn, where violence and chaos reigned, often caused by Trussell's rival Samuel H. "Cap" Hyman. By 1862 Trussell was running his own crooked faro gambling houses in Chicago, as well as Buffalo, New Orleans, and New York, employing his political influence to secure police raids on his rivals and betting heavily on horse races.[38]

In 1866, Trussell bought a half share of the great eight-year-old gelding Dexter for $7,000. The son of Hambletonian 10, trained by the outstanding horseman Hiram Woodruff, and driven by future turf Hall of Famer Budd Doble, won twenty-five of twenty-six races that year and went on to amass forty-nine victories in fifty-three career races. Trussell got so involved in racing that he abandoned Mary A. "Mollie" Cosgriff, mother of his child, forcing her to become a madam. On September 4, when George was celebrating Dexter's victory over rival George M. Patchen at a concert saloon, Mollie entered and shot him dead. Dexter went on to set mile world records for both trotting under saddle in 1866 (2:18) and in harness in 1867 (2:17.25).[39]

Cap Hyman ran his own racetrack at Sunnyside, a resort in the town of Lakeview, three miles north of Chicago. The locality was best known for his Sunnyside Inn, a popular establishment with the demimonde, as well as his racecourse. The Sunnyside course generally drew lower-quality horses, although it was an attractive, high-quality facility, described by the *Tribune* in 1867 when it opened as "one of the prettiest, half-mile tracks in the country." A steeplechase race there in the fall of 1867 drew some thousand spectators. However, supporting the racetrack bankrupted Hyman in 1873.[40]

The Irish, Gambling, and Syndicate Crime

After the Civil War, the Irish began to supplant native born southern Americans in the business of horse race gambling. About 17 percent of the population in 1850 was German, mainly well-paid skilled workers, who resided in heavily German neighborhoods that facilitated their adjustment to life in America. They were slightly outnumbered by the Irish (20 percent), but soon surpassed them. Chicago had around

240,000 Irish residents in 1900, compared to 470,000 Germans. The Irish newcomers were largely poor, unskilled, and subject to considerable prejudice. As late as 1900, nearly 70 percent were manual workers. In the late nineteenth century, ambitious unskilled and uneducated Irishmen often turned to jobs in construction, politics, policing, and crime to get ahead. The emergence of urban Irish crime syndicates affiliated with Democratic Irish bosses like New York's Richard Croker of Tammany Hall provided young Irish bookmakers with financing and protection for their illegal initiatives.[41]

Crime historian David Johnson argues that the Irish employed a more businesslike approach to illegal enterprises, like bookmaking compared to the flashy southern blacklegs who preceded them. The Irishmen invested time and money in building relationships with Irish politicians, sportsmen, and the underworld in cities across the country, and especially Boston, Brooklyn, Chicago, and New York. Irish involvement in sports gambling reflected their bachelor subculture that supported drinking, gambling, and whoring. An interlocking community emerged between gamblers, policemen, politicians, and the courts for mutual self-interest that led to the rise of crime syndicates that employed political protection to advance their illegal enterprises.[42]

Offtrack betting was always illegal and widely opposed. Yet it thrived as a well-organized, illegal enterprise, a "victimless crime." Historian Mark Haller defined an illegal enterprise as a business that sells "illegal goods and services to customers who know that the goods or services are illegal," such as prostitution, and especially gambling, and is well protected by an alliance of machine politicians, policemen, and underworld figures. Haller asserted that illegal enterprises have three main features that underlie cooperation among the entrepreneurs: the systematic corruption of police and politicians who oversee the business and provide protection, overlapping connections among illegal businessmen that help them pool resources to get started and expand, and such internal economic factors as risk taking, specialization, and diversification. The illegal enterprises typically operate as crime syndicates, which Haller described as "a system of cooperation so that many retailers are backed by the same group of entrepreneurs."[43]

Haller asserted that from around 1880 through 1905, "in many neighborhoods, it was not so much that syndicates influenced local political organizations; rather gambling syndicates *were* the political organizations." They were very important in organizing and financing professional sports, vice, and commercialized nightlife.[44]

Haller further pointed out that three patterns emerged among the predominantly Irish American gambling syndicates in the last third of the nineteenth century. In the first case, Mike McDonald, a local gambler kingpin in the 1870s, became a neighborhood party leader. Then around the turn of the century, certain notable gamblers, such as Jim O'Leary, who dominated offtrack gambling on the South Side, gained close ties with prominent politicians and local policemen to protect their interests. Finally, there was the case of prominent politicians, notably Alderman "Bathhouse" John Coughlin, boss of the Levee District, who used his political clout to get involved in supervising gambling operations. These Irishmen got their start as precinct workers or bookmakers' runners or clerks.[45]

The Dexter Park Racetrack

The prosperity engendered in Chicago by the Civil War stimulated new interest in turf sports among the nouveau riche interested in establishing racing stables and the masses eager for excitement and entertainment. It all came together a few blocks from the Union Stockyards opened in 1865, about six and a half miles from downtown, just outside the city limits. The yards ultimately encompassed 475 acres from Thirty-Ninth to Forty-Seventh Streets. Before 1848, when the first public stockyard was open, cattle were pastured at land outside various taverns until shipped out of town and butchered. Thereafter, several more public stockyards were opened owned by various railroads that shipped cattle. The slaughtering of livestock skyrocketed during the Civil War, when there was a huge need for processed meat for the Union army. This growth led to consolidation and modernization at the Union Stockyards, which opened in 1866. John B. Sherman, one of the prime movers, and the Union Stockyards' first manager, was also instrumental in building a racecourse on adjacent company property at Forty-Fourth Street and Halstead Avenue, named for the great trotter Dexter. Sherman anticipated the track's proximity to the Union Stockyards, its excellent rail connections, the nearby Drovers' Hotel, and other essential facilities would make the facility attractive to horse owners. George B. Mansur directed the two-year construction and then managed the course. He was also an alderman from 1867 to 1869 and director of the city prison.[46]

The Dexter Park Association operated the course under President William F. Tucker, head of the Stockyards Bank. The $50 membership provided free access to the track's stands, clubhouse, and sheds and free admission for wives or girlfriends. Dexter Park originally had two separate tracks, one for five-day thoroughbred meets consisting of heat events of one to four miles over a softer and more elastic seven-furlong surface (seven-eighths of a mile) and a second harder and smoother one-mile trotting track considered among of the finest in the country. There were two grandstands, one seating 1,500 men and the other 200 women, to preserve moral norms. However, the seating area was poorly designed, leaving the afternoon sun in the face of spectators. Racing fans got to the track from the center of town by carriages, a thirty-minute train ride, or an hour-long horse-car ride. The grand opening, scheduled for Saturday, July 4, 1867, was rained out, so it opened two days later with about 1,000 in attendance.[47]

Dexter Park's next season began on July 3, 1868, with a thoroughbred meet attended by some 2,000 fans. The leadoff event was the $500 City Railroad Purse, sponsored by a local transit line. The racing crowd differed from the trotting audiences, drawing more out-of-staters, Englishmen, and Canadians. The holiday crowd on the following day drew 7,000 people, including so many women that an overflow crowd in the ladies' stand forced many into the main grandstand. However, the overall turnout was disappointing, which the *Spirit* partly blamed on trotting folk worried that a successful running meet would be detrimental to their sport.[48]

Dexter Park had only trotting in 1869. Club members had access to a clubhouse replete with balconies and rooms amply lined with glass windows. The 1870 meet started poorly, drawing a dismal audience of 150 to opening day, which the *Spirit* blamed on recent questionable races. The facility was leased that summer to the White Stockings, Chicago's first professional baseball team. The ball club moved to downtown Lake Front Park the next year, when it joined the new National Association of Professional Baseball Players, baseball's first professional league.[49]

The continuing interest in harness racing was reflected by the many local residents who drove their own trotting horses for work and pleasure. In 1869 two foreign tourists identified Chicago as particularly "noted for its fast trotting horses, the wide, level, straight and withal softly paved streets, being eminently suitable for the rapid movements of the crowds of spidery vehicles, coursing along at the extraordinary pace of fifteen to twenty miles an hour," faster than most trains. Nationally, harness racing was in the midst of a great boom. The number of harness races in the United States and Canada in the period 1869–75 tripled to 3,304.[50]

In 1871 the new Dexter Driving Association (DDA), led by David Gage, C. B. Farwell, and James B. Sherman, leased the course for $35,000 over ten years. Two years later, a ladies' grandstand opened with 1,000 reserved seats for women and their escorts, along with a ladies' refreshment room. The association's 71 members included such notables as General Phil Sheridan and *Tribune* publisher Joseph Medill, but collectively the members did not constitute a core of the city's elite. One year later, 100 new memberships were opened up for a $30 fee.[51]

The DDA fell out of favor by 1874, despite four-day meets with trotting and racing for $21,000 in purses. The *Tribune* criticized the judges' slow work and the presence of stockyard rowdies. The *Spirit* admired the club's terrific physical plant, but found the meet less than an eminent success, reflecting the impact of the national financial panic of 1873 that began a six-year depression. The sports weekly also noted the track's sketchy reputation "as the jockeying ground of tricksters and the harvest field of gamblers. . . . [V]ery few honorable gentlemen cared to patronize the doubtful sport where speed and merit were held in check to satisfy and gratify dishonest avarice." Still, the *Spirit* applauded Mansur for trying to get conditions in order, rebuilding public confidence in his facility, and almost breaking even.[52]

By 1876 the *Spirit* was completely dissatisfied with Dexter Park's ambiance, accommodations, location, and accessibility: "Under the most favorable circumstances, you are liable to be smothered with that unbearable stench from the stock yards and packing houses." Thousands of Chicagoans who owned horses never drove to the track because "the drive is a dusty, unpleasant, and sometimes dangerous" journey because of the need to cross railroad tracks. South Side pedestrians walking to the track had to cross a half mile of railroad tracks carrying freight trains bound for the stockyards. The *Tribune* completely agreed with that assessment. The more well-off carriage trade was turned off by the unpleasant trip to the track, while clerks and small businessmen were put off by their long workdays and the 25-cent cost of public transportation.[53]

The *Tribune* was more supportive of the 1876 season because the two meets were run honestly and offered good-size purses, although attendance was only fair and probably insufficient to produce a profit. In fact, the newspaper suspected that attendances were never enough to make money. The purses for the first 1875 meet were pretty comparable for trotters ($3,700) and runners ($3,000), but the gap widened markedly at the next meet ($13,800 to $1,550), discouraging thoroughbred owners. In 1876 the track's pool seller sold about $150,000 on all events, sharing his 3 percent commission ($4,500) with the track management.[54]

The 1877 season began on a sour note on opening day when racing officials found that one of the trotters scheduled to run was a ringer and was disqualified. Nonetheless, 8,000 attended the races on July 4, the largest crowd in some time. Despite the meet's shameful start, the *Tribune* considered the season "the most successful and encouraging . . . ever . . . in this city, and has given to legitimate turf sports an impetus," patronized by the best people. Nonetheless, Sherman and Tucker rated the meet a failure and, despite hosting other events like polo (a sport newly introduced in the United States by publisher and sportsman James Gordon Bennett) and shooting to bolster revenue, decided to leave the business. They got out of their lease from the Union Stockyards, and the site was subsequently used to expand the meatpacking industry.[55]

The *Spirit* considered Dexter Park's closing as a black mark on Chicago's standing as a sporting town and also on the local breeding industry: "Why a great city, with half a million of inhabitants, and wealth untold, should fail to keep pace with sister cities [particularly St. Louis] in popular amusements and sports is not easy of comprehension." Chicago "was the centre [*sic*] of a region unsurpassed for its horse breeding interests, within her own limits there were hundreds of speedy trotters and some runners, and her citizens took an exceptional interest in the sports of the turf."[56]

The *Tribune* agreed with the *Spirit*'s analysis, as did letter writer "King-Bolt," who considered Chicago's lack of a thoroughbred course a poor reflection on the booming city, especially since other municipalities with half its population had racecourses. The *Tribune* agreed with King-Bolt's call for a new racing association to build a trotting track at an eighty-acre site near Lake Michigan in the town of Lake, where there were cheap land, accessible utilities, and quality transportation, including frequent streetcars, 10–15-cent rides from downtown via the Illinois Central Railroad, and scenic roads. In 1884 that location became the site of the new Washington Park racetrack.[57]

Equine Sports Move to the West Side

In May 1878, H. V. Bemis, of the Bemis and Curtis Malting Company, and con-game artists Harry Lawrence and Morris Martin, owners of the largest wholesale liquor, wine, and cigar house in the West, organized the Chicago Jockey and Trotting Club (CJTC) with nearly four hundred members. The principals claimed their goal was to emulate the elite American Jockey Club (AJC) that operated New York's Jerome Park, and the Maryland Jockey Club of Baltimore, which ran Pimlico, but the CJTC was never in their league, though it did get into full-fledged thoroughbred racing.[58]

The CJTC officers represented a more prestigious group than the membership. The president was prominent attorney and former Republican state senator S. K. Dow, backed by Vice President Samuel J. Medill, managing editor of the *Tribune* and brother of former mayor Joseph Medill, publisher of the *Tribune*. Its secretary was Dr. Nicholas Rowe, editor of *Chicago Field* (renamed *American Field* in 1881). The CJTC was supported by a thirteen-member board that included six journalists who could help promote the track, two hoteliers, and several prominent businessmen, all successful. However, their stature was far below that of the AJC board members, which the CJTC hoped to emulate.[59]

The CJTC constructed the Chicago Trotting Park (CTP), an eighty-acre, $75,000 facility, with funds ostensibly advanced by Harry Lawrence and Morris Martin, though half of the seed money actually came from Bemis's loans. The site was considered ideal since sixty acres was considered the necessary size for a racecourse, plus there were no impediments to hinder construction. It opened in 1878, leased for twenty years, three miles west of downtown, just west of the south end of Central Park, at Madison Street and Crawford Avenue. Central Park was then the centerpiece of the West Side Park system, designed by architect William Le Baron Jenny. He is best known today as the father of the American skyscraper, having designed in 1884 the ten-story fire-resistant Home Insurance Building, supported by a steel frame. The park was renamed in 1881 for martyred president James Garfield.[60]

The CTP featured a mile-long trotting track around a running track, a stable for 150 horses, a clubhouse, and a ten-thousand-seat grandstand, four hundred feet long and sixty feet wide, with a west front to avoid exposure to the sun and windows in the back for greater ventilation. A four thousand reserved-seat Swiss-style "select stand" for club members and other favored fans was adjacent to the clubhouse. Club members could park their carriages in one of three hundred stalls protected by locking doors to prevent thievery, a big innovation compared to the open sheds at Dexter Park. Admission was $1 for a grandstand seat and an additional 50 cents for a seat in the reserved select stands. A pass for the season was $5.[61]

2. Inaugural meeting of the Chicago and Trotting Club in 1878. The poster highlights the racing schedule for harness and thoroughbred horses and its grandstand's design. Original color print by John B. Jeffery, Printing and Engraving of Chicago. Library of Congress Prints and Photographs Division, Washington, DC, LC-USZC2-258.

The West Side track's environs were a big advance over Dexter Park, since it was much more accessible, and located next to a beautiful suburban-style park near the city limits, instead of the foul-aired stockyards. Well-to-do racing fans enjoyed traveling there in their own carriages along beautiful east-west drives like Madison, Washington, and Monroe Streets. Travel was inexpensive from the Loop via the Van Buren, Randolph, and Madison streetcars. The Madison route, which left downtown every two minutes, was extended by the city council right to the racetrack. The Illinois Central had a station twelve hundred feet away. The Northwestern Railroad constructed a branch line to the track, and the Chicago, Burlington & Quincy (CB&Q) ran a switch from its main line north to the track, thereby accommodating up to eight thousand spectators an hour from the South Side.[62]

The upscale Republican *Inter Ocean*, with the seventh-largest circulation of any English-language newspaper in Chicago, claimed the opening of the track drew more attention than any prior western sporting event, drawing thousands to the city, including many country folks who delayed their normal fall visit to Chicago to see the races. Ten thousand people attended a free open house at the grounds on October 6, two days before opening day, just to inspect the facilities and watch the trotters work out. This open house was a good public relations move, unlike in St. Louis, where proprietors charged fans 25 cents to visit their new track.[63]

Opening day drew more than six thousand spectators. The grandstand and clubhouse were in fine order, although other preparations were incomplete. Security was provided by thirty-five Pinkertons and a police contingent. Several hundred carriages were on the grounds, but most fans came on the Madison Street trolley. Trotting races began at 1:30 p.m., enabling men to put in a morning at work and then go to the track. However, the day opened under a cloud because of concern over fixed races. The owner of Jennie C. went through three riders in different heats because he was suspicious about her performances. He finally placed Jennie C. under a police guard to prevent any tampering.[64]

The next day again drew six thousand spectators and ten thousand on the fourth day. The meet was highlighted on day three, October 10, by the inaugural Chicago Derby. It drew a nationally renowned field, in which Rarus pulled a wagon, Great Western, under saddle, and Hopeful, in a sulky, raced mile heats, won in three straight heats by Hopeful. The *Tribune, Inter Ocean,* and *Spirit of the Times* reported an attendance of thirty-five thousand, which is hard to believe. The *Washington Post* and *Washington Star* estimated fifteen thousand, while the *New York Sun* reported estimates between twenty-five and forty thousand and chimed in at thirty thousand, calling it an "almost unprecedented assemblage" and reporting the facility "one of the best-appointed racing institutions in the country." The *Inter Ocean* proclaimed, "No grander evidence of Chicago enterprise and Chicago appreciation was ever known." The *Tribune* bragged about the wonderful Anglo-Saxon crowd that was present. The *Spirit* reported that the grandstand was filled with "the most respectable looking body of men that we have ever seen upon any track, while the ladies' stand and the immense balconies of the club-house . . . are crowded with the elite, fashion, and beauty of Chicago."[65]

The track's management reported a very lucrative four-day meet with profits of $20,070.46. Membership fees came to $11,850, the gate brought in $22,264, entrance fees brought in $7,400, and concessions amounted to $3,000. The biggest expenses were purses ($14,800), followed by advertising ($3,572), wages ($717), the band ($275), and hay, oats, and straw ($212). The report omitted such important expenses as mortgage payments and maintenance costs, and the receipt column did not report fees paid by pool sellers Ira E. Bride and W. R. Armstrong to run the on-track gambling. They paid the track $50 per day for bookmaking at trotting meets and $100 for thoroughbred races, plus 1 percent of the commissions paid on auction pools and 40 percent on pari-mutuels. Bride & Armstrong netted $67,645 from 1878 through 1883. Rumors abounded that the real director of betting at the track was Mike McDonald, who ran a "wheel of fortune" (roulette wheel) at the track.[66]

The *Tribune* and the *Spirit* both applauded the CTP for its out-standing field of horses, large purses, and sparkling races. The club paid a 30 percent dividend on the original investment in its second season ($22,500), nearly identical to the profit reported in 1878. The CJTC also staged its first thoroughbred meet in 1879, receiving 391 nominations for stakes races. Seven thousand attended the Chicago Trotting Park race on June 25, the largest crowd for a running race in the city's history, which seemed to mark a major step in the beginning of racing's dominance over trotting in the Windy City.[67]

Up to this point, mixing trotting and thoroughbred races had not been profitable for the turf industry. The CJTC preferred trotting then because harness owners were charged entrance fees amounting to 65 percent of the cost of purses, while thoroughbreds were entered for free and thoroughbred owners expected larger purses.[68]

Following the meet, avid horseman and nationally renowned the-atrical entrepreneur J. H. "Jack" Haverly, well known for his min-strelsy productions and ownership of such theaters as Brooklyn's Niblo, New York's Haverly, Chicago's Adelphi (rebuilt after the Chi-cago Fire), and the Columbia, opened in 1880, purchased Lawrence and Martin's interest in the racetrack for $39,300. Jack was previously well known as an avid auction-pool participant who for a time would put as much as $1,000 into the pool to ensure himself the favorite in the race. This gambit was no more sinful to him than gambling in the futures market. He became the majority stockholder, followed by H. V. Bemis, who had $11,000 in CJTC shares, and secured for him-self a four-year lease on pool and other gambling-booth privileges. He denied rumors his involvement was purely commercial, promising to donate profits to charity.[69]

The *Spirit* was uncomfortable with Haverly's takeover because it generally opposed profit-oriented tracks and was against a single individual controlling the majority share in any racetrack. The *Spirit* recommended that jockey clubs reinvest their profits to improve facili-ties and promote "honorable and enjoyable sport" and warned against proprietary managers who sought high admission fees that exceeded purses so sponsors would not have to directly put out money to attract horsemen. The track's response was that stakes events (contests in which the prize is at least partly composed of entry fees put up by owners of entered horses), without additional funds, would not attract the best horses.[70]

In 1880, the CJTC adopted a *Spirit* recommendation that all events become stakes races because previously win and place prizes had been pretty similar. Thereafter, winners got 65 percent of the purse, with 20 percent for second. The track opened on June 19, drawing some fifty-five hundred spectators of all social backgrounds. Wealthy club members watched from places in the clubhouse, while their wives sat outside on the full upper balcony. The *Tribune* reported that such "an assemblage . . . showed conclusively that, when properly conducted, racing is popular in Chicago."[71]

Nonetheless, attendance was disappointing, particularly among women. The *Spirit* blamed the local press, especially the *Chicago Times*, which had built its reputation by covering scandals, for unfair criticisms of thoroughbred racing, to wit "that the running turf folk are composed chiefly of stupid ignorant Negro boys, gamblers, drunkards, bullies, and braggarts, and that good breeding, politeness, common sense, and gentlemanly deportment are conspicuously absent from the running turf."[72]

The 1880 season did not go well because meets at second-tier tracks like the West Side track often struggled because of mismanagement, poor programs, and inadequate accommodations. Despite the positive reviews of opening day, the grandstand was barely accessible because it had few entrances and narrow stairways. Women complained that their facilities were insufficient and that their "select stand" was too far from the action and too close to obnoxious pipe smoke. The stables' wooden floors were dangerous for horses, which often got agitated by crowds they saw passing by. Furthermore, the club had foolishly sold off the pool-selling and refreshment privileges, worth $15,000, which would have covered the track's ongoing losses for 1879 and 1880, which came to $13,463.[73]

Betting Formats at the Tracks

Bets at antebellum races were often between social peers, though there were sometimes professional gamblers at the track who took wagers from individuals. The first American who took bets off the track was Dr. Robert H. Underwood, a Jewish veterinarian born in Dublin, who migrated to the United States around 1851, eventually settling in Lexington, Kentucky, where he trained young trotters. In 1855 Underwood was introduced by New Orleans gambler Price McGrath to a betting system that became known as auction pools and made it a popular betting format. At that time, many bettors were not settling their bets, and stakeholders often absconded with the money bet. In this new betting format, a professional gambler organized a pool covering individual races and "auctioned" off an option to the highest bidder to select whichever horse he wanted to bet on in that race. The pool seller would follow this betting opportunity with new auctions on the other horses in a race. If no one bid on the less regarded horses, the pool operator could offer an auction on the "field," which consisted of all the unselected horses. The auctioneer could then repeat the process and organize more pools, keeping a 3 percent service charge. Underwood brought this betting format in 1863 to the new Saratoga Springs racecourse, organizing auction pools on and off the track. Three years later, Underwood took bets in Manhattan for races at the newly opened Jerome Park Racetrack at "poolrooms" (for pooling the bets together) on and off the track. It was the first time that term appeared in the press, not to be confused with pool halls, where cue-ball games are played. The auction pool system had three disadvantages: the odds were determined only once the bidding was completed, bettors needed a lot of money to win an auction for the best horse, and it paid off only on horses coming in first. Wealthy bettors, not surprisingly, favored auction pools over other betting formats because it gave them more control over the pool, particularly control over the betting favorite.[74]

Large, crowded downtown poolrooms soon became popular in Chicago and New York. Charles L. Dubois was Chicago's first offtrack pool seller, operating in the mid-1860s in Alderman Tom Foley's saloon. "Future pools" were a popular innovation. They took bets on upcoming races, typically prestigious stakes events staged either in Chicago or out of town. Poolrooms were banned in Chicago and elsewhere but would become a cornerstone for the rise of syndicate crime, protected by pay-offs to the police and the influence of powerful political machines allied with the underworld. The penalty for operating a gaming room was not less $100 for the first offense, at least $500 and six months in the county jail, and at least $800 and two to five years in the penitentiary.[75]

Another important betting format was bookmaking, first used in England around 1840. A bookmaker working at a racecourse paid a fee to the track or its agent for the right to take bets. He stood on a raised platform inside a stall with a large blackboard, posted his odds on competing horses, and recorded wagers in a notebook. He took a fixed percentage, usually 5 percent off the top, and divided the remainder among the winning bettors. A successful bookie needed to post attractive odds that would draw bettors to support numerous horses in the race. A bookmaker's goal was to create a "balanced book" that assured him a profit, regardless of whichever horse won. Bookmaking was introduced in the United States after the Civil War by Philadelphia gamblers, who took bets on cricket, regattas, and trotting. In 1871 James B. Kelly of New York became the first bookmaker to set odds on a horse race, and one year later bookmakers worked at Jerome Park. This system was soon dropped, however, because wealthy bettors preferred the auction pools that they could dominate.[76]

The final major betting system was the pari-mutuel, invented in 1865 by Parisian perfumer Pierre Oller, who believed that professional gamblers offered unfair odds. His system accepted bets from all comers at a fixed price that were placed into a pool, with the winnings, less Oller's 5 percent fee, going to everyone who wagered on the winning horse. Approximate odds were reported while the bets were taken, tabulated by simple totalizers (devices that added up the amounts bet on each horse and then figured out the odds), which gave bettors a sense of what their potential winnings might be. The odds constantly changed as more money was bet. Wagers were usually a minimum of

$5. The tracks briefly tried to run this system, but found that professional oddsmakers or bookmakers could do a better job. In 1874 Jerome Park sold the privilege of operating a pari-mutuel to the well-known gambler and politician John Morrissey for $12,500. The pari-mutuel was considered a democratic form of betting compared to the auction pool, since every bettor could wager on any horse, including the favorite. However, there were problems with counterfeit tickets, the betting odds were uncertain until the betting was closed, and big bettors felt their heavy wagers depressed the odds.[77]

New Management for the CJTC

The CJTC sold its operations in early July 1880 for $50,000 to a new syndicate, the Chicago Driving Park Association that also assumed Haverly's three-year $15,000 lease. The jockey club revived the name of the old Civil War–era racing association. CDPA treasurer H. V. Bemis became the largest of 134 stockholders, which included well-known local businessmen, but just a single millionaire, and publishers of two Republican newspapers, the *Staats-Zeitung* and the *Inter Ocean*. Brewer John H. McAvoy was the second-largest shareholder and combined with Bemis held a majority interest. Capital stock was set at $100,000, of which $60,000 was collected by the time of purchase. The building and tracks were bought for $50,000, leaving $10,000 in the treasury. Bemis and his partners put up an additional $10,000 to cover the CJTC's outstanding debts.[78]

The new regime started out well, with the first two dates averaging about nine thousand spectators, undoubtedly because admission was cut from $1 to 50 cents. However, the venture was a financial disaster since they had limited revenue sources, especially as Haverly still controlled the ancillary privileges. By late September the CDPA was $42,000 in debt. Creditors included the Pinkerton Agency and various newspapers where the Chicago Driving Park had advertised, including $5,000 owed to the *Times* and $3,200 to the *Tribune*.[79]

The CDPA made a big mistake that summer by heavily investing in short-distance racing that emphasized speed while facilitating more races and more betting. The *Tribune* pointed out that the Midwest was a trotting area. Management should continue staging five-day meets and not run an overly lengthy fourteen-day meet featuring events with substantial purses for brief races that did not interest local fans. Chicagoans did not like attending four hour-long racing dates with races that took only about twelve minutes to complete. They were said to prefer four-mile heat racing and other events of two or three miles.[80]

The fall meet opened with merely three hundred spectators and just one pool seller. The track was in prime shape, but there was such inept driving that disgusted fans left early. Racing aficionados were also disappointed with the concessions. The *Inter Ocean* complained that the "refreshment stands have been turned over to a gang of unblushing robbers. . . . A thin glass of beer, composed largely of foam, could not be got for less than ten cents. Bad cigars were sold at first-class prices, and attenuated sandwiches are sold for fifteen cents when five would be liberal." The meet had one memorable event on September 18, when railroad magnate William H. Vanderbilt's great trotter Maud S. raced the clock to set a new world's record for the mile at 2:10.75.[81]

In 1881 the four-hundred-member jockey club opened its trotting season on a beautiful day, with ten thousand in attendance. Membership cost $20. Private boxes, seating four to six, were available in the grandstand for $1 each. However, the CDPA offered just seven days of harness racing (with fifty-four heats) compared to twelve days of racing in 1880. There was also a week of flat racing. Overall, the club reported grossing $31,278, with just $13,049 in expenses, leaving a net profit of $18,229. Then in 1882 the trotting season made $20,000 and in 1883 claimed a positive balance of $6,983.[82]

The *Spirit* reported a large female audience in 1882, who "not only add to the attractions of the occasion, but their presence has a tendency to restrain the too violent demonstration of the enthusiasm of a mixed crowd." However, the afternoon *Daily News*, the city's most popular daily, with a circulation in 1890 (229,363) triple the *Tribune*'s (75,000), was far more critical. The *Daily News* was the turf's strongest detractor in Chicago, reflecting publisher Victor Lawson's

Table 1
Chicago Driving Park Association Profits, 1881

Meet Receipts	
Running meeting	$9,888
Membership	5,920
Clubhouse, bar, and privileges	6,211
Summer trotting meeting	9,259
Total	$31,278
Meet Expenses	
Rent	$1,900
Insurance	986
Taxes	248
Expenses	9,288
Running 1882 meet	207
Postage	420
Total	$13,049
Profit	$18,229

Source: Chicago Tribune, December 4, 1881, 15-1. Original tabulation errors corrected.

crusading philosophy against vice and misgovernment. The paper disparaged streetcar service to the track as unpleasant and inconvenient. Riders had to cope with long waits, dirty cars, and insolent conductors. The Daily News disapproved of gambling and alleged swindling and frauds at the track. It censured management's failure to enforce the rules proscribing liquor sales and the presence of minors, who, according to Mayor Carter Harrison, needed written parental permission to attend. The press disapproved of the fleecing of spectators, who expected admission to cost 50 cents, but had to pay double for any spot where they could actually see the racing. They also attacked the concessionaires who charged an exorbitant 10 cents a glass for ice water.[83]

After the end of the fall flat-racing season, a consortium represented by track secretary D. L. Hall bought H. V. Bemis's 52 percent
of the capital stock, worth $52,000, for just $37,000. The syndicate
consisted of Hall, W. R. Armstrong, R. C. Page, and John Forbes, who
got the board of directors to extend Bride & Armstrong's contract to
run the betting until the end of the track's current lease and added a
wheel of fortune charging $500 each day the track was open. Bemis
still remained active in racing, becoming president in 1884 of the new
$50,000 *Chicago Horseman*, a thirty-two-page turf weekly, with a cir-
culation of seven thousand. By the end of 1883, the track had assets
of $131,958 that were nearly all structural improvements, but had so
many liabilities that it was in the black by just $6,983 and declared no
dividends. The professional gamblers associated with the track made
out well. One-third of the $18,000 made by the wheel of fortune went
to the operator and the rest to Hall's syndicate, which also shared in
Bride & Armstrong's $17,000 fee for running the gambling. The *Daily
News* decried the new gambling format that it felt had no business at a
respectable racecourse.[84]

CRIME BOSS MIKE MCDONALD AND THE TURF

In 1873, before Lawrence and Martin went into the racing game, they
partnered with up-and-coming gambler Mike McDonald to establish
"the Store" at 176 Clark Street in the heart of the post-fire downtown,
conveniently located across the street from the County Building. The
"Store" became the city's premier gambling emporium. Mike bought
out his partners in 1877, which helped propel him to become the first
head of syndicate crime in America.[85]

Mike was born at Niagara Falls, New York, in 1839. He apprenticed
as a boot maker, but also worked as a Buffalo hack driver, cooperating
with swindlers who cheated unsophisticated travelers. McDonald subsequently left home and sold sweets and newspapers on the Michigan
Central Railroad. Mike arrived in Chicago by 1861 where he worked
the confidence game, and ran a low-class saloon in the Richmond
House, near the Central Railroad Depot, which became the nerve

3. Mike McDonald, king of
gamblers. McDonald (1839–1907)
used his clout and organizing
ability to found syndicate crime
in Chicago. Reprinted from
Hugh S. Fullerton, "American
Gambling and Gamblers," 34.

center for con men seeking unwary arriving travelers; and opened a
downtown faro game. He also helped thieves enlist in the army collect
a bounty and then abscond.[86]

McDonald and the Rise of Syndicate Crime

According to historian David Johnson, the idea for organizing the
local gambling business probably started in 1870 with McDonald,
future alderman John Corcoran, owner of a modest hotel and operator
of two faro games, and Alderman Thomas Foley, a billiard champion
who owned the finest billiard parlor in the world, a saloonkeeper, and
cofounder and first manager of the White Stockings. After the Chicago
Fire, McDonald opened a thieves' hangout on State Street and moved
on to the West Side, a partner in John Dowling's saloon and gambling
house, providing police protection. He reputedly cleared $100,000 in
less than a year. By 1873 McDonald headed an association to regulate
competition and arrange mutual protection among the city's leading
gambling halls. As Johnson points out, "McDonald became the broker
for necessary services required by Chicago's underworld."[87]

McDonald's prominent role in the underworld was further mani-
fested when he and his partners opened the Store. The first floor
had a saloon, the second was Chicago's largest gambling hall, and
the two upper floors were a boardinghouse. The three partners also
gained total control of the city's bunko (swindling) business that made
$900,000 to $1 million from unsuspecting marks. From then on, no
one could break into that trade without paying them for instructions,
police protection, and legal aid. Twenty percent of their profits went
to the police for protection, 40 percent to the ropers who found the
marks (people who got cheated), and 40 percent to the firm.[88]

The Store's ground-floor saloon served for fourteen years as Chicago's sporting center and a major meeting place for politicians and
underworld toughs. Mike became the linchpin in the growing nexus
between the sporting world, urban politics, and syndicate crime. At his
apex he reportedly had some two thousand gamblers paying him off. A
major reason for his success was that he was also becoming an important political boss who helped select and elect political candidates and
then employed them as his puppets. However, the press exaggerated
his power when it claimed he "ruled the city with an iron hand," since
he was certainly not omnipotent or as powerful as his contemporary
bosses in New York's Tammany Hall.[89]

McDonald originally had serious rivals in the gambling business,
but he found ways to form alliances with his competition. One of his
biggest foes when he was building his syndicate was Harry "Prince
Hal" Varnell, a prominent politician, gamester, and horseman, known
for surrounding himself with elegance. The Chicago-born Varnell got
into politics as a young man and was rewarded in 1880 when county
commissioners hired the twenty-eight-year-old as warden of the
Cook County Insane Asylum in Dunning. Varnell ran it as a patronage haven for McDonald's followers and as a virtual country club for
friends, relatives, and political cronies. He provided a clubhouse atmosphere, with regularly scheduled dances, complemented by refreshments from the asylum's unlicensed drugstore. County commissioners
spent so much time enjoying themselves at the asylum that it seemed
some lived there. The facility's reputation became so bad that in 1886

state's attorney Julius Sprague Grinnell initiated an investigation of the county asylum, poorhouse, and hospital that resulted in Varnell and several other public officials being sentenced to the Joliet state penitentiary. After Varnell was released, he opened a saloon at 126 Clark Street and then bought the entire building at 119 Clark. The prince spent more than $100,000 just on furniture and operated the most elegant gambling hall in the city. The second floor was embellished with "wood carvings, marbles and bronzes, paintings, and rich tapestries." The gambling hall, open twenty-four hours a day, employed twenty-five faro dealers and fifteen croupiers. His political clout came from the young "Bathhouse" John Coughlin, elected First Ward alderman in 1892. However, despite his powerful protection, Prince Hal was closed down in the mid-1890s during Mayor John Hopkins's antigambling crusade.[90]

McDonald's main foes were brothers Al, Jeff, and George Hankins, who reportedly earned $20,000 a month from their gambling halls. They were sons of a McHenry County farmer who had previously tried to make their fortune out West, engaging in mining and mercantile and saloon businesses, before drifting into gambling. In 1869, Al and Jeff opened what was then the city's most elegant gambling house at 125 North Clark.[91]

The Hankins brothers were avid sportsmen. Al was an athlete who later bred gamecocks and financed prizefighters and pool players. He began buying thoroughbreds in the 1870s and was considered by the *Tribune* as the area's most outstanding owner and breeder. George also got into racing with Johnny S. Campbell in the Chicago Stable, one of the city's preeminent jockey clubs and one of the most successful in the United States. It was an unusual partnership because some of the horses were collectively owned, but others were individually retained. Rivals, especially in New York, did not like or respect Hankins or Campbell, gamblers who played for high stakes. The *New York Mail and Express* wrote, "Their horses run in and out, in unaccountable fashion." Some of their horses were owned collectively, but others individually. One of their top riders was Jimmy McLaughlin, best known as the chief jockey for the Dwyer brothers of New York, who won six Belmont Stakes. In 1888 the Chicago Stable won $97,873 in purses, highlighted by Macbeth II's victory in the Kentucky Derby. However, the firm split up, in October, with Hankins buying out Campbell for $10,000. George brought new faces into the Chicago Stable, which struggled in 1890, barely meeting expenses, though it did win the American Derby, worth $18,000, with favorite Uncle Bob, bought just prior to the race for $15,000 (plus $2,000 if he won). Hankins sold his interest in the stable at the end of the year, earmarking the profits toward financing a racetrack.[92]

The brothers were the strongest holdouts against McDonald's gambling trust. They believed their elite clientele put them above McDonald's associations and were unwilling to pay McDonald's crowd one-third of their profits. But when McDonald agreed to cut his syndicate's share of their profits to 25 percent, the brothers signed up. His expanded organization nearly monopolized bookmaking at Chicago-area tracks and totally controlled offtrack betting. During the 1890s, only independent bookies affiliated with McDonald's gambling trust prospered, notably Jim O'Leary, son of Mrs. O'Leary of Chicago Fire fame, and William "Silver Bill" Riley, reputedly the first Chicagoan to operate a gambling hall just for horse-race betting. His most astute client in the mid-1880s was "Pittsburgh Phil Smith, who became the most outstanding handicapper in North America. He died with a fortune of $3.25 million.[93]

McDonald and Chicago Politics

Mike McDonald became heavily involved in Democratic politics after the Civil War, and his participation increased after the Chicago Fire when Mayor Charles Medill tried to impose strict moral standards upon the citizenry, such as enforcing Sunday blue laws, curtailing liquor consumption, and limiting gambling. Medill's infringements on personal liberty incensed the mainly Republican German American voters and the overwhelmingly Democratic Irish. In 1873 McDonald switched to the new and short-lived People's Party under mayoral candidate Harvey D. Colvin, then the city treasurer. The People's

Party stood for personal freedom, which appealed to working-class Germans and Irishmen. McDonald masterminded the gambling syndicate's prominent role in Colvin's victorious campaign against acting mayor Lester Bond, capturing 60 percent of the vote. McDonald was rewarded when the new administration promoted a wide-open city that gave saloonkeepers, pimps, madams, and gamblers free rein. However, the moral reformers regained power in 1876 under Republican Monroe Heath, who curbed personal freedoms and dramatically increased anti-betting raids.[94]

McDonald and prominent criminal attorney Alfred Trude brought many of the People's Party supporters back to the Democratic fold, supporting Samuel Tilden in the 1876 presidential election. According to biographer Richard Lindberg, McDonald "was warmly regarded by influential city attorneys, judges, and politicians as a master organizer who resurrected the moribund Cook County Democratic Party" in the post–Civil War era. He and Trude played a major role in the next mayoralty campaign of 1879, electing Carter Harrison the first Democratic mayor of Chicago in fourteen years. McDonald was comfortable with Harrison, who opposed Sunday blue laws, restrictions on alcoholic beverages, and the suppression of vice. Carter believed that gambling was rooted in human nature and preferred regulation over termination.[95]

Following Harrison's election, Mike McDonald became party treasurer and chairman of assessments for the Democratic Central Committee, putting him in charge of raising money for the party. Yet Mike continued using his clout in support of the underworld. Chicago had no citywide political machine then, unlike New York's Tammany Hall, led by "Honest John" Kelly, but both the Democrats and the Republicans had powerful ward bosses. McDonald was regarded as a major party figure, exemplified by his role in helping make twenty-nine-year-old inspector William McGarigle police superintendent in 1880, who responded by actively working to protect Mike's interests. Two years later, McDonald spent $50,000 to support McGarigle's unsuccessful race for county sheriff. McDonald was a close ally of several committeemen, including party secretary

"Chesterfield Joe" Mackin, a gambler and saloon owner who reportedly introduced the free-lunch system to Chicago's taverns. In 1883 McDonald and Mackin were the powers behind the election of city clerk Michael Ryan.[96]

McDonald and his cronies were important financial backers in the early Harrison reelection campaigns. In 1881 Harrison met with several Chicago sportsmen at a national convention of American firemen. He told them that he would not run for reelection for less than a $10,000 campaign donation. He got his money. Two years later, his price went up to $15,000, which Mike McDonald, Al Hankins, and other prominent gamblers put right into his hands. Then in 1885 a group of gamblers appeared at the mayor's home with $15,000. Harrison asked for another $5,000, but the sporting crowd, composed of fans and gamblers, balked this time. He won that election over Republican judge Sidney Smith by just 375 votes, and his opponent called for a recount. Harrison hit on the gamblers again, this time for $7,000, threatening to "throw up the sponge." They paid him off.[97]

In the four years prior to Harrison becoming mayor, the police under Colvin (1875), and under reformer Republican John Heath (1876–78), did not make fighting gambling a prime concern. From 1875 through 1878, there were 1,841 gambling arrests compared to 7,850 for prostitution, were mainly for faro and card playing. Colvin had a gambling index of 44, while Heath's ranged from 42 to 26. During Harrison's first four terms (1879–87) there were 4,719 arrests for gambling violations and 17,989 for vice, though the yearly ratio of gambling to vice did drop from 1:8 in 1879 to 1:2 in 1887. Harrison scored the lowest Gambling Index (22) among all Chicago mayors over his first four terms than other mayors in their tenure, for their careers for the years 1879–87, and lower than any single year until Ed Kelly (13) in 1934.[98]

The *Chicago Tribune* considered McDonald their equivalent of John Morrissey, the former sportsman, gambler, and Tammany leader. A letter to the *Indianapolis Journal* claimed that McDonald controlled "75 to 100 saloons, and scores of gambling halls, and virtually owns 1,000 votes." The *Tribune* claimed the correspondent underrated his importance "to the degeneracy and degradation to which politics have been brought to this city" by the McDonald-led Democratic Party, whose "value to the party far exceeds that of a dozen Harrisons."[99]

McDonald and Harrison did not see eye to eye on many matters. Harrison occasionally went after some of the worst gambling halls, including rooms owned or protected by McDonald, as in 1885 when he ran for reelection, seeking the support of reformers.[100] The two had another big falling-out in 1893 when Harrison tried to embellish his public image and regain the mayoralty after a four-year hiatus by distancing himself from McDonald and his crowd. Even then, McDonald, titular boss of the Eleventh Ward and a Cook County committeeman until 1892, raised money from gamblers backing Harrison. He claimed his support for Harrison was worth five thousand votes. Mike also played a big role in the nomination and election of John Peter Altgeld as governor. Historian Ray Ginger, Altgeld's biographer, considered Mike "the decisive recruit to his cause." After the election, McDonald resumed managing his syndicate, collecting a fixed percentage of profits from all gamblers and confidence men for protection from police interference.[101]

McDonald and the Sporting Life

Mike had a wide range of illegal sporting interests besides horse racing. According to one barroom bettor, "Some of them races were so fixed you could smell the brakes smokin' when the jocks pulled a hoss on the turn fer home." Racing dominated the betting scene by far, but other sports that provided a venue for betting included baseball, boxing, and professional rowing, a popular spectator sport in the 1870s and 1880s that lost its standing because of numerous fixed races. One of McDonald's first ventures into sculling came in the early 1870s when he brought in New York gambler, sports promoter, and murderer Jere Dunn to organize illegal races on the lakefront. He became a booking agent for John L. Sullivan and other fighters and regularly gave tips on boxing matches to help McDonald with his betting. McDonald, in turn, kept him in touch with top attorneys.[102]

McDonald allegedly participated in an effort to fix the St. Louis Brown Stockings–Chicago White Stockings game of August 24, 1877, won by Chicago, 4–3. Charles C. Spink, sports editor of the *St. Louis Globe-Democrat*, claimed McDonald conspired with two Brown Stockings to predetermine the outcome. The intermediary was reportedly National League umpire L. W. Burtis, seen socializing with McDonald in Chicago a few days earlier. McDonald reportedly mailed "a considerable sum of money" to Burtis, who placed a large bet on Chicago. Burtis purportedly sent a telegram to McDonald: "Buy wheat. Smith is all right. Jones will assist." Burtis never officiated in the Majors after that season.[103]

Spink later claimed the Browns lost because two players who had advised friends to bet on the White Stockings made pivotal errors "at precisely the right moment." After the game a McDonald assistant was followed by a private detective to a St. Louis saloon backroom, where he allegedly paid off the players. The following game was also supposedly fixed, but when the Browns captain learned of the plot from a St. Louis "sharp," he switched a suspected conspirator to a different position, which frightened his teammates to play up to form. St. Louis won the game, which cost McDonald dearly.[104]

McDonald was also closely tied to Chicago promoter Charles E. "Parson" Davies, who staged indoor sports like pedestrianism (long-distance racing) and pugilism, which, when conducted by professionals, was illegal. In 1881 Davies brought in rising heavyweight contender John L. Sullivan to exhibit his skills in a "sparring" match at McCormick Hall, with McDonald as master of ceremonies. One month later, McDonald refereed a match starring young Sullivan, and afterward McDonald and Davies tried to match Sullivan with American heavyweight champion Paddy Ryan, promising to bet $5,000 on the challenger. They were unsuccessful, and the bout was instead promoted by publisher Richard K. Fox of the *National Police Gazette* on February 7, 1882, at Mississippi City, Mississippi. McDonald and Davies switched their allegiance and put their money on Ryan, who lost. Chicagoans afterward arranged a benefit for him. McDonald remained active in boxing for several years, and on February 13, 1889, he refereed the Billy Myer–Jack McAuliffe world championship light-weight fight, scheduled for an unannounced site that turned out to be North Judson, Indiana. Attendees included some one hundred members of the Chicago Board of Trade and, according to folklore, so many aldermen that the city council recessed.

McDonald Goes Legit

In the late 1880s, even while the McDonald-Hankins bookmaking syndicate dominated the metropolitan racetracks, McDonald was breaking away from some of his old connections, having earned $2 million from his criminal dealings. He branched out into more legitimate enterprises, selling the Store in 1888 to Parson Davies and gambler Harry Perry and getting involved in downtown real estate. Two years later, he became part of the syndicate that built the Lake Street line, the city's first elevated railroad. In 1891 McDonald purchased the *Chicago Globe*, a Democratic newspaper, for $109,000, which he ran for more than two years. He also bought a Lemont quarry and used his political influence to get contracts to supply local governments with sand, stone, and gravel. However, he did not entirely exit the sporting life, founding the Garfield Park Racetrack in 1891 and remaining active in the gambling business.[105]

Mike's Personal Life

Mike died a rich man in 1907, but he had a very unhappy private life. His first wife, Mary Noonan, shot and killed a police officer who was investigating the family's apartment, but was acquitted. She later ran off with an actor to San Francisco and later fled to Paris with a priest. McDonald divorced her in 1888. Ten years later, Mike married a local burlesque dancer, Dora Feldman, daughter of Jewish immigrants, previously married at eighteen in 1888 to Sam Barclay, a Major Leaguer (1884–89). The divorced entertainer met Mike in 1893 and married him five years later when he converted to Judaism. In the late 1890s, Dora began a decadelong affair with Webster Guerin, then a high school student. Their affair lasted until 1907, when she shot him to death. Mike died that year and left her $25,000 for her trial, which resulted in an acquittal. McDonald, who had converted back to Catholicism, left an estate estimated at anywhere from $490,000 ($13,491,246 in 2020) to $2 million, of which Dora got one-third as his widow.[106]

Conclusion

Equine sports were popular in Chicago in the city's first half century, providing attendees with opportunities to wager on their favorites, thereby demonstrating their expertise in evaluating horse flesh, and the extent of their manliness, by backing their judgment with their wagers. Before the Civil War, there were several short-lived race-courses that hosted brief meets lasting about a week, built and operated by prominent men who were comfortable with harness racing, a useful, democratic sport that did not carry the cachet, or the costs, of thoroughbred racing.

The early trotting tracks were intended to make money, or at least break even. Men like William B. Ogden, Charles P. Chapin, "Long John" Wentworth, and David A. Gage believed that operating a track demonstrated their public interest in their community, while displaying their personal wealth and social standing. They expected political connections would help secure them inside access to real-estate data for their track site and preferential action from the city council on taxes, licenses, and other related matters.

Harness racing in Chicago made important strides after the Civil War and began to draw national attention with the local ownership of Dexter, the preeminent trotter of the nineteenth century, and then the opening of Dexter Park, named for the great horse, at a site in the stockyards neighborhood. However, the facility was not of the highest quality and was supplanted by the Chicago Jockey and Trotting Club, with its finer amenities and easier access. The sport still struggled, though harness racing was legal, even if the gambling was not, and men of some distinction were in charge. The wagering was run by men of questionable integrity and relied on the political clout of its backers in the mid-1870s, the McDonald gambling trust. The syndicate provided bookmakers with capital, racing news, bondsmen, attorneys, and protection against municipal interference and facilitated raids against rivals in return for payoffs and political support at election time.

As the 1880s began, the Chicago turf scene was not commensurate with the city's stature as the nation's fourth-largest city, especially given the Chicago's open-mindedness and the strong ethnic working class's opposition to restrictions on personal freedom. Harness racing, except for a few rich sponsors like publisher Robert Bonner and railroad tycoon Commodore Vanderbilt, was on the decline as an urban sport, rapidly becoming primarily a rural diversion, increasingly identified with county fairs. There was a strong appetite among Chicago's high society for a thoroughbred racing club in the 1880s that would gain members, status, and prestige. This quest for public recognition led to the emergence of the greatest racing organization in the Midwest, the Washington Park Club.

2

The Chicago Elite and the Rise of the Washington Park Club, 1883–1889

Chicago had a lot to be proud of by 1880, having made remarkable strides in rebuilding itself after the Great Fire. Chicago had 503,185 residents, a 59.4 percent increase in a decade. Chicagoans were delighted by the city's reconstructed housing system, the coming in 1882 of a huge cable-car system, the growth of the Union Stockyards in conjunction with the railroad freight business, the astonishing industrial expansion, and the growth of its banking and commercial base centered in the thriving downtown, which was the financial and cultural center of the city. Local boosters were also prideful of such institutions as its daily press, the park system (1869), the public library (1872), the National League's White Stockings champion teams (1876, 1880–82, 1885–86), and the Chicago Academy of Fine Arts (1879), renamed the Art Institute of Chicago three years later.[1]

Chicago was still a young city, whose business elite were virtually all men of new or recent money, unlike Boston, Philadelphia, or New York, whose privileged people were still mainly "old money." Nouveau riche Chicagoans demonstrated their social status by emulating elite easterners by engaging in favorable marriages, residing in lavish homes at prestigious addresses, leading a lifestyle of conspicuous consumption, and participating in philanthropy. They also joined exclusive convivial men's clubs that emphasized business, like the Chicago Club (1869), politics such as the Union League Club (1879), culture such as the Calumet Club (1878), and sports such as the Washington Park Club (1883). Membership confirmed and enhanced their stature.[2]

Membership in sports clubs endowed less status than the most prestigious urban men's clubs, although polo and yacht clubs were very close to the top and racing and athletic clubs not far behind. Prestigious American jockey clubs dated to the 1730s and 1740s and remained important social institutions in the South, like Charleston's South Carolina Jockey Club and the Metairie Jockey Club of New Orleans up through the coming of the Civil War. The sport of kings had recently enjoyed an enormous revival in New York State, beginning in 1863 at upstate Saratoga, and continued in the metropolitan area when new elite jockey clubs built elegant racetracks in New York, Brooklyn, and nearby Long Branch, New Jersey. They became models for elite jockey clubs in Baltimore, Louisville, and Chicago. Gilded Age nabobs spent huge amounts of money establishing stables and jockey clubs because they enjoyed the thrill of racing, the accompanying excitement of gambling, and the social cachet of membership in the horsey set. Membership in elite jockey clubs provided social status and opportunities to socialize with the right people and displayed one's wealth when riding to the track in a luxurious horse-drawn carriage, sitting in a box seat on opening day, socializing with their peers at the clubhouse, or getting mentioned in local newspapers. The racing set was made up snobs who reveled in a pastime that, according to sociologist Thorstein Veblen, exemplified conspicuous consumption and was "expensive, . . . wasteful and useless," though horsemen did rationalize the sport as a means to promote the breed.[3]

THE FORMATION OF THE WASHINGTON PARK CLUB

Chicago's first jockey clubs primarily sponsored harness racing. Membership offered some status, but far less than membership in the leading thoroughbred racing clubs in major American cities. By the early 1880s, elite Chicagoans wanted to set up a higher-status racing association comparable to the finest jockey clubs in the land. On February 10, 1883, several of the city's principal citizens organized the Washington

Map 1. Location of Chicago racetracks in the years 1840–1904 in *Chicago Railroad Map of 1890*. Reprinted from *Rand McNally Standard Atlas of the World* (Chicago: Cambridge, 1890), 104. Map image courtesy of Barry Lawrence Ruderman Antique Maps—www.RareMaps.com.

MAP LEGEND FOR CHICAGO AREA RACETRACKS, 1844–1904

Track	Dates	Address
1. Chicago Racetrack	1844–47	26th St. & Indiana Ave.
2. Garden City Track	1854–62	36th St. & Indiana Ave.
3. Brighton Trotting Park	1855–72	38th St. & Western Ave
4. Chicago Driving Park	1863–66	31st St. & State St.
5. Dexter Park	1867–77	42nd St. & Halsted St.
6. Chicago Trotting Park	1878–85	Madison St. & Pulaski Ave.
West Side Park	1885–90	Madison St. & Pulaski Ave.
Garfield Park Racetrack	1891–92	Madison St. & Pulaski Ave.
7. Washington Park Club	1884–1904	E. 61st St. & S. Cottage Grove
8. Hawthorne Race Course	1891–1904	3501 S. Laramie, Cicero.
9. Roby Race Track	1892–1904	108th St. and State Line
10. Harlem Racetrack	1894–1904	Collier Ave. & 74th St., Harlem
11. Worth Racetrack	1901–1904	111th St. & Ridgeland, Worth

Park Club at a meeting chaired by James Van Inwagen, son-in-law of Charles Lewis Tiffany, the preeminent American jeweler. The meeting raised more than $100,000 to build a world-class racecourse with $5,000 coming from Samuel Allerton, a leading figure in the stockyards and railroad consolidation; soap and baking manufacturer N. K. Fairbank; Marshall Field, the department-store mogul; and Murray Nelson, a major grain commissioner and prominent Republican Party leader. A particularly important figure at the meeting was Albert S. Gage, who had a wholesale millinery business and was an experienced owner of thoroughbred horses. They anticipated setting up an elite racetrack on the South Side exclusively for thoroughbreds based on the model of New York's Jerome Park.[4]

The WPC never called itself a "jockey club," until the late 1890s, unlike New York's American Jockey Club or Brooklyn's Coney Island Jockey Club (CIJC) did, since its primary goal was to "promote good fellowship among its members, by providing a club-house and pleasure grounds for . . . social intercourse; and, further, to encourage by providing the proper facilities, raising, improving, breeding, training, and exhibiting horses, at meetings to be held . . . each year." Their main intent was social rather than promoting racing. According to one member, "Our original idea was a sort of country club to which we could resort for pleasure or a drive, and in Winter for sleighing parties. Racing was the fashionable amusement and we took it up. . . . But while we are bent upon making it the great racing ground of the West, if not of the union, we are determined to maintain the social side." The founders did not intend to hold extended meets or make a lot of money, because "they have a higher purpose than mere hippodroming," though they certainly did not want to lose money.[5]

The WPC immediately got widespread national attention. The *Spirit*, for instance, was effusive in its praise: "Never since the formation of the American Jockey club in 1866, has the sport received such an impetus. . . . It has laid out a course which will have no superior, and the social features which distinguish the American are to be reproduced in the club-house and numerous other features which will render the membership desirable to the best elements of Chicago society, and place racing under its auspices on that high plane of refined and cultivated surrounding which have ever been conspicuous at Jerome [Park]."[6]

Civil War hero General Philip H. Sheridan, the current US Army commander in chief, was the WPC's first president. His vice presidents were Allerton; Fairbank, president of the prestigious Chicago Club; John W. Duane, president of the Merchants Loan and Trust Bank; and A. S. Gage. The politically connected banker John R. Walsh became treasurer, and J. E. Brewster, an experienced racing man, was appointed secretary and general manager. Brewster was a native of Massachusetts, who had recently moved to Chicago from New York to operate the J. E. Brewster Straw Works with 160 employees. He got into racing in 1869 with Colonel David McDaniels and Gage in the McDaniels' Confederacy, an important racing stable (1869–78) that won three straight Belmont Stakes (1871–73).[7]

The Washington Park Racetrack was capitalized at $100,000 (40 percent of the CIJC), divided into a thousand shares of $100 each, and had 174 stockholders. The original 114 incorporators included such notable men as Marshall Field, hotelier Potter Palmer, industrialist George W. Pullman, and lumberman Martin W. Ryerson. The club was run by its 23-member board of directors, overwhelmingly native-born white Protestants from upstate New York. Eight were millionaires, but just 4 were experienced racing men, reflecting the WPC's original emphasis on sociability over commercialized sport. The first 200 members paid a $150 initiation fee, while others were charged $200 and had to pass a rigorous vetting process that allowed blacklisting by prior members. Annual dues were $40. By 1884 the WPC had raised $174,000 just from initiation fees and dues.[8]

Chicago's social and economic elite flocked to the club. In 1890, for instance, the WPC had 762 local members, 28 nonresident members, and 2 in the military. They were among the richest and most prestigious Chicagoans, overwhelmingly from the upper class (83.8 percent). They included the crème de la crème of Chicago society, with names like Field, Kimball, Leiter, Palmer, Ryerson, and Swift particularly well represented. The elite constituted 38.6 percent of the total membership (see table 2). In 1892, 96 of the city's 278 millionaires were members, a number exceeded only by the Chicago Club.

Table 2
Washington Park Club Members' Social Status, 1888

SOCIAL RANK	NUMBER	PERCENTAGE
Elite	294	38.6
Upper class	345	45.3
Upper middle class	99	13.0
Middle class	14	1.8
Unknown	10	1.3
Total	762	100.0 percent

[a]Error due to rounding off.
Source: Membership list drawn from *Chicago Clubs, Illustrated*, 71–72. For biographical material, see Washington Park Members' Biographical Sources in bibliography.

They not only were extremely wealthy but also had the most prestigious occupations, belonged to the most esteemed men's clubs, were
the most eminent philanthropists, and resided on the most desirable
South Side streets, namely, Michigan (131), Prairie (86), and Calumet
Avenues (32), which had the city's most fabulous mansions.[9]

Historian Frederic C. Jaher, an eminent scholar of the American
upper classes, rated the WPC among the city's leading half-dozen
metropolitan clubs. Memberships often overlapped and were passed
down to the next generation. The WPC was well represented in such
top clubs as the Calumet (with 111 members), Chicago (220), Union
(44), and Union League (159).[10]

WPC members were employed in the highest-paying and most
prestigious occupations. Some, like Potter Palmer, owner of the
eponymous department store as well as a major real-estate investor,
worked in more than one field at a time. In 1890 the WPC included
124 members of the celebrated Chicago Board of Trade, the world's
first commodities exchange, which then had about 1,900 members
who paid $10,000 ($283,293 today) to join, a significant investment.
The most common primary occupation (see table 3) was commission
agent (125), which involved buying and selling commodity futures.
There were 84 men in merchandising, one-third of whom were

Table 3
Washington Park Club Members' Occupations, 1888

Commission agent	125
Merchandising	84
Attorney	58
Manufacturing	50
Real estate	48
Lumber	43
Packing	38
Railroad	31
Total	477

Source: Study data of 762 Washington Park Club members, 1888.

wholesalers (28) and two-thirds retailers (56) who sold dry goods to the public in department stores and specialty firms. Attorneys were third (58), which reflected the importance of contracts in a corporate, manufacturing, and commercial city, as well as the varied opportunities available for lawyers beyond law firms. Next were 50 manufacturers, whose factories ranged from clothing to steel. There were 48 involved in real estate, a flourishing business in this era, exemplified by the appreciation of downtown land prices by 700 percent between 1877 and 1892.[11]

Club membership in 1890 was nearly 90 percent white Anglo-Saxon Protestant. I found no Scandinavian members, 22 Irish, and 53 Germans, all heavily working-class groups. A high proportion of the Irish and German members were prominent in the liquor business, a trade in which they were locally and nationally well represented. The WPC did not have a single Jewish member when it was founded or any members of color. One year later, the press reported critically on news that the two prominent Jews proposed for membership ended up among the five blackballed applicants. Club secretary J. E. Brewster publicly declared, "No Jews would be admitted to the club," even though there were prominent local Jews very interested in racing. This snub drew considerable negative public attention, and considerable pressure was placed on the WPC to reverse its policy. Four Jews were admitted in 1886, including Moses Bensinger, vice president of the Brunswick-Balke-Collender Company that manufactured billiard tables and son-in-law of founder John Brunswick. Four more Jewish men were added by 1890.[12]

The prejudice against Jewish membership was no surprise. There was historically substantial anti-Semitism in the United States among people of all social classes and groups. Anti-Semitism was especially strong among the elite and the horsey set. Yet there were a handful of Jews involved in antebellum thoroughbred racing, and after the Civil War New York's highly respected American Jockey Club had a Jewish president, August Belmont, the renowned financier and national Democratic leader, who married the daughter of Commodore Matthew Perry. The AJC in 1873 had at least 8 other Jewish members.[13]

The WPC rejection came shortly after elite American anti-Semitism had become nationally recognized in 1877 when international banker and philanthropist Joseph Seligman was rejected access to the Grand Union Hotel in Saratoga, New York. Probably the most ardent anti-Semitism among horsemen was among members of The Jockey Club (TJC), an organization founded in 1894 to work with the new New York State Racing Commission one year later to help supervise thoroughbred racing in the state. The Jockey Club had no Jewish members until 1951.[14]

The WPC bought eighty acres in 1883 of swampy land south of the city (bounded by Sixty-First and Sixty-Third Streets, South Park and Cottage Grove) in Hyde Park township (midway between Woodlawn and Englewood) at a cost of $120,000. The site's viability for racing was first mentioned in the press in 1878 because property values there were cheap and the area had good transportation. Prominent architect Solon S. Beman, a WPC member, builder of the renowned Studebaker Building in 1885 (today the Fine Arts Building), the new town of Pullman, and several structures for the Columbian Exposition, and Nathan F. Barrett, the noted landscape engineer, designed the facility with its one-mile track and $40,000 eight-thousand-seat two-tiered grandstand (like New York's Jerome Park). It was five hundred feet long, making it the largest in the United States.[15]

The course's centerpiece was a luxurious $50,000 three-story clubhouse, the biggest in the country, which had a café, wine rooms, a timbered-ceiling grand dining room, seven private dining rooms, a ladies' parlor, a veranda, a covered balcony, and bedrooms on the third floor. By comparison, one year later, Albert Spalding, owner of the White Stockings, spent just $30,000 to build the six-thousand-seat West Side Grounds at Congress and Loomis Streets. Racing fans sitting in the clubhouse and the grandstand, and standees on the front lawn, enjoyed perfect views of the track. The *Spirit* rated the course as perfect in its lines, curves, and turns, with dark, pliable elastic soil for the horses to run on. There was also a three-quarter-mile private driving track for club members to ride their roadsters. Admission to the track and grandstand cost $1, a reserved seat was $1.50, a season

4. Washington Park Clubhouse in 1884. It was said to have the finest facilities and ambience of any in the United States. Reprinted from *Chicago Clubs: Illustrated*, 70. Digital Collections, University of Illinois at Urbana-Champaign.

ticket cost $10, and a private box for four was $10 a day or $60 for the entire meet. A program cost 10 cents.[16]

The WPR's inaugural eight-day meet began on June 28, running on alternate days through July 12, featuring ten stakes races. However, skeptical elite eastern stable owners chose to not ship their finest horses to the meet. Charley Bush and Ira E. Bride purchased the meet's gambling privileges for the exorbitant price of $35,240 ($4,405 a day) and posted a $25,000 bond to guarantee their work. They charged bookmakers working inside the track a daily $100 fee and got a proportionate amount from the gamblers running auction pools and pari-mutuels. By comparison, the betting privilege at Brooklyn's Sheepshead Bay track in 1893 went for $3,000 a day, and the Long

Branch course in Eatontown, on the Jersey Shore, charged $4,000. It was estimated that $110,000 a day had to be bet at the WPR for the bookmakers to break even, which was easily achieved. WPR spectators regularly spent about $95,000 at auction pools, around $200,000 at the pari-mutuel tables, and another $200,000 with the forty to fifty bookmakers present.[17]

Opening day, June 28, was a beautiful early summer day and a great success with nineteen thousand in attendance, far exceeding any previous race in the city. The *Tribune* reported that the first train bound for the track left the Illinois Central Depot at 1:00 p.m. with a heterogeneous crowd of pleasure seekers: "The portly-looking elderly man of business in white hat and vest, throwing to the winds his financial cares, was out for his holiday and looked to be enjoying it to the full. The wealthy speculator and gambler, the low-salaried clerk, the store-keeper, and the son of toil, alike bent on pleasure, jostled one another in the scramble to get on board." Women were underrepresented on trains because "the gentler sex having evidently preferred the more select method of reaching the course—by means of carriages and horses." They were fashionably attired, with flowers and plumes in their hats and bonnets.[18]

There were five races on opening day, four sprints and one heat race. The betting scene was "one of the wildest imaginable," dominated by auctioneers, although there were also about fifty bookmakers and pari-mutuel men. The beer and whiskey stands were busy. The *Tribune* gave more coverage to the crowd than to the races, with detailed attention to the clothing of Chicago society, including Mrs. Carter H. Harrison and Mrs. Potter Palmer. The paper thoroughly described the various carriages elite spectators rode on their way to the track, including Victorians, landaus, broughams, and summer phaetons, along with more modest box buggies, fancy surreys, and rockaways, and reported that Mayor Harrison appeared astride his Kentucky thoroughbred. The character of the clubhouse crowd was rated as comparable to what one would find at a big race at the CIJC's Sheepshead Bay or a gala at the opera.[19]

5. Isaac Murphy, greatest jockey of the late nineteenth century. Cigarette card for Goodwin & Co. tobacco manufacturer. Library of Congress Prints and Photographs Division, Washington, DC, LC-DIG-ppmsca-55327. Produced by Geo. S. Harris & Sons, lith., [1888].

The highlight of the day was the inaugural one-and-a-half-mile American Derby, the richest stakes race of the year for three-year-olds. Eighty-two horses were originally nominated for the race, but only twelve appeared. Modesty captured the $11,000 first prize, a rare major victory for a filly. She was trained by J. W. Rogers and ridden by the great African American jockey Isaac Murphy, one of the highest-paid athletes in the United States, who earned $20,000 in 1882 and about $10,000 in 1884. This fee included a $4,000 retainer fee by one of the nation's most prominent stable owners, Edward Corrigan, who guaranteed Murphy up to 10 percent of their winning purses. Corrigan even paid him when he rode for other owners the customary $25 for winning and $10 for losing.[20]

Washington Park's first season was a great success measured by the quality of the races, the attendance, and the excellent $87,000 profit. The press estimated that the average attendance after opening day ranged from 4,166 and 5,166, topped by more than 10,000 on the Fourth of July.[21]

THE PROPRIETARY TRACK

An 1884 booster guide to Chicago bragged that the six-year-old West Side's eighty-acre track facilities, including a fifteen-thousand-seat grandstand, was worth $200,000, a huge exaggeration over its real value. The Chicago Driving Park Association was concerned about the upcoming competition from Washington Park and budgeted more than $180,000 in advance of the upcoming season for expenses, of which nearly 80 percent went to purses and stakes. However, the standardbreds actually raced for a reported $280,000, including entrance fees, far more than any trotting course in North America. In mid-May, a month before Washington Park opened, the track's directors announced their unanimous intent to introduce Sunday racing after consulting with supportive trotting and thoroughbred owners. Management claimed, rather disingenuously, that Sunday racing was for the intellectual, physical, and moral benefit of fans. The real reason was that the jockey club entered the 1884 season with a $20,000 debt, had huge expenses, and needed to borrow money to stay in business. The CDPA had high hopes of drawing big working-class crowds on Sunday because that was their day off, making the facility much more accessible to blue-collar workers than any other day.[22]

Sunday recreation was a controversial issue in nineteenth-century America. Conservative Protestants, including Baptists, Congregationalists, Methodists, and Presbyterians, believed that righteous behavior required keeping the Sabbath holy. They supported the "American Sabbath" that limited activities on the Lord's day to religious and moral actions. These revivalists felt threatened by the more liberal Protestant denominations, like Episcopalians, Catholic immigrants who adhered to a "Continental" view of the Sabbath that allowed recreation after church services, and Jews who observed their Sabbath on Saturday. Chicagoans enjoyed a relatively liberal Sabbath, typical of larger midwestern cities that were more open-minded than eastern and southern cities and where immigrants and their children (77.9 percent of Chicago in 1890) had considerable political clout. However, Chicago did not have Major League Sunday baseball until 1893 because Albert Spalding, owner of the Chicago White Stockings, and the majority of National League owners, believed that its middle-class WASP fans preferred a strict Sabbath. These attitudes were not shared with the rival American Association, founded in 1882, which appealed more to working-class fans and scheduled games in St. Louis and Cincinnati.[23]

The West Side track's president was Washington Hesing, a Yale man, publisher of the *Staats-Zeitung*, and a prominent German American politician, who switched his political affiliation from Republican to Democrat in 1880. He was a big backer of Sunday racing. Hesing pointed to the growing popular support for Sunday amusements in several western European countries and certain American cities, notably New Orleans, which already had Sunday racing. Hesing recommended that working people use their leisure time on Sundays to enjoy innocent amusement at the racetrack instead of vile theaters, saloons, or gambling dives: "There are an immense number of young men, clerks, bookkeepers, and professional men, who would gladly attend a horse-race but who never can have even a half-holiday. Of this class there are many who keep a horse and buggy and who may be seen on the drives every Sunday afternoon."[24]

Hesing intended to charge adults fifty cents and children twenty-five cents for admission on Sundays and prohibit the sales of pools, games of chance, and whiskey "so that the middle classes can take their families out, bring their lunch with them, and spend the better part of the day on our grounds." In 1884 the track hosted two June Sunday performances of the Buffalo Bill Wild West Show to bolster profits and provide an entering wedge for Sunday racing, but did not stage horse races on Sundays.[25]

Local Protestant clergymen responded with apoplexy and delivered many critical sermons. No minister supported racing on Sunday, not even liberal ministers such as Reverend George Batchelor of Unity Church, who supported rational Sunday recreation at libraries, museums, and parks because "it is the most dangerous one [day] of the week for young men in a great city like this." The Reverend David Swing of the Central Church, the era's most popular Chicago cleric, declared that "Sunday for races and bull-fighters would be like a Sunday for vice—just set apart especially for sinners. They might as well change the name of the day and call it Sinday."[26]

Hesing's proposal received nearly universal condemnation from the mainstream press. The *Chicago Freie Press* took their fellow German to task for supporting Sunday racing, which might make difficult more legitimate entertainments. Even sports periodicals criticized Hesing. The *Spirit* criticized Sunday racing given prevailing social values that discouraged entertainment on the Sabbath. The *New York Clipper*, another major national sporting weekly, offered lukewarm support, pointing out that afternoon racing at distant tracks would not interfere with morning churchgoing, but "there is really more need for ball-playing or for concerts on Sunday than there is just yet for horse-racing."[27]

The *Chicago Daily News*, which never supported gambling in any fashion, joined the more "responsible" citizens in opposing Sunday racing and warned that such a notion would discredit the sport. It predicted that the proprietary track, mentioned in the press for the first time as the West Side Driving Park (WSDP), would not draw respectable workingmen, but "will be the retreat of fast young men and lewd women, the spot to which the scum of this great city will naturally float."[28]

In the summer of 1884, the CDPA secretly leased its track to William K. Emmett and his syndicate from January 1885 through August 20, 1885. Emmett was the son of a New York judge who arrived in Chicago in 1875 and made his living running the Academy of Music, which was both a well-known school and a popular site for musical entertainment. Emmett was a great sportsman who raced horses, but faro playing ruined him, and he lost up to $10,000 at a single sitting. However, he recouped his funds by betting heavily on the 1882 John L. Sullivan–Paddy Ryan championship heavyweight fight. Emmett intended to operate an "Electric Hippodrome" during the summer that would feature two harness races and a chariot race nightly. However, it never took place.[29]

Emmett's syndicate was composed of bookmakers and pool sellers, whose poor work marred the track's reputation. Pool sellers occupied the most prominent parts of the grandstand where ladies and gentlemen congregated. The CDPA's standing was further hurt by the presence of a huge grog shop below the grandstand that was "always full of swearing, boozy men" and a similar class of women. The occasional presence of Mike McDonald serving as a race starter or timekeeper probably did not help, either. Fields that summer were small, and the many rumors of chicanery badly hurt attendance. There were days when $7,500 races brought in less than $500 at the gate. The low point came on October 10, when only two hundred people attended the races.[30]

The track was sold at public auction on January 23, 1885, for $23,000, "almost given away" for less than half of what it was really worth, to satisfy the claims of various creditors. A group who already held $14,000 of the track's $20,000 mortgage bought the track, led by Benjamin F. Campbell, vice president of the Chicago West Division Railway Company. His partners included Kansas City streetcar magnate and horseman Edward Corrigan, CJTC president S. K. Dow, George G. Newbury (a partner in a plumbing and steam-fitting business), and distiller DeWitt H. Curtis. The new management was supposed to be a big improvement over the old owners, who staged suspicious races, failed to pay purses, and repudiated debts. However, Billy Emmett remained in charge of racing operations, which was certainly not reassuring to the driving park's fans. He did make one sound move, requiring owners of stakes entrants to put up 5 percent of the purse as an entrance fee, which resulted in bigger purses and larger fields of high-quality horses.[31]

In the spring of 1885, the CDPA hosted three Wild West shows on Sundays and two days of racing. In response, more than two thousand people, including Marshall Field, signed a petition urging the city to halt Sunday racing. On June 17, Mayor Harrison announced that Emmett had agreed to halt Sunday racing, though state's attorney Julius Grinnell secured a temporary injunction against Sunday racing just to be sure. Grinnell argued that Sunday racing was so popular that streetcars were crowded with revelers and drunkards on their way to the track, harming the repose of the community and the pleasant Sunday pleasures of Garfield Park. He presented affidavits from thirty residents and property owners who claimed the track had a negative impact on their neighborhood, causing property values to drop by up to one-third. Local residents were concerned about safety, feeling especially challenged on Sundays, when increased streetcar and carriage traffic endangered pedestrians.[32]

Edward Corrigan and Chicago Racing

Edward Corrigan was born in Ireland in 1842 and migrated with his family at a young age to Kansas City. He started out as a railroad laborer in the West and worked his way up to become a railroad contractor. Afterward, Ed joined his brothers to construct and operate a major part of Kansas City's street railway system. An "incorrigible character" and maverick, "Corrigan was an ill-tempered sort who was known to crack his cane over a man's head rather than consider the

6. "Blind John" Condon (1854–1915) and "Big Ed" Corrigan (1843–1924). Condon, one of Chicago's most successful gamblers and racetrack owners, had a long-standing feud with Corrigan, one of the biggest operators of racetracks and racing stables in North America. Reprinted from Hugh S. Fullerton, "American Gambling and Gamblers," 35.

other's point of view." Once when his workers threatened a strike, he invited four negotiators to see him, "knocked them out," and announced the pending strike was canceled.[33]

Corrigan as a young man owned and raced trotters for recreation before graduating to thoroughbreds in 1874 and eventually owned a 503-acre Kentucky breeding farm. He moved to Chicago in the early 1880s and became Illinois's leading breeder and racer of thoroughbreds. His horses appeared in some of the most lucrative and prestigious races across the country and also in England, earning about $2 million in purses and stakes, including such prestigious events as the 1890 Kentucky Derby, won by his stallion Riley. Ed became known as the "Lorillard of the West," because his horses dominated western racing, just as tobacco magnate Pierre Lorillard ruled the eastern circuit.[34]

Corrigan went on to become not just a leading horseman, but one of the preeminent track owners in the United States, starting with his investment in the West Side track, before relocating in 1891 to the southwest suburb of Cicero, formerly known as Hawthorne, two blocks from Chicago. As we shall see, he encountered considerable troubles in Chicago with rival track owners, his own partners, and local politicians and became known as a "turf disturber." Corrigan later owned courses in San Francisco, Kansas City, and New Orleans.[35]

Unfortunately for Corrigan and his partners, the CDPA lost money during its 1885 spring meet. Beginning in September, it was mainly known as the West Side Park (WSP) or West Side Driving Park. The *Spirit* attributed the losses to declining interest in trotting, widely considered too slow and less exciting than thoroughbred racing. There was also competition from the WPR, which made about $30,000 in 1885 because it had good attendance and cut operating expenses by about $15,000.[36]

Washington Park's Summer Meets, 1885 and 1886

The American Derby on June 27, 1885, drew a crowd of ten thousand people (surpassed a week later by the July 4 races, with twenty-five thousand spectators), serviced by thirty bookmakers. Chicago's elite was so taken by the WPR that in the three weeks leading up to the meet, C. P. Kimball's manufacturing company sold twenty-six millionaires new carriages so they could ride in style to the track on Derby Day, even if there were not enough English coachmen to drive them. The city's upper crust were all there for opening day and were entertained in the clubhouse by the army's First Regimental Band, with selections from Offenbach operettas. The *Inter Ocean* reported that "such a display of fashion, elegance and wealth and beauty had never been seen upon any race course in the country."[37]

The *Tribune* believed that a big part of the WPR's success began with the pleasure of riding carriages to the track down shaded Michigan Avenue with its elegant homes, west along Thirty-Fifth Street to the broad Grand Boulevard, and then on through South Park Avenue to the course. On opening day and Derby Day, the streets were lined with Chicagoans, eager to catch a glimpse of Chicago's elite and their beautifully gowned girlfriends, wives, and daughters.[38]

7. Washington Park Club official program, summer meeting, 1885. At least two of the three jockeys were African Americans. Washington Park Club, 1885 lithograph. Original in color. Chicago History Museum, ICHi-065472.

Isaac Murphy repeated as the winning Derby jockey, riding Volant, owned by Elias J. "Lucky" Baldwin, who had made his fortune in California mining and real estate. Murphy, then at the apex of his profession, was originally scheduled to ride the expected favorite, Corrigan's Ten Stone. But the stallion was scratched, freeing Murphy to ride another mount. Afterward, Murphy switched from Corrigan to Baldwin's California Stables for a $5,000 retainer.[39]

By 1886 the WPC had spent more than $500,000 on the racecourse, and membership rose to 789 men of high status. Total stakes reached $120,000, one-third more than any midwestern or western track. Bride & Armstrong paid over $50,000 for the valuable betting privilege. They supervised auction pools and pari-mutuels and 30 bookmakers who were charged $100 apiece. The meet, highlighted by

Murphy's third straight Derby victory, this time on Baldwin's Silver Cloud, certified Washington Park as one of the top American racing venues. Baldwin rewarded Isaac by raising his retainer fee to $10,000 and giving him carte blanche to select other mounts. The opening-day crowd for the American Derby was about 20,000–25,000, surpassed on July 5 when nearly 30,000 Chicago fans attended the holiday event.[40]

While the WPR was a big success, management did encounter some difficulties, such as the mistreatment of animals. President John G. Shortell, president of the Humane Cruelty Society (HCS), believed that jockeys employing whips and spurs were barbarians: "If the cruelties practiced on the horse on the race-course were done in the streets . . . the perpetrators would be arrested." Certain WPC members, along with the HCS, criticized steeplechase events that employed dangerous stonewalls, hurdles, and water jumps. Shortell explained, "I think it is illegal to force the poor animals over ditches and barriers of different kinds, compelling them to attempt jumps, which they are physically incapable of accomplishing."[41]

There were also other problems, including drugs and fixed races. On July 17, Corrigan entered his filly Pearl Jennings in a three-quarter-mile race that was below her class. When she came in third, Corrigan and others thought the horse had been drugged. One month later, "Texas Tom" Redmond was arrested for trying to poison Corrigan's mare Lizzie Dwyer in a conspiracy involving Corrigan's stable-man and two stable boys working with a gambler named Donaldson. The plot was foiled after a clerk discovered a telegram giving the conspirators the go-ahead, and he forewarned Corrigan.[42]

The Selling of the West Side Driving Park

While Washington Park prospered, and even expanded into trotting matches, its competition, the West Side Driving Park, fell on hard times. The WSDP closed down in 1886, except for amateur racing. Its fall was attributed by the *Spirit* to the track's loss of integrity: "There is no trotting track in this country to-day that has seen as many bare-faced steals."[43]

The track was sold at the start of September 1887 to the Chicago Fair and Trotting Breeders' Association (CFTBA), a $50,000 corporation ostensibly established to stage turf sports, inspire agricultural and mechanical fairs, and encourage the breeding of trotting horses. However, its primary aim was to promote gambling. The firm was run by Corrigan, assisted by club secretary David Waldo, and bookmaker Joseph Ullman. The site's new owner was Judge Lambert Tree, a distinguished Democratic politician, jurist, ambassador, and art patron. He rented the West Side track to the CFTBA for $7,000 and turned the facility into a running track.[44]

THE CHICAGO POOLROOM

Poolrooms in the late 1870s and 1880s were concentrated downtown at Gamblers' Alley (bounded by Clark, Madison, LaSalle, and Washington). Downtown bucket shops were previously also prominent there, but they moved out of the area by 1887 under pressure from the Chicago Board of Trade, the New York Stock Exchange, and the state legislature. Bucket shops were offices where clients could make "bets in the form of orders or options based on current exchange prices of securities or commodities, but without any actual buying or selling of the property."[45]

There were then seven poolrooms and sixteen saloons in Gamblers' Alley. The poolrooms were busy for nine months a year, but business declined in the winter because there was little racing then outside of New Orleans. They serviced up to five thousand clients a day, six days a week, from 10:00 a.m. to 10:00 p.m., closing for dinner from 6:00 to 7:00 p.m. Bookmakers took bets as low as a dollar, auction pools for five dollars, and pari-mutuels and combinations at ten and twenty-five cents. The auctions charged winners an 8 percent fee and combination holders 10 percent. A combination bet could entail picking the win and place horses in a single race, winners in two different races, or other permutations.[46]

The press uniformly decried the poolrooms as illegal offtrack betting. For instance, an 1879 *Tribune* editorial entitled "Gamblers'

Alley Pool-Rooms" claimed that professional gamblers were "living and thriving upon the ignorance and gullibility of the [amateurs]. No efforts are made to conceal the poolrooms, and no efforts were made . . . to break them up. The city has never been so disgraced for contempt for . . . laws against gambling as it is to-day." The editors blamed new mayor Carter Harrison and his police for inaction. The result was that "100s of sports and blacklegs have come to Chicago assured the city is wide open."[47]

The *Tribune* averred that "the poolrooms are the most corrupting of all gambling institutions, because they are operated as though pool selling were a legitimate business, and thus attract the presence of young men who would not consent to enter a faro-bank or keno-den." Chicago bookies took bets on not only horse racing but also baseball, pedestrianism, rowing, and even political elections. The *Tribune* indicated that the rooms are almost always crowded with "all manner of people," ranging from mechanics and laborers to bookkeepers, clerks, merchants, government officials, "and a large number of colored men." The problem became so grave that many prominent businessmen hired detectives to shadow clerks suspected of frequenting poolrooms and then fired them as a warning to other employees.[48]

Poolrooms operated brazenly, with doors wide open. The *Tribune* particularly blamed the police, who could have easily detected the crimes if they wanted to, and the courts that barred the police from breaking down poolroom doors and making arrests without warrants. The paper recommended that moralistic clergymen worried about such trivial matters like Sunday streetcars should instead concentrate on fighting gambling. In the late 1870s, reformers, discouraged by the criminal justice system's failure to halt offtrack gambling, petitioned Springfield to shut the poolrooms. However, they were unsuccessful, encountering strong opposition from gamblers' lobbyists and progambling Democratic Chicago legislators.[49]

Gamblers' Alley attracted slumming young men like Carter H. Harrison II, son of the mayor, who found its ambiance resembled western frontier towns. In the summer of 1882, on vacation from Yale Law School, he found himself nearly broke and owed his father $100.

He went to the WSDP with his father's passes to bet and hopefully make money to pay off his debt. Young Carter wagered his only $3 on a long shot recommended by a racing tout (a self-styled racing expert who recommends his favorite horses at the track for a piece of the action) and won at 25–1. Thereafter, Harrison regularly frequented "Silver Bill" Riley's basement poolroom that specialized in auction pools. His best moment came when he bet a 50-cent combination on three races and won $354. He ended up $1,200 ahead by the end of the summer. Harrison continued to go to the track in the future, but went broke in 1885.[50]

Few poolroom raids occurred in Mayor Harrison's first years as mayor, and the business flourished throughout his eight-year term. They were widely located downtown, and there was even one inside a building behind the Chicago Opera House. When the first major poolroom raids of 1885 began on June 5, Harrison was vacationing at Hot Springs, Arkansas. The police halted nearly all South Side gambling, except for a few protected facilities that did a booming business with their competition shuttered. Harrison then brazenly took credit for halting the gambling and promised to surpass Republican mayors Joseph Medill and Monroe Heath in his antigambling efforts. But since Harrison was closely tied to the local gamblers, the gaming rooms were soon back in business.[51]

The crusading *Daily News* initiated its own poolroom investigation that summer. It described the clients as a tough crowd of broken-down gamblers, second-rate politicians, third-rate saloonkeepers, unemployed bartenders, peddlers, and hawkers. Harrison responded by promising to turn up the heat, but actually did next to nothing. The press reported the occasional jackpot like the 25-cent combination bet in 1887 that paid $170. Such a bonanza encouraged hundreds of small bettors to try their luck.[52]

In 1887 the biggest of the poolrooms in Gamblers' Alley, and another two located elsewhere, belonged to politically connected Silver Bill Riley. It accommodated as many as two thousand people on a busy day, as much as all the other poolrooms combined. The colorful entrepreneur, who wore a $90 London-made overcoat and a $2,000

gemstone in his polka-dot necktie, was a vice president of the Western
Bookmakers' Association (WBA) that tried to monopolize betting at
several major tracks. Riley's room claimed to keep out minors, but
bootblacks, newsboys, and other youth would sneak in or ask African
American men or other adults to make a bet for them. Riley supported
the idea of licensing poolrooms and claimed he was willing to spend
as much as $10,000 a year for a license because that system would help
him gain market share.[53]

The Midwest's leading racing organization, the American Turf
Congress (ATC), founded in 1883 (also known as the Western Racing
Congress), came out against poolrooms in 1889, recommending banning telegraph transmissions of race results to poolrooms. The local
press supported its plan. One expert claimed that $50,000–$60,000
was bet at Chicago poolrooms the evening and morning before races,
often on out-of-town events. Such bets directly competed with WSP
bookies like Joseph Ullman, who operated "foreign books" at the
track, taking bets on out-of-town tracks.[54]

The Antipool Bill

The legality of racing in Illinois was a highly contentious issue, as
it was in every racing state. Racing opponents were concerned about
the abuse of animals, race fixing, and especially the gambling, considered an integral part of the racing experience. Pietistic Protestants
believed that horse-race gambling was sinful and weakened character.
They believed gamblers coveted other people's property and sought
to amass material goods without gainful labor, which was equivalent
to stealing. British historian David Dixon further points out that
gambling "refuted the concept of divine regulation and purpose" by
appealing to chance. Anthony Comstock of the New York Society for
the Suppression of Vice (established in 1873) was one of the leading
foes of gambling, though he was best known for the Comstock Laws
of 1873 that suppressed the dissemination of obscene literature and
birth-control information through the US mail. He focused on New

York poolrooms. Another major opponent of the New York poolrooms was the Reverend Charles Parkhurst, of New York's Madison Square Presbyterian Church (1880–1918), who was elected president of the Society for the Prevention of Crime in 1891.[55]

A second group of gambling opponents consisted of social reformers who were motivated mainly for secular reasons. They included social gospelers (liberal clergymen who hoped to apply Christian ethics to solve urban social problems) as well as more non–spiritually minded criminologists, social scientists, businessmen, and feminists who hoped to ameliorate the era's prevailing economic, social, and political problems. They wanted to clean up betting in horse racing because they believed such entertainment was socially disruptive, with the potential for a loss of self-control and a failure to perform hard work. They thought that racetrack gambling facilitated a culture of chance that had dangerous repercussions such as destroying families, overturning the integrity of working-class leaders, and facilitating the rise of syndicate crime, with the accompanying corruption of politicians and police. One brazen example of how the gambling fever corrupted men was the arrest in the summer of 1886 of Robert Newman, treasurer of Local 14 of the Cigarmakers' Union, who stole $2,000 from the local and ended up gambling it away at Washington Park.[56]

The press continued to steadfastly oppose offtrack gambling, lambasting poolrooms as the second step on the road to perdition after on-track wagering. The *Tribune* in 1887 chastised poolrooms for demoralizing thousands and pushing promising young men to crime: "men who have disgraced and beggared their families, men who have gone to the penitentiary as embezzlers, men who have sought refuge in the suicide's grave—all as a direct result of pool-room gambling." The Republican *Chicago Evening Journal* hoped that the state would first go after the cheap gambling halls: "Popular sentiment may compel effective legislation against the catch-penny pool-rooms in which so many youngsters take their first downward step, and under this the more respectable pool-rooms may be crowded out."[57]

The Chase Act and the Gibbs Amendment

The responsibility in the United States for drawing up laws to regulate or prevent gambling belonged to state legislatures. The US Constitution gave state governments the responsibility for policing their residents, while in the case of foreign countries it was usually the job of the national government. The legislatures of northern state governments in the post-Reconstruction era were staunchly Republican in the North and Midwest and increasingly single-party Democratic in southern states. In the Midwest, the dominant Republican Party mainly represented small-town white Anglo-Saxon Protestant voters who espoused traditional conservative social values on such issues as Prohibition, prostitution, gambling, and public education. They had a tight hold on the Illinois state government, making passage of laws supporting racing difficult to secure. The Democrats were strongest in cities with large immigrant and Catholic populations. Illinois had only one Democratic governor between 1865 and 1913, John Peter Altgeld, elected in 1892, the only year between 1860 and 1908 that the state went for a Democratic presidential candidate.[58]

The state legislature was historically a strong Republican bastion. Altgeld's coattails helped produce a Democratic-dominated senate in 1893 for the first and only time from 1878 to 1932. The Illinois General Assembly was controlled by Republicans from 1864 to 1913, except for 1891–94. Representation was highly gerrymandered in behalf of rural farming areas and small-town districts that were dominated by a conservative electorate. Republicans also took advantage of the state's unique system of cumulative voting that dated to 1870. Each legislative district elected three representatives, and each voter cast three votes, distributed any way they wished, including a "bullet," or three votes for one candidate. This format helped Republican candidates in traditionally Democratic districts secure one of the three seats. As a result, Chicago was severely underrepresented by 29 percent in the assembly, which had 153 seats. However, its number of seats in the senate, which had 51 districts, was much fairer. Yet there were probably more Republican senators from the city than expected because of the bullet voting system.[59]

At the start of the 1887 legislative session, the Citizens' Association (CA), founded in Chicago in 1874 and best known for promoting civil-service reform, worked with various clergymen on a bill to close all horse-racing betting facilities, emulating transformative propositions under similar consideration in New York. Representative D. C. Chase, a Lake County Republican, introduced a bill based on a proposal drawn up by CA attorney W. C. Grant to punish anyone engaged in the business of betting $1,000 or more with a fine or one year in jail or both. Certain WPC members raised money to block the Chase bill, which they feared would end betting on horse races, knowing that racing could not continue without betting. Poolroom spokesmen were also totally against the bill, which they derided as "religious poppycock." Rumors popped up that a dozen poolroom operators raised funds to defeat the bill, and another tale emerged that gambling supporters tried to blackmail legislators to block the proposed law. Nonetheless, the Chase bill passed the assembly by a huge majority (105–8).[60]

The *Tribune* felt the preponderant support reflected public sentiment against gambling. The racing men's strategy was to focus their attention on the senate, but the *Tribune* was not worried about the outcome. The editor was pleased that the proposition to forestall horse-race gambling did not exempt fairgrounds and driving parks that featured harness racing or that betting at a racecourse was considered any less immoral than offtrack betting: "'Book-making' and betting on horse-races and ball games are certainly no less demoralizing in the immediate presence of the races or games than they are two miles away."[61]

Cook County Republican senator George A. Gibbs ostensibly took charge of passing the Chase bill in the senate. Observers expected that senate foes would try to kill the proposal and preserve horse racing by amending the act and then sending it back to the Illinois House of Representatives too late for reconsideration. Instead, the senate totally emasculated the bill and turned it upside down into an act *advancing* racetrack interests while maintaining the ban on offtrack betting. Gibbs offered an amendment doubling the fine for bookmaking or pool selling to $2,000, while adding a codicil exempting the fine if the gambling took place *inside* an incorporated fair or racetrack association within twenty-four hours of a scheduled race. Gibbs's modification followed the lines of the Ives racing bill working its way through the New York state legislature. This radical amendment meant that Illinois racecourses would not be liable to the state proscription on offtrack betting.[62]

Gibbs's proposal was vigorously supported by course operators who needed on-track betting to survive. The altered bill would give their operations an aura of respectability and legality. The act implicitly distinguished track bookmakers as men of integrity compared to disreputable and still illegal offtrack poolrooms, whose owners fleeced their clients. This line of reasoning also supported the idea that people who took the trouble to attend races were supporting the advancement of the breed and took an interest in the sport that transcended the act of gambling, unlike the clients of offtrack bookmakers who were simply interested in betting. Ideally, passage meant that racetracks would henceforth monopolize the wagering on horses and offtrack betting would be eliminated, but that was not going to happen.[63]

The senate approved the Gibbs amendment by a staggering vote of 38–1. The revised measure was sent back to the house, where despite the radical modifications it was easily adopted by a vote of 98–22. Why would the legislators agree to the major changes in the revised act? Did they not understand the ramifications? How many votes were bought by the racing interests? We don't know. Representative Frank J. Wisner, Democrat of Cook County, certainly thought a "gang" in Springfield used their boodle to gain passage "to crush out bucket-shops and pool-rooms" to promote pool selling at Washington Park. On May 31, Republican governor Richard J. Oglesby signed the Chase-Gibbs bill (also known as the White Act), and it went into effect on July 1.[64]

The new law was expected to greatly bolster racing in Chicago. Besides the Washington Park summer meet, the West Side course announced two trotting meets and one running meet. A few days after the bill was signed, the new Illinois Jockey Club (IJC) was incorporated and announced plans to hold a four-month meet at a new mile course near Lincoln Park. The incorporators included Charles E. Coburn, a former county commissioner, and Louis H. Cohen. According to the *Tribune*, "The local Hebrew population, who are excluded from membership in the Washington Park Club, will give it solid support."[65]

The city's eight poolrooms and the men and boys involved in the offtrack betting business were concerned about their future. Prominent poolroom operators expected the WPR would nearly monopolize pool selling in Chicago and charge bookmakers premium prices for space at the track. They were also suspicious about the IJC, which might simply rent a downtown lot and run "a lot of old plugs for a $10 stake, and . . . [sell] . . . pools and events all over the country." Another possibility was that the IJC would lease the struggling West Side Driving Park. However, in the end, the IJC simply disappeared.[66]

The *Tribune* criticized the new law as class legislation since it was the first Illinois statute to violate the doctrine of uniformity by legitimizing an act in one location that was barred elsewhere: "The clerk who cannot take the time to attend the race is a gambler and a criminal if he takes a 'flyer' on the result, but his employer who belongs to the club and can command his time, may go behind the fence with a gay multitude of the 'best people.'"[67]

The *Tribune* anticipated that the law would make it futile to contest offtrack betting parlors, even with the new antipool sections of the Chase-Gibbs Act, especially because respectable citizens, free to gamble at the tracks, would set a poor example for children and the working class: "If there should continue to be gambling in Washington Park and the West Side Driving-Park—resorts for respectable gentlemen and their families—it would be useless to attempt its prevention in down-town pool-rooms." I would add the new law turned professional bookmakers to taking bets in states like Illinois and New York into legitimate businessmen, as long as they limited their enterprise to race tracks.[68]

The future of the poolrooms took a severe hit when incumbent mayor Carter Harrison bowed out for "health reasons" just a day or two before the April election. The Democrats did not run a candidate and largely lined up behind reform Republican John A. Roche, who campaigned against the gambling menace. Roche trounced Socialist candidate Robert Nelson, 68.2 percent to 31.7 percent. Once Roche took office, he prodded the police to fight the gamblers. In June the authorities closed six prominent poolrooms, including resorts owned by Al Hankins, Sid McHie, Edward Corrigan, and Pat Sheedy. Roche was said to have cleaned up Gamblers' Alley as well. Nearly all local poolrooms went out of business by July 1 because of police pressure and the expected impact of the Chase Act that was about to go into force. Mayor Roche closed down the poolroom business, along with faro and roulette parlors. The poolroom scene became so quiet that the only article in the 1888 *Tribune* on poolrooms was a report that several local workers moving to St. Paul to work for Shaw & Branigan at the "Tremont Exchange."[69]

Racing after the Gibbs Amendment

Washington Park

The local tracks were excited about the legalization of on-track gambling and the ongoing proscription against offtrack wagering. The West Side track reopened for trotting, and the WPR worked hard to publicize its upcoming meet, putting up about $71,000 in added prize money and hiring artists to produce promotional racing posters and other materials to advertise the track. The WPR received particularly laudatory reports from the *Spirit* prior to the summer season for its integrity, quality of events, and positive impact on Chicagoland racing. The *Spirit* claimed the WPR was promoting thoroughbred racing in Chicago, just as the AJC's Jerome Park had already done for New York: "The club has taken up the sport and elevated it . . . [and has] made it the favorite recreation of the most refined people of the midland metropolis."[70]

So many fans attended the $14,000 American Derby on June 25 that management opened the infield for the first time to accommodate the overflow crowd, generously estimated at thirty thousand. The race ended in a stunning upset by 50–1 long shot C. H. Todd, owned by the prominent breeder Ali Ben Haggin, a rich California attorney, rancher, and partner of George Hearst in a major mining firm. Bush & Bride supervised the betting privileges that netted the WPR more than $10,000 that day from bet takers. They included some forty bookmakers from across the country, who paid a minimum advance fee of $100 a day for five days to cover wagers. About a dozen men sold $5 pari-mutuels, and some gamblers ran auction pools. There was also speculative combination betting that offered odds against two or more horses, from which the WPR got a 5 percent cut. Many elite fans watched from their carriages and sent a footman into the betting ring to make a wager for them. No official pools were sold inside the elegant Palmer House as in the past, but Riley's big poolroom was full of business.[71]

The press gave a lot of attention to spectators, especially women at a time when few participated in sports or attended sporting events. The coming of the races to the South Side track broadened the female audience to include "the wives and children of honest, respectable merchants, and others in the great middle class."[72] Women from the demimonde who had a lot of free time in the afternoon were also often reported at the races as well, especially in the *Daily News*, which was always ready to disparage the sport. As the *Tribune* pointed out, in the paternalistic style of the day:

> It was a day for pretty women and a day for new gowns, and there were plenty of both. There were five women to one man at the clubhouse, and the women sat around in state and looked bored and had little yawns, behind big fans. They were five men to one woman on the grandstand, and the women laughed and chatted and flirted and held little levees and received compliments and made little bets and had a jovial time. Some of the clubhouse ladies did a little betting, too—but it was serious betting. . . . [W]omen never buy anything but Paris mutuels. Betting more complicated than that leaves them in a fog.[73]

The *Tribune* published two feature stories after the 1888 Derby that made fun of female fans titled "Scenes at the Grandstand: How the Women Select the Horses on Which They Bet" and "The Girls at the Races." Women mainly attended on Saturdays with a male escort who usually bet on their behalf, covered their losses, and divided up any winnings. These women spectators also bought advice from tipsters for 10 cents. Women betting on their own accord reportedly selected horses by color, beauty, a cute name, sentiment, or based on the jockey, especially if it was the famous Isaac Murphy.[74]

Despite the jovial atmosphere of Derby Day, heavy betting led to serious problems. Seventeen-year-old Robert G. Lydston, a son of wealthy parents, was arrested the next day, just before the Gibbs Act went into effect, for embezzling $200 from his employer, Fitch, Hunt & Co., to pay for gambling debts. A constable took him home to speak to his father and to secure bail money. The lad excused himself, went up to his room, and shot himself through the heart for having disgraced the family. "Like many another promising youth," noted the *Chicago Times*, "Robert Lydston was a victim of the gambling craze. The money which he purloined from his employers found its way to the pool-rooms and the race-course, where it was absorbed by the blacklegs infesting those resorts."[75]

Two days later, the *Chicago Times* ran a major article sarcastically titled "Respectable Gambling at Washington Park," claiming that the state antipool law had given the track a monopoly in the wagering business, with the exception of the Chicago Board of Trade and an unnamed popular resort, probably a poolroom or bucket shop, for "sportive preachers, speculative ladies, high roll members of the Board of Trade, blacklegs, peculating clerks, and graduating school for ambitious suicides." The reporter identified many disreputables at the track such as "Jennie" Goodrich with her paramour, African American P. B. S. Pinchback, the former governor of Louisiana, who was associated with the notorious Louisiana Lottery.[76]

Favorites dominated the meet, resulting in short odds, averaging 1–2 (and as low as 1–20 in one race). The *Times* took particular notice of closing-day results, traditionally the day when pool sellers and bookmakers fleece bettors, trying to get even. One bettor took six winners with combination bookies in which he predicted the first three finishers in a race, an unbelievable run of luck, or a tale of fixed races.[77]

Racing on the West Side

Beginning in the summer of 1888, the West Side course was known just as the West Side Park. It staged a twenty-day summer meet under the largely unknown James Winters, who ran a real-estate and insurance agency. Winters claimed he had once lost $56,000 speculating in a coal-mine deal. Admission was 50 cents. Purses were promised to average $1,500 a day for four flat races and one steeplechase event. The contests had sufficient entries to fill the races, drew good crowds, and had plenty of bookmakers to take bets. However, there was a lot of concern about the races' integrity. Three of four events involving the Campbell and Fenton stable were reportedly fixed. By the meet's end, it appeared that horsemen would think twice about racing there again.[78]

Despite concerns over fixed races, business at the WSP was so good that Winters extended the season. However, his bubble burst when constables tried to appropriate some of his personal property for "old debts." He then skimmed $8,600 from the track's profits and skipped out on his creditors. He left some bookmakers in charge, and they soon ended the meet in its forty-sixth day. Despite all, the track ended in the black.[79]

Racing integrity was a national concern, as always. For instance, one year later, millionaire turf man Captain Samuel S. Brown, a founder of the Brooklyn Jockey Club, blamed the widespread concerns on dishonest bookmakers, jockeys, and starters: "As long as a number of owners that I could mention are tolerated on the turf, these things may be expected. My belief is that a large majority of the jockeys who are riding today are crooked, and that a majority of the races are jobs [fixes]. It could hardly be otherwise when gamblers are allowed the betting privilege, and at the same time control horses and run them in nearly every race."[80]

Washington Park in 1888

Washington Park in its fifth year still offered the highest purses in the West. It expected to draw more than seven hundred horses for its spring meet, although there were only six hundred stalls available at the start of the season. WPR's success led to the addition of a second thoroughbred meet in the early fall and a trotting meet in late August. About ten thousand attended the first day of harness racing but few club members, partly because they preferred thoroughbreds, but mostly because they were on vacation. The *Spirit* felt the club could do better if there were more Chicago horsemen to bolster local interest. The fall racing fell below expectations, at best breaking even because of competition from the West Side Park and the second-place White Stockings ball club.[81]

Overall, the legal Chicago gambling scene at Washington Park was quite active and profitable. WPR's bookmaking privilege went for $3,000 a day, compared to $2,000 in St. Louis and $2,400 in Louisville. The season started with forty-one bookies who paid $95 a day to operate, but so many favorites came in that half the bookies left before the meet ended. Chicago and St. Louis were the only western cities that had pari-mutuel betting, but it was less popular than anticipated and barely covered expenses. Two years later, Washington Park hosted an average of forty-nine bookies a day during the twenty-five-day meet that produced $117,050 for the jockey club, plus additional fees for auction pools and pari-mutuels.[82]

The 1888 American Derby was worth $17,000, compared to just $4,850 for the less prestigious Kentucky Derby. Owner Lucky Baldwin won his third American Derby with Emperor of Norfolk, ridden by Isaac Murphy, his fourth winning Derby in five years. The track continued to draw a wide variety of Chicagoans, including fans from the city's small African American community. The press seldom commented on the black presence at the track and then usually in a deleterious fashion. For instance, the *Tribune* pointed out that Pinkertons had previously received many complaints against men and boys, especially African Americans taking bets for women and then running off with the money. The Pinkertons were on the alert when they spotted an African American making bets for women in the grandstand, and a fight ensued with him. The accused party was badly beaten and then thrown out. The fray, the *Tribune* reported, left "the colored men on the grounds . . . much excited. They talked wickedly, but were over-awed by the force of the Pinkerton men present."[83]

Most of the African Americans working at Washington Park and other American tracks then were lowly paid stable hands such as grooms, exercise riders, handlers, and stall cleaners, but there were also a few black trainers and many well-compensated jockeys such as Isaac Murphy. There were at least 117 black jockeys after the Civil War, including 15 of the first 28 winners of the Kentucky Derby. One of the finest was Anthony Hamilton, who won 154 races in 1891, the second-highest number of victories among all American jockeys.[84]

The Revitalized West Side Park

In 1888 Ed Corrigan reorganized the management of West Side Park, taking over full control of racing operations and bringing in gambler Bill Riley, vice president of the year-old Western Bookmakers Association, to work with him. The WBA had forty members who sought to deal directly with racetracks to secure betting privileges instead of going through intermediaries who leased the gambling concession and then sublet the rights to individual bookmakers. The WBA also intended to serve as a pressure group to protect members from arbitrary rulings by racing officials.[85]

The West Side track charged 50 cents admission, which included free access for its reportedly motley crowd, to the grandstand, betting grounds, and clubhouse. Twenty bookies paid $75 a day to work the track, which largely covered the management's purses. The cheap admission prices facilitated family outings, especially on Saturdays, when crowds approached six thousand. The *Times* applauded family parties as "a marked feature in the big, roomy, old-fashioned grandstand, such as can seldom be seen at the more austere track on the south side."[86]

The West Side Park usually opened after the WPR's summer meet and went on for three months, with hopes of clearing $50,000. The two clubs had poor relations, especially after Corrigan was briefly suspended from the rival course in 1887 for alleged discourtesies to racing judges who had warned his jockeys not to go easy on their horses. Then hostilities heated up after Washington Park expanded its fall season to compete directed with the WSP. In addition, WPR treasurer John Walsh, publisher of the *Chicago Herald*, castigated Corrigan as a swindler in his paper.[87]

Opening day at WSP on July 16 drew more than ten thousand "jammed inside the betting shed like sardines in a box, and it was nearly as thick in the open ground between the betting shed and the track." A loud, cracking noise was heard after the third race, and some people mistakenly started yelling, "The stand is falling." The *Tribune* described it as a "ludicrous riot" that some spectators thought was the work of anarchists. A near riot followed as people rushed for safety. Remarkably, no one was hurt, and despite the chaos no money was stolen in the betting ring. The racing resumed once order was restored.[88]

On September 27, 1888, a fire broke out at WSP at about three in the afternoon during a race, leading to a panic among attendees. The fire department arrived in thirty minutes, but had a hard time getting water to fight the blaze. Fortunately, no animals or people were hurt. The clubhouse and the grandstand were saved, but 176 stalls burned. After a brief time, the races resumed. Damages were set at $8,000–$10,000, some of which was covered by insurance. No cause was ever found, though two suspicious youths were seen running from the scene of the fire.[89]

Public safety at wooden semipublic buildings was a huge national concern, especially in Chicago at this time, scene of the catastrophic 1871 Great Fire. Racetracks were constructed of flammable materials that posed a danger to the thousands sitting in wooden stands and to the hundreds of thoroughbreds stabled in wooden stalls. Wooden baseball parks were an even greater concern. There were more than twenty fires at Major League ballparks in the 1890s, including Chicago's West Side Grounds in 1894.[90]

The National Racing Scene in 1888

According to *Harper's Weekly*, one of the most respected American periodicals with a circulation of around a hundred thousand, thoroughbred racing was doing superbly, citing the WPC clubhouse as "undoubtedly the most pretentious and best appointed jockey-club quarters in the land." The periodical claimed that $37.5 million was spent in 1888, based on an average attendance at "reputable" tracks such as Washington Park, Jerome Park, Sheepshead Bay, and Monmouth, of five thousand (far higher than the "average" American track). Fans typically spent 50 cents for transportation, $1 for admission, and $1 for refreshments and incidentals, and half of them would make bets, averaging $10. *Harper's* estimated that $25,000 changed hands for each of six races at the reputable courses. It also pointed out that the breeding business was booming, as evidenced by the record $38,000 price for the yearling King Thomas. It also indicated the growing number of outstanding tracks around the country, not to mention breeding farms, particularly in Kentucky and California. It estimated that the courses in New York and New Jersey constituted a $2 million investment. The top courses employed around six hundred people, and the leading jockeys made about $12,000 a year.[91]

THE LONG 1889 SEASON

The Legislature Reconsiders the Gibbs Act

Before the 1889 racing year was under way, an effort was made to overturn the Gibbs Act. In March Senator Orville F. Berry (R–Hancock) with the support of Senator E. L. McDonald (D–Morgan) sought to halt all bookmaking, which he thought was worse than the bucket shops. On the other hand, racing advocates such as Senator W. J. Campbell thought the Gibbs Act too weak, since he and his partners in the Hamilton County fairgrounds had been fined for allowing gambling at their track. Critics blamed the millionaires behind the WPC in blocking the bill, though it was also opposed by breeders, who felt it would lower the value of their horses, and it was seen as a foolish act to limit the recreational options of visitors to the upcoming World's Fair.[92]

The Illinois House of Representatives also considered altering the state's racing laws. Democratic representative Frank J. Wisner sponsored a bill to amend the Gibbs Act and close down racing at county fairs. There was a brief debate between the men promoting individual rights and those legislators wanting to protect foolish bettors that almost led to blows. In the end, the measure was sent to die in committee.[93]

The Racing Scene

Chicago's 1889 racing season started on May 14 and lasted 128 days, with 779 races. Washington Park ran 25 days and West Side Park 103. The tracks combined for $356,000 in purses, second only to New York. The highlight was the American Derby on June 22, which drew thirty thousand spectators. The race was won by Spokane, who had previously captured the Kentucky Derby. The biggest gates were typically on Saturdays, when a lot of fans who worked only a half day would go to the track. The *Tribune* recommended that such a summer afternoon respite was a great escape from the office, revitalizing one's health and energy.[94]

Unfortunately, Derby Day ended poorly because of inept work by racing judges on the final race of the day. Red Light, leading from the start, finished first by almost a full length. However, the judges awarded the victory to Baggage, who appeared to most onlookers to have finished sixth. Jockeys, owners, and spectators all demanded a correction, but the judges "cavalierly . . . refused to correct their blunder." The presiding judge, responsible for reporting the first-place finisher, thought the winning jockey had 7 on his arm (for Baggage), not the 3 for Red Light. The error was admitted the next day, and the track awarded Red Light's owner the equivalent of the purse and paid off holders of the winning betting stubs. The *Spirit* blamed the error on the track's policy of honoring distinguished citizens as judges regardless of their vision, concentration, or experience.[95]

The WSP's owners that year subleased the track from themselves for $15,000 ($8,000 more than the annual rent), under the name of the West Side Trotting Association (WSTA) and leased the betting concession to the WBA. Patrick Sheedy, a local poolroom operator, claimed that Corrigan netted $185,000 clear at the West Side races, "all on book making."[96]

The *Spirit*'s highly regarded reporter "Broad Church" covered Chicago racing for the weekly. He gave the West Side track an overall positive assessment, despite obvious flaws: "Some people sneer at the Corrigan track and intimate that the races are crooked and that jobs [fixed races] are plentiful." The journalist recognized that cheating did occur at the track, "but I wish there was as vigilant management in every track as there has been at the West side. Unlike some other tracks I could name, there they take the bull by the horns and if the management is satisfied that an owner or jockey is not running to win, he is ordered away," even if they end up at "so-called high-toned tracks."[97]

CONCLUSION

Chicago in the late 1880s was the racing capital of the Midwest, mainly because of the Washington Park Club, which immediately became one of the city's most prestigious men's clubs, expanding the social and cultural world of the local elite and providing a new means for upper-class families to conspicuously display their wealth. Its track, which sponsored the American Derby, one of the greatest and richest races in the world, was quickly recognized as one of the most outstanding American courses, with one of the finest clubhouses anywhere. The track's opening helped confirm Chicago as the second-leading American city. In addition, the growing interest in flat racing undergirded the WSP at a time when harness racing was losing a lot of popularity, enabling the West Side proprietary racetrack to survive and earn some impressive profits as a thoroughbred course, despite some rough years of poor management. The Chicago turf also benefited substantially from the Gibbs Act that legitimized the business of horse racing and on-track gambling and clearly proscribed turf wagering off the track. The legal fortunes of the racing business seemed etched in stone, but it would not be the case for long. The new situation encouraged the McDonald syndicate to soon jump into the business of running a race-course and employ its clout to displace the WSP. Furthermore, the Chase Act proved inadequate to destroy the illegal offtrack betting business, which, while briefly struggling, flourished in the hands of the politically well-connected McDonald syndicate that employed its political might to protect itself and curtail competition.

3

Politics, Gambling, Syndicate Crime, and the Chicago Turf, 1890–1892

As the United States entered the last decade of the nineteenth century, there was little doubt that Chicago was a world-class city, with all their finest attributes and all their major problems. The population was 1,099,850, having increased by a staggering 25.5 percent in a decade. Chicago had the fifth-most inhabitants of any city in the world, following London, New York, Paris, and Berlin. Its rapid urbanization led to infrastructure and development problems that outpaced nearly all cities. Its population was 40.5 percent foreign born, second only to New York (42.2 percent) among American cities with more than 80,000 residents. Among residents classified as white, 78.9 percent were immigrants or children of immigrants, mostly from Germany, Ireland, Great Britain, and Scandinavia, with increasing numbers from Bohemia, Italy, Poland, and Russia. The city had a highly stratified social structure, topped by a small wealthy WASP elite enriched by industrial capitalism, particularly banking, commerce, finance, commerce, manufacturing, and real estate. The economic expansion required a big growth in middle-class occupations such as accounting, management, and engineering, but most people were employed at modest or low-paying jobs. Seventy percent of workers were blue collar, half of whom were semi- or unskilled, laboring six and even seven days a week, ten to twelve hours a day. They worked in iron and steelyards, meatpacking yards, and sweatshops. The lowest 29.3 percent of workers made an average of just $376 a year.[1]

The city in 1889 underwent dramatic physical growth, expanding from 35 to 185 square miles by annexing surrounding towns and villages, facilitated by the expanding private mass-transit system that made possible longer middle-class commutes to work. The upper class could afford to live in wealthy suburbs such as Lake Forest and Winnetka, accessible to work by rail lines, or choose homes near downtown in elegant neighborhoods on the near South Side. Land use became highly specialized, especially downtown in the central business district, which was the center of government, commerce, and culture, as well as the hub of mass transit. The extremely high cost of land and technological innovations led to the rise of skyscrapers that housed corporate headquarters, government offices, department stores, and hotels. The CBD was also the site of important commercialized recreational facilities, including opera houses, theaters, symphonic halls, museums, and, yes, poolrooms and billiard parlors. Also, just outside the CBD was the Levee District, the politically protected center of such vices as prostitution and gambling.[2]

The wealthy CBD was surrounded by three radial residential rings. The poorest and newest immigrants lived in densely populated slums, often adjacent to industrial areas where they worked. The slums had poor-quality housing, inadequate urban services, labor unrest, ethnic hostility, and high mortality and crime rates. Next came the "zone of emergence," originally inhabited by working-class Irish, Germans, and Scandinavians where families lived in modest homes in safer and healthier neighborhoods with better government services. Male residents of these two regions who liked to gamble on thoroughbreds were well served by local handbooks at saloons, candy stores, and newsstands. Finally, there was the middle-class "suburban fringe," inhabited by white Anglo-Saxon Protestants, residing in spacious homes situated on large lots on the edge of town. These were clean, safe neighborhoods, with excellent schools, beautiful public parks, and high-quality public services.[3]

The prevailing social, economic, and especially political developments had an important impact on the racing scene. People who went to the tracks or the downtown poolrooms had more discretionary time and income than most residents, while those who frequented neighborhood handbooks earned little money, worked long hours, and were subjected to insecure work schedules. Upper-middle- and upper-class racing fans took advantage of improved roads, riding carriages to the tracks, though most people rode cable cars, trolley cars, and commuter trains. Social values and attitudes, which were based on class, education, religion, and ethnicity, influenced people's attitudes toward racing and gambling, with the upper and lower classes more open to betting on racing than the heavily Protestant middle class.

Regrettably, there are no hard data and little impressionistic data on the social origins of racing crowds. Certainly, people of all social backgrounds went to the races and made bets outside the track. The wealthier fans were seen at Washington Park for the big races, and their names were reported in feature stories about the American Derby, but their numbers were small. Lower-class folk mainly attended races at the proprietary tracks and did a lot of their betting in their neighborhoods with handbooks. But many people in the standing-room sections at Washington Park were working class, and members of the demimonde were in the grandstands. Middle-class men and women regularly went to the races, although Chicago's leading opponents of racing and gambling were also middle class. A 1903 editorial in the *Tribune* described its editors' take on the social backgrounds of racing fans: "Probably over 50 per cent of the men one meets in a day—in street cars, in barber shops, in hotels, barrooms, cigar, or periodical shops—are talking races. It is no exaggeration to say that 40 percent of the middle class salaried men and boys of Chicago bet on the races."[4]

Corrupt local politicians had a significant impact on racing and gambling in the city. However, contrary to conventional wisdom, Chicago's municipal government was not overwhelmingly Democratic. The city elected two Republican mayors in the 1890s, and the city council had Republican majorities for half of the decade. On the other hand, the general presumption that several aldermen, regardless of political affiliation, were dishonest, and sold their votes to the highest bidder, was accurate. The Democrats mainly appealed to working-class voters, especially the Irish, who were big gamblers, and the recent newcomers from eastern and southern Europe, while Republican organizations depended on middle-class white native-born American and German and Scandinavian artisans. There was no citywide machine, but prominent Democratic and Republican ward bosses had a lot of power, dispensing patronage to party workers and protection to underworld figures involved in illicit enterprises, like offtrack gamblers, who helped finance their operations.[5]

Political influence played an important role in racing in the early 1890s, starting with a big fight between Mayor DeWitt Cregier and owner Edward Corrigan of the West Side Park, followed by the successful effort by politically connected bookmakers to push Corrigan out of the city. He was supplanted on the West Side by Mike McDonald's syndicate, which turned the WSP site into a financial bonanza. However, the public became so disgusted with Garfield Park's management and the track's low-life clientele that a successful campaign was fought to close the outlaw track despite the ownership's strong political protection.

Mayor Cregier and Chicago Racing

In April 1889 Democrat DeWitt Clinton Cregier, a former chief engineer of the Chicago water system and commissioner of public works, defeated incumbent mayor Republican John A. Roche, an ardent gambling foe. Everyone knew Cregier's victory was owing to the support of local gamblers who wanted a new regime friendly to illegal wagering. A week before the election, the *Tribune* explained, "Cregier was a defeated man. . . . His Campaign Committee was destitute." But after wealthy "friends" rescued him, Cregier reconsidered his opposition to reopening closed gambling houses and promised professional gamblers they could resume business. The *Tribune* admitted that "while there is not and cannot be any written proof of a bargain, there is sufficient circumstantial evidence to show that one was made between the gamblers and someone who held Cregier in the hollow of his hand."[6]

Cregier's new vision was credited to Mike McDonald, who served as campaign chairman, with George Hankins as his deputy. According to the *Tribune*, "Mr. McDonald exercised the talents which have made him famous and wealthy." He collected around $6,000–$8,000 from New York gamblers and $30,000 in all for the campaign. Mike's aides worked hard to turn out the vote and made sure supporters voted often for Cregier.[7]

Cregier won a surprisingly large victory with 55 percent of the vote. Immediately after he took office, gambling houses, closed for two years, reopened. Poolrooms particularly enjoyed a resurgence and, except for an occasional raid, remained open. Yet the authorities were less helpful to gamblers than under Harrison because certain disgruntled bettors were permitted to seek revenge against pool operators by hiring private detectives and constables to batter down doors, smash furniture, and otherwise interfere with offtrack betting.[8]

By late July, Gamblers' Alley seemed back in business. The *Tribune* ran an article that gave the addresses of fifteen gambling halls and estimated there were at least twenty in operation. Some did not even have a guard at the front door to weed out the clientele and prevent raids. George Hankins, one of the major gambling-hall operators, did because he wanted to keep out professional gamblers, while promoting business among inexperienced working-class bettors. He employed eighty-two men at his poolroom at 134 Clark Street, at a weekly cost of $2,350, while also spending $153 on gas and other incidentals. The staff included four managers ($200), eighteen dealers ($630), twelve roulette croupiers ($360), and one bouncer.[9]

The *Tribune* belittled Mayor Cregier's efforts to shut down poolrooms in April 1890, one year after his election, and initiated a new call for their elimination. The police then periodically raided unprotected pool sellers, but when a protected room was scheduled for an incursion, the owner or manager would be forewarned so that the principals would not be present. Arrested men would be fined by a police justice, and their attorneys would then appeal the case to the criminal courts, placing the matter in the hands of the state's attorney. A trial would follow some months later, and, if convicted, the guilty poolroom men further appealed, first to the appellate court and then to the state supreme court. If the conviction was upheld, poolroom owners, who usually remained in business during the entire legal process, paid the fines and lawyers' bill, which they considered a virtual "license fee" to remain in business.[10]

Cregier came under strong pressure to close the local poolrooms during the course of the WPR's 1890 summer meet. The demands came from some of his own main backers, notably the Hankins brothers, who ran books at Washington Park and wanted to limit offtrack competition. The authorities responded by warning poolrooms one month before the WPR summer meet to close or get raided.[11]

An exception was made for handbooks, small-time bookies who recorded their transactions in small notebooks (hence the term *handbooks*). Handbooks were mainly located in working-class neighborhoods, where they were nearly ubiquitous. These bookies hung out wherever men congregated, such as saloons, pool halls, or candy stores, giving the shop owner a small percentage of his profits. They also met clients on the street and employed solicitors (runners) to take bets inside factories and offices. Certain bookies catered specifically to women, especially in offices or cafeterias. The handbooks paid off after the race or the next day. At best they paid off using track odds reported in local newspapers, but typically paid off below track odds and nearly 25–40 percent less for a long shot.[12]

Handbooks ran independently or affiliated with a crime syndicate that provided protection from the police, speedy reports of race results, the opportunity to lay off large bets with bigger bookmakers, access to attorneys, and bonds for arrested workers. A bookie relied heavily on his reputation to sustain a working relationship with clients, but there were dishonest bookies who regularly cheated clients, such as taking losing bets after post time when they already had the results.[13]

Corrigan v. Cregier

The 1890 spring meeting at West Side Park was generally uneventful. The twenty-two bookmakers at the track paid $100 a day to operate, and the foreign book paid $150. Then toward the end of the WPR summer season, the "word" went out that the authorities were going to be less vigilant fighting offtrack gambling. This news led to the reopening of poolrooms on July 21 in direct competition with WSP bookmakers. The average track attendance of about three thousand spectators a day was hurt by the reopened downtown poolrooms. The *Chicago Post* estimated that city poolrooms cost West Side Park $5,000 a week in lost revenue, or about $50,000–$60,000 for the summer season.[14]

Corrigan asked the illegal entrepreneurs to close during his meet as they had for Washington Park, but they refused: "We have done enough for Cregier in shutting down during the Washington Park races, so that he might keep faith with some of his political backers. We do not propose to close down for you, even if the Mayor should ask us." Corrigan claimed that pool representatives offered him $700 and a share of profits to cease selling pools at his track. When Ed threatened to push for the enforcement of antipoolroom laws, George Hankins and Mike McDonald promised retaliatory raids, which the *Tribune* took seriously: "They evidently spoke with authority. They are putting their threat into practice. They control the police force."[15]

The WSP saw no point appealing to city hall because of the gamblers' clout. Instead, Corrigan went on the offensive and called on William "Billy" Pinkerton of the Pinkerton Detective Agency to attack illegal rooms on his behalf. McDonald, Hankins, Johnny Condon, and other leaders of the gambling combination tried to convince Pinkerton to stay out. "Of course, we know you never sleep," McDonald told Pinkerton, "but couldn't you just wink now and then for a month or so?" Pinkerton responded, "We never wink."[16]

One of Corrigan's main supporters in the antipoolroom fight was partner Joe Ullman of St. Louis, a former butcher who became a successful horse breeder. In 1887 he sold his two-year-old gelding Raceland to August Belmont, the renowned thoroughbred owner, and Raceland became the nation's top stakes champion. In 1892 Ullman opened and managed the East St. Louis racetrack, which became a successful proprietary course. Joe's primary involvement with the WSP was operating its foreign book that in 1890 reputedly made $600,000. The Hankins-McDonald gang placed a lot of pressure on Ullman, who eventually agreed to pay 60 percent of his profits for protection. Despite that price tag, Ullman was so successful that in 1896 the *New York Times* rated him the best in the United States.[17]

Corrigan's pressure on Mayor Cregier got municipal officials to threaten offtrack room operators with arrests on July 22. However, the grand jury would not vote any indictments based on evidence amassed by private detectives or go after the small fry. The jurors were focused on McDonald and his cohorts, and even the mayor and police chief, for allowing poolrooms to reopen. The grand jury transposed itself into a court of last resort and ruled that the Gibbs Act was constitutional. One juror explained, "The two race tracks are within the city limits, and we cannot see why the pool-room business is wicked in one part of the city and an innocent pleasure in another part."[18]

On July 30, Corrigan's attorney applied for an injunction restraining Cregier and the police superintendent, Frederick H. Marsh, from interfering with gambling at the WSP, pointing out that downtown pool selling was going on under police protection at a cost of $125 a week per poolroom. Cregier denounced the charges, asserting he was supported by the Chicago Law Department's opinion that foreign books on the tracks were illegal. It was probably the first time a private company made such accusations of malfeasance in court against a Chicago mayor.[19]

The *Tribune* took Cregier to task for allowing six downtown rooms closed by former mayor Roche to reopen and urged the administration to go for the big fish and not the auctioneers, money changers, telegraph operators, or messengers. Another editorial criticized city prosecutor Johnny May as being nearly the equivalent of a gambling-trust attorney. When he prosecuted poolroom men the year before, May sought convictions under a weak city law that levied a maximum $200 fine compared to the more severe state law that carried a $2,000 fine and a year in jail. On August 3, the administration responded to Corrigan's harassment by terminating his amusement and liquor licenses for allowing, if not fostering, illegal pool selling at his track.[20]

Cregier invited one hundred prominent personal and political friends to a meeting on August 9 to discuss the Corrigan situation, but only twenty-five showed up. He told them that corporation counsel C. L. Hutchinson had determined that Corrigan was "acting lawlessly in employing private detective agencies to protect his race-track gambling," and the mayor wanted their support. The audience was visibly uncomfortable that Cregier had placed them in an awkward position because they did not believe the police had done a satisfactory job in fighting the poolrooms and that Cregier was fighting Corrigan for personal reasons, and thus not properly doing his job. The consensus was that Corrigan was still a public benefactor for fighting the downtown gamblers, even if only for his own business interests. The *Tribune* chastised Cregier for incompetence compared to his more effective predecessor, Mayor John A. Roche. The paper even rated him below Carter Harrison, who had rationalized his weak stand against enforcing the antigambling codes by claiming that implementing reform would actually create worse evils than illegal betting. Nonetheless, the *Tribune* credited the mayor as honest and outspoken and said he "behaved like a man."[21]

Cregier recognized that he had become the subject of considerable ridicule and decided to leave Corrigan alone on the pool-selling issue. More important, Washington Park was scheduled to reopen on August 13, and gamblers tied to the administration, like George Hankins, wanted to sell pools there, and the track management wanted their business. City hall worked out a deal with Corrigan, who dropped his complaints against Cregier, and in return Ullman was permitted to sell his foreign pools. Corrigan further protected himself with a temporary restraining order that prevented interference by the mayor, the police superintendent, or their agents with his racetrack's gambling, saloon, and amusement licenses.[22]

THE COURTS AND THE GIBBS ACT

At the end of October, circuit-court judge Murray F. Tuley ruled on test cases regarding bookmaker C. J. Brownlee, convicted of taking bets outside of a racetrack, and Joe Ullman, charged with bookmaking and selling foreign pools at the WSP as well as maintaining a

Chicago bookmaking and pool-selling facility. Tuley ruled that the Gibbs Amendment was unconstitutional because it violated an 1869 state statute prohibiting gambling and the keeping of gambling places and contravened the 1870 state constitution by giving certain groups special privileges. Tuley explained that Gibbs was, in effect, a special act, granting exclusively to county-fair and racehorse associations the right to keep gambling places within their enclosures at certain times and giving anyone involved immunity from the general law barring betting on races or selling pools. Tuley also ruled that an obscure new city law that fined anyone selling illegal pools just $50–$200 was also unconstitutional since it was a mere slap on the wrist, intended to help city poolrooms remain open.[23]

Tuley's verdict was considered a crushing defeat for Corrigan and a sweeping victory for the poolroom men, putting them on the same footing as other racing gamblers, making them all illegal. Judges prior to Gibbs did not interpret pool selling as gaming, and thus not subject to the general statute on gambling. Corporation counsel Jonas Hutchinson interpreted Tuley's ruling to mean that pool selling was "ordinary, every-day gambling, just the same as faro or poker," which made all racetrack gambling illegal.[24]

Tuley's judgment was not the panacea sought by the antigambling forces. However, it did hinder Corrigan's plan to operate three separate tracks in 1891 and jeopardized Washington Park's operations as well as a plan by bookmakers to open a track in the Grand Crossing neighborhood on the South Side. Experts expected that tracks without betting could not afford to operate because of the lost fees paid by bookmakers and an anticipated 50 percent drop in attendance.[25]

Washington Park in the Early 1890s

In 1889 Chicago annexed the town of Hyde Park, where the Washington Park Racetrack was constructed in 1884. The area surrounding the racetrack was not yet highly developed, but the opening in 1882 of the South Side Wabash–Cotton Grove cable line led to a big housing boom in the area. Land values dramatically appreciated so much that the Washington Park Racetrack was offered $850,000 for its land, but rejected the offer. The *Spirit* suspected that the tracks would hang on until after the World's Fair to take advantage of the tourist boom and by 1895 would divide up the sites into building lots.[26]

The WPR made substantial improvements in 1890 to keep up with its growing popularity. The betting quarters were extended by more than sixteen thousand square feet on the east end of the grandstand, making it easier to find a bookie. Several thousand seats were added to the grandstand, briefly making it the largest in the country. The *Chicago Evening Post* described it "as elegant a race track as may be found anywhere within a 500-mile radius."[27]

WPR president Harry F. Wheeler, head of the Chicago City Railway, reported the meet was the most profitable ever, despite an early summer heat wave and a brief Illinois Central strike. Overall attendance was up by several thousand, and the daily gate rose by $600–$700. The American Derby attracted a reported record audience of fifty thousand, with about sixty-five bookmakers taking bets. George V. Hankins's stallion Uncle Bob captured the nearly $16,000 prize, and he picked up another $25,000 in wagers. The meet was highlighted by Racine racing a mile in 1:39.5, breaking a thirteen-year-old world record.[28]

Charles S. Bush of New Orleans again supervised the bookmaking. Local poolroom man Pat Sheedy offered $20,000 for the privilege of making books on foreign races but was rejected because the Chase antipool law barred bets on out-of-town races. Betting was extremely heavy, with bookmakers covering at least $60,000 on every race. The press felt that so much action led to considerable chicanery, more than at the less respected WSP. Wheeler responded that the number of frauds had not risen, but was just more apparent. A WPR director asserted that "last year the jockeys decided which horse should win. . . . This year the bookmakers' combination decides."[29]

The Hankins crowd was mainly blamed for the decline in form. They entered horses from six different stables and constituted the majority of competitors in several eight-horse races. Their interconnections encouraged and facilitated intrastable conspiracies, or at least the appearance of evil plots. For example, on July 15, George V. Hankins's best stallion, Santalene, went off as a prohibitive 3–5 favorite in the feature race. Eighty percent of the bettors backed Santalene, but he was upset by Atticus, a 10–1 common platter (horses in a race that can be claimed for a specified price). The racing judges immediately called in Hankins, his trainer, and the jockey to explain. They determined that Hankins had heavily bet on his horse to win, but that his stallion was insufficiently trained for such a competitive race.[30]

Local sportswriters were dissatisfied with the stewards' report, especially since Atticus's reputed owners were a front for Al Hankins, George's brother. As one St. Louis bookmaker warned, "Never put a nickel on a race where a Hankins horse is entered."[31]

According to the *Tribune*, "The public and the WPR members must know that if the Hankins Stable is to figure on their grounds and the Hankins brothers are to control the track there will be nothing but jugglery . . . and all semblance of fair racing will be defeated by rascally trickery. It is therefore high time for the Washington Park Club to decide whether the park is to be utilized by gentlemen for fair and square racing or by professional gamblers for swindling."[32]

Bookmakers were disappointed with the meet because they believed dishonesty had cost them money. One-fourth of them were losers, one-fourth broke even, and one-half made money. After ten days the number of bookmakers dropped from sixty-five to forty-two because of high fixed costs ($95 a day fee to operate, plus $65 for other expenses) and the risk of crooked races. Some felt they could do better as bettors than as bookmakers. As the *Tribune* rightly pointed out, "Bookmakers prefer square racing, because if they cannot depend upon the public form of horses, they are all at seas and must meet trickery with trickery." The bookmakers also complained that the WPR had been unfair to them because their fees helped cover the added money donated by the club for stakes events.[33]

Closing West Side Park

Efforts to Reform Racing and Pool Selling

In February 1891, Democratic representative Sol Van Praag from Chicago's notorious First Ward, and a close colleague of Mayor Cregier, introduced a racing bill in the legislature thought to be primarily aimed at Edward Corrigan. The bill sought to ban winter racing, limit meets to thirty days, and levy a 5 percent tax on gross revenues, to be distributed to county fairs to promote the improvement of the breed of horses, cattle, and sheep. However, it failed to pass. Other bills were presented two years later by Representative Daniel S. Berry (R–Carroll County), a racing foe, but also failed to pass.[34]

The direction of thoroughbred racing in Chicago was about to change, but not because of the Tuley decision, which had a longer-term impact. The immediate issue in 1891 was Corrigan's protracted fight against Mayor Cregier, the city council, the police, and politicians connected to Mike McDonald and his gambling trust. Corrigan's future on the West Side was tenuous because of the power of the McDonald crowd, who saw Corrigan as an intransigent intruder from Kansas City who would not negotiate with them. Corrigan expected his political opponents and their politically connected downtown gamblers would harass him in every way possible to force him out of business so they could take over his racing site. The final blow came when Judge Lambert Tree announced the doubling of the WSP's rent from $7,000 to $15,000. Corrigan and partner David Waldo saw the writing on the wall and announced at the start of January 1891 that they would dismantle the WSP. However, they were not going out of business, but relocating to a new site.[35]

Corrigan's new firm, the Chicago Racing Association (CRA), built a new racecourse chosen "to get out of reach of the blackmail or legislation . . . of the [City] Council." The location was just outside Chicago's southwest border in the village of Hawthorne (the southeastern part of the town of Cicero), between Thirty-Fifth and Forty-Eighth Streets, an area inhabited almost completely by working-class immigrants. The 103-acre track site cost $160,000 ($1,553 an acre), and the CRA spent $50,000 to build the track, stands, and stables as well as purchase essential equipment. The land was about the same distance from downtown as the WPR and was well served by commuter railroads that ran just three blocks away, including the Illinois Central, the Santa Fe, and the Chicago, Burlington & Quincy. The CRA issued $500,000 in capital stock in $5,000-unit shares. Corrigan owned half of the stock; former West Park commissioner John Brenock, a part-owner of the track site, owned a quarter share; and his son-in-law, poolroom operator John Burke, owned nearly as much. Brenock had recently been in the public eye for assaulting his neighbor Edward Swiney with a baseball bat, and nearly killing him, after discovering that Swiney, a married man, was enamored with Brenock's granddaughter. The facility was officially named the Chicago Jockey Club Park, but everyone knew it as the Hawthorne Racetrack.[36]

Corrigan's nemesis, Mayor Dewitt Cregier, came up for reelection in April and encountered a stiff challenge from Republican Hempstead Washburne, former city attorney (1885–89) and the son of an eight-term congressman. A third strong candidate was Carter Harrison, coming out of retirement as an independent Democrat. Cregier again turned to local gamblers for financial support. The sporting crowd knew that Washburne was committed to suppressing gambling, so the Gamblers' Trust and its allies amassed a $25,000 fund to secure Cregier's retention.[37]

The election was one of the most complicated in Chicago history. There was a fourth candidate, reformer Elmer Washburn of the local Citizens' Party, who promised to take the police out of politics. He was a former Chicago police superintendent and head of the US Secret Service, as well as president of the Union Stockyards National Bank. His name was very similar to the Republican aspirant, and many voters saw him as a potential spoiler. Hempstead Washburne won the election with just 28.8 percent of the vote, edging Cregier (28.6 percent) by just 399 votes, with Harrison third (26.4 percent).[38]

Largely forgotten today, Hempstead Washburne was an outstanding reform mayor who immediately turned the screws on gambling,

8. The American Derby, 1916, Chicago. Hawthorne racetrack was closed from 1905 through 1908. It was bought by Chicago politician and book-maker Tom Carey. It was opened as an experiment for a few days from 1909 through 1912 and again in 1916 for the American Derby and again closed until a thirteen-day meet in 1922. Library of Congress Prints and Photo-graphs Division, Washington, DC. Photograph. https://www.loc.gov/item /2007663748/. Copyright Kaufmann & Fabry, 1916.

ordering police superintendent Fred Marsh to close every gambling house in the city. Marsh failed that impossible mission and was replaced by Major Robert W. McClaughry, former superintendent of a Penn-sylvania reformatory. On April 28, instructions went out to the ranks to warn major gambling rooms to close immediately or be raided and have their property confiscated. The gamblers complied immediately, and by early afternoon 150 men were out of work. Only Sid McHie and John O'Neil's gambling halls stayed open, and they both closed later that day after the finish of out-of-town races.[39]

On May 20, the CRA opened for business at the new Hawthorne racecourse, with a mile-long track and a three-hundred-foot-long double-decked grandstand that seated ten thousand, with lunch coun-ters, bars, and a telegraph office underneath. The beautiful grand-stand, set off from the homestretch at an acute angle to allow everyone to see without standing, was one of the first brick-built racetracks and rated as one of the best and safest in the country. Admission cost seventy-five cents to a dollar. The betting ring was fifty feet away, with space for nearly a hundred books. Hawthorne also had a two-story clubhouse with sleeping apartments and a reading room, café, and buffet. The track attracted high-quality horses and by summer had stalls for 680.[40]

Local authorities tried to put the squeeze on the new track. Cicero's trustees denied Corrigan a liquor license, but when Hawthorne opened the concessionaires still sold alcoholic beverages. The town police raided the track in June, but found only coffee, lemonade, and mineral water for sale. Village board president S. A. Rothermel kept up the attack and had the authorities arrest Corrigan, Brenock, the restaurateur, and two bartenders for operating without a license.[41]

THE WASHINGTON PARK SCENE

On June 19, the day before the opening of Washington Park, Mayor Washburne announced he would not interfere with pool selling there or at the new Garfield Park track that replaced Corrigan's on the West Side. His position was that, notwithstanding the Tuley ruling, Gibbs legalized on-track gambling. Washington Park secured a license at the nominal cost of $50 for one month, less than the $58.44 license fee for its saloon, operated by Gardner Spring Chapin and James Jefferson Gore, owners of a renowned downtown tavern that was a popular hangout for handbook men.[42]

The American Derby on June 20, 1891, drew 39,613 spectators, including 34,954 tickets purchased at the gate or sold by the Illinois Central, three tickets for each of the 853 club members, and 2,100 complimentary tickets for the press, owners, and horsemen. Sixty-six bookmakers worked the betting ring, where space for 2,000 bettors proved insufficient. Bettors wagered some $2 million on the American Derby in just thirty minutes. Nearly the entire first three pages of the next day's *Tribune* were devoted to the race and the crowds. Names of some sixty-four groups who came by horse-drawn vehicles were identified, plus two parties that arrived by private train cars. Strathmeath, the 2–1 favorite, captured the $19,000 first prize.[43]

Washington Park ran a successful meet, with profits estimated at $200,000, double the original capitalization, a superb return on investment. The triumphal meet was no surprise to the *Spirit*: "Very liberal patronage was natural enough for the racing was of the best, and the good order and decorum . . . were akin to the proprieties observed in a well-regulated opera-house. Catering to the self-respecting and reputable classes goes a great way in insuring both popular and permanent support in conducting any species of amusement, and notably that allied to the turf." Still, the *Inter Ocean* warned bettors about crooked bookies who bet against their own horses.[44]

On July 10, Alfred "Monk" Overton became the second jockey in the world after England's Freddy Archer (1877, 1882) to ride six winners in one day. Overton was one of the fifteen or so black jockeys who were considered among the finest sixty riders in the United States. However, they encountered a lot of racial prejudice, particularly by white jockeys, who did not want them competing for lucrative mounts and tried to intimidate them off the track. White riders at Chicago's Harlem Racetrack in August 1900 forced the great Jimmy Winkfield and his horse into the guardrails during a race, injuring both. Journalists did not totally dismiss black jockeys' skills, but often underplayed their accomplishments and belittled their intelligence by quoting them in dialect. Stable owners stopped hiring nearly all the African American jockeys, compelling star riders to work abroad and the rest to fade out of the occupation by the early 1900s.[45]

THE RISE OF GARFIELD PARK

Corrigan's flight from the West Side only briefly left the area without racing. At first, the WSP buildings were dismantled, and the public expected developers to divide the site into building lots. Yet some seven thousand Chicagoans followed racing as a business, and there was ample demand for another track. Just a few days after Corrigan announced he was leaving Chicago, two young North Siders fronting for George Hankins's bookmakers' syndicate secured a ten-year option on the old site at $15,000 for the first year (identical to

Tree's offer to Corrigan), $20,000 for the second, and $25,000 for the third.[46]

Garfield Park and Political Clout

The Garfield Park Club (GPC), named for the adjacent public park, was incorporated in late May 1891 by George Hankins and John Condon, with a capital stock of $300,000. The club planned to spend $150,000 for the stands and the clubhouse and reportedly actually spent $200,000. The major shareholders were all professional gamblers: Sid McHie (15 percent), a future millionaire also active in the local bucket-shop trade; George Hankins and Mike McDonald (12.5 percent each); Al and Jeff Hankins, Condon, and Harry Varnell (10 percent each); and Paddy Ryan (5 percent). Varnell also got the liquor concession. They opened Garfield Park Racetrack, which became known as the "bookmakers' track," on July 20. The course was one of the fastest in the United States. Washington Hesing, the prominent publisher and Democratic politician, who ran in the 1893 primary for mayor, was the West Side track's first president.[47]

The new owners had enormous political influence, primarily through Mike McDonald, Varnell, and Condon and their association with Johnny Powers of the West Side Nineteenth Ward (1888–1903, 1904–27), a future racetrack owner, and "Bathhouse" John Coughlin. Coughlin served as an alderman of the downtown First Ward from 1892 until his death in 1938. He was the longest-serving councilman until surpassed in 2014 by Edward M. Burke. Five years later, he was joined as ward alderman by "Hinky Dink" Mike Kenna (1897–1923). They were known as the "Lords of the Levee," rulers of Chicago's vice district, located just south of downtown and renowned for its gambling halls and brothels. They were all Irish Democrats and leaders of the "Grey Wolves," city councilmen who preyed on the defenseless public, trading votes for favors and using their power to make money, legally through "honest graft," or illegally, if necessary.[48]

The term *honest graft* was created by New York Tammany boss and state senator George Washington Plunkitt in the early 1900s,

referring to moneymaking opportunities available to government officials that were legal, such as employing inside information for their
own personal advantage. According to Plunkitt, "I seen my opportunities and I took 'em." This inside information might involve buying
land the city intended to buy for a public park before the city closed
the deal. Plunkitt deplored "dishonest graft," such as stealing from the
city's coffers.[49]

Bathhouse John Coughlin was fascinated by the turf and spent
a lot of time and money at the track, following in the footsteps of
older brother Joe, a track worker as a teenager who became a capable
handicapper. In the early 1880s, when John went into politics and the
bathhouse business, he became a good friend of Washington Park
jockeys and trainers who gave him tips on fixed races, termed "boat
rides." In 1885 he bought his first horse and eventually owned a racing stable with as many as sixty horses. Bathhouse raced his horses at
local tracks and maintained a box at Washington Park. Bathhouse and
Hinky Dink were also heavily involved with boxing promoter Parson
Davies, who regularly paid them off so he could stage bouts at racetracks, saloons, and armories.[50]

John Condon

One of the most important Chicagoans involved in the rise of Garfield
Park was John Condon. He was a poor boy from Logansport, Indiana,
who started out as a barber. Sam Doll, a local gambler, took an interest in him and enabled him to learn the art of dealing faro. Doll and
Condon moved to Chicago in the 1880s and opened a gambling hall.
Condon became one of the first men to learn the importance of police
connections to promote and protect his illegal business against interlopers like horseman Edward Corrigan.[51]

Condon soon became a close associate of McDonald's and the
man to see if one wanted to enter the gambling business, especially
the poolroom trade. The *Tribune* credited him with dividing up the
city "by natural and racial lines," figuring out the best locations for
high-class gambling palaces and setting up a district to promote such

popular games like craps, faro, and stuss ("Jewish faro," which was dealt by hand).[52]

Condon became a major figure in the poolroom trade, using his political connections to "fix" problems, and was involved in such important gambling palaces as the "Store" and the "House of David." He, of course, got part of the action. He was particularly involved with the local poolrooms and even owned a bucket shop. He became a millionaire and one of the leading investors in racetracks in Chicago, Montreal, New Orleans, and Oakland. John was the principal owner of the Harlem Track, which in 1897 was the only course open in metropolitan Chicago. Condon reputedly made $100,000 in just eighty-eight days. Six years later, he reputedly tried to take over the betting at Washington Park along with Hinky Dink Kenna and Tom McGinnis. He sent a message to WPR treasurer John R. Walsh demanding control of the field book for $100,000 and the rest of the betting privileges for an undetermined amount. This figure was an enormous amount, but he was reportedly paying $500 a day elsewhere for less profitable, but lengthier, meets. Condon warned Walsh that Mayor Harrison would bar gambling at the track unless the deal was approved. Walsh refused.[53]

Community Opposition

Garfield Park's opening was vigorously opposed by clergymen, moral reformers, and local residents who owned nearby single-family brownstones. The track's detractors, who had been none too happy about Corrigan's track, filed a suit to block the new course. They claimed that in the past, "the stench from the stables polluted the air; shouts, jeers and the sound of brass bands were heard" at their homes. They asserted that the gambling at Corrigan's track brought into the neighborhood "a crowd of thieves, confidence men, loafers, tramps, beggars, and adventurers, and at all hours of the day and night houses were visited by beggars who sometimes carried revolvers to extort alms or food." They claimed the old West Side Park was an "intolerable nuisance" that, besides racing, also hosted dog fighting and boxing and that their wives and children "could not venture from their homes for fear of violence or insults at the hands of the mob."[54]

Given the local residents' disapproval of the Corrigan regime, it was ironic that their strongest ally was Corrigan, who wanted revenge against the new owners for forcing him to move. On June 4, Corrigan pleaded with Mayor Washburne to deny Garfield Park a license, pointing out that Chicago's Park Act required the West Side Board of Park Commissioners to approve "any horse-racing, gambling, or obnoxious or dangerous business or amusements within 400 feet of said boulevard and parks."[55]

On June 26, seven neighborhood property owners living within a block of the site filed for an injunction against the new track, complaining that virtually all the prospective owners were pool sellers or bookmakers, including notorious keepers of common gambling houses. The petition asserted that the new track was not established to improve the breed, develop speed, or promote sport, but purely to encourage gambling "and of gaining large profits thereby." The document asserted the course's presence would depress property values; attract "all classes of low people, thieves, prize-fighters, abandoned women, tramps, and other disreputable characters"; and be as great a nuisance as the old West Side Park. The West Park commissioners thereupon sought an injunction against the new track, claiming it was a cover for unlawful gambling that would harm the usefulness of the park and ruin the neighborhood with "vast crowds of objectionable persons."[56]

The track's attorneys, who included former three-term Republican US senator Lyman Trumball, defended the syndicate, admitting the track existed for betting purposes, but pointed out that the Gibbs Amendment permitted wagering at racecourses. The lawyers argued that the site had been used for racing since 1878 and denied that the area was thickly settled, since three streets adjoining the course were nearly vacant and the fourth already had several saloons. Finally, the advocates asserted that the owners' occupations were irrelevant. On July 10, Judge Tuley, who a year before had ruled against betting at WSP, seemed to overrule himself, denying the injunction, since the racetrack was not ipso facto a nuisance, and no one had previously complained about racing there in the previous thirteen years. The city council then proceeded to award the necessary building permits.[57]

The Inaugural Season

The Garfield Park opened up with a five-thousand-seat double-spired grandstand (with plans to expand to twenty thousand seats), two running tracks, and a clubhouse that may have been the model for the double-spired grandstand track at Churchill Downs built in 1895. It appeared to have been designed after the Brighton Beach racetrack in Brooklyn, though some felt the grandstand was similar to the Clifton, New Jersey, course since it was prepared for winter racing with glass walls and steam heating. Every seat offered a fine view because the architect designed the structure to use light roof supports that required less pillars than other tracks. The betting ring had space for one hundred slate writers and was rated as one of the most commodious and accessible in the West. The stables provided excellent accommodations for the racehorses, with 777 dry, well-ventilated, and roomy stalls. Admission to the course was $1, which seemed expensive at a time when unskilled workers made $1 a day—it was four times the cheapest White Stockings ticket—but free passes were commonplace. Management advertised Garfield Park as the "closest track to downtown," merely a ten-minute ride once the new Lake Street elevated train was completed. McDonald's biographer Richard Lindberg claims the track's presence was an impetus to the completion of the line.[58]

The GPC did not operate under the jurisdiction of the American Turf Congress or any other racing organization, which made it an "outlaw" operation. However, the track managers were experienced racing officials, most notably course superintendent and presiding judge Colonel Meriwether Lewis Clark Jr., a well-known member of Louisville society, grandson of the renowned explorer William Clark, and the president of the ATC. Judge Clark's Garfield Park salary exceeded that of every American court judge. He is best known today as the founder and first president of the Louisville Jockey Club, which in 1874 leased land from his mother's family, the Churchills, for a racetrack. The first Kentucky Derby was raced one year later. The GPC purposely set up its first schedule to directly compete with Corrigan's facility. Garfield's typical program had five events with purses amounting to $3,300.[59]

The press coverage of Garfield Park was mixed. The *Tribune*, which was a big critic of the track, and not a big fan of gambling, and the *Inter Ocean* regularly sent reporters to Garfield Park. The *Inter Ocean* did not believe in doing away with pool selling at the track since it believed state law permitted it. It thought the working class should have a chance to bet, just like the upper class had at Washington Park, and provided respectful coverage of its operations. Prior to the start of the 1892 season, a *Tribune* editorial took the *Inter Ocean* to task for criticizing gambling on the editorial page yet offering readers betting tips.[60]

The *Chicago Times* supported Garfield Park at first since it promised a good entertainment option for tourists attending the upcoming World's Fair and provided a convenient site for local racing fans who lived in the middle-class neighborhood. Publisher Carter H. Harrison had previously been close to many of its principals, though he had fallen out with McDonald. Perhaps the former mayor has his eyes on another election campaign and was looking for allies. The crusading *Daily News*, on the other hand, did not cover the races at Garfield and gave it little attention, perhaps because the management and its business were beneath contempt.[61]

Opening day, July 20, drew a huge crowd of fifteen thousand, although, the *Spirit* noted, "The four hundred are not out in force." The track's only larger gate that year was for the $10,000 Garfield Stakes, when sixteen thousand were admitted for free. From my tabulation of press reports, it seems that Chicago weekday crowds drew about forty-six hundred spectators, while Saturday races drew about eight thousand. However, those statistics are misleading considering the large numbers of passes doled out, especially at Garfield Park, which often took in no more than $200 from weekday gates.[62]

The Hawthorne–Garfield Park Rivalry

When Garfield Park opened on July 20, Corrigan retaliated by opening Hawthorne for free. However, his track drew only about three thousand, mainly sightseers. Half of the audience were women, who normally made up closer to 10 percent of its crowds. Professional gamblers that day did not expect much interest from racing enthusiasts, and only seven bookies were present, mainly taking just $1 bets. Hawthorne's audiences did improve over the next few days, drawing many new fans, including families taking advantage of the new liberal admission policy. Admission was free on thirty-two days of the forty-two-day summer meet, which enabled families to enjoy fresh air and a day at the races. Overall, attendance was nearly the same as at Garfield Park during the week, probably about forty-five hundred, but less on Saturday, when it passed eight thousand just once.[63]

Corrigan promised no compromise in his war with Garfield Park and bragged that he was prepared to lose up to $500,000 to win his competition with "the bookmaker's track." Broad Church of the *Spirit* was not sanguine about a situation that boded ill for both tracks, "especially with the conditions of free admission and relentless rivalry." He felt that Garfield Park was better located, but that Hawthorne had a considerable following from its days on the West Side.[64]

Garfield Park responded on August 8 to Hawthorne's admission policy by opening a free two-thousand-seat auxiliary grandstand. The community opposed the innovation, fearful the policy would attract degenerates. The supplementary stand had a separate entrance and its own betting ring, restaurant, and bar. However, the view of the finish line was less visible compared to the main grandstand.[65]

Hawthorne had already made about $50,000 in the spring. The summer meet started out well in early August, but thereafter attendance declined, even with the frequent free admissions. Hawthorne was hindered by infrequent and expensive train service that cost five times the trip from downtown Chicago compared to Garfield Park. The CRA abruptly closed on September 7 after forty-two days of summer racing because it was losing $1,400 a day during the summer meet, or about $58,800 total. This figure came to a total loss for the year of about $8,800. The closure was unexpected because Corrigan had promised to remain open until November at any cost and then, after a brief hiatus, resume racing in the winter. Personally, Corrigan made out all right since his stable won $23,500 in purses at Hawthorne meet and because of the $55,000 he made by running a foreign book.[66]

The *Spirit* described the Hawthorne meet as a "heroic struggle against peculiarly adverse circumstances," since mounting losses came despite its excellent ambiance, intolerance of ruffians, good training facilities, integrity of the races, and superiority of its horses compared to nearly all western tracks. The sports weekly applauded Corrigan for running his operations with a stern hand, far superior to the despotic GPC, and blamed politics for many of Corrigan's problems: "The Tweed and Tammany rings of New York in their palmiest days were babies in comparison to the clique of Chicago, who have strained every source known to the order to down Mr. Corrigan. Every dive, barroom and thug ugly of the Garden City were in league against him, in fact so bitter has been this element that most of the public resorts boycotted his racing cards, so that patrons were obliged to wait the morning papers to see the entries at Hawthorne."[67]

Garfield Park and Year-Round Racing

There were many complaints during the 1891 season about possible fixes at Garfield Park, odd decisions by racing judges, and dubious methods employed by its operators. Judge Clark was highly regarded and worked hard to bolster the track's reputation for integrity, instituting a system of patrol judges stationed along the track to watch for dishonest riding. Nonetheless, racing fans did not trust the outcome of races, not surprising given the course's ownership by bookmakers whose character was not highly regarded.[68]

This lack of public confidence in Garfield encouraged many critics to request that Mayor Washburne remove its license and halt the gambling. In early October, the track's opponents, probably either Corrigan or certain downtown poolroom operators who felt the track was taking away too many of their best customers, organized raids by private detectives at Garfield Park. Most of the twenty-five arrests made over a three-day period were jockeys, but among those individuals nabbed were Mike McDonald and Al and George Hankins, charged with violating state anti-pool-selling laws.[69]

Garfield Park was scheduled to run into late November, despite the cold Chicago temperatures. Colonel Clark claimed that attendance in the first sixty-five days of racing there surpassed 300,000, or more than 4,600 a day, a higher daily average than any American track. If we accept Clark's report, there was a big decline in November when the weather got a lot colder. My daily count for November, based on attendance reported by the press, came to 2,533 spectators, including about 1,500 regulars. Garfield was then the only western track open, starting early, at 1:00 p.m., because of the declining daylight. These events did not draw a lot of betting action, even though the bar and the betting ring were enclosed and heated. Consequently, the 27 bookmakers there had virtually no business, and the track reduced their daily fee. The only real action was with the extremely lucrative foreign book.[70]

The *Tribune* critically covered the fall races with headlines such as "Tricks of the Stables," discussing how racing teams with just one or two horses changed their names almost daily to evade paying forfeits for not fulfilling their obligations or to confuse the betting public. "Running in the Fog" described a day when the mist was so strong that horses could not be identified until the finish line. Racing was often so specious that headlines screamed "All Bets Declared Off," "Ruled Off for Fraud," and "Another Queer Race."[71]

The prevailing public sentiment backed the national press, anti-cruelty societies, and various regulatory racing organizations in strongly opposing winter racing. The *Inter Ocean* and some other papers stopped printing results from Garfield. The paper supported horse racing when honest and safe, but "there are conditions necessary to true sport. One is that it shall not be cruel. Another is that it shall be honest. The racing at Garfield Park is not honest and it is cruel. It cannot be honest for no owners of a horse worthy of the name of a racer would permit it to put forth the best efforts, or indeed, any efforts at all upon such a track as Garfield Park offers in this season of alternating mud, and snow and frost. Weather conditions, including frosts, made late fall racing difficult, if not impossible."[72]

On November 17, for instance, only one race was run because the track was frozen solid. Nonetheless, the track directors decided by a one-vote margin to institute winter racing, a radical and unwise decision in a city with Chicago's climate. But, as far as management was concerned, expanding the racing calendar provided more opportunities to separate bettors from their money.[73]

Winter racing then was rare in the United States, mainly limited to warmer climates such as New Orleans. In 1884 Brooklyn's Brighton Beach experimented with winter racing, as did Guttenberg, New Jersey, in 1885. Six years later, New Jersey's two outlaw tracks, Guttenberg and Gloucester, both staged winter racing. Gamblers interested in these winter events were mainly limited to downtown poolrooms or neighborhood bookies to bet on the limited winter races.[74]

There were days when the snow was so heavy that plows had to be run around the course to make a path for the racehorses. The racing even occurred during frosts. One day the track's surface was so frozen that the racing was canceled after the first race. In response, Garfield Park implemented the "Guttenberg Plan," named after the New Jersey track, winterizing the course's surface with sand and salt to make a safe slush for bad weather. The track also planned to lay steam pipes under the entire track, heat parts of the grandstands with radiators, and build a six-foot overhang on the front of the grandstand to protect against the elements. However, when projected costs reached $70,000, well over the $45,000 originally budgeted, these improvements were abandoned.[75]

On December 3, the city council, under pressure from Mayor Washburne, passed an ordinance to prevent Garfield from reopening after the current three-month meet ended on December 12. Garfield Park's directors voted by a margin of one vote to go ahead and still stage winter racing, making it the only western track operating in late November. The decision was chastised by sportswriters from across the country. The season ended in December one day earlier than planned, after the West Side Park commissioners called for a halt on the seven-furlong (3/4-mile) main track that was located 398 feet from Garfield Park, 2 feet less than the minimal distance permitted by law. Fifteen park police officers and twenty-five patrolmen were sent to the racecourse to make sure the regulation was not violated. The track reached a compromise with the authorities and rescheduled the remaining races on the inside track, which was 401.5 feet away from the park. Shortly thereafter, the track closed for the winter.[76]

Four days later, a bill introduced by Alderman John Kenny back in October to bar bookmaking and pool selling in Chicago, including inside racecourses, was approved, 45–4. Anyone found betting or selling pools on races, or betting inside a racetrack, was guilty of a misdemeanor and received a fine of $100 to $500. Another proposal to block horse racing by running streets through the courses was not approved.[77]

Garfield Park's Profits

The conventional wisdom was that Garfield Park was "like a gold mine," earning from a minimum of more than $440,000 to $1 million, which would have been biggest yearly profit of any nineteenth-century track. The *Tribune* published a lot of financial data on the Garfield Park course, accounting for 113 of the 119 days of racing (excluding just December when business was down). Purses and money added to stakes came to $443,280, or about $3,923 a day. Management spent about $75,000 to shape up the track and put it into racing competition, $35,000 on various other improvements, $60,000 for labor costs (including the president's salary), and $15,000 for rent. The expenditures came to $628,280. Garfield Park was one of the most expensive and most profitable proprietary tracks in America.[78]

The track netted an enormous amount of money, but not from the gate, which made only about $150 a day ($17,850 for 119 days of racing), since so many people were admitted free. The large attendance did lead to big profits from concessions and a fortune from the gambling. During the summer, the bar brought in about $1,400 a day

Table 4
Garfield Park Profits, 1891

Expenditures	
Purses	$443,280
Track preparation	75,000
Improvements	35,000
Labor costs	60,000
Rent	15,000
Total	$628,280
Receipts	
Gate	$17,850
Bar	107,800
Western Union fee (est.)	19,000
Bookie fees	226,100
Foreign book	600,000
Total	$970,750
Total profit	$342,470

Source: Chicago Tribune, November 30, 1891, 6-3.
Note: Cost of construction is not amortized.

for 60–70 days (about $91,000), down to $300–$400 a day when the weather got colder (about $16,800). The track also made money by selling racing information to Western Union clients.[79]

By comparison, in 1891 the prestigious Morris Park Racetrack, operated by the New York Jockey Club, received $1,600 a day from Western Union, which was then servicing 84 poolrooms in New York and 120 elsewhere. The twenty or so bookmakers at Garfield Park each paid $95 a day, or $1,900 day, about $226,100 for 119 days. They fared extremely well, especially since only three downtown poolrooms remained in business in late fall. But the major source of revenue was by far the track syndicate's foreign book that reportedly brought in nearly $600,000, a huge return. The total profit shown in table 4 is $342,470, though the real profit is likely greater, since the data for purses does not account for any money paid in entry fees by horse owners. Of course, this figure does not account for the cost of construction of the facility, which was at least $150,000. No one expected the track would survive for just a year and a half. One type of enterprise that particularly thrived from Garfield Park's success was pawnbrokers. They reportedly loaned $1.5 million to bettors, including small businessmen, boys, and women, though many of them could not repay their debts.[80]

WESTERN UNION AND THE TURF

A key factor in the racing business in the late nineteenth century was Western Union, which paid racetracks a fee to secure the results of North American races for a consideration that it then sold to newspapers, poolrooms, and bookmakers across the continent. Western Union was founded in 1856 by Hiram Sibley and Ezra Cornell. Five years later, they opened a transcontinental telegraph line, operating as a common carrier. The ticker became a primary revenue source, supplying financial news to stockbrokers, banks, and bucket shops, and provided sports news to newspapers and other interested parties. By 1887, 87 percent of the company's revenue came from business messages, mostly to speculators and racetrack gamblers. Three years later, President Norvin Green of Western Union told Congress that his firm grossed $700,000 just from New York City poolrooms. As historian David Hochfelder points out, "It is striking that a majority of Western Union's ticker business came from gambling in bucket shops, horse-race gambling parlors and saloons—and that its president openly acknowledged this in congressional testimony."[81]

Hochfelder dates the initial use of telegraphy and gambling sports to the February 7, 1849, boxing match between American champion Thomas Hyer and "Yankee" Sullivan at Pond, Maryland, that Hyer won in eighteen rounds. By 1876, when the National League was formed, Western Union was supplying gambling halls and saloons with baseball results. Thirteen years later, Henry Clay Ditmas, a former Western Union racetrack messenger, developed the idea of securing the exclusive right to distribute racing news, primarily from the three major Brooklyn tracks, to poolrooms throughout the United States and set up Western Union's new Racing Bureau. His ability to secure a monopoly on the sale of Brooklyn racing news may have been helped by his close friend John Y. McKane, the political boss of the Gravesend section of Kings County, who was heavily involved in protecting bookmakers and boxing promoters in Brooklyn. A similar monopoly was obtained for western tracks by E. S. Gardner. The messages at first were just race results, but Western Union soon added detailed data on changing betting lines and descriptions of entire races.[82]

The dissemination of racing information became an increasingly elaborate and complex enterprise. The *New York Times* in 1891 estimated that Western Union made between $1 and 2 million a year, probably an inflated figure. A telegraph operator at the track sent data to Western Union's main office, and then it would be resent by another wire either directly to distant poolrooms or to a central receiving station in a big city like Chicago, from where the news would be transmitted to local poolrooms and handbooks. Western Union became an essential element in the illegal business of offtrack betting, although it was itself a legitimate enterprise legally selling information as a common carrier.[83]

RACING IN SOUTHERN ILLINOIS

Chicago bookmakers in the early 1890s were directly involved in thoroughbred racetracks downstate in East St. Louis, a suburb St. Louis, and across the state line in Indiana. The East St. Louis Jockey Club opened a three-quarter-mile course in 1892, led by president and noted bookmaker and plunger (high-risk gambler) Alex F. Ullman and his brother Joseph, the track's general superintendent and also a well-known bookmaker. The club had important clout in St. Louis through Ed Butler, the city's Democratic boss and the principal lobbyist in the Missouri state legislature. Butler was a co-owner of the track site who reportedly got 10 percent of its profits. The track became

extremely popular because it was just fifteen minutes from downtown
St. Louis by electric streetcar and operated a foreign book, which was
banned in Missouri. The initial meet averaged more than two thousand spectators.[84]

The track went year-round in 1893 with a free gate and purses that
averaged $1,700 a day. A new track was built the following year that
offered free admission. The course was naturally sandy, drained well,
and endured frost or rain. Its two-thousand-seat grandstand, encased
in glass, was climate controlled. In April 1894, winter racing was a
political issue in the local St. Louis elections when the People's Party
tried unsuccessfully to push out the protrack Citizens' Party. The
track went out of business in 1895, like Chicago's suburban courses,
part of a nationwide reform push against horse-race gambling.[85]

A second downstate track opened in nearby Madison, eight miles
from St. Louis, on October 29, 1892. Cole Ullman, Joseph's brother,
in partnership with a future town mayor, owned the Madison County
Fair and Racing Association that operated the five-furlong Madison
Race Track, but it was open for only a few days. One year later, on
November 30, 1893, the new $30,000 Madison Turf Association (MTA)
opened, operated by St. Louis racing entrepreneurs S. W. Adler and
Andrew "Cap" Tillies, two Jewish cigar dealers, and their partner, Ital-
ian Louis Cella, a saloonkeeper and bookie. They became known as
the CAT syndicate and eventually owned most of the St. Louis tracks
and several other midwestern courses.[86]

The MTA's track was on a site leased from a local street railway
company for $600 a week. The grounds had a naturally sandy soil that
made it winter viable. The CAT had considerable political clout from
another partner, businessman Charles D. Comfort, a former St. Louis
councilman, who was closely connected to Mound City mayor Cyrus
P. Walbridge. Opening day drew about ten thousand spectators, an
awesome turnout. The MTA was a low-budget operation that initially
charged no admission fee, and the average purse was just $150. Atten-
dance ranged from twenty-five hundred to seven thousand. However,
Madison was considered an outlaw track that did not associate with
any regional racing organization, and it went out of business in 1895.

The track introduced a newly patented starter developed by Chicagoans George Hankins and Harry Romaine that lined up horses behind
a rod that extended across the track. When the starter signaled all was
ready, a cord was pulled, the rods flew up, and the horses took off.[87]

GARFIELD PARK'S EARLY-SEASON STRUGGLES

Washington Hesing stepped down as president of Garfield Park in
January 1892. The *Tribune* felt he had been an active executive who
presided over its meetings and occasionally went into the judges' boxes
after races to influence results. Hesing reportedly looked after his
share of the profits, but displayed "as much business acumen as any
short card gambler quarreling with his partner over his share in their
victim's money."[88]

Hesing was replaced in a public relations move by respected attorney George A. Trude, a man of such stature that after Mayor Harrison
was assassinated in 1893, he was considered as a possible replacement.
The track had big expectations for the upcoming year after the banner
1891 season and spent $25,000 to enlarge the grandstand to seat nearly
seventeen thousand, more than triple its original capacity. Management also increased the number of stalls to more than fourteen hundred, double that of Washington Park. The jockey club planned to
open in late May, close during the WPR meet, and then run until
November 1, with races worth an astounding $714,000.[89]

Garfield Park's ambitious plans were problematic given its scan-
dalous reputation, the ongoing conflict with the West Park Board
of Commissioners, the opposition of rival Edward Corrigan of the
CRA and, most important, Mayor Washburne's announcement in
early April that he would not grant any racing license for more than
thirty days. Al Hankins anticipated no problem in getting a license
but announced that if thwarted, as the track was, Garfield Park would
simply pay the small $50 daily fine and continue operating.[90]

That summer former mayor Carter Harrison, owner and editor of
the *Chicago Times*, lashed out against Garfield Park for its questionable
methods and dubious management, and especially his old associate,

stating: "Mike McDonald is an unscrupulous, disreputable, vicious gambler, a disgrace, and menace to the city. He should be driven from the city and the race tracks forever." Harrison was subsequently denounced by newly elected city council member Bathhouse John Coughlin, who stood up in the city council to protect Garfield Park.[91]

When the spring season began, the GPC signed a secret $124,000 one-year contract to work with three or four local poolrooms. Opening day on May 21 drew a modest crowd of forty-two hundred, even though admission was free. There were some twenty uniformed officers present, but they did not interfere with the gambling. Law enforcement offered a stronger presence two days later, but there were only twelve hundred spectators. On May 25, the authorities closed down the foreign book. Garfield Park chose to close until Decoration Day (renamed Memorial Day in 1968), celebrated on May 30, since the authorities would be too busy with parades and crowds elsewhere. Opening day drew around five thousand racing fans and forty-two bookmakers.[92]

Garfield Park's summer meet did not measure up, failing to draw many top stables. Its biggest race was the $17,000 Garfield Park Derby for three-year-olds on June 17, which drew eighteen thousand spectators and forty-five bookmakers. Corrigan, who had not raced at Garfield the year before, entered three horses in the derby, drawn by its enticing purse. John Condon's staff at the track arranged an even-money bet for local fans that none of Corrigan's horses would come in among the top three. Corrigan unwisely took the bet himself on a day when there was a wet track, and his entries all lost. Corrigan reportedly lost between $200,000 and $300,000, which only exacerbated the conflict between him and John Condon.[93]

Washington Park in 1892

The WPR was a great success in its first eight years, but its fans were concerned that since the value of the site had appreciated to about $1 million, a 15 percent increase in just three years, the club might sell the land. However, management had no intention of leaving and instead spent $50,000 on major improvements. The grandstand was expanded by forty-five hundred seats to a capacity of sixteen thousand with a grand promenade behind it, standing room was tripled to twenty-one thousand, and a new paddock was built. Special attention was also given to the interest of women fans. A women's restaurant was opened, and bridges were constructed to enable women arriving by the Illinois Central or cable car to bypass the betting ring on their way to their seats.[94]

Washington Park's betting concession continued to go to Bush & Bride, who dealt with about sixty-five bookies, three-fourths of whom belonged to the Western Bookmakers Association. This arrangement produced about $185,000 for the track. This amount was nearly double the $103,000 for the betting concession at Cincinnati's Latonia Racetrack for its spring and fall meetings.[95]

The 1892 season was highlighted by the American Derby, attended by more than forty-five thousand fans. The elite came out in such numbers that the *Spirit* felt the local press newspapers needed society reporters there almost as much as sportswriters. The *Tribune* gave its usual extensive coverage to the elite, citing the names of everyone seated in the sixty-eight grandstand boxes and the sixty-three annex boxes. The thirsty crowd was serviced at the beverage concession by two hundred people selling hard liquor, wine, beer, pop, and buttermilk. Hungry spectators ate at an adjoining restaurant that sold peanuts, hot tamales, and "mystery" sandwiches.[96]

The *Tribune* published an anonymous article on Derby Day purportedly written by a woman who described herself as a smart and knowledgeable baseball fan. She found the derby a bit mystifying, explaining that horse racing was "in the same category with a variety of pronounced unsavory subjects of which well-bred young women are supposed to know nothing." The author enjoyed the rituals of the sport, beginning with the drive out to the track, the coaching parties, and the sociability of the clubhouse. However, she did not understand much that took place inside the course or else found it pretty stupid. For instance, she was quite sorry to hear that three horses had been scratched and was confused when the horses went to the post, but there was no post to be seen. The article's tone strongly suggests the author was actually a man assigned by his editor to make fun of women spectators.[97]

Journalists elsewhere actually gave more serious attention to women fans. In 1893 the *Brooklyn Eagle* published an article titled "Gamblers in Petticoats: A Study of the Women of the Race Track," which seriously examined women's ability to make bets and enjoy themselves at the track. One year later, renowned journalist Nellie Bly attended the elite Saratoga meet in upstate New York and reported about the wicked sport in the *New York World*. She was critical of women gambling and of the painted women at the track.[98]

THE DEMISE OF GARFIELD PARK

Garfield Park was closed during the WPR meet. On July 15, Harry Varnell's agent gave the city collector $150 for a three-month permit. However, the collector, acting on the advice of Mayor Washburne and Police Superintendent McClaughry, refused to grant a license. The track unsuccessfully applied for a writ of mandamus to compel the mayor to issue the certificate. As Garfield Park's planned reopening approached, with or without a license, Mayor Washburne stepped up his fight. Administration spokesman John Cooke presented an ordinance to the city council on July 18 to close the racetrack by barring the granting of a license or permit to any racecourse operating inside the city limits or selling foreign pools. He claimed that "residents complain that the betting pools cause disreputable men and women to loiter in the neighborhood." Alderman Coughlin spoke up for Garfield Park, contending, "You can't do that! You can't shut up a man's property. . . . It's . . . un-American" and also unfair, since the track brought millions of dollars to the city.[99]

Garfield Park reopened without a license on July 25 despite severe pressure from the mayor and McClaughry, who declared that without a license there would be no racing if admission was charged. Six thousand spectators got in free that day. Ninety-seven bookies attended, but probably no more than two hundred bets were made, discouraged by the presence of nearly a hundred policemen on hand to prevent ticket selling and betting. A test case was orchestrated after the fifth race when one bookmaker put up his slate and took a bet. He and his three assistants were arrested. The track was closed the next day and reopened on July 27, but with just twenty-three bookies. The arrested men were released on August 9 by Judge George H. Kettelle, who ruled they were innocent of any crime since the city's gambling laws did not bar pool selling.[100]

One day later, just before the city council began its summer recess, Chairman Johnny Powers of the Finance Committee, known as the "prince of boodlers" for his work as chief dispenser of political payoffs, proposed an act to circumvent the mayor's licensing powers. His bill called for racing associations to pay a $100 license fee with meets permitted between May 1 and November 1. His supporters included several Republicans who believed it was unfair to deny Garfield a license after having issued one to Washington Park. Thirty-eight of the sixty-eight aldermen approved the measure.[101]

Mike McDonald then brought $3,000 to city hall to secure a thirty-day license, but was rebuffed at the city clerk's office. An assistant city clerk informed him that the mayor's order not to grant a license had not been withdrawn, nor had he signed Power's bill to permit a license to Garfield Park. In fact, Washburne vetoed the Powers scheme, explaining that it left the authorities with insufficient power to interfere with the management of amusement sites should there be conduct detrimental to good morals and the public peace. Powers responded, "We must have races in Chicago. It is a sport center and the great majority of people favor racing." Forty-six votes were needed to override the mayor, but the Garfield Park gang was assured of only thirty-three. The track's proponents believed the racing season would be salvaged anyhow. They assumed, incorrectly, that the bill automatically became law ten days after the veto since the council was going on recess. In any event, the GPC advocates figured that management would stall long enough to get in most of its meet.[102]

Both Hawthorne and Garfield Park reopened on July 28. Hawthorne advertised six Illinois Central trains from the Union Depot

(255 West Canal Street) along with three trains on the CB&Q, arriving in twenty-five minutes. Hawthorne reopened with Frank James, the former outlaw and brother of Jesse James, as assistant starter. Grandstand tickets cost seventy-five cents. But only around ten bookmakers were present. Garfield Park had seven Chicago & Pacific trains leaving from the Grand Central Station (Fifth and Harrison), including an express train that arrived in eighteen minutes, but a cheaper option was the Madison Street Cable that went right to the entrance. The Garfield bookies did considerable business at the track and did not encounter a lot of competition from the few offtrack poolrooms operating on the sly.[103]

The reopening was vigorously opposed by community activists. West Side churches held an anti-Garfield protest meeting on July 31 at St. Paul's Episcopal Church. Bishop Samuel Fallows of the Reform Episcopal Church presided, declaring that the track was "the one big blot on the West Side." He asserted that most embezzlements in Chicago were the product of betting losses, that crooked gambling at Garfield Park was worse than the infamous Louisiana Lottery, and that neighborhood property values were declining. The protesters approved a resolution congratulating the city council for fighting the gamblers and drew up antiracing petitions.[104]

The Garfield Park situation came to a head on September 2 when Police Superintendent McClaughry, acting on a petition from local businessmen and clergymen, ordered a raid on Garfield Park for operating without a license and for permitting gambling. Police Inspector Lyman E. Lewis and 100 officers surrounded the track after the first race and arrested 33 people, including track manager Clark, his secretary, the race starter, and several jockeys. Coughlin and Varnell bailed them out, charging that Corrigan and former mayor Harrison, who they claimed might be a part-owner of Hawthorne, were behind the raid. The defendants freely admitted that the track opened without a license but claimed they did not need one, since no admission was charged, and that the defendants were not responsible since they were not stockholders. They also complained that McClaughry's actions were unfair since he had never acted against "his friend Corrigan" or Washington Park. The press applauded the raid.[105]

The next day, a Saturday, some 6,000–7000 attended the races despite the raid the day before, and the presence of 150 police officers. According to the *Tribune*, "There was never a stormier afternoon on a racetrack than that at Garfield Park yesterday." The races did not go on as scheduled at 2:00 p.m., even though the track had gotten an injunction against police interference, but Inspector Lewis countered it, declaring he had warrants against track authorities for keeping a disorderly house if racing was resumed. The only betting was on out-of-town races and the upcoming Sullivan-Corbett heavyweight boxing championship fight. There the matters stood until 5:00 p.m., when the judge's bell rang, signaling jockeys to mount their horses. The police immediately went to work, arresting Hankins, Varnell, and as many employees as they could catch. Colonel Clark then announced that all bets were off, though the foreign book continued to operate. The crowd dispersed after the foreign races were accounted for. Mike McDonald then gave a public rant, denouncing Carter Harrison, Ed Corrigan, Superintendent McClaughry, and everyone else who opposed Garfield Park. He blamed the raid on Corrigan, who he claimed was tight with McClaughry and the Republicans, and urged all racing fans to vote Democratic in the next election.[106]

A Sunday editorial in the *Tribune* applauded the Friday raid against "a vile resort of the lowest type, a nest of thieves, burglars, confidence men, and lewd folk." They constituted "a veritable charnel-house for morals, a den in which were killed off all the good and noble sentiments that were originally entertained by its frequenters."[107]

On Monday, September 5, racing resumed. Once the crowds were inside, Pinkertons closed and bolted the front gates to keep out the police. Two races were staged without interference. Then around 3:30 p.m., by which time the authorities were convinced gambling was going on, a huge complement of 500 policemen arrived. They stormed and smashed the gates with axes, raced into the track, and surrounded the betting ring with paddy wagons. The authorities arrested 800 people and incarcerated 125, including 25 gamblers, 25 jockeys, Colonel Clark, George Hankins, Harry Varnell, and Michael Coughlin, Bathhouse's older brother. It was one of the largest raids in Chicago history. Mike McDonald made bond for the track officials.[108]

Thirty-three people were tried the following day. The courtroom largely focused on the strained relationship between the mayor and his police superintendent. Washburne testified that McClaughry had told him that Democrat James E. Burke, whose brother owned 25 percent of the CRA, had promised $50,000 to the Republican campaign fund if the city closed Garfield Park. The track's attorneys portrayed this testimony as an effort by the superintendent to bribe the mayor. McClaughry then gave his version, explaining he had heard gossip that Garfield Park would come up with $50,000 if the track could remain open and guessed that Hawthorne would produce a similar amount to close Garfield. He denied that Burke had made any such offer.[109]

Only fifteen hundred people attended the races that day. Some two hundred or more policemen moved in shortly after 4:00, before the start of the third race, intent on capturing horse owners and stablemen. The police entered the course as they had the day before and loaded their wagons with track personnel, bookmakers, and spectators. At least sixty-five people were arrested. As the officers prepared to leave, a police whistle was heard coming from the southwest part of the grounds, and then a shot rang out. Then more whistles and more gunfire. Inspector Lewis ordered his men to the danger scene. The police were worried that the action was coming from the stables of millionaire horseman and Texas Ranger James M. Brown of Lee County, Texas. Brown was renowned for his work as the Lee County sheriff (1878–84), when he rid the area of horse thieves, road agents, and murders. But he was also known for gambling with such notorious gunfighters as John Wesley Hardin. He had twelve notches in his pearl-handled .44 and was reported to have warned the day before that anyone trying to arrest him or his employees without a warrant, or interfering with his stable, would be shot. A warrant had reportedly been issued by the governor of Texas to bring him back to stand trial for a violent crime.[110]

Three or four policemen encountered the fifty-three-year-old former lawman at a barn, yelling insults at the authorities. He had supposedly threatened to kill anyone trying to arrest him without a warrant. Brown shouted, while twirling his pistol, that no one was going to stop the races. When three policemen confronted him, the old Ranger shot a number of rounds, and then fled, chased by six officers. Officer John Powell encountered Brown and told him to halt and when he did not took a shot that whizzed by Brown's head. The Texan spun around and fired back, killing Powell with three shots, and then shot Officer Henry McDowell, who also died. Brown was soon surrounded by more policemen and shot at officer William Jones, but his gun jammed, and Jones killed him.[111]

The track did not try to reopen the next day. Superintendent McClaughry's determination to close the track was confirmed by the violence: "If police officers cannot enter the park in the discharge of their duty without being killed, it is time the park was closed." An inquest ruled the shooting was justifiable because the officers felt they were in danger, with Brown shooting the first bullet. However, the *Spirit* found the killing a "little short of murder," since Brown had the right to defend himself. McDonald's *Chicago Globe* agreed: "Jim Brown died like a man. . . . [He was] shot down like a dog . . . by the offal of a crime-cursed city."[112]

Meetings were held on the West Side by ministers, businessmen, clubwomen, and journalists who endorsed closing the track. Attorney Ephraim Banning asked an antitrack rally at Van Buren's Hall, attended by a thousand men and fifty women, "Are we to support a corrupt and degrading influence in our midst? Are we to allow our property to be depreciated and our community to be desecrated by these thugs and blacklegs? Our street cars are congested and our women cannot ride . . . without being insulted by the mob." The gathering applauded the superintendent for his work and urged that he and the mayor stand firm against "this great gambling infamy."

A Committee of Fifteen was organized to pressure the city council against Johnny Powers's proposal to license Garfield Park over the mayor's veto.[113]

On September 12, the city council met and discussed the Garfield Park situation. Alderman Peter J. Ellert called for an investigation of the Brown episode, supported by John Coughlin's wild antipolice harangue. The proposal was defeated. Then the council upheld Washburne's veto of the Powers racetrack license ordinance (44–22), which, after the Brown incident, never had a chance. Thereafter, Garfield Park's political supporters gave up the fight. The *Tribune*'s next-day headline declared, "The Reign Is Ended."[114]

The *Spirit* blamed the Garfield Park management for its demise, having killed "the goose that laid the golden egg." The year before, "they continued the racing into the cold months and compelled poor, suffering brutes to race over a frozen track, or, in arctic weather drag their weary limbs through a beastly track deep in slush and snow." This season the track opened up "and a better equipped race-track it would be hard to find anywhere," but it had created too many enemies.[115]

The track halfheartedly tried to get an injunction to prevent its termination. However, Judge Lorin C. Collins ruled against the GPC, asserting that the track needed a license to operate. He also asserted that the Gibbs Act permitting gambling at the track was unconstitutional.[116]

The Committee of Fifteen was not satisfied with just shutting down Garfield Park. They wanted the city to suppress all racing. The closing of Garfield Park encouraged the Reverend O. P. Gifford of Immanuel Baptist Church to redouble his efforts against gambling at Washington Park, a worse evil, because "the rich law breaker is the more dangerous . . . because of his better means of evading the punishment of the law." However, that outcome was not in the cards.[117]

On September 17, Republican police justice Charles W. Woodman, who was adjudicating cases emanating from the police raid the prior week, reported a $300 bribe offer from McDonald to make sure he ruled in favor of the defendants. He also said that Mike promised to use his influence with the Democratic State Central Committee to get him reappointed. McDonald denied the story but was put on trial for bribery before a justice of the peace. The case was dismissed by a Democratic judge.[118]

The Resurgence of Hawthorne Park

Hawthorne operated for seventeen days in the spring of 1892, twenty-seven in the summer, and sixty-seven in the fall under the direction of its well-known starter, Colonel Phil Chin, compared to twenty-five for Washington Park and fifty-nine for the abbreviated Garfield Park season. Corrigan was the leading money winner at his own track, with $71,409 (sixty-nine wins in 288 races), followed far behind by George Hankins ($14,540) and Bathhouse John Coughlin ($6,000).[119]

The closing of Garfield Park brought Hawthorne into greater prominence. The *Chicago Daily News* estimated that about six thousand Chicagoans were "race-struck" and would go anywhere to bet on a race, including a suburban track. The absence of Garfield enabled Hawthorne in October to resume its normal 75-cent admission policy and cut way back on awarding passes. On the other hand, closing seemed to energize suburban opposition to Hawthorne, which seemed the next most vulnerable target for reform. There was a mass meeting on September 29 in Oak Park against the track and the nearby saloons. Attendees resolved that the township should close the track for corrupting the entire community. There was also a strong negative response to the expansion of the foreign book to offer bets on the upcoming presidential election that led to more public meetings in the Cicero area to block a new racing license for Hawthorne.[120]

In mid-December the Garfield Park crowd initiated a long-anticipated effort against Corrigan and his associates, swearing out a warrant for the arrest of Hawthorne's track officials and the operators of its foreign book. However, their detainment hardly deterred Hawthorne, which introduced winter racing, even during snowstorms when bettors could barely see the horses. Henry Wilson, who worked winters at Hawthorne, remembered forty years later the brutality of winter racing. He estimated weekday attendance at about three thousand and as many as seven thousand for Saturdays. Spectators included teenage boys, often bellhops who got season passes when Hawthorne flooded local hotels to distribute to their guests.[121]

The *New York Times*, a strident opponent of winter racing, vigorously chastised Hawthorne: "The cruelty of winter racing was never better exemplified than during the big snowfall at the Hawthorne track. . . . One jockey had his ear so frozen that it required three hours of application of snow to thaw it out. Other jockeys could do little more than cling on to their saddles in the races. Horses shivered at the starting post and clearly suffered. . . . Meanwhile the spectators hugged the stoves on the glass-enclosed betting ring. But the bookmakers were kept busy."[122]

On July 31, 1892, with the future of Garfield Park up in the air, Chicago pool sellers announced the establishment of a new track by Hammond, in Lake County, Indiana, thirty minutes by train from the Loop, which would open in November and operate until spring. The ninety-acre site belonged to Edward H. Roby, a Chicago railroad attorney, who had bought six hundred acres in 1873. The track site extended from 107th Street on the north end to 112th on the south side. The western boundary was the state line with Illinois, and the course extended a half mile on the east side.[123]

RACING IN INDIANA

John Condon, the prominent Chicago racing and gambling entrepreneur who was responsible for bringing organized gambling into Northwest Indiana, and Paddy Ryan, a former Chicago policeman and bookmaker, were the principals in the new Indiana Racing Association (IRA) (later the Roby Fair Association). It was purportedly a $400,000 corporation, half of whom were Garfield Park shareholders. The IRA's president was Chicago alderman Ernest Hummel of Hegwisch, chief executive officer of the Indiana Railroad, a partner in the South Chicago Brewing Company, and a future Chicago city treasurer.[124]

The Chicago entrepreneurs became known as the Columbian Athletic Club, although locals knew them as the "Roby Octopus," a politically clouted group who got their tentacles into Hammond's racing. They were big supporters of local Democrats, including Mayor Thomas Hammond (1888–93), a local banker and future congressman. Their track and poolroom enterprises ran undisturbed. Lake County was well known among racing fans as a site for racehorse betting, even though pool selling was a misdemeanor, with a $500 fine. The city charged the local track only a daily $20 license fee, one-fifth of what it probably should have been. The new course had strong political connections, ranging from Hammond's mayor to other leading officials who had a say in naming the track manager. The track was also involved in local businesses, particularly newspapers that promoted the sport.[125]

The Hammond track donated funds to the local Democratic campaign chest to ensure noninterference from local authorities and influence in the state legislature. Lake County politics was historically not terribly contentious, but with the coming of racing a lot was on the line. The position of sheriff, according to the *Tribune*, "will be worth more than the job of being a member of the Chicago City Council." Indiana newspapers opposed Roby, describing its organizers as "gamblers, convicts, jail-birds," the fans as "lewd fellows of the baser sort," and the entire project as "one of the most impudent, infamous gambling schemes ever devised."[126]

The new jockey club built a $100,000 racetrack in Hammond, Indiana, on a site costing $270,000. The entrance was one mile across the state line and fifteen miles from the Loop. The course was also fifteen miles from the county seat of Crown Point, sufficiently far away to make it hard for the authorities to check out violations. Chicagoans got to the track by a fifty-cent railroad ride (later reduced to twenty-five cents), a Chicago cable line that connected to an electric streetcar, or a forty-five-minute ride by steamer from downtown. The track had a 1 1/16-mile circumference, along with a one-mile trotting inside the longer course, and a five-thousand-seat, 352-foot grandstand modeled after Washington Park, with space for ten to fifteen thousand spectators. The betting ring was underneath. The roof was self-supporting, so there were no columns to obstruct spectators' views. There were stalls for five hundred horses. The side of the grandstand facing the track was enclosed in glass and steam heated by twelve furnaces for winter racing. There were a clubhouse and an electrically lit betting ring, bar, and restaurant under the stand. A grandstand seat cost fifty cents.[127]

On opening day, November 12, there were twelve bookies at work serving four thousand spectators. The track was mainly soft, yielding sand and not adequate for galloping. It took Chicagoans two hours to get back downtown. One reporter found that women outnumbered men in the grandstand for much of the day. They bet with uniformed young men with a sign reading "Official Pool Buyer" who walked up and down the grandstand aisles.[128]

Attendance ranged from two to three thousand, with space for twenty-eight bookies, who took bets on local and out-of-town races. Roby's course was one of seven American tracks operating in the winter of 1892–93. Horsemen claimed it was not cruel to employ working horses year-round and that horses were more comfortable racing in the cold than in summer heat. The track started out a financial loser, which utilized a free admission policy to bolster attendance. However, the betting was light and the train service unsatisfactory. Roby temporarily closed in mid-February 1893.[129]

The Economics of Thoroughbred Racing

In 1892 the major American racecourses had stakes and purses of $4,647,608, with all bets exceeding $432 million (see table 5). Approximately $300 million was bet at eastern tracks and poolrooms, while $132,180,400 was wagered in the West, composed of $97,280,000 at the tracks and $34,960,400 off the tracks. Chicago alone accounted for $52,180,400 (39.5 percent) of all western betting and 51.1 percent of all on-track betting. Some 95.4 percent ($49.8 million) of Chicagoland's thoroughbred betting took place in its 195 days of racing, with an average daily handle of $265,592. The offtrack betting was estimated at $2.4 million, or about $12,300 per racing day. Experts believed that the actual money in circulation was less than 25 percent of the total bet because of the fast action and continual turnover each afternoon.[130]

When it came to purses, the three Chicago tracks in 1892 collectively gave out $788,676 (average $262,677), a huge amount, but still well behind New York's four major tracks ($1,256,454, an average of $314,114). Washington Park's purses came to $182,517, eleventh nationally, but only fourth highest in Illinois after Hawthorn (fifth), Garfield (seventh), and East St. Louis (eighth), which ran much longer meets. The WPC reportedly earned $200,000 in 1893 ($5,715,733 in 2020), a huge return, but well behind the elite Coney Island Jockey Club in 1894 ($287,915). The *Tribune* estimated that during the meet, its sixty bookmakers covered about $1,750 per race, or $14.4 million for the 146-race season. Overall, Washington Park Club fans bet $14,792,500 in just 25 days (97.5 percent of all WPR action), including auctions ($300,000), combinations ($37,500), and the only pari-mutuels ($25,000) in Chicago. It had no foreign books.[131]

Hawthorne offered $362,252 in prizes in its 111 days of racing, with typically five races per day. The proprietary Gloucester, New Jersey, track was number one, with $483,800, followed by Coney Island (Brooklyn), Morris Park (NY), and Monmouth (NJ). Hawthorne had only nine bookies for the spring and summer and eighteen in the fall. Track goers bet $760,000 with bookies in the spring, $1,386,000 in the summer, and a hard-to-believe $9,828,000 in the fall. This figure came to about $1,000 per race for each bookie in the spring and summer and $1,600 in the fall. Hawthorne's spring and summer action on out-of-town races averaged $12,000 and then rose to $30,000 a day during the fall, when there was less competition from downtown poolrooms. That increase was a prime reason for operating tracks in cold weather. In all, $14,677,500 was bet at Hawthorne, including $2,558,000 in foreign books (17.4 percent) and $165,500 (1.1 percent) in combinations.[132]

The *Tribune* estimated that a complete season for Garfield Park in 1892 would have cleared $1 million just in the foreign book. Garfield Park ran a 30-day meet in the spring with 161 races with purses of $132,125. There were about forty bookies at the track, whose average handle per race was $1,500. The foreign book averaged $40,000 a day and $1,000 for combinations. During the spring, $10,890,000 was wagered (including $8,440,000 with the bookies and $1.26 million

Table 5
North American Thoroughbred Racing Purses,
January 1–November 19, 1892

Brooklyn (spring)	$170,200
Brooklyn (fall)	149,090
Brighton Beach	88,600
Coney Island (spring)	220,020
Coney Island (fall)	217,492
Denver (spring)	34,640
East St. Louis	235,300
Garfield Park (spring)	132,125
Garfield Park (summer)	111,496
Gloucester	483,800
Guttenberg	214,300
Hawthorne (spring)	72,135
Hawthorne (summer & fall)	290,117
Latonia (spring)	132,645
Latonia (fall)	90,650
Lexington (spring)	34,350
Lexington (fall)	16,500
Louisville (spring)	39,525
Louisville (fall)	14,194
Memphis (spring)	43,680
Monmouth Park	403,535
Montreal	4,000
Morris Park (spring)	198,999
Morris Park (fall)	212,053
Nashville (spring & fall)	86,345
New Orleans	49,350
Sacramento	2,000
San Francisco	77,350
Saratoga	129,610

Table 5 (Con't.)
North American Thoroughbred Racing Purses,
January 1–November 19, 1892

St. Louis (spring)	179,270
St. Paul	73,780
Toronto	3,000
Washington (spring)	28,300
Washington (fall)	17,000
Washington Park (Chicago)	182,157
Miscellaneous, including South Side Track, St. Louis; Madison, IL; Roby, IN; Denver (summer); Kansas City and various western tracks	210,000
Total	$4,647,608

Source: Chicago Tribune, November 20, 1892, 7-3.

with the foreign books). The 29-day summer meet had 150 races (curtailed by police interference) worth $111,496 in purses. Bookies on the average covered $1,400 per race. The foreign books, operated only on 22 dates because of police interference, pulled in $880,000 in bets, while the total handle at the combinations was $150,000. The summer meet took in $9,430,400, making a total of $20,320,400 for 1892, the most of any Chicago track, despite hosting only 59 dates.[133]

During Garfield Park's 178 days of operation over two years, the track spent $150,000 for the racing plant and $95,000 for operating expenses, and it gave out nearly $600,000 in purses and stakes. Fixed costs included the refurbished grandstand, salaries owing to the presiding judge Clark ($125 a day) and starter Charles Pettingill ($100 a day), $80,000 owed (at $10,000 a month) to Western Union for the foreign book until April 1893, and $70,000 in rent since the lease had two more years to run. While the numbers don't add up, the *Tribune* estimated total expenses of $730,000.[134]

Total receipts came to $1.35 million, derived from several sources. Each day the track made $600 for the information sent out to foreign poolrooms (which each paid $10 a day for the news), $350 from the bar, $200 in gate receipts, $4,000 from bookmakers, and a whopping $500,000 from the foreign book in 1891 (16.7 percent less than the previous year's estimate) and at least half that much in 1892. According to the *Tribune*, the profits came to $620,000 (not counting legal costs, campaign contributions, or the cost of the plant) for its two seasons. The GPC reported that it lost $90,000 because of high overhead expenses. Employing the amended 1891 *Tribune* data, we come to Garfield Park making $710,000 in 1891 (not counting legal costs, campaign contributions, or the cost of the plant). This amount would certainly be by far the most of any American track in the nineteenth century and just does not seem realistic. In any event, the profits were apparently so extraordinary, why didn't the GPC make more of an effort to compromise and stay in business?[135]

CONCLUSION

There was a lot of money to be made in Chicago racing in the early 1890s, legally and illegally, part of a widespread boom in the turf, especially in the East. New Jersey had six major tracks then, and business was so good at the outlaw Guttenberg track near Manhattan that it netted about $200,000 from the fall of 1890 through the winter of 1891. New York City's four major tracks combined to gross $576,917, led by the Coney Island Jockey Club with $206,667, and paid handsome dividends. The racetracks' success carried over to the breeding industry, and in 1893 there were more than twenty breeding farms worth more than $200,000.[136]

Washington Park flourished because of its prestige and the high-quality racing and was one of the most profitable jockey clubs in the United States. It did not have major political clout like top eastern tracks, but the antiracing movement in Chicago that targeted Garfield Park was not yet considered a dangerous threat to its future. Furthermore, the WPR seemed secure financially because of the organization's wealth, its big profits, and the sharp appreciation in the value of the track site. While the legality of racing was uncertain because of court decisions challenging the constitutionality of the Gibbs Act, there was no strong pressure as of 1892 to halt elite racing.

The political connections of entrepreneurs operating proprietary tracks were significant. The McDonald crowd had a lot of important connections that protected their offtrack gambling and enabled them to force Edward Corrigan to move his jockey club out of Chicago. Corrigan continued to struggle against political foes at his new track in Cicero and with Mayor DeWitt Cregier in Chicago. The bookmakers' syndicate at Garfield Park started out well in 1891, taking over the West Side site, building their own facility, and making huge profits. However, management overplayed its hand the following year by cheating the customers, mistreating the local community, abusing their horses, and disrespecting Mayor Washburne. The track was closed not because it violated state antigambling laws, but because the mayor became convinced it was a crooked operation that cheated fans, abused animals, permitted violence, and mistreated its West Side neighbors. Garfield Park so alienated the general public that Mayor Washburne refused to grant it an amusement license, and despite the track's substantial political clout, the enterprise was doomed. But hardly anyone saw this development as a forerunner of Washington Park's future as Chicago got ready for the Columbian Exposition and what promised to be the greatest meet in western turf history.

4

Washington Park and the Tenuous Status of the American Turf, 1893–1894

Midwestern racing fans greatly anticipated the coming of the 1893 season following the demise of the nefarious Garfield Park Racetrack and the highly promoted summer meet at the Washington Park Racetrack to complement the World's Columbian Exposition. The World's Fair commemorated the four hundredth anniversary of Columbus's landing in the New World in 1492, but had nothing directly to do with the history of Chicago. Nonetheless, city leaders wanted to host the fair to promote Chicago as a world-class city raised like a phoenix from the destructive 1871 fire and to encourage its economic development. Local boosters and the city government promised Congress it would raise more than $20 million if awarded the right to stage the event. They also argued that Chicago surpassed New York in the quality of its air and water, housing for tourists, transportation, and potential sites.[1]

The fair was an enormous success that advanced Chicago's public image and encouraged advancements in science and technology, architecture, urban planning, the fine arts, and scholarly discourse. Chicago's outstanding architects, engineers, and urban planners created a six-hundred-acre fair that was a glorious international exposition composed of a beautiful white city of neoclassical buildings, canals, and lagoons, exhibitions of fine art and mechanical arts that hosted international scientific and humanistic conferences and publicized mass culture. Today, World's Fairs no longer have the significance they once had. Instead, major cities have gotten away from competing to host international expositions and instead seek to certify their progressive character by such megaprojects as building sports stadiums and hosting the quadrennial Olympic Games.[2]

The local track management, especially the Washington Park Racetrack located close to the World's Fair in Hyde Park, hoped that large numbers of the expected crowds, which turned out to be twenty-seven million (78.2 percent paying) in six months, would spend some of their free time in the afternoon at the nearby Washington Park track. The WPC made a major effort to promote their elite course and share in the exposition's glory. They figured it was a golden opportunity to make a big splash in thoroughbred racing and enhance Washington Park's prestige in national and international turf circles. The 1893 meet was highlighted by the $60,000 American Derby, with $49,500 to the winner. This enormous purse had been exceeded only by the Futurity Stakes at Brooklyn Sheepshead Bay Racetrack, a six-furlong sprint for two-year-olds from 1889 to 1891. The single richest race was the 1890 Futurity won by Potomac, ridden by African American Anthony Hamilton, who was elected to the Racing Hall of Fame in 2012. Potomac, owned by August Belmont Sr., the renowned banker and Democratic politician, won a record $67,675.[3]

Few, if any, students of racing could predict at this time that thoroughbred racing was about to hit a major bump. American thoroughbred racing was staged at an average of 190 flat tracks from 1882 through 1889, though about 85 percent were extremely obscure and used for no more than five days a year. The number dropped to 110 in 1892 and averaged 151 from 1892 through 1896 (see table 8 in chapter 5). In regards to Chicago, Washington Park's great success turned out to be short-lived because public pressure compelled its closure in 1894, which foretold the coming doom of the turf in metropolitan Chicago and other major racing sites. Moral reformers were then engaged in a nationwide campaign to halt horse racing because they considered the gambling associated with the sport a mortal sin. Social reformers opposed the gambling because they believed it was a big social problem that destroyed the families of working-class gamblers, corrupted municipal governments, and helped finance the rise of organized crime. The main foci of the anti-horse-racing forces in the mid-1890s were the major flat-racing states of Illinois, New York, and New Jersey, which all had several racecourses that included some of the most prestigious courses in North America, drew the largest crowds, and attracted the best racing stables competing for the most lucrative stakes.[4]

HORSE RACING, GAMBLING, AND POLITICS

The 1893 Mayoralty Election

Horse-race gambling was a major issue during the 1893 mayoralty campaign. Carter Harrison, running in his seventh campaign, was opposed at the Democratic nominating convention by Washington Hesing, former president of the Garfield Park Racetrack and postmaster of Chicago (1894–97), and former mayor DeWitt C. Cregier, all proracing politicians and all connected with Mike McDonald. Hesing, not surprisingly given his background, supported horse racing. He promised not to discriminate against Hawthorne, his former enemy (though as Chicago mayor he had no jurisdiction there), though he claimed the authorities had acted unfairly toward Garfield Park. He wanted to license gambling halls, rein in the worst attributes of wagering, and make betting on horses respectable. Cregier was long identified with McDonald and the city's bookmakers and as a foe of Edward Corrigan of the Hawthorne track. Harrison's ties with McDonald dated to the late 1870s, although they had fallen out for some time. The *Chicago Tribune* opposed both Hesing for his connections to the Garfield Gang and the track management and Harrison as "an insufferable, bombastic, egotist," who did not have a worthwhile platform. The editors further claimed that local citizens wanted an active, public-spirited man who would run the city "on business principles without any regard to politics, political patronage, sports, or boodle." All the English-language morning dailies except the *Chicago Times*, which Harrison owned, regularly castigated him "as an associate of gamblers, a conscienceless politician, a weak-minded and insanely egotistic old man."[5]

The press targeted Harrison because he was the primary contender. Besides his connections to McDonald, the newspapers beset Harrison for betting on racing, not opposing pool selling at the tracks, and failing to quash the gambling interests in his prior terms. Harrison did not believe that on-track gambling could be eliminated, but thought that it should be regulated when too obnoxious. He criticized racetracks for offering bets on foreign races and free liquor to entice betting, permitting late closing hours, and allowing the presence of juveniles. Harrison argued that Washington Park merited special consideration because it was run by a public-spirited, elite social club led by prominent, moral men; only had a single monthly meet; was not profit oriented; and drew a respectable audience who could afford to lose bets. As he pointed out to the *Daily News*, at Washington Park, "I have seen the majority of the crowd be respectable people, while at . . . [Garfield] they are very disreputable. At Washington Park it is a great sight to see a well-dressed society lady betting on her favorite horse and clapping her pretty hands when he comes in first. At Garfield this cannot be seen, for the demi-monde prevails." He also claimed that if there were any evils at the elite park, the problems were one-twelfth of Garfield's, which was much more accessible and opened twelve months a year. Harrison handily won the nomination at the party convention on March 7, with 531 votes to 93 for Cregier and 57 for Hesing.[6]

Carter Harrison went up in the general election against wealthy Republican Samuel W. Allerton, who had made his fortune in slaughterhouses, banking, and streetcars. Allerton was supported by the *Tribune* and most of the newspapers because he stood for reform, economy, and efficiency. The Harrison family that owned the *Times* certainly did not support Allerton, vigorously chastising him for racing connections as a director and shareholder in the Washington Park Club. He was said to aspire to its presidency and had shared in its profits drawn from its many bookmakers who outnumbered those at Garfield Park. The *Times* also pointed out that "members of this newspaper collaboration [the anti-Harrisons] are shareholders in [the WPC]" and accused them of publishing "malicious falsehood charges" against Harrison. The *Times* further pointed out that the anti-Harrison clique included the *Globe*, owned by the notorious Mike McDonald.[7]

The press (excepting the *Globe*) continued criticizing Harrison for his long-term relationship with boss Mike McDonald, with headlines like "Mike McDonald Has Bought Carter Harrison." A reporter discovered a copy of a suspicious letter signed "M. C. McDonald" supposedly sent to Harrison that called for a big meeting "on important business." The newspapers claimed McDonald and other gamblers had raised at least $100,000 from their fellow disreputables to protect their illegal enterprises, that George Hankins gave Carter $5,000 in return for a pledge to reopen Garfield Park, and that McDonald was running the mayoralty campaign. Harrison denied all these charges late in the campaign at a big Democratic rally at the Auditorium and promised he would never reopen Garfield Racetrack.[8]

On April 4, Harrison easily won the mayoralty, 114,237 to 93,148, in a record turnout. Afterward, Carter announced his intent to close down gambling in the city, but the conventional wisdom was that his election meant a wide-open town. Some local gamblers resumed operations right after the election, and certain out-of-town bookies moved to Chicago. They were all surprised on April 21 when Police Superintendent McClaughry, a Washburne holdover, notified gambling-hall managers that there would be no favoritism like in the past and divulged his plans to establish a special secret-service force and a special detail to smash any operating betting rooms.[9]

The State Legislature and Horse Racing

Early in the new 1893 legislative session, when Democrats controlled both branches, Representative Daniel S. Berry (R–Savannah) introduced an antipool bill to void the Gibbs Amendment because gambling at races by women and children, especially at the WPR, where racing was conducted "under the guise of respectability, . . . leads them on to the paths of destruction from which they can ever be recovered." The *Daily News* and *Inter Ocean* both vigorously joined the crusade against the gambling menace. The *News* disagreed with Harrison, who supported Washington Park and Hawthorne, claiming that "Washington Park is no better than Garfield park and Hawthorne classes with the Guttenberg, Gloucester, and the East St. Louis tracks." It also pointed out that Illinois was not a breeding state, the WPC had no noted turf members, and the leading local stables belonged to the notorious George Hankins and Edward Corrigan. One critic added that "the gambling at Washington park is a greater evil than at Roby or Hawthorne simply because it is the elite who gamble there instead of the common classes." At the end of March, the house passed Berry's antipool bill by a resounding 124–8, despite its Democratic majority.[10]

However, experts reported that the senate was evenly divided on the Berry bill, with 27 senators already strongly opposed to changing the Gibbs law. Furthermore, the Berry bill's passage was considered unlikely because of the influence of thoroughbred owners, breeders, and racetracks, who spent an estimated $35,000 to influence the vote, along with the opposition of many harness tracks in small towns owned by homegrown businessmen and well-to-do farmers protective of their locality's racing tradition. On April 19, the Berry bill was derailed when it was sent to the Chicago Senate Committee on the Judiciary to die, along with other antipool bills.[11]

The *Tribune* attributed the defeat of the antiracing bills to the economics of racing: "This State is filled up now with little racetracks at the more important towns, which give meetings of two- or three-weeks' duration each year. Without pool selling they cannot pay their purses, and most close up." There were a total of thirty or so racetracks in Illinois, which explained why the Horse Breeders Association and owners of state's minor tracks opposed the Berry bill. The *Tribune* was right about the opposition of small-track owners to the bill, but failed to point out that those tracks staged meets of just five days or fewer. The big-track managers hoped that instead of just blocking the passage of antiracing legislation, the general assembly ought to approve a proracing bill. Otherwise, thoroughbred racing would be in trouble, as it was in New York, where poolroom titan Peter De Lacy was trying to break up the big-time courses controlled by the Board of Control that opposed his offtrack gambling interests. The cost of buying the votes needed to pass a new law to permit two months of racing was estimated at around $60,000–$100,000.[12]

THE WASHINGTON PARK SEASON

The much-anticipated 1893 meet was outstanding by every measure. There were some important innovations, including the presence of thirty Chicago policemen inside the track on Derby Day, as well as at the gate, the betting ring, and the clubhouse, ostensibly to prevent pickpocketing. Another innovation was in the betting operation. Management chose to auction off the betting privilege that ended up much more profitable than hiring an agent to license bookmakers and pool sellers as in the past. The public sale was won by Minneapolis gambler Frank Nutting Shaw for an astounding $100,000, outbidding the Association of Western Bookmakers. Shaw was best known for operating a secret poolroom syndicate under the guise of the Mercantile Telegraph Company, ostensibly seeking to corner betting privileges at leading western tracks. Shaw had already bought the betting privilege at the Latonia racetrack in Covington, Kentucky, across the Ohio River from Cincinnati. The *Daily News* castigated the decision to put Shaw in charge of the WPR gambling, since he was a "dead-sure-thing gambler, who did as much if not more than anyone connected with that august organization [Washington Park] to make racing disreputable last season." Shaw raised the fee for bookmakers' access to the betting ring to $150 a day, justifying the high price because he limited the number of available slots. The number of bookmakers dropped from seventy on opening day to only thirty-seven by the end of the season, most of whom lost money. The big drop reflected the public's dissatisfaction with the bookmakers' reliability, but also the negative impact on racing of the panic of 1893, which led to one of the worst depressions in American history.[13]

The American Derby on June 24 was one of the great events in North American racing in 1893. It was such a grand affair that the *Tribune* devoted its four front pages to the race and the accompanying spectacle. According to the *Spirit of the Times*, horses' entrance fees for the Derby were $500, compared to $200 from 1884 to 1886 and $250 from 1887 through 1892, which was again the fee in 1894. The 325 horses nominated for the Derby produced $33,055 in entrance fees (approximately $101 per horse) that was applied to the race's stakes, along with about $27,000 from the track. In addition, the WPR put up about $30,945 for the purses for the Isabella Stakes and the *Columbus* Handicap later in the meet to further induce top eastern stables to send their finest horses.[14]

A *Tribune* writer asserted that "Chicago can claim preeminence as the sporting center of America . . . [and] Derby day in Chicago has come to be recognized as the great sporting event of America." A reported record forty-seven thousand attended, despite the elevated $2 admission fee. Racing secretary Brewster justified setting the high ticket price because that was what theaters and other amusements did for special attractions. There were sixty-eight bookmakers in attendance, plus seven pari-mutuel machines, including two for straight betting, two for place betting, and three for show money. The WPR took in about $94,000 in ticket sales, plus another $8,000 for pool privileges and $10,000 for private boxes and other privileges. The track netted $81,055 for the day after paying overhead expenses.[15]

The feature event went off at 5:50 p.m., more than two hours after the scheduled starting time. The start was first delayed by twenty-seven minutes because of an argument between Corrigan and the Marcus Daly–David Gideon stable over who owned the services of renowned African American jockey Monk Overton. Corrigan ended up having Monk arrested for breach of contract, and he missed the race. Then starter Charles Pettingill, one of the finest race officials in the United States, had a terrible time getting the horses under way since there were an unbelievable twenty-five false starts. The fifteen-horse Derby was captured by John E. Cushing's ill-tempered Boundless, a 6–1 favorite, ridden by noted jockey Snapper Garrison. Cushing's horse earned him $50,000.[16]

The Sunday papers criticized the long wait to start the Derby, but reported nothing askance in the running once the race finally began.

However, on Monday, both the *Daily News* and the *Mail*, neither of which had Sunday editions, claimed Shaw fixed the race. The *News* also claimed that elite fans were warned not to bet on the race and that Americans were unwilling to let their big event go to Strathrose, an English horse, owned by the Duke of Beaufort. The *Mail*'s dramatic and vitriolic coverage was reprinted in the British *Sporting Times* with a screaming headline: "STRATHROSE WAS JOBBED: Beaten at the Post by Unsportsmanlike Methods and Pocketed in the Race." It asserted that Shaw had plotted Boundless's victory over the favorite, Strathrose. However, the story was totally inaccurate. Strathrose, who came in last, went off at 15–1.[17]

The *Daily News* was the city's strongest racing foe and published a scathing front-page critique of Derby Day, headlined "Demireps at the Derby." An editorial called the day a disgrace and described the track as a "moral fester" with the usual complement of petty criminals, professional gamblers, cardsharps, and the "frail sisterhood," consisting of thirty-eight black and white prostitutes whom the *Daily News* named, and their associates, and singling out the famous madams Eva Cohen and Carrie Watson, who drove up in a tallyho.[18]

The paper was offended that "colored women were mixed in with the white women [in the grandstand] and they talked together like a happy family. The white women also talked to colored men and colored women to white men as though the Derby put them all on one general level." The *Daily News* did admit there was nothing the WPC could do to keep out "the class of people who frequent Garfield and Hawthorne . . . thugs and gamblers, men from the cheap boarding houses and low saloons." It even praised the club for trying "to reach the great respectable middle class . . . who are prosperous in business and try to save money. . . . And above all it was to reach the families of all three classes."[19]

The *News* followed up with more critical front-page stories over the next few days that included negative comments about the WPR from nearly thirty prominent people, with special attention to minors betting at the races. The track's $50 daily license stipulated that the only minors allowed on the course were jockeys. Mayor Harrison

A PICTURE OF WASHINGTON PARK THAT TELLS ITS OWN STORY.

9. From the reform-minded *Chicago Daily News*, an ardent critic of gambling, belittling the elite Washington Park Club for its mistreatment in 1893 of youthful spectators. Reprinted from *Chicago Daily News*, July 1, 1893, 1.

urged racing fans before the Derby not to take their children to the races because it was an unfit environment for them, but neither city policemen nor private security guarding the gates stopped youth from entering. Hundreds of minors attended the race, drank beer, and gambled at "a dollar a throw" with bookmakers who took dollar bets. The reporter claimed these youths were mainly downtown office workers, "and it is a matter of common knowledge in police circles that nearly all the petty thievery in this city during the summer months can be traced directly to gambling at the Washington park fixed-race joint."[20]

On July 1, the *Daily News* ran a large front-page cartoon describing how Washington Park was under the control of betting concessionaire Frank Shaw. The graphic depicted the presence of many loose women, minors drinking, and bookmakers taking bets. The accompanying article claimed that property values near the track were much lower than in similar communities and called the racecourse "the most despicable dive in the city of Chicago." The *News* claimed that the track occupied 20,400 square feet of Cottage Grove Avenue that was public land the track had illegally taken when the site was part of the Hyde Park township and demanded its return.[21]

The *News* denied that Washington Park was run more honestly than other venues and excoriated the management for hiring officials who had made their reputations at disreputable tracks, such as the notorious Frank Shaw and racing judge Joseph Burke, a veteran of the crooked Guttenberg track. Furthermore, it asserted that few favorites won races there because horses did not run close to form, questioned the honesty of the three stakes races on Derby Day, and rated the meet's final day as no better than contests at the outlaw New Jersey tracks.[22]

The *Daily News* also reported widespread unhappiness among WPC members who did not want its respectable name lent to such dubious goings-on and were dismayed at the presence of the demi-monde. It claimed many clubmen were so disgusted that they wanted to close the track. They were also supposedly dissatisfied with declining dividends, which track officials blamed on the panic of 1893.[23]

The *Daily News* did have a few good words for the track's physical plant, admiring the fast track with its excellent soil; the elegant clubhouse, lawns, and walks; the betting ring; and especially the paddock. "But with this ends all that can be said in favor of the track." The racecourse was criticized as too narrow and "just about fit for a county fair." The *Daily News* unfairly chastised the WPR as cheap and lacking first-class facilities, particularly an undersized grandstand, and compared it poorly to elite eastern tracks that "have elegant buildings, [while] Washington park has a rookery."[24]

The *Daily News* begrudgingly admitted at the end of the racing season that there were fewer scandals at western tracks than eastern ones and that some betting problems had abated at the city's poolrooms. However, it singled out clerks wagering at the track as a serious social problem because it led to embezzlements and petty thefts. The editors recommended local merchants emulate St. Paul businessmen who hired detectives to check if clerks were going to gambling places and then dismissed those who bet on the races.[25]

Most other commentators gave a much more positive evaluation of the WPR, including Mayor Harrison, who believed the lengthy preparations for the meet gave "the Columbian season . . . an éclat surpassing any previous meeting. The season has been orderly and well conducted and the mayor's injunction as to minors has been obeyed." He felt the track's expectations of a big bump from the World's Fair, which many other local businesses anticipated, were too optimistic and that the declining economy was leaving Chicagoans with little discretionary income for amusements. The mayor agreed with Secretary Brewster that the fair actually hurt attendance because it "served as a counter attraction to our normal race-going population . . . very many of whom utilized their holidays in visiting the Exposition instead of Washington Park."[26]

The *Spirit of the Times*, which may have been Washington Park's biggest supporter, rated the meet the greatest ever in America. Five or six world records were established, and the *Spirit* considered three-year-old Morello's victory against more experienced horses in the Wheeler Handicap on the last day of the meet, "age and weight considered, probably . . . the greatest race ever seen." Morello tied the world record of 2:05 for a mile and a quarter, previously achieved by Salvador at Sheepshead Bay in 1890. Salvador had the advantage of being four years old, raced at 122 pounds (his weight for age), and competed in a match race. Morello went off at 9–5, but the favorite was "queen of the turf," four-year-old filly Yo Tambien, winner of fourteen of sixteen races in 1893. She and her stablemate Maid Marian were coupled (a bet for one covered both) and went off at 6–5. The *Tribune* reported the meet drew a track record 325,000 spectators (a daily average of 13,000), equal to three of New York State's three top tracks (Saratoga, Gravesend, and Sheepshead Bay) combined.[27]

The meet was expensive to run, with an average daily purse of $11,172, totaling $378,000, double the 1892 prizes. The daily winnings were by far the most generous of any American track, with the Coney

Island Jockey Club a distant second at $9,330. The basic admission price was $1 ($2 for opening day), which, if the reported attendance estimates were accurate, brought in $370,000. The clubhouse cost $1,000 a day to maintain, amply covered by the $40 dues paid by its more than seven hundred members. Concessions were an important source of revenue, especially the $100,000 fee for the bookmaking privilege and the $30,000 rent for the barroom. These receipts alone came to $528,000. One of the more important sources of revenue that day was the entrance fees to stakes events, which covered more than half of the Derby's purse.[28]

Washington Park's only local rival, the Hawthorne course, operated all winter and spring until the WPR opened in late June. Hawthorne then reopened at the start of August and remained open until a December 2 snowstorm. The suburban track had 259 days of racing in 1893, with purses averaging $2,400 each day, and crowds of about three thousand, including sizable female audiences, said to be as large as any New York track.[29]

The 1893 racing season ended with Washington Park as one of the preeminent racing sites in the entire United States. While profits were down from the record 1892 season, the WPR reportedly paid the highest dividends of any American jockey club in 1893. Attendance was a track record, and, in addition, the facility also hosted the finest harness-racing meet in the nation. Few would have expected that a few months later the track would close down.[30]

The Trials and Tribulations of Chicago-Area Racing in 1894

The Chicago racing season opened optimistically in February 1894 across the Indiana state line at the town of Roby, where Chicagoans had bet on races since 1892. The depression that was putting millions out of work did not seem to dampen public interest in gambling. The course was then operated by the newly formed Roby Breeders Association, with a capital investment of $27,000 and rent of $10,000. Shareholders were all Chicago bookmakers, including the new track manager, George

Hankins; treasurer James O'Leary; and Leo Mayer, originally from St. Louis, who each owned 20 percent of the stock. Johnny Condon, Samuel Doll, Harry Perry, and Charles Smith each had 10 percent.[31]

James Patrick O'Leary, the "Gambler Boss iv th' yards," was ultimately the most important of the partners. He was born in 1869 to Patrick and Catherine O'Leary, whose barn at 137 DeKoven Street was where the Great Chicago Fire of 1871 began. The family was originally blamed for the fire, ostensibly started when their cow knocked over a lantern, but recent research proved the conflagration was started by Daniel "Peg Leg" Sullivan, the first person to report the blaze. Eight years later, the family moved to the stockyards district to avoid prying reporters. Young Jim first worked at the Union Stockyards and then for local bookmakers before opening a gambling resort at Long Beach, Indiana, in the late 1880s that failed.[32]

O'Leary made his big stake by successfully backing Jim Corbett over John L. Sullivan in the 1892 heavyweight championship fight and subsequently opened a multipurpose saloon at 4183–85 South Halsted Street opposite the main entrance to the stockyards. His business included a restaurant, billiard room, bowling alley, barbershop, Turkish baths, and the biggest poolroom in the city, which increasingly became his focus. O'Leary bragged that his two-story edifice was "fireproof, lightning-proof, bombproof, burglarproof, and police proof." It was protected by a steel door, secret passages, steel-walled rooms, a trapdoor, and a fake chimney for a fast getaway. A lookout at the door scrutinized potential clients, though a tip of a few dollars often helped secure entrance. The facility took in as much as $10,000 a day in $2 or more bets, with a lot of action on out-of-town races. O'Leary was shameless about his operations, routinely admitting his illegal operations every eighteen months because it was the statute of limitations for gambling crimes.[33]

Roby was an unpretentious racecourse, and public expectations were low. Its main appeal was the foreign book on winter races in New Orleans and Hot Springs, Arkansas. The Daily News forewarned, "It looks as if Roby would be the Guttenberg of Chicago," employing unskilled jockeys described as "stable boys," needing training and experience and low-quality horses. Yet the *News* considered Roby one of the best winter courses when it came to jockey safety and the ability of its sandy-soiled track to stand up well to rain and slush.[34]

Garfield Park's Last Hurrah

In April the Garfield Park Racing Association made noise about resuming operations, either at its old site or at a new location just west of the city. West Side men's clubs opposing those plans protested to Mayor John Patrick Hopkins: "This track is operated by an infamous and disreputable gang. It menaces the peace of the West Side. . . . It is a question of decency against outrage."[35]

Hopkins had just recently been elected mayor in an emergency election in December 1893 to replace the martyred Carter Harrison, assassinated by a disgruntled job seeker two days before the closing of the World's Fair. Republican councilman George B. Swift replaced Harrison as interim mayor and then ran against Hopkins to fill Harrison's term. The city's first Irish mayor won by the narrowest of margins, 112,959 to 111,660. Hopkins was a self-made man who rose from humble origins, starting out in Chicago as a machinist who opened up his own business in 1888, and went on to become a multimillionaire. Racing played a small part in the campaign, though sportsmen were concerned that Swift would halt horse-race gambling in Chicago and send it off to Indiana.[36]

The city council reconsidered Garfield Park's status in mid-April 1894. Political observers expected that the Republican majority would fulfill their recent campaign pledge to promote honest government and block a return to racing at Garfield Park. On April 16, veteran Republican alderman James L. Campbell presented a resolution asking the mayor to not relicense the track, during which he was repeatedly interrupted by three of Garfield Park's chief aldermanic supporters, Louis I. Epstean, John Coughlin, and John J. Brennan.[37]

The issue was apparently serious enough that half of the next day's *Tribune* front page was devoted to the discussions. A delegation of one hundred West Siders opposed to Garfield Park spoke and repeated the old criticisms of the track. Republican alderman Martin B. Madden, city council president from 1891 to 1893, president of the Finance Committee for seven years, and a prominent businessman, asserted that the races had been conducted there by a "disreputable and infamous gang." The council voted against reviving Garfield Park, 37–24. Some vengeful Garfield Park supporters called for adding Washington Park to the resolution, as did some Republican aldermen who opposed both tracks, but it failed.[38]

Two days later, Mayor Hopkins announced he would not issue Garfield Park a racing permit. He topped off that statement by ordering the extension of streets into the track, which made the question of racing there moot. Hopkins took into account the West Side residents' complaints and the wishes of landowner Lambert Tree, who had recently successfully sued Hankins and McDonald for $35,000 in back rent. The gambling kingpins claimed they were under no obligation to pay the debt because of municipal interference since Tree had knowingly rented the site to them for an illegal purpose. The Chicago Committee on Licensing recommended that the mayor not license Washington Park and that no racing license be issued without council approval, which the entire council approved. However, Hopkins did not sign off, and the bill was not enacted.[39]

Racing at Hawthorne

Hawthorne was not an issue in the April 3, 1894, township election when Charles E. Piper of Berwyn, state president and national treasurer of the five-year-old Epworth League (a Methodist young adult association for individuals eighteen to thirty-five), was elected president of Cicero. Yet there was considerable speculation about his plans regarding the racecourse, and there was scuttlebutt that the track had "fixed" him. Piper spoke out following his inaugural against the racetrack evil and promised to support the board if it wanted to drive out horse-race gambling.[40]

Community opposition to the track was growing, especially among Cicero's church and temperance people, and it was rumored that the year-old Chicago Civic Federation was joining the fight. The CF was founded by such prominent citizens as Jane Addams of Hull House, businesswoman and philanthropist Bertha Honore Palmer, and banker Lyman J. Gage, president of the Columbian Exposition, to deal with the city's political and moral corruption and to promote economic development and government fiscal restraint. In mid-May, Chairman W. G. Clark of the CF's Committee on Morals issued a plan to suppress gambling and set up the Committee on Gambling to examine local and regional gambling laws, investigate the Chicago gambling scene, and prosecute gamblers.[41]

Hawthorne opened on May 1, eighteen days earlier than originally advertised, with six races, starting at 2:15 p.m. The *Tribune* declared that "the racing given there is, bar Washington Park, the highest class in the West." However, one week later, a meeting at the Austin Presbyterian church to suppress the secret sale of liquor in the north end of town initiated an antiracing campaign after resolutions were approved condemning the track.[42]

Hawthorne's early opening led to a racetrack war with Roby, which responded with a free gate. The *Tribune* anticipated this conflict would turn about once machine Democrats tied to the proprietary racetracks lost control of the state legislature to reform Republicans. The years 1893–94 were the first time that both branches of the Illinois General Assembly had been Democratic since the Civil War. Shortly thereafter, the courts shuttered the local tracks, just days prior to the legislature passing laws making track gambling illegal. As the *Tribune* pointed out, "Racetracks are not any too kindly thought of just now anyhow, and when the managers themselves get to fighting the enemies of racing are given a grand opening to do the sport an incalculable harm."[43]

Hawthorne and the American Turf Congress

Hawthorne had problems dealing with the Kentucky-dominated American Turf Congress that regulated midwestern racing was a pressing problem in racing circles. In late May, Hawthorne and Washington Park jointly applied for admission. The ATC had recently decided to admit only one track per city, but Washington Park successfully got the rule rescinded. However, after the WPC was voted in, and Hawthorne's admission came up, the WPC did not stand by its pact with the suburban track and failed to support Hawthorne's application for admission. The ATC originally offered Hawthorne and the brand-new Harlem track (located west of Chicago between Maywood and Oak Park) a license permitting them to operate under its rules, but without membership, which gave them no say in setting ATC policies. Corrigan was humiliated and rejected the offer.[44]

One reason the ATC turned down Hawthorne was that it permitted foreign books. The ATC ostensibly opposed foreign books, but since the ATC admitted St. Paul and New Orleans, which also had foreign books, that explanation did not hold water. Furthermore, the ATC formed an alliance with the newly established and highly prestigious Jockey Club, an organization established by leading New York horsemen to regulate eastern thoroughbred racing, and it did not oppose foreign books. Oddly, while the ATC opposed foreign books, it did support offtrack betting, ordering member tracks to have turf reporters present. They were paid $10 a day and could supply forty to fifty poolrooms with racing information, earning the tracks at least $400 each day. As the *Tribune* noted, "Compared with foreign books on race tracks the poolroom is a monstrous evil. Evidently the Turf Congress doctors are quacks."[45]

The ATC also rejected Hawthorne because its rules barred tracks owned and operated by a single person. Corrigan was certainly Hawthorne's public face, but he owned just half its stock. On the other hand, the Louisville Jockey Club was nearly completely controlled by president M. Lewis Clark, and the St. Louis Fair Grounds Association leased its complex to Frank Shaw, who pretty much ran everything there, including the $100,000 betting privilege. The *Tribune* believed the real problem was that the eleven-member ATC was worried that admitting Hawthorne would give too much influence to Chicago jockey clubs who might ally with St. Louis and St. Paul courses to form a rival western-based alliance detrimental to Kentucky racing interests.[46]

Corrigan thought there were other factors for the Chicago Racing Association's rejection, including his blunt criticism of Clark and ATC president Van L. Kirkman, head of the Nashville track; his opposition to ATC rules that barred winter racing north of Nashville; and the jealousy of ATC members of his far-flung racing empire, which included the opening in late 1895 of his $300,000 Ingleside track in San Francisco as the home of the elite Pacific Coast Jockey Club. Finally, Corrigan felt the ATC wrongly labeled Hawthorne as an outlaw track because it had always been extremely generous to horsemen. By his account, Hawthorne offered $657,392 in purses in 1893 compared to New York's Gravesend, considered a free-spending enterprise, at just $258,650, or the next two most liberal western tracks, Washington Park at $281,300 and Latonia at $204,000. The CRA that year put up more added money for purses than the rest of the ATC combined. In the end, the ATC held a second meeting in Chicago when it reconsidered the status of Chicago's two proprietary Chicago courses and unanimously voted in Hawthorne and the new Harlem track.[47]

The most important power for any turf organization, including the ATC, was the authority to declare a racing club an "outlaw" because of some flagrant unprofessional actions and decisions, such as knowingly permitting fixed races. The consequence for the cited track was that anyone racing a horse, riding a horse, or training a horse there would be banned from all member tracks. That summer the ATC, under pressure from St. Louis's South Side Race Track Association, declared the two southern Illinois courses outlaw tracks. The Mound City's track operators had fought with Joseph Ullman ever since he opened the East St. Louis Jockey Club and were especially mad at him for running a 364-day meet in 1893. Ullman followed that meet with 108 days of racing and arranged free train service from downtown to his track for St. Louis racing fans.[48]

THE COMING DEMISE OF WASHINGTON PARK

Pressure mounted in the spring of 1894 to close Washington Park, even though it was one of the most prestigious men's clubs in the Midwest, if not the United States; sponsored the finest thoroughbred meets in the nation west of New York City; and returned big profits. However, the track was on shaky grounds because of local circumstances and the growing national opposition to gambling at racetracks. Certain lower-court jurists such as Murray F. Tuley had pronounced the Gibbs Amendment unconstitutional because it granted certain rights to on-track bet takers that it did not grant to offtrack bookmakers. Furthermore, the city had proved in 1892 that it was ready to close racing facilities when it shut down Garfield Park.

The spirit of reform in Chicago got a big boost in March 1894 with the publication of British journalist William T. Stead's *If Christ Came to Chicago*, a muckraking account of local vice that sold one hundred thousand copies in its first two weeks. Stead was the former innovative editor of the *Pall Mall Gazette* and the *Review of Reviews* and had earned a stellar reputation as an investigative journalist. He was well known for his studies of slum life and childhood prostitution in London. His book mainly focused on the Near South Side Levee District, where gambling and prostitution went on unhampered by authorities paid off by the local vice lords. Stead's goal was to clean up the moral cesspool in city hall, the Levee District, and elsewhere in town.[49]

Stead discovered that respected property owners owned buildings in the vice district that they rented to professional gamblers and madams. He provided detailed maps locating the principal gambling houses and brothels. The publication engendered quite a brouhaha among reformers, who in the summer of 1894 pressured the police to take action against the city's fifteen hundred to two thousand professional gamblers. All the notable gambling houses were busy, including the downtown rooms of Harry Varnell and John Condon. Varnell's annual expenses at 129 South Clark included $10,000 in rent and a yearly payroll of $161,496. His hall offered customers faro, roulette, poker, and other games with a staff that included steerers (who lured in customers), lookouts, bouncers, bartenders, twelve roulette operators, and twenty-four dealers.[50]

But reform was going to be difficult because these gamblers were closely tied to local machine politicians, policemen, and judges.

Furthermore, the general public and police officials agreed the authorities had more important concerns than victimless crime. In addition, the police appreciated the additional income received from payoffs to look the other way and were themselves ardent bettors. For instance, in the summer of 1894 many policemen regularly bet at the Calhoun Place poolroom, west of the stage entrance to the Chicago Opera House, near the Central Police Station, which was frequently passed by beat patrolmen and detectives coming and going to city hall. They could hear the calling of out-of-town races, yet never interfered because the resort had immunity. Manager Jere J. Driscoll was a reputed former lieutenant of San Francisco's "Blind Boss" Christopher Buckley, and his experiences there made "him a valuable man in certain political connections."[51]

Antigambling reformers, having successfully shuttered the well-protected Garfield Park in 1892, now targeted Washington Park, which they felt, despite its fame and success, was vulnerable because its management and membership lacked the commitment, political clout, or fortitude to withstand a full-frontal attack. Furthermore, success against the elite track might create momentum for further attacks on local vice.[52]

The assault on Chicago racing was part of a major national effort to kill thoroughbred racing and gambling. The fight centered in metropolitan New York, which was the national capital of racing, and next door in New Jersey, a major center of racing, where there were six thoroughbred tracks. They included the prestigious Monmouth Park Association's Long Branch racetrack, four proprietary tracks located close to Manhattan, and the infamous Gloucester track, just eight miles across the Delaware River from Philadelphia. New Jersey was a heavily Democratic state and controlled the governorship from 1869 through 1896. In 1893 the state's Democratic machine was in firm control of the state legislature and passed the Parker Acts that empowered local government agencies to license racecourses. But a political realignment occurred in the following fall election in which horse racing's legality was a major concern, along with such other social and cultural issues as prohibition, Sunday blue laws, and compulsory education. The state courts ruled the Parker Acts unconstitutional, and the newly elected Republican majority in the legislature enacted new antiracing laws in 1894. These actions killed New Jersey racing for nearly fifty years. Chicago reformers would watch and learn from developments there.[53]

Two of Chicago's leading local gambling foes were the Reverend W. G. Clarke, pastor of the Campbell Park Presbyterian Church, who first became well known in 1890 delivering antigambling sermons, and his fellow Presbyterian Dr. Carlos Martyn of Hyde Park. Clarke in 1894 led the Civic Federation's crusade against gambling and was considered the local equivalent of New York's Charles Henry Parkhurst. Clarke chaired the Civic Federation's Subcommittee on Gambling of the Committee on Public Morals. He agreed with Steed's estimate that there were more than fifteen hundred professional gamblers in Chicago and over a hundred gambling houses.[54]

In late April, Dr. Carlos Martyn preached to his congregants against licensing the nearby Washington Park, which he described as bordered on one side by a grog shop and a brothel, and between them "men sail into perdition, as the ancient mariners used to sail between Sylla and Charybdis out into storms and shipwrecks." Martyn described the track as "a lively section of hell," frequented by "two classes—the fleecers and the fleeced." He criticized the gamblers who frequented the track, along with their flashy escorts, and decried the wagering that encouraged people, especially youth, to get something without earning it. Martyn decried the poolroom operators as "scientific scoundrels, whose religion is illicit gain and whose ritual is plunder." Martyn considered the city's poolrooms as feeders for the tracks by encouraging people to bet without even going to the races, though in reality the poolrooms took business away from the tracks. He claimed the betting scene was part of a multimillion-dollar business that included Western Union, track men, and the railroads and urged South Siders to protect themselves like the West Siders who had taken on Garfield Park.[55]

Reformers pressed Mayor Hopkins to halt racing at Washington Park by rejecting its license renewal. A delegation of well-known businessmen residing near the track called on him, claiming to represent owners of millions of dollars of property harmed by the track's presence. They told Hopkins that "there was a time when the track helped that section but that time has long since passed. Now it is a positive detriment. . . . If we erect a building, we cannot get desirable tenants because there are so many toughs and blacklegs hanging about. People who would improve their property do not do so and will not until the park is subdivided."[56]

The South Side Anti–Race Track Association organized a mass meeting on May 10 at the Isabella Theater to denounce the jockey club and plan how to pressure Mayor Hopkins to reject the license application. A leading antiracing foe told the press that the main difference between Washington Park and Garfield was the former had a sprinkling of respectable leaders "who use these races as a cover to their vices." The association argued:

> The fact that the Washington race-track has a prominent membership makes it much more hurtful in its influences on the young and susceptible members of the community who are led into gambling and kindred vices by the example of men whose names should stand for morality and honesty. . . . Yearly at its meetings are dumped on a respectable and quiet residence community a mass of humanity, gamblers and disreputables and the off-scourings [sic] of the earth. . . . This club becomes the common meeting-ground between supposed respectability and total depravity. Women of loose character swarm the grounds and hold sway where the young men of the city are here led into gambling and evil associations, and the air of semi-respectability given it by its . . . prominent members. This race-track is a blot on the south [side].[57]

The audience, composed of neighborhood residents and nearby Hyde Parkers, also included many proracing advocates who thought the meeting was for open discussion. Organizers, worried their presence would create a heated meeting, called in a dozen policemen for security, but the gathering became so animated that the officers called for backup. A near riot developed until the proracing advocates went elsewhere to continue their own conversation.[58]

Dr. Martyn spoke out against the track and its traction allies, concerned that "the comfortable homes erected by honest citizens . . . were threatened by an abomination in the way of a racetrack. The racetrack brought gamblers and bad women into Hyde Park and laid snares for the young men." Other critics estimated the track's presence lowered property values by $1.5 million, making the surrounding area barely sellable. Cottage Grove Avenue's value by the track was $125 per foot, but would have been $200 to $300 without the track. The 82-acre track site, originally purchased for $100,000, was itself then worth about $1.64 million ($20,000 an acre), a healthy appreciation in just a decade. The racing foes asserted the higher evaluation was unconnected to racing but reflected the neighborhood's high quality; its proximity to the spectacular 372-acre Washington Park, designed and built by renowned landscape architect Frederick L. Olmsted in 1870; and the area's significantly improved mass-transit facilities.[59]

When the friends of the Washington Park Race Track reconvened next door, longtime area resident W. R. Whitehair pointed out that property values had actually appreciated with the coming of the track. Other speakers noted that the course was managed by leading Chicagoans who operated it on a higher basis than other area tracks. The gathering backed a petition signed by seven hundred local property owners urging the mayor to grant the license, which he did.[60]

As Derby Day neared, the *Spirit* reported, "Public sentiment against racing grew less obtrusive and gave way to the popular and enthusiastic support that is usually accorded to so great an event." Management did not seem concerned about community opposition and planned seventeen big stake races worth $145,000 and a total purse of $252,200. Frank Shaw lost the gambling concession, which was leased to the firm of Bush and Johnson, the former having previously managed betting at Washington Park. They reduced the daily fee charged bookmakers back to $100.[61]

The ongoing depression did not seem as if it would hinder elite racing fans, whose wives planned for weeks their gowns, hats, and matching parasols. One milliner alone made fifty gowns, mostly delicately tinted silks or lace, with ribbon-trimmed muslins. The *Tribune*

10. An early American Derby at the Washington Park Racetrack. The fore-ground depicts a prosperous family outing. Reprinted from *Harper's Weekly*, August 1, 1888, 577. From a photograph by J. W. Taylor.

expected the clubhouse and lawn "to look like a large French flower garden." The day before the race, the *Tribune* published the names and locations of every upper-box holder. More society people were out of town than normal for summer vacations, but attendees arrived in liveries they owned or had rented at a cost of $10 to $75. The track secretary reported more than twelve thousand applications for passes, but fewer than two hundred were given out.[62]

On opening day, June 23, the Derby drew an estimated thirty-five thousand. The attendees included people of modest means, who, the *Tribune* pointed out, "exchange weeks of wages for two minutes of pleasure," some spending a week's earnings to ride in elegance to the track. One should not forget that the huge crowds included large numbers of middle-class people who enjoyed the wonderful ambience of a derby and, of course, the gambling. While a lot of the middle class may have been opposed to horse-race betting, the enormous crowd at stakes events did include a large middle-class audience. Well-dressed clerks and aspiring businessmen went to the track with male friends for an afternoon of diversion, and middle-class men rode out to the track on carriages with elegantly dressed and well-coifed dates for a pleasurable afternoon. Middle-class families also attended the races with young children. A few years later, Fannie Kessner, a young and respectable Jewish South Sider, gladly attended the Derby with her two brothers and other relatives. They had a portrait taken of her sitting in a carriage with them.[63]

Early comers to the track were entertained by Adolph Rosenbecker's twenty-five-piece orchestra. The afternoon started with a startling victory by the mare Peytona, who won at 100–1 odds. The American Derby was won in an exciting upset by Rey El Santa Anita at 40–1, owner "Lucky" Baldwin's fourth Derby winner. The *Daily News* speculated that jockey E. Van Kuren's brilliant winning ride might encourage bettors to develop a new gambling philosophy that gave greater credit to the skill of jockeys than they previously had and less to the horse. Baldwin's win was worth $19,875 of the $25,000 purse, a big drop from the rich 1893 race, owing in large part to the dismal economy. The gambling was mostly with bookies, although less than usual, and just 251 $5 pari-mutuel tickets were sold on the race.[64]

Despite the meet's promising start, the first week of racing did not go well. The next racing day drew the smallest crowd in years, "quiet and orderly, showing little or no enthusiasms when the races were lost or won." Indeed, the *Daily News* reported that Washington Park's first week looked "as if racing in Chicago had ceased to be a popular sport." Attendance was light, the fields small, purses down, and the betting insignificant.[65]

Washington Park's declining business was hurt by the absence of charismatic horses and jockeys, but mainly by the panic of 1893 that resulted in four million unemployed nationally. Chicago itself was in the midst of the Pullman strike by four thousand workers that ran from May 11 to July 20. Thirty people were killed in Chicago, and $80 million in property was destroyed. Local transportation was disrupted, notably overcrowding on the alley el and cable cars, which certainly did not help people taking public transportation to Washington Park.[66]

Interest in the sport actually picked up during the second week of the strike, perhaps because Chicagoans wanted a momentary escape from the labor strife. Washington Park's average daily attendance in 1894 of six thousand was less than half the record-breaking 1893 season, but still surpassed the banner 1892 season. There was heavier gambling than ever at any western track. The WPR made a good profit, although it was only about one-third the record returns of the previous season. The track was coming off two extraordinary seasons, during which time management did a superb promotional job, and matching those years would have been difficult regardless of the depression.[67]

The local press still wrote favorably of Washington Park in 1894, claiming it did the best it could under the circumstances. Even the *Daily News* lauded the track for promoting honesty and stakes events whose winners set record times. Washington Park still outdrew the prestigious Sheepshead Bay racetrack at Coney Island, the only major New York facility to draw large crowds, though they all finished in the black, and four tracks earned at least $75,000. Broad Church of the *Spirit* concluded that "Chicago has now become . . . a great racing center, probably the most important in the country."[68]

The year 1894 was a difficult period nationally among sporting enterprises, though the New York tracks still made out well. The elite Coney Island Jockey Club made $125,000, Morris Park $75,000, and Jerome Park, in its first year, $15,000. The main proprietary tracks also did well. The Brooklyn Jockey Club made $100,000 at Gravesend, and the Brighton Beach Racing Association took in $90,000. The proprietary tracks also did well in 1894. The Brooklyn Jockey Club made $100,000 at Gravesend, and the Brighton Beach Racing Association took in $90,000. However, racetracks outside of Chicago and New York struggled financially. Major League Baseball had fared decently the year before when the panic began, with eleven of twelve National League teams making a modest average profit of $12,708. Most also made money in 1894, as people sought relief from the bad times. However, in the next few years, National League franchises lost money, partly owing to internal problems of a weakly competitive and unwieldy twelve-team league and also because of the aftermath of the damaged economy.[69]

MORE COMPETITION: THE NEW HARLEM TRACK

The Chicago racing scene got a lot more crowded that summer with the opening of a new southwest suburban track operated by the Chicago Fair Grounds Association (CFGA), whose president was William Martin, a bucket-shop owner. The main financial backer was George V. Hankins, the well-known bookmaker and racing man, said to have invested nearly $300,000 in the track. His wealth was estimated at $2 million, including $750,000–$1,000,000 in stocks, bonds, and some eighty Chicago flats. He lived in a $150,000 mansion on fashionable Michigan Avenue.[70]

The CFGA raced on an eighty-two-acre site purchased in December 1893 for $93,500, just beyond the city's limits, in the village of Harlem (bounded by Collier Avenue, Twelfth Street, West Seventy-Fourth, and West Seventy-Sixth). The track cost at least $170,000 to construct, nearly three times the White Stockings' $60,000 newly built West Side Grounds. The CFGA chose the suburbs to avoid Chicago's licensing laws and congested transportation, which contributed to Garfield Park's woes. The Harlem Track, twenty-five minutes from downtown via the Wisconsin Central, was also accessible by seven other routes from the Loop. One year later, the electrified Metropolitan el was opened, further improving transportation options.[71]

The new track, modeled after the elite Morris Park that opened in Westchester County, New York, in 1889, had a four-hundred-foot-long, fifteen-thousand-seat grandstand with seventy-two boxes. Admission was just 75 cents to promote interest during the depression. Amenities included a restaurant, four public bars where free lunches were served, and a private bar. The betting ring had space for seventy-five to a hundred bookmakers, although in 1894 no more than thirty

GRAND STAND.

11. Harlem Racetrack grandstand, June 1901. First opened in 1894, the proprietary track was controlled by John Condon. Reprinted from "Improvements at Harlem Race Track," *Chicago Daily Tribune*, June 9, 1901, 19.

usually worked the track, except for opening day. The mile-long track was made of black loam and considered safe and fast, with excellent drainage. There were five daily races, with purses averaging $500, as at eastern tracks. Security was supplied by uniformed policemen and about fifty plainclothesmen.[72]

Hawthorne was displeased with the new competition, but agreed to a truce. The west suburban tracks agreed to race on alternate weeks, an arrangement the *Tribune* approved because it promoted temporary cordiality and encouraged a friendly rivalry. The paper also pointed out that the scheduling was unusually convenient for horse owners who could now stable their horses at one track and race them at both.[73]

The opening-day crowd was described by the *Daily News* as "Garfield Park greatly improved," including not just the "usual contingent," but also "those who go to see racing for the sport itself." Harlem's daily crowds averaged three thousand, and Hawthorne also did well, except in the betting ring. Hankins diversified the racing by adding trotting and pacing events.[74]

The racing community was shocked on August 25 when Harlem's betting ring was bombed, injuring three people and causing a panic among the fans, especially when two more explosions soon occurred. The violence reminded Chicagoans of the Haymarket Riot of 1886 and other recent anarchist attacks. However, these blasts were not political but rather a diversion for a robbery. A man tried to steal the cash box of the "Chicago Club," a bookmaking concern, when the bomb went off. He escaped into the crowd.[75]

The *Spirit* rated the Harlem Racetrack's initial season a great success both on the track and at the box office, making expenses. Attendance was higher than expected, there was a lot of betting, and national records were set at six furlongs and the mile. However, the *Daily News* was pretty critical of both Hawthorne's and Harlem's fall meetings, which it described as of "the catch-penny cards of continuous racing," since there were no stakes events or particularly interesting special races.[76]

On October 21, George V. Hankins announced that he was disposing of his interests in saloons, two important gambling houses, and his one-fifth share in Roby to give full attention to Harlem and his half-interest in a Kentucky stable. The *Tribune* claimed that outside of Mike McDonald, "No man has ever waxed so rich from gaming profits as George V. Hankins." James O'Leary succeeded him as president of Roby.[77]

CAN RACING SURVIVE?

The effort to halt racetrack gambling in Chicago was ratcheted up several degrees on June 30 when the grand jury indicted several WPR officials for keeping a gaming house "where persons of disreputable character congregated." In addition, John Brenock, Edward Corrigan, and Joe Ullman were all charged with gambling violations at Hawthorne.[78]

Fighting offtrack poolrooms also got a lot of attention that summer. The *Tribune* felt that offtrack betting was the most demoralizing business associated with racing: "On a race track a foreign book only adds to the interest of the patrons of such a course . . . like the sideshow of a circus. . . . In a poolroom it is different. The horses on the boards and the odds laid are the only attractions; it is a gambling place pure and simple."[79]

The antigambling movement gained widespread support by the end of the summer, with a lot of publicity resulting from Civic Federation raids on poolrooms. The CF began on September 19 a series of daily raids by bringing hired constables into suburban Evanston, but made its main forays downtown at betting parlors like the Hankins & Wightman gambling house and the notorious House of David, a downtown restaurant, saloon, and gambling den founded in 1874 by noted sportsman "Genial" David Thornton, who died in 1884.[80]

On September 22, four constables went to Hawthorne to serve warrants for pool selling on Corrigan, Burke, and Brenock and on Ullman for his foreign book, presumably in retribution for Corrigan's support of the CF's fight against downtown gamblers. Corrigan blamed the incursion on O'Leary, whose Back of the Yard operations was recently raided even though he was paying the police $200 a month for protection. Hawthorne was forewarned about the raid, and management called in Cicero justice of the peace Adam Trapp to meet them at the track so they could make their best deal, bail at $200.[81]

The Civic Federation had widespread support for its antigambling drive, including the press, organized labor, and Mayor Hopkins. The American Federation of Labor backed the Chicago Trade and Labor Assembly in declaring that gambling should be stopped at dinner-pail (working-class) games on Clark and Dearborn, in palatial hotels, and at "that blot upon the map of Chicago, that great Monte Carlo of America, Washington Park . . . , where on last Derby day poor fallen women, drunken with the frenzy of the horse races and with the wine freely distributed, amused themselves by throwing wine bottles at the waiters' heads."[82]

The *Tribune* called for a strong crusade against all forms of gambling and saw no reason to discriminate between gambling houses and racetracks: "If anything, the tracks were far worse because the gambling-house makes no pretense of being other than it really is. . . . The Washington Park club throws around itself a cloak of respectability and even of fashion, while in reality it is a kindergarten where many a young man takes his first lesson in gambling. They get their education from the bookmakers and when they have completed their curriculum in pools at the race tracks, they are graduated into the gambling-house."[83]

Antigambling groups organized meetings to halt gambling at upper-class men's clubs, racetracks (especially Washington Park), and the Board of Trade. The Trade and Labor Assembly organized a Saturday-night meeting with the Society for the Suppression of Gambling and the Anti–Race Track Association at Bricklayers' Hall. The Reverend Carlos Martyn told the meeting that the best way to attack legalized gambling venues like the Board of Trade was to start with Washington Park: "This is the great gambling place of the aristocracy, and they consider it their stronghold." He anticipated a lot of support from real-estate interests and recommended cutting streets through the track and fighting it as a common gambling place and a public nuisance.[84]

By mid-October, the authorities seemed to be finally taking serious steps against poolrooms. Sheriff James H. Gilbert ordered raids, including a massive one against the House of David by officers equipped with sledgehammers, axes, crowbars, and battering rams. The racing crowd welcomed the efforts to close poolrooms, expecting it would bolster track attendance, but following the raid against Hawthorne, the sportsmen quickly realized the reformers were also after them. Track operators were also worried by the recent halting of racing in New Jersey that might become a model for Illinois and the bad reputation given Illinois racing by the outlaw tracks in East St. Louis and Madison, where gambling was wide open. Local jockey-club leaders became convinced that the sport needed new legislation to better protect their interests.[85]

Harlem and Hawthorne withstood the pressure of the antiracing forces, but an unseemly legal matter arose at Harlem, where stewards ruled thoroughbred owner Henry Simon off the track for fraud. Simon secured a restraining order from Judge Philip Stein on October 22 that allowed him to buy a ticket into the track and race his horses. The *Spirit* injudiciously pointed out that Stein was the only Hebrew judge in Illinois, "and in him the Hebrew instinct of caring for his own people seems to be strongly developed." These proceedings brought to mind bookmaker Louis Cohn, who had sued Washington Park after he was refused admission. The court in that case ruled that management *could* deny admission to objectionable characters.[86]

The Closing of Washington Park

Delegates attending the mid-October meeting of the ATC were stunned by news that Washington Park was closing. On October 13, President Wheeler called a special closed-door meeting of the WPR board of directors to consider halting operations at the track. Ten of twenty-three directors attended, including treasurer John R. Walsh, Frank S. Gorton, and John Dupee, who with Wheeler were most responsible for track policy. The WPR had been considering its future for about six months, and the discussions were accelerated by the decline of racing and legal barriers being raised against the sport, particularly in New Jersey and New York; CF's attack on racetrack gambling; the impending closing of fields for 1895 stakes events; and lower-court rulings since 1890 that Gibbs was unconstitutional. In addition, the WPR needed funds to promote lobbying if it intended to help fight against new anti-pool-selling bills expected in the upcoming legislative session. The directors felt the club could no longer maintain its character and standards, especially since a number of dubious American racing clubs had been run purely and simply as gambling ventures and even operating in the dead of winter, such as Garfield Park in Chicago and Gloucester and Guttenberg in New Jersey. But most of all, Wheeler was anxious that the upcoming grand jury would indict him and other track officials. The WPC had previously been indicted as a corporation on gambling charges, though the case was thrown out because of faulty construction. Wheeler himself was arrested the previous summer for running a gambling facility. The detainment humiliated Wheeler and embarrassed and annoyed the WPC's leading racing men. A brief discussion followed Wheeler's presentation, and then the directors present voted to cancel the upcoming racing season. Stockholders then debated the future use of the site, such as the possibility of turning it into a country club with facilities for tennis, polo, and harness racing or simply dividing the land into lots and selling it for homes.[87]

Observers agreed that the anticipated sharp fight in the Illinois General Assembly over horse racing was a major cause for the jockey club's decision. Washington Park had been through a couple of legislative scrapes and did not relish another. The WPR supported the position of trotting and agricultural interests that sought a law limiting race meets to thirty days and taxing gross receipts, in emulation of New York's Ives Law. But Wheeler did not want to work with the proprietary tracks that were committed to continuous racing from April until November. Furthermore, he and Corrigan recently had a big falling-out because the latter believed Washington Park had previously not borne its full share of lobbying the state legislature or helping his track gain acceptance in the American Turf Association. As one WPC member told a reporter, "The mere fact that we, in order to exist, would have to form an alliance offensive and defensive with Hawthorne and Harlem was obnoxious to nearly every member of the club."[88]

Internal factors also contributed to the sudden decision, including the recent death of racing secretary Brewster, who did most of the work organizing meets, a task most racing directors abhorred. The track had been well managed, and despite the occasional glitch, the races were well orchestrated and of the highest integrity. Some directors claimed the closure occurred because the WPR could not sustain its high standards in the presence of less desirable race goers, especially clients of foreign books. The *Tribune* attributed the divesture as a result of the board's decision to separate the club's social and racing features and make it more like a country club, as its name indicated, instead of a jockey club.[89]

Many WPC members empathized with Wheeler, who had received a lot of public abuse and harassment. One member pointed out that "the officers of the club have been placed in constant jeopardy; every season they have been threatened with arrest, and some newspaper or other has always a criticism for the Washington Park club." Since 1893 many members interested only in the social aspect of the club had protested the racing, complaining about the heavy expenses that resulted. Club member Dr. F. C. Greene estimated that only one-fourth of the members cared about racing and attended just on Derby Day. President Wheeler became over time increasingly sympathetic to the club's influential antiracing faction that strongly opposed racing.[90]

On the other hand, member J. B. Walker, president of a railroad-car manufacturing company, was highly critical of the closing, irate that only stockholders were consulted. "It is simply a business transaction with them. . . . No one except stockholders is glad the club is to be closed up. The racing has brought thousands of dollars and consequent prosperity to Chicago. It has built up this section of the city to a great extent. What similar resort will be left in Chicago after the Washington Park club is abolished? . . . I consider it a blow to the whole city."[91]

The WPR's eleven-year run was a great success, providing a recreational facility for the upper class and thousands of other citizens. It enhanced the social status of its members, promoted thoroughbred racing, and boosted Chicago's public image. The average derby purse was $17,709 and the total annual purses averaged $163,043 a season, peaking at $343,520 in 1893 (table 6). The track's property was worth about $1.5–$2 million, and the club annually earned a handsome 12 percent profit on its investment. From 1888 through 1894, the WPR made $100,000 to $150,000 each year, topping off at $200,000 in 1893. No dividends were issued until 1892, since all profits were previously reinvested in improving the facility. Then for three years, stockholders received $50,000, a 50 percent return on the original investment. The WPR's 2,500 shares were worth $250,000, or $100 a share. The

Table 6
Washington Park Club Purses and Values of American Derby, 1884–1894

YEAR	DERBY-WINNER PURSES	ANNUAL PURSES TOTAL
1884	10,900	$66,910.75
1885	9,770	83,560.00
1886	8,360	170,255.50
1887	13,940	111,496.75
1888	14,590	108,788.75
1889	15,690	142,028.50
1890	15,510	147,334.75
1891	18,860	172,190.75
1892	17,180	173,655.00
1893	50,000	343,520.00
1894	20,000	273,735.00
Total	$194,800	$1,793,475.75

Source: *Spirit of the Times*, January 1, 1898, 732.

principal stockholders then were Wheeler (320 shares); John Dupee of the Board of Trade (300); the estate of Dupree's former partner, Charles Schwartz (460); hotelier Albert S. Gage, the man most responsible for the WPR's creation (300, including proxies); and treasurer John R. Walsh (200).[92]

The *Tribune* at the time of closing appraised Chicago racing at its all-time peak and lauded the WPR as "the most disinterested turf organization in America, high of class, liberal and a benefactor to the American turf," and said its members were the top American jockey club "by reason of what it did and the quality of the sport its rich fights attracted." The *Tribune* compared the local racing scene favorably to New York, the national center of thoroughbred racing, because "Chicago has no multitude of tracks, merry-go-rounds, or electric-light excuses for gambling" that New York had, along with its high-class tracks. By contrast, in Chicago "there have been but three race tracks. All have profited richly, the courses have been well managed, and the general racing clean." Apparently, the writer had forgotten about Garfield Park and the city's early tracks.[93]

The Closure's Impact

The sport of kings in the United States suffered a huge blow with the closing of Washington Park. A few other elite tracks had recently closed. In 1889 Baltimore's elite Pimlico, founded in 1870 by Governor Oden Bowie, and site of the prestigious Preakness, shut down, unable to compete with the New York and New Jersey tracks and threatened by the upcoming opening of the Benning Race Track in Washington, DC. Jerome Park, New York's first elite course, closed in 1894 and became a reservoir, already supplanted by Morris Park, whose site was annexed to the Bronx in 1895. Also, in 1894, the elite Monmouth Park and the five proprietary New Jersey racetracks were closed by court decisions, followed by the legislature's banning of gambling at the races.[94]

The Washington Park closing shook up the racing community in Chicago and beyond. The shuttering was different from the ending of Garfield Park, which nearly everyone, except its bookmaker owners, their political friends, and the lowlifes who frequented the track, considered a positive action. The WPC had promoted gambling, year-round racing, political corruption, and the immoral behavior of the sporting crowd, without promoting the public interest. Washington Park's demise was expected to hurt breeders, stable owners, racetrack workers, and the other racecourses in Cook County.

COMPARING AMERICAN AND BRITISH RACING

The strong American opposition to horse-race gambling was quite different from Great Britain, the historic center of thoroughbred racing that by 1839 had 153 racetracks. Top American breeders, jockey clubs, and racetracks looked to the British as a role model. The mother country was still close to the United States economically, politically, linguistically, culturally, and religiously. The British had a strong puritanical tradition, sustained in the nineteenth century by evangelical nonconformist Protestant denominations; maintained a Victorian culture that considered prostitution and gambling immoral; and observed a strict Sabbath. Yet when it came to the aristocratic sport of horse racing, there was one rule for the rich and another one for everyone else. The British elite who dominated racing did not consider their own gambling a moral issue. As racing historian Mike Huggins points out, "Racing and respectability went hand in hand." The most privileged tracks rarely closed. Four of the five classic events—the Epsom Downs Oaks (1779), Epsom Derby (1780), Newmarket £1000 Guinea Stakes (1814), and £2000 Guinea Stakes (1809)—have been contested every single year since they were founded. The oldest major event, Doncaster's St. Leger Stakes (1776), was halted only in 1939 following the start of World War II.[95]

Huggins found greater support for racing among the middle classes than historians believed, participating as entrepreneurs, officials, spectators, and bettors because even during the Victorian era they were more interested in pleasure than generally recognized. They were less supportive of evangelical nonconformist Protestantism and less unified in their opposition to gambling than typically credited.[96]

Certainly, important segments of the British middle class, such as businessmen, religious leaders, and social reformers, were always concerned about the working class wagering on racing, especially by the 1830s and 1840s, once the sport became more commercialized with enclosed tracks and more available to the working class, who could afford admission fees at proprietary tracks. Reformers promoted rational recreations, endorsing sports through muscular Christianity, reading for self-improvement, and engaging in artistic pastimes for self-expression. Such uplifting recreation was considered an outstanding substitute for vile amusements like gambling. Racing for the lower sorts was problematic because it supposedly led to absenteeism from the workplace, encouraged breadwinners to waste scarce family resources, abetted criminality, and weakened individual morality.[97]

In Great Britain the protection of public behavior was a national, not a local, matter, decided in London, unlike the United States, where it was determined at the state or local level. The American federal government did not decide national moral policy, including regulating or banning gambling, but Parliament in 1853 passed the Betting House Act that banned the establishment of gambling houses to accept wagers on horse races and barred bookies from working in betting houses, showing lists of horses in a race, or advertising their business. However, as the law's title indicated, the state did not interfere with on-track betting, conducted mainly by the upper middle class and the elite. The Betting House Act also left untouched well-known betting sites like Tattersall's, where only members could bet, often wagering among themselves rather than via a bookie. The new law failed to halt the targeted offtrack betting, because the wagering moved out of the gambling rooms into the streets and public houses, where it continued clandestinely. A generation later, Parliament passed the Betting Act of 1874, banning the publication or distribution of any materials promoting horse racing, but it had little impact on working-class wagering.[98]

Another big difference between American and British reform of horse-race gambling was that there was no single-minded American organization fighting racecourse wagering, as there was in Great Britain. In 1890 nonconformists, labor leaders, and such reformers as industrialist and social investigator Seebohm Rowntree, future Labour prime minister Ramsay MacDonald, and economist J. A Hobson established the National Anti-Gambling League, which primarily focused on fighting blue-collar wagering on horses. The NAGL was concerned about the recent growth of working-class gambling on racing, abetted by the growing number of profit-oriented tracks, rising real incomes, the growing racing press, and widespread illegal offtrack credit bookmaking. The society's critique of wagering was based less on morality than on the social effects of gambling and actually first focused on the bad example of elite betting rather than direct action against working-class gambling. The NAGL pressed Parliament, which led to an investigation by the House of Lords' Select Committee on Betting of 1901–2 and culminated in the 1906 Street Betting Act that permitted offtrack betting by well-off people (like members of Parliament) who could keep an account with large bookmakers and call in bets. The act barred cash bets, mainly affecting working-class punters (British gamblers, especially the ones wagering with book-makers), by making them subject to fines and imprisonment. The act also gave the police new powers to enforce the law. But the plan went for naught since there was so much neighborhood support for gambling that the police found it practically impossible to enforce the new edict. Furthermore, bookmakers and their local agents got around the law by relying on credit betting, which the act did not banish. In 1907 the authorities prosecuted 3,008 cases of illegal betting, but only eight men were imprisoned for violating the law.[99]

Racing around the world was rarely ever interrupted by national governments run by aristocrats and the extremely rich who shared a common culture that included an infatuation with the elite sport of thoroughbred racing and gambling. Racing in the British Empire outside of the UK and Canada, in Australia, Hong Kong, India, Ireland, Jamaica, Kenya, New Zealand, Singapore, and South Africa, occurred mainly at elite courses, where it was dominated by ex-pats and the local upper class. Thoroughbred racing was also popular in late-nineteenth-century Austria-Hungary, France, Italy, and Russia, as well as outside Europe in Argentina, Brazil, Chile, China, Egypt, and Mexico. But the history of racing was different in the United States.[100]

The American opponents of horse-race gambling focused their efforts almost entirely on local regimes. Ethnocultural moral issues in the United States such as prohibition, prostitution, and gambling were overwhelmingly dealt with at the state level. The absence of the federal government in regulating the turf placed the racing industry at a severe disadvantage. Gerrymandered state legislatures were heavily overrepresented and predominantly controlled by social conservatives from rural districts and small towns who were opposed to betting.[101] Tactically, the racetracks usually needed to secure new laws to protect their sport since most state laws opposed gambling. Racing foes won out by staying the course, putting pressure on local officials to carry out laws against on-track betting. Even in New York, New Jersey, and

Illinois, where betting at racecourses was at one time permitted, all the states eventually banned the sport. However, getting the authorities to halt offtrack betting was another story.

Conclusion

In 1893 the Washington Park Club organized one of the greatest meets in nineteenth-century racing in hopes of benefiting from the large number of tourists in Chicago for the Columbian Exposition. It was highlighted by the American Derby, one of the richest races for three-year-olds on American turf, drawing a reported record audience of about 47,000, and among the great social events of the year. The WPR itself outdrew the Chicago franchise of the National League (renamed the Colts in 1890), whose attendance was 223,500, about 3,605 a game). This amount was just 68.8 percent of the WPR's total. In addition, the proprietary Hawthorne track ran one of the longest meets in American racing history (259 dates), generating an attendance of approximately 777,000. By any statistical measure, thoroughbred racing was the favorite spectator pastime of Chicagoans. Yet the season drew a lot of caustic criticism from the press, especially the reform-minded *Daily News.*[102]

The 1894 racing season struggled in the midst of the depression, but there was enough optimism to allow the opening of the new suburban Harlem Track. But then the highly profitable and prestigious Washington Park closed because its directors and members, only a small proportion of whom were active horsemen or stable owners, did not have the will or the intestinal fortitude to stand up and fight the reformers. Most WPC members were mainly interested in the social aspects of club life and more leisurely sports, like golf and tennis, rather than horse racing. These upper-class Chicagoans had other ways to certify their status and demonstrate their manliness and were not prepared to go to the barricades to protect the sport, especially if it meant working with the entrepreneurs who ran the local proprietary tracks. By contrast, in New York, whose new state constitution of 1894 explicitly banned gambling at racetracks, the movers and shakers behind the elite tracks were deeply committed to their sport and successfully fought to keep it alive when doing so seemed impossible. Stockholders and directors of the major New York jockey clubs were far more committed to the sport than the men of the WPC. They were more likely to be breeders or racers, including some of the leading racing men in the entire United States, and had far stronger political influence. Elite horsemen like financier August Belmont Jr., son of the former chairman of the national Democratic Party and a prominent figure in the Democratic Party in his own right, went to work with powerful Tammany Hall leaders, including boss Richard Croker, himself a major stable owner, to save the sport by passing the innovative Percy-Gray Act in early May 1895 to circumvent the constitutional ban. The new law put thoroughbred racing under the supervision of the New York State Racing Commission, the first state sports regulatory agency, empowered to license tracks and divide racing dates in cooperation with The Jockey Club, a new voluntary organization based in New York City that was responsible for enforcing the rules for thoroughbred racing. It may have been the first time a state agency comanaged a public enterprise in partnership with a nongovernmental agency. Despite the retention of racing in New York, the closure of the wonderful Washington Park, one of the finest and most profitable elite racecourses, followed the end of racing in New Jersey and left the Chicago turf, and the American turf in general, on an unsteady footing.[103]

5

The Fall and Rebirth
of Chicago Racing, 1895–1899

The successful fight in 1894 against Washington Park, the closing of the New Jersey tracks, and the near collapse of racing in New York encouraged reformers in 1895 to step up their fight against the turf and the gambling menace. Illinois tracks were in their weakest legal position in nearly a decade, especially after a state supreme court ruling on January 15, 1895, confirmed Garfield Park secretary Joseph Swigert's 1892 conviction for running gambling at the course. He had been fined $100 by a justice of the peace, which the criminal court confirmed. The appellate ruling meant that bookmaking inside an Illinois track constituted a crime. Racetracks were recognized as gambling houses, making track officials automatically keepers of a gambling house. Corporation counsel John M. Palmer considered the decision a deathblow to racing since the ruling meant that the Gibbs Act was now certainly unconstitutional. However, most observers did not expect the racing situation to change, since they anticipated the legislature would rescue the beleaguered and desperate, albeit well-connected, operators of the Hawthorne and Harlem tracks. These observers turned out dead wrong because all Illinois tracks were closed in 1895. No one could predict the sport's future, but within a few years the Chicago tracks were back in business.[1]

THE LEGISLATURE AND RACING

In the mid-1890s, New York was unchallenged as the dominant center of thoroughbred racing because of the presence of such elite racecourses as upstate Saratoga Park, Sheepshead Bay in Brooklyn, and the Morris Park track in a part of Westchester, annexed to the Bronx in 1895. New York's elite tracks hosted most of the finest American stakes races that drew the best stables and top jockeys. There was also Brooklyn's Gravesend track, the leading commercial course in North America, and the lesser proprietary Aqueduct and Brighton Beach courses. As previously mentioned, the New York turf's legitimacy was severely threatened by the new 1894 state constitution, but politically powerful racing interests protected the sport through the Percy-Gray Act. However, few other state governments backed their local thoroughbred racing industry in the late nineteenth century.[2]

An ardent effort was made in Illinois by optimistic turf men when the general assembly convened in 1895 to support thoroughbred racing, but their lobbying ended up a failure. Several proracing measures were introduced in hopes of legalizing at least a minimum one-month meet at each local track without a foreign book, but all failed. Advocates were probably not realistic considering that the general assembly had just gone from predominantly Democratic, a nearly unique moment in nineteenth-century Illinois political history, to mainly Republican as per the norm. The incoming house was 92–61 Republican and the senate 33–18. Racing interests focused their attention on Senator John Humphrey's (R–Orland Park) bill introduced on February 27 that proposed that any association organized to improve the breed could hold race meetings for ninety days with betting on local and foreign races. Hawthorne and Harlem backed the bill, but the Washington Park Racetrack, which had already closed racing operations, and with a tradition of twenty-five-day meets, opposed long-term racing and did nothing to help the Humphrey bill.[3]

Senator Homer F. Aspinwall (R–Freeport) introduced a rival plan drawn up by the Civic Federation's attorney and Arthur Caton, president of the Northwestern Trotters Horse Breeders' Association (NTHBA), founded in 1885. Aspinwall's scheme as amended banned foreign books, limited pool selling and racing at fairgrounds to thirty days, and punished violators with fines up to $1,000 per day or thirty days in jail. The bill seemed to have substantial Republican support and was given a good chance to pass because it was drawn up in favor of harness-racing promoters. Many senators agreed with harness-track managers in midsize cities like Aurora and Rockford and in smaller towns who felt that races at county fairs, a popular rural tradition, merited special consideration.[4]

Humphrey's bill passed the senate on March 21, 27–18, though with just 11 pro votes from Cook County. The *Tribune* was shocked that the antigambling Republicans "would have the hardihood, nerve, gall, or whatever you please to call it, to vote for this foul proposition." The *Tribune* disputed the pro-Humphrey argument that the measure favored farmers and county-fair associations, pointing out that the bill was really in the interest of bookmakers, touts, and thoroughbred tracks in East St. Louis and Cook County. The Republican mouthpiece claimed that $100,000 might have been spent on gaining proracing votes by bookmaker and track operator Joe Ullman and by Chicago's Hankins crowd to protect their interests. The *Tribune* railed against the Civic Federation and its friends, who apparently made a deal to support the racing bill in return for votes for a civil-service bill that passed the senate.[5]

The *Tribune* interpreted the senate passage as "a continuation of the disaster and ruin these tracks have brought to many homes. It means defalcations, embezzlements, and, judging by the events of the past, murder. The enormity and infamy of this measure are beyond comprehension. . . . It is the most beastly bill that ever-achieved prominence in an Illinois Legislature." The *Tribune* warned that if the three-fifths Republican house approved it, the party would have a hard time in the next election, since the party would have forfeited its status as the ethical political party and defender of public morals.[6]

The Humphrey bill was sent to the house Livestock and Dairy Committee whose members were completely divided on it. The *Tribune* expected the committee to favorably report on that measure, and the tracks also anticipated the entire house would approve the bill. Moral crusaders, abetted by both the rural and the urban press, mobilized to block the bill. Fundamentalist clerics like Dr. P. B. Henson of Chicago's First Baptist Church delivered sermons against the racing bill, calling it one of the vilest and most corrupt pieces of legislation ever considered. He pointed out that many families were ruined by racetrack gambling, leading them to pawn their furniture and jewelry. R. W. Bland, secretary of the Chicago Preachers' Association of the Methodist Church, sent the assembly a copy of antiracing resolutions adopted in the name of 266 ministers and 100,000 Chicago church adherents. Concerned evangelical Chicago clergymen petitioned Democratic governor John P. Altgeld to veto the Humphrey bill should it pass the legislature.[7]

The collective opposition had a big impact, breaking the momentum behind the proracing proposals, and as a result the Humphrey bill languished in committee. At the start of June, racing and trotting interests met to break the logjam with a compromise bill to allow racing for sixty days without foreign books, but the prevailing ill will among racing men made it hard for them to form a cohesive alliance. The thoroughbred crowd believed that trotting men arranged a raid on Harlem in May and promised, in response, that if no favorable racing bill passed, they would fight pool selling at trotting tracks. The WPC no longer opposed the racing bill, but did nothing to advance it and continued to refuse to cooperate with Edward Corrigan or George Hankins, weakening support in Springfield for the proposed law. The *Tribune* thought that a $20,000–$30,000 "corruption fund" might be enough to ease the bill out of committee, an indication that the house had been bought by Chicago gamblers. However, the bill never made it to the floor.[8]

Legalized Racing as a Revenue Bill

On July 9, the Illinois General Assembly reconvened in a special revenue session. Chicago's three track managers tried to come up with a program to legalize race meets with betting, agreeing to support thirty-day meets. The proposal drew positive attention from various businessmen, including railroad managers, hotel keepers, restaurateurs, and saloonkeepers who benefited from the trade of sportsmen. The *Tribune* reported that "the sight of hundreds of people going to

Milwaukee daily and spending their good coin there . . . is a sight that makes the most conscientious of shopkeepers grimace with despair." The Great Northern Hotel's manager claimed the absence of racing cost his inn $1,000 a week and Chicago businessmen $40,000–$50,000 a week. The *Tribune* responded critically, indicating that any hotel dependent on "the patronage of racetrack gamblers, touts, blacklegs, and swindlers for a continued existence" should be shut down.[9]

A number of new bills were drawn up to legalize racing, with Representative Lawrence Kilcourse's (R–Chicago) proposal the most passable. He created a sensation by introducing a racetrack pool-selling measure cloaked under the guise of a revenue bill, seeking sixty-day meets with regulated pool selling and a 3 percent tax on paid admissions. The *Tribune* strongly opposed the bill as an entering wedge to legalize faro, craps, and poker. The bill died in committee.[10]

The racing outlook was becoming desperate. Chicago racing appeared to be "Dead as a Door nail," with negative repercussions for the economy. According to one racing man, "Never within the last fifteen years has Chicago been so dead as at present. . . . Without a race meeting going on there is nothing to draw transients to the city." This argument foretells the rhetoric of contemporary sports promoters justifying municipal support for their private sports businesses as venues to generate revenue from tourists and locals looking for a fun time.[11]

THE 1895 RACING SEASON

The problematic situation in Chicagoland racing encouraged local turf men that winter to focus some attention on Northwest Indiana, where Roby and the nearby gambling houses were opposed by Democratic governor Claude Matthews and the Civic Federation. Matthews, a leading candidate for the Democratic nomination for president, lost on the sixth ballot to William Jennings Bryan, who delivered an electric address at the convention. Matthews was warned his political career would be destroyed if he continued fighting Roby. James M. Sellers (D–Crawfordsville) introduced into the legislature Matthews's plan limiting racing to three fifteen-day meets at any single track, banning a club from sponsoring more than three meets that had to be sixty days apart, and proscribing winter racing. The measure passed the legislature, and Matthews signed it.[12]

The Indiana racing season began in mid-April with racing sponsored by the Roby Fair Association. Then James O'Leary and his associates in the Roby Breeders' Association secured a fifteen-day lease from track owner Edward Roby beginning on May 2 that they subleased to President Louis Tolman of the Hammond Fair Association. This sublease was a sham because Tolman worked for O'Leary, and his staff was identical to the RBA.[13]

The Suburban Tracks

Hawthorne and Harlem picked up Washington Park's lost racing dates and some of its stakes events. Hawthorne staged the Chicago Derby and boosted its value from $5,000 to $25,000, Harlem ran the $20,000 National Derby, but the prestigious American Derby was discontinued. The successful fight against Washington Park invigorated reformers' desires to further curtail racing and betting, and the area's two remaining tracks soon found themselves in trouble.[14]

The upgraded Hawthorne course opened for business on May 1. Management dropped for a couple of days the normal $1 admission fee to the grounds and grandstand to forestall a rumored raid. This free admission helped build the audience to around three thousand. Fans traveling from downtown by the Illinois Central or the Chicago, Burlington & Quincy paid 25 cents for their round-trip ride. On May 10, a free date, the Civic Federation raided Hawthorne. The Roby crowd supported the raid, retaliating for Corrigan's decisions to stage a competing meet in May and for blocking Western Union transmission of his race results to Roby. The CF's warrants were based on evidence amassed by its investigative agents on track gambling, no longer protected since the *Swigert* decision overturned the Gibbs Act. The raid was led by William T. Baker, president of the Chicago Board of Trade and the former chief executive of the World's Fair, and abetted by former Illinois attorney general George Hunt, an attorney for the

CF, Chief Deputy Sheriff Charles W. Peters, and 175 newly sworn-in sheriff's deputies. Corrigan, Brenock, Ullman, and 28 others were arrested. The next day, admission was reset at 50 cents.[15]

The two suburban Chicago tracks responded to the raid by calling for the closing of the Board of Trade, which they claimed was the greatest gambling institution in the United States. The next day only 1,200 spectators made it to Hawthorne, and bookies had little action. No admission was charged on the third day so the track could be more competitive with Roby, and Hawthorne attracted 3,000 fans and 20 bookmakers. The CF staged another raid on May 11 with 175 deputies. Thirty-one people were arrested, including Corrigan, Brenock, and Ullman, and the bookies closed their stands. Afterward, the track announced it was suspending events for two weeks in anticipation of a new racing bill being passed.[16]

Harlem opened a couple of days later with many misgivings, having just built a $300,000 track that cost $2,500 a day to operate. Its management followed closely the racing situation in New York, where local tracks had circumvented the ban on gambling in the new state constitution through the Percy-Gray Act.[17]

The Harlem Jockey Club tried to survive by compromising with its critics, cutting out the foreign book, and altering the betting format. Bookmakers used markers to bet with people they knew well and settled up after the races or else used the English system of oral betting in which no cash changed hands until the next day. Harlem was so worried when the CF took out new warrants that it closed indefinitely on May 16. This closure meant a potential significant financial loss for the town that had already gotten about $10,000 from the Chicago Fair Grounds Association for the right to operate, covering the cost of such essential public services as street paving, sewers, and police.[18]

Hawthorne resumed racing on June 4 with a free gate that drew 2,500. The 7 bookmakers, two field books, and a combination book encountered no interference. The disappointed *Tribune* attributed the resumption of betting to the grand jury's recent failure to indict bettors recently arrested there and encouraged the CF to continue its fight because "wives and children have had the benefit of wages which otherwise would have been squandered at Hawthorne or at Harlem."[19]

Ten days later, George Hunt sought a permanent injunction against Hawthorne barring any gambling at the track. The court ruled on June 14 that the Chase Act did not affirmatively allow gambling, and so Section 127 of the criminal code that banned gambling was still in effect. Then on June 22, the grand jury issued indictments against Corrigan and Brenock and dozens of bookmakers, including Ullman, George Hankins, and Sid McHie. The tracks saw they were knocking their heads against the wall with no relief in sight. So, two days later, Hawthorne and Harlem declared all 1895 stakes off, which seemed to mark the end of Chicago racing.[20]

Negative national repercussions were anticipated. George Hankins asserted that Chicago's closure would cut the value of American horses by at least $100 million. Harlem's secretary Joseph A. Murphy saw the impact first at Tattersall's, a $300,000 sporting arena (Sixteenth and Dearborn) built in 1891 for horse shows, political conventions, and prizefights. Sports bettors commonly met there to settle their wagers. Following the end of Chicago racing, the value of Tattersall's average horse sale dropped from $500 a head to $50–$75. Racing experts figured that the sport in Chicago would not resume for two or three years. The end of racing also led to the temporary closing of the four-page *Daily Racing Form*, first published in Chicago on November 17, 1894, by former *Tribune* journalist Frank Brunell. The paper focused exclusively on racing, with news stories, gossip, and the first horse-racing charts ever published. Brunell resumed publication in 1896, and the *Racing Form* went on to become the turf's paper of record.[21]

The apparent end of racing in Chicago gave impetus to meets in Detroit, Milwaukee, and Kenosha, Wisconsin. Kenosha's four-thousand-seat Ideal Track, fifty miles from the Windy City, was run by Chicago bookies, and Milwaukee's track was run by gamblers Charles S. Bush and Henry Johnson, who had previously controlled the betting at Washington Park. They had spent $30,000 a few years earlier to convert a site in suburban West Allis, where there had been horse racing since 1876 and was used for the state fair since 1892, into a modest racing plant. Their two-week meet was comparable to Roby, but with lower-quality horses and jockeys. Chicagoans got to the track by boat or a ninety-seven-mile, two-hour special train from the Loop directly to the track gates for $2.50, which included a $1 admission ticket. However, the racing there was short-lived because the state passed an antigambling law halting it in 1897.[22]

Despite the turf's political failures in Springfield, the Harlem course ran an experimental meet beginning on August 8, charging 50 cents for admission, with five $200 races each day. The track hoped to daily draw a few thousand fans and pay expenses from the gate and concessions, but expectations went unrealized. Five handbooks took bets, including Joe Ullman, without the track's approval, publicizing their odds on a large blackboard and limiting transactions for strangers to cash. Spectators could also bet with betting commissioners or wire wagers via Western Union to a Covington, Kentucky, bookmaker.[23]

On August 14, the Civic Federation secured an injunction from Justice Walter Gibbons, restraining gambling and betting at Harlem. Two days later, the Harlem Jockey Club ended its meet after losing about $8,000 and averaged only around a thousand spectators a day. Harlem announced it would be closed until 1897. The track tried unsuccessfully to dissolve the injunction, claiming the court had no jurisdiction and was engaging in improper interference with the rights of a corporation.[24]

The *Spirit* was greatly disappointed by the demise of Chicago racing, blaming ill-advised actions regarding racing legislation that aroused public hostility, and the deepened, intensified press opposition, for creating adverse conditions for the turf. The weekly thought it was bizarre for Chicagoans to question racetrack gambling while investors at the Board of Trade "can bet tens of thousands that wheat or corn will go up or down, and no questions are asked as to whether the transaction is a gamble, pure and simple. But just offer a $2 bet on a Chicago race-track and one is promptly gobbled for doing a criminal act."[25]

The antiracing *Daily News*, on the other hand, exulted in the outcome. It attributed the collapse of racing to greedy track managers, the impact of the *Swigert* case, and raids that enforced the antigambling laws. The paper claimed that racing was more of a legal question in Illinois than in New Jersey and New York, which both had more legislation regulating the turf than any other sports and where, unlike other athletic activities, "thoroughbred racing has become almost hopelessly mixed up with politics."[26]

The ending of Chicago racing encouraged Edward Corrigan to focus his attention elsewhere, but not back east, where he was reviled. In 1890 Corrigan purchased Huron from the prestigious Belle Meade stud and entered him in the upcoming Lawrence Futurity. However, the stewards of the Coney Island Jockey Club ruled that since Huron's previous owner had withdrawn him from the race, he could not compete under Corrigan's colors. His well-known attorneys William F. Howe and Abraham Hummel, two of New York's leading criminal lawyers, secured an injunction that got the horse into the 1891 race, and he came in second by a neck. However, the CIJC did not recognize the outcome, refused to pay Corrigan the second-place money, and barred his stable from the Sheepshead Bay track for suing the jockey club. Corrigan then got a restraining order, claiming the CIJC had stigmatized him and deprived him of a chance to race at New York tracks through its influence with the Board of Control, the agency that ran eastern racing before the founding of The Jockey Club. The case ended up in superior court, which ruled against Corrigan because the Board of Control was not a quasi-public operation, like a utility company, but a private corporation and was free to choose its own way to do business.[27]

The *New York Times* in 1895 claimed that Corrigan, along with New York poolroom king Peter De Lacy, had done more to bring thoroughbred racing into dispute than anyone, except for Guttenberg's Big Four, the machine politicians who ran that corrupt New Jersey track, located just nine miles from Midtown Manhattan. Corrigan was "a pugnacious and vindictive representative of the lowest type of the men who have infested the turf—a true type of the turf gambler, for whom no one had the least respect." Corrigan and his allies "brought the sport into such disrepute that the organization of respectable citizens known as the Civic Federation was brought into being to crush him and his *allies out of existence*." The *Times* urged New York turf men to avoid Corrigan's Ingleside track and hoped that he would be forced out of that track, just as President Gottfried Walbaum, a bookmaker with important political connections, had been forced out of Guttenberg. Corrigan admitted a long-standing friendship with Peter De Lacy, the millionaire "poolroom king" of New York, but denied encouraging him in his war with The Jockey Club to promote offtrack gambling. Furthermore, Corrigan objected to the negative caricature because his Hawthorne racing "was clean and decent, and the objectionable characters that went there were very few compared with the hordes that frequented other tracks."[28]

The closing of the Chicago racetracks left local racing interests in disarray. The main hope for restoring racing seemed to lie with new laws, but the legislature would not meet again until 1897. The racing crowd had to be satisfied with third-rate tracks in Indiana or Wisconsin. But the shuttered racetracks did not mean the death of offtrack gambling, whose political connections kept them running. Reformers kept an eye on the gambling scene but were also busy trying to clean up other vices, especially prostitution, while fighting Chicago's corrupt political machines, especially the "Grey Wolves" on the city council.[29]

Chicago Gamblers Look Eastward

Harlem's demise left western Indiana with a monopoly of racing in metropolitan Chicago. In July the Indiana Supreme Court sustained the Sellers Act, passed earlier in the year. The judges clarified the act that stated a track owner could not sublet his track to other parties to circumvent the law and hold additional meets there. This ruling led to court injunctions against racing at Roby, a raid on August 24, and arrests of several Chicago bookmakers. Hankins, Condon, and other Chicagoans then decided to circumvent the Indiana gambling rules, establishing a new corporation in September, the Lakeside Jockey Club, which got a three-year lease on the Roby track for $12,000 a year and the option to buy the track for $280,000.[30]

Chicago racing men and certain Whiting residents came up with another ploy in September to promote racing by leasing 150 acres from Jacob Forsyth near the state line, one-half mile from Roby, where they set up the new three-quarter-mile Forsyth course. Then at the end of the month, a third syndicate course opened in Hammond, the mile-long Sheffield Racetrack, managed by Hankins and backed by John Brenock and John Burke. It had primitive amenities, but the breezes off Lake Michigan made the facility more bearable in the heat than the other Indiana courses. These three tracks drew as many as five thousand spectators to their races.[31]

Thereafter, Indiana racing went on nearly continuously, moving every fifteen racing days to another site. These tracks made their money primarily from the foreign book, which made about $1,000 a day. In May 1896, Governor Claude Matthews and Attorney General William A. Ketchum moved on Lake County's "infected district." Ketchum took the tracks to trial and convinced the Indiana Supreme Court that even though the three tracks had different stockholders, they were essentially one and the same operation, run by the same people, with the same racing judges, bookmakers, and horses. The court agreed, and the tracks soon closed. However, one year later, Ketchum determined the tracks were located several miles apart and decided not to interfere with the Lake County racetracks.[32]

HARPER'S WEEKLY AND THE REPUTATION OF THE WASHINGTON PARK CLUB

While in 1896 the WPC had been closed for two years, it still had an outstanding national standing. It was the subject of an extremely glowing evaluation by Chicago-reared author H. C. Chatfield-Taylor in the highly respected *Harper's Weekly: A Journal of Civilization*, one of the most important periodicals of the late nineteenth century. The weekly was founded in 1857 primarily as a political magazine, but was also well known for covering foreign news, topical essays, humor, and fiction. It was heavily illustrated to appeal to both the educated and the less literate, reaching a circulation of about 160,000 in 1870. One of its main missions was to promote modern values to its readership.[33]

Chatfield-Taylor pointed out that the WPC was founded when "a country club or a club for out-of-door sports was unknown in Chicago" and provided a model for the creation of upper- and upper-middle-class country, golf, and cycling clubs. He admired how its superb race meets immediately drew huge crowds and how Derby Day "once became the great function of the year."

> Until its opening society had been without a gathering-place, and it may be safely asserted that with the inauguration of the Washington Park Club, Chicago laid aside the garb of an overgrown village and began to assume the aspect of a great city. . . . Probably no race-course in America has ever, from a purely social stand point, attained the prominence of the Washington Park Club. The scene on the lawn before the club-house became almost comparable with the enclosure at Ascot or the lawn at Goodwood [prestigious British racecourses], while as many as fifty thousand spectators crowded the grand stand and paddock.

Harper's deplored the track's closure owing to unwise decisions by the state legislature. But the club remained open year-round for coaching and sleighing parties. In 1894 younger members set up the Chicago Polo Club and developed an excellent field for play, abetted by parties drawing other members and ladies. One year later, the WPC established a nine-hole golf course, thereby turning a racing club into a uniquely accessible "full-fledged country club" inside the city limits.[34]

Bringing Racing Back to Chicago

As the 1896 racing season came to an end, the outlook for Chicago racing looked dismal. The Chicago Racing Association management was in total disarray and held its first board meeting in four years. Corrigan's partners believed that he used his complete and secretive control of its assets for his personal ends. Ed's conflict with Brenock and the Burkes dated back to the fall of 1894, when Corrigan approved a $50,000 loan by the CRA to his partners, backed by their racetrack stock, to buy cattle from meatpacker Samuel W. Allerton. Eighteen months later, they still owed $29,000. Then in early 1895, Brenock invested $25,000 in the Forsyth racetrack in partnership with John Condon, Corrigan's bitter enemy, which only worsened their relationship. Corrigan gained some revenge in 1897 when he convinced the American Turf Congress to require all Chicago-area tracks to offer purses of at least $400, too expensive for the Forsyth course.[35]

When the board meeting began on September 21, Brenock asked Corrigan to submit a thorough financial statement, which Corrigan refused, as he had in the past. Corrigan shortly thereafter drew a pistol and pointed it at his associate, who left the meeting with the Burkes. Brenock soon instituted several unsuccessful lawsuits against Corrigan, including one seeking to place the track under receivership because he claimed Corrigan had taken at least $70,000 from the CRA for his personal use to fight racetrack opposition and secure a racing bill. Such expenditures were hardly for "personal use," but were necessary expenses for a jockey club amid a struggle.[36]

The racing situation only worsened when in December the NTHBA, which had paid out more than $650,000 promoting harness racing in its twelve years in operation, announced it was closing. It had lost $12,500 in the past two years and would not stay on unless the legislature passed a bill allowing pools at race meets.[37]

The Legislature and the Fight to Restore Racing

Despite recent setbacks, racing fans were optimistic in early 1897 about the renewal of racing, partly fed by rumors that traction mogul Charles T. Yerkes, who was involved in trying to get the city council to extend the length of his streetcar franchises, planned to build a racetrack to generate business for his North Side line and use his clout to secure proracing laws to protect his investment. Yerkes never built a track, but in the late nineteenth century streetcar lines often operated or helped finance baseball parks and amusement parks to promote traffic along their routes.[38]

The *Spirit* in February called on the WPC to take the initiative to secure proracing laws, but it seemed uninterested. WPC secretary James Howard reminded the *Spirit* that the club's objective was "good fellowship among its members" and that racing was secondary. He pointed out that "while the majority of our members are enthusiastic supporters of racing, there is a considerable element in the club which cares little for it. . . . The club is thriving as an organization and anyone . . . who imagines that the stopping of racing affects the success of the club is deluded." Howard asserted that the facility was becoming more like a big country club and had dropped racing "because we felt we could no longer afford to be made a target of by those whose only interests in the sport was mercenary, and whose vicious tendencies prompted them to attack us and thereby destroy racing altogether in this state." He asserted that the club did not intend to lobby for legalized racing and had no plans to resume racing until the sport was legitimized.[39]

Despite Howard's pronouncement, the political battle over horse racing quickly heated up in Springfield, where a number of bills were introduced to legalize horse racing with on-course gambling that would raise money for the state by taxing the tracks. These bills were designed as revenue measures that would appeal to taxpayers concerned about the state's need for money. Senator Patrick V. Fitzpatrick (R–Cook County) drew up a promising bill in January on behalf of the NTHBA, and the presumed backing of the WPC, which shared members with the harness group. Fitzpatrick proposed a 2 percent tax on track gross receipts, thirty days of racing at each track, and the banning of pools on foreign races. This proposal was different from the Missouri Breeders' Law passed later that year that ostensibly sought to promote the breed and racing, while barring offtrack betting by legitimizing horse betting only at racetracks with a state-licensed bookmaker.[40]

Senator Fred E. Harding (R–Monmouth) introduced a proposal on March 10 to allow corporations organized to hold competitive horse races of "speed and endurance" to make books and sell pools. He called for a 4 percent tax of their gross, with 75 percent going to agricultural societies and the rest toward state-fair prizes. Representative Lawrence Kilcourse (R–Chicago) offered a bill that called for sixty days of afternoon racing at mile-long tracks from May to November where books and pools were permitted for a modest $50 daily fee to the state and 2 percent of the gross to the home county. Offtrack bookmakers or pool sellers would be banned, with violators fined a minimum of $200 and 30–180 days in jail. Kilcourse's bill was supported by Hawthorne and the old Garfield Park crowd, several of whom were highly visible in Springfield. The License Committee favorably reported his bill after amending the length of meets to thirty days.[41]

On May 5, Senator Patrick V. Fitzgerald (R–Cook County) introduced a bill to license pool selling at track meetings of thirty days or less between May and November, with a 5 percent tax on gate receipts. It was similar to the other proposals, but considered the best deal for the state and most likely to pass. All Chicago racing interests endorsed this bill that the Livestock and Dairy Committee amended to proscribe winter and evening racing and lower the tax to 2 percent. Horse owners who had forgone millions of dollars in lost purses and breeders fees and suffered at least a 40 percent drop in prices since 1894 supported the bill. So did hoteliers and other businessmen who claimed that Chicago merchants had lost $5 million a year in trade because of Washington Park's closure.[42]

The Fitzpatrick bill seemed on the way to passage in the senate, but expectations were low in the house, where Speaker Edward C. Curtis (R–Kankakee) was geared to block it. However, the measure never got that far, going down to a stunning 32–9 defeat in the Republican-controlled senate. Fitzpatrick blamed the debacle on the presence of too many antiracing Christians in Chicago, but others thought that Indiana money was generously employed to block the bill to prevent competition with its tracks. The "out-of-state money" came from Chicago bookmakers operating in Indiana. Many legislators were also rankled by the opening of a bookie-controlled track in Joliet. The *Spirit* blamed Fitzgerald's defeat on the corrupt political system in

Springfield that acclimated corrupt state legislators to expect huge bribes to support legislation, such as the reportedly $250,000 spent to support gas company consolidation and the $750,000 behind the Allen Street bill authorizing the Chicago City Council to extend Charles Yerkes's streetcar lease for fifty years.[43]

Racing and the 1897 Mayoral Election

Horse racing played a notable role in the 1897 mayoralty election. The main Democratic contender was Democrat Carter H. Harrison II, graduate of Yale Law School, who helped run the *Chicago Times* with his brother. The leading Republicans' options were jurist Nathaniel C. Sears, an organization candidate selected by "Blond Boss" William Lorimer's faction, detested for supporting Charles Yerkes's traction interests, and independent Republican patrician John Maynard Harlan, a lawyer and city councilman. His father and son, both named John Marshall Harlan, were both justices of the US Supreme Court. Harlan, who advocated political, moral, and social reforms, supported tighter regulation of traction companies, closing saloons on Sundays, and halting gambling, won Lorimer's support. He was also backed by the prestigious Municipal Voters League, renowned for its recent fight against the "Grey Wolves," including Coughlin, Kenna, and Powers, who enriched themselves by helping award electrical, gas, telephone, and transit franchises to private businesses. The MVL was formed in response to the Grey Wolves awarding a franchise in 1895 to Ogden Gas, a paper company, to pressure the current franchise holder to buy up the rights to operate.[44]

The politically inexperienced Harrison was popular among his father's working-class supporters, spoke to his German constituents in their own tongue (he was educated in Germany), and attended a Catholic church with his Catholic wife. He curried favor with athletes by participating in hundred-mile bicycle races and promised to support cyclists' political interests, such as building good roads. Harrison positioned himself as a populist, yet worked closely with

Democratic-machine politicians. Coughlin, Powers, and McDonald considered him "one of the boys," a supporter of a wide-open city, who would not suppress gambling and opposed political changes pushed by the National Municipal League. Turf fans hoped that Harrison's election would mean an end to puritan rule and the passage of a law legalizing horse racing.[45]

After Harrison won the Democratic nomination with heavy machine support, over Alfred S. Trude, the renowned criminal attorney, the *Tribune* bitterly noted, with a little exaggeration, "Never in the history of Chicago have the gamblers and the interests allied with them—saloon men and racetrack people—taken as active an interest in politics as they are showing in the spring election." Though Harrison did not acknowledge the gamblers' support, they were so confident before the general election that a number returned to their old haunts, while options were already being sought on prime potential sites for gambling halls. John Condon, for instance, reopened his old headquarters at 110 North Clark Street, and George Hankins re-leased his old location over Mike McDonald's "Store."[46]

Harrison won a hard-fought election with a huge majority. He captured a plurality of the vote (50.2 percent), handily defeating Harlan (23.5 percent) and Sears (20.1 percent), who split the Republican ticket. The *Spirit* interpreted Harrison's election less as a victory for the Democratic machine than as an impressive social statement by the electorate that boded well for Chicago racing: "The . . . Democratic victory in Chicago is almost universally recognized as a popular protest . . . against a Puritanical regime that was repressive in its intolerance and repugnant to individual liberty and freedom" and encouraged support for a proracing bill in Springfield.[47]

Harrison did not immediately cozy up with the sporting crowd upon taking office. Nonetheless, scores of gambling rooms opened and operated without interruption except for faro and craps, which the police considered too gross to be allowed. In late July, Harrison had Police Superintendent Joseph Kipley order George Hankins to close his new poolroom and betting parlor or face a raid, a signal to other gamblers to keep their operations more clandestine. This closure marked the end of Hankins as a major force in gambling circles. Hankins, always among the more aggressive gamblers, had gone broke in 1896 and turned over his property, including $1.3 million in real estate, to Mike McDonald to pay off his debts. He also divided up the renowned Hankins-Johnson stable, with Johnson taking the racing horses, while Hankins kept the Kentucky breeding farm.[48]

McDonald had remained active in politics after the demise of the Garfield Park racetrack, supporting John P. Altgeld's drive for governor. His patronage army of saloon Democrats and gamblers worked ardently for the candidate, and his *Globe* was the strongest pro-Altgeld English-language paper. He kept his spot as Eleventh Ward representative to the Cook Country Democratic Party until the end of 1892. However, he and the elder Harrison had never reconciled. McDonald got out of the gambling business, but always remained available to help his old friends, especially when it came to posting bond to get them out of jail. When Mike died in 1907, he was worth about $1.5 million, the equivalent of about $41,346,000 today. By contrast, many of his famous peers in the gambling business ended up broke.[49]

A Racing Experiment in Joliet

The sport of kings returned to Illinois on May 19, 1897, at Joliet's Ingalls Park, previously the site of two years of uninterrupted trotting races. L. E. Ingalls, a prominent real-estate agent and partner in the Joliet Economy Light and Power Company, built the track in 1892 at a site two and a half miles from the center of town and about thirty-five miles from Chicago, an hour by train. R. L. Allen, former secretary of the Chicago Fair and Trotting Breeders' Association, a former warden at the Joliet penitentiary, and an ex-employee of Ingalls, was course superintendent. Chicagoans reached the track via rail lines that ran right past the track. The *Tribune* rated it the equal of "any race track in the State, except in its buildings." The grandstand was four hundred feet long, with three thousand chairs and room for a thousand more. Ingalls Park was notable for the racetrack bed, composed of blocks of sod twelve inches square and two inches thick, covered with four inches of black loam, which was previously employed only at the $100,000 Narragansett Park, the fast trotting surface in Providence, Rhode Island.[50]

The Joliet meet was promoted by the same men who operated Indiana's tracks, including John Condon, Bob Allen, and John Brenock, who paid Ingalls $200 a day in rent. The "boys" were closely connected to the Will County sheriff and prosecutor who did not interfere with their operations. Money was said to have changed hands to clinch the deal. A lively meet opened with five races, employing horses drawn from the recently concluded races at Forsyth. Opening day drew 2,000 spectators from Chicago and 150 from Joliet and Will County, including local farmers and their families who sat in their vehicles, like at county fairs. There were 9 bookmakers, two field books, a combination book, and a thriving foreign book.[51]

The fifteen-day meet was comparable to the Roby-Gloucester-Guttenberg meets, which meant the quality of the horses was modest and the integrity of the races questionable. Chicago turf men were rankled that there was racing outside the metropolitan area, but not in Chicago or its suburbs. The Joliet community benefited directly from the track's presence. Farmers sold oats and hay to the racing stables, and about 600 residents worked at the track, spending money in town for food, shelter, recreation, and other personal needs. The track sold only lemonade and soda pop, leaving a lot of business for local saloonkeepers.[52]

RACING RETURNS TO THE WINDY CITY

Harlem's owners decided to reopen in the summer with little fanfare, encouraged by the election of Mayor Carter Harrison II and the uninterrupted meet at Joliet. The *Spirit* anticipated no local or state interference, leaving the Civic Federation as the main opponent. The business dealings at this time were more than a bit murky. On July 3, President William Martin of the CFGA sold the eighty-acre Harlem course to attorney William H. Allen for $150,000. Allen then leased the track to James Anglin, a front for the syndicate that had run Harlem in the past and more recently the Joliet and Indiana tracks. John Condon became general manager and journalist Martin Nathanson secretary. Allen soon sold the track to Paddy Ryan, who after the season sold it to Condon for $180,000. These machinations were probably intended to circumvent some old Harlem debts and injunctions. The conventional wisdom was that despite the failure to get a proracing bill out of the general assembly, there would be no interference from racing opponents, including the financially strapped CF, unless neighborhood residents took the initiative.[53]

The Harlem track surface required considerable preparation after two years of inactivity before reopening on July 14. The *Spirit* reveled at the revival of what it considered a beautiful facility, which boded well for Chicago, "the [future] Mecca for Western turfmen." The *Tribune* was also upbeat because of its high regard for presiding judge M. Lewis Clark, the twenty-minute special train ride from downtown, and the special police appointed by the township of Proviso to guard the track. Its main concern was the absence of quality horses because out-of-town stable owners were unsure the meet would go on. However, there were eventually about five hundred horses at the track.[54]

Opening day at Harlem drew just four thousand spectators, a big disappointment given high press expectations and management's ardent promotional efforts, including giving hotels thousands of complimentary tickets for their "sportively inclined" guests. About a dozen bookmakers were present, including O'Leary, who operated a foreign book with action on races at Brighton Beach, at the Oakley racetrack opened in 1889 named after its Cincinnati neighborhood, the St. Louis courses, and the Canadian tracks at Fort Erie (five miles from Buffalo) and Windsor (three miles from Detroit).[55]

Management further tried to bolster attendance by paying Edward Corrigan $9,000 to keep Hawthorne closed and promise not to embarrass Harlem. In the meantime, Corrigan's irate partners, Brenock and the Burke brothers, acquired a 25 percent interest in Harlem. The American Turf Congress meeting in late July approved important rule changes, including banning foreign books and requiring minimum

$400 purses, supposedly aimed at the Newport, Rhode Island, and Harlem tracks. Two months later, the American Turf Congress readmitted Washington Park and Hawthorne, which had lost their memberships after not operating for three seasons and two seasons, respectively. Colonel Clark went to the meeting worried the CFGA would not be readmitted to ATC membership, having only recently paid back entrance money for its canceled 1895 stakes events. Clark and Corrigan got into quite a contretemps there after Clark asserted that Corrigan was not keeping to his agreement to not hamper Harlem because he had proposed rule changes Clark opposed. Corrigan and Clark started calling each other liars, and then Clark, who had a violent history, pulled out a revolver and threatened Corrigan.[56]

On August 4, the Harlem Track inaugurated Ladies' Day to further bolster attendance and elevate its status and repeated it one week later. The custom began in Atlanta in 1886 at the Peach City's Minor League ballpark, when women were allowed in free when attending with a male escort. The *Chicago Evening Journal* gushed over the marvelous experiment: "The spacious grand stand was filled with interesting and wholesome looking family groups entering into thorough enjoyment of the races, filling their lungs with the fresh prairie air, and listening to the music of Banks Cregier's really excellent orchestra. There is no pleasanter spot in Cook County for a day's outing."[57]

Three days later, when new ATC rules went into effect, Harlem had 2,912 admissions, including 536 complimentary tickets (18.4 percent), producing a paid gate of $1,782. The *Tribune* estimated Harlem's daily expenses would be $2,400, consisting of $400 for salaries and other general expenses and $2,000 for added purse money (another $400 was contributed by bookmakers; see table 7). Purses for the eighty-nine-day meet came to $214,450. The *Tribune* conservatively projected that a Harlem audience of 1,500 paying $0.75 for admission would bring in $1,125; gamblers' fees, $1,800; the sale of race results to poolrooms, $500 (considerably below the $800-plus level at similar completed tracks); and other fees, $400. The daily fees amounted to $3,825, which less the $2,400 in expenses produced a daily profit of $1,425, or $126,825 for the entire meet.[58]

Table 7

Anticipated Harlem Racetrack Daily Gross Income and Expenses, 1897

Expenses

General expenses	$400
Purses	2,000
Total	$2,400

Receipts

Admissions (1,500 @ $0.75)	$1,125
Bookies (15 @ $100)	1,500
Field book	300
Refreshment privileges	250
Programs and smaller privileges	150
Information sold to poolrooms (50 @ $10)	500
Total receipts	$3,825
Total profits	$1,425

Source: *Chicago Tribune*, August 2, 1897, 4-5.

The 1897 season did not end up with Chicago's three racetracks on good terms. In September, Washington Park and Hawthorne were among the six out of fourteen tracks that voted to keep Harlem out of the ATC because of "jealousies and rivalries." Members remembered that Colonel Clark had denounced the ATC president when Harlem's membership bid first came up and how he had threatened Corrigan.[59]

The *Spirit* considered the meet well run, decorous, and free of ruffianism, unlike the riotous behavior of the Board of Trade, where "cold blooded gambling is . . . allowed in the commercial exchange and bucket shops. Why should the racetrack, with its salubrious, exhilarating enjoyment, be placed under ban?" Condon's obituary claimed he made $1 million during the three months of racing, which seems a big exaggeration given the *Tribune* statistics.[60]

Chicago racing seemed primed for the future at the end of 1897 when Mayor Harrison announced his support of first-class racing and gambling because it would be a harmless boost to the local economy. He further proposed that the best thing for the town would be a thirty-day meet at Washington Park. According to Harrison:

> It would be worth $1,000,000 annually to the city and it would not hurt a soul. . . . It will shock some of the goody-good people, but such a race meets right here in Chicago, run the right way, would be a wonderful thing for the city.
>
> I tell you we are getting too goody-goody in these parts. There is such a thing as killing yourself with your own virtue. . . . Chicago needs an awakening and a first-class race meet is something that would make better times in every way.
>
> Suppose the boys did bet a few dollars at the races. If they can't do it at Washington Park they will at Harlem or in Indiana, or they'll go East and spend it at the race there. Rest assured that a man who is going to spend his money the wrong way won't be kept from doing it by putting a high board fence around the city. What's the use of going to a horse race unless you spend a couple of dollars on a bet? I wouldn't go if I couldn't.[61]

The Reopening of Washington Park

State senator Patrick V. Fitzgerald's revised his old bill to legitimize racing for the 1898 legislative session, proposing a seven-month racing season starting on May 1, with forty-five-day meets, a 5 percent tax on gross receipts, and betting on the premises, but no foreign books or evening races. Racing men, as always, expected it to pass, especially since it seemed the tracks were unified behind the bill. However, the WPC did not go to bat for the bill, which died in committee. Club member Will J. Davis, manager of several prominent Chicago theaters, favored the proposal because halting racing "has cost the city millions." Furthermore, it reflected poorly on American intelligence that "with all our vaunted superiority over Europe, we cannot use what common sense we have and properly regulate instead of killing a sport that appeals to every class of people and is second to none in popularity."[62]

Despite the setback, the tracks' plans for a vigorous racing season went on unabated. In March, Condon's syndicate announced it would begin the spring season in early May at Lakeside. Then on April 7 came the news local and national horsemen were awaiting—the unanimous vote by WPR directors to reopen Washington Park. The board never explained its reasons, but was undoubtedly convinced that reopening would dramatically enhance the club's prestige, be very lucrative, and encounter little or no interference from the authorities or reform groups like the Civic Federation that had more pressing issues than gambling on their mind.[63]

The club planned a scaled-down meet with modest daily purses of at least $400 a race, like at Harlem, and just a $10,000 American Derby. Condon bought the betting privileges for $60,000. The directors were not worried about violating gambling laws since the gamblers would copy the popular eastern model of betting without bookmakers' stands or slates, with no cash passing hands, and settling bets off-course, thereby circumventing the penal codes. The *Spirit* figured Mayor Harrison and other Chicago leaders would raise no objections because "no association in the country did more for the cause of sport through the high-toned liberal policy of its officials."[64]

Edward Corrigan, who had been in San Francisco operating his Ingleside Racetrack, announced the reopening of Hawthorne after the WPR meet. This news was not well received in the racing community because his fellow horsemen detested him for regularly entering his own steeds in races below their class to gain easy victories and gambling coups. Corrigan was also on the outs with Yerkes and other prominent streetcar executives who had urged Condon, whose track generated a lot of traffic, to buy Hawthorne. The traction operators knew Corrigan would never sell to his old enemy, so they schemed to negotiate through John W. "Bet-a-Million" Gates, the barbed-wire promoter, oilman, and America's most famous "plunger" who was worth more than $40 million at his death. He was on good terms with Corrigan, who often gave him inside tips. Gates met Condon and agreed to help finance a takeover of Hawthorne. Corrigan offered to sell for $335,000, but Condon would not go higher than $310,000, and the deal fell through.[65]

Condon hired noted Chicago boxing writers and referee George Siler as his track's press agent to help publicize his track. Harlem's betting concession went to a powerful bookmaker syndicate that employed an experienced oddsmaker whose probabilities were adopted by other bookmakers. This scheme hindered clients from shopping for better odds by scanning the boards of competing bet takers who gave identical odds. This policy turned off many clients and eventually hurt business.[66]

The twenty-six-day Harlem meet was competitive and cleanly run, but attendance was down, except for Decoration Day, and the track made virtually no money. The *Spirit* blamed the outcome on the experiment with syndicate odds making, along with the start of the Spanish-American War in late April. Another possibility was that many fans were waiting for the reopening of the glamorous Washington Park Racetrack.[67]

Chicago spruced up in anticipation of the WPR's reopening. In early June, local department- and clothing-store windows displayed apparel labeled "for the Derby." On opening day, June 25, there was a virtually unprecedented demand for carriages and other elegant transportation, with elegant Victoria carriages renting for $15–$25 and coaches for up to $100.[68]

Twenty-three thousand spectators attended the Derby renewal in which Coat bested Warrenton by a nose to win the $9,000 first prize. The thirty-one bookmakers present included O'Leary, "Social" Smith, George Rose, Bill Riley, Riley Grannan, and Jewish bookies Maxey Blumenthal, Abe Levy, and Kid Weller. There were also eight field books, including one run by former western lawman Bat Masterson. Condon advised bookmakers to put up their slates with their firm's name clearly marked, but without prices, to circumvent anti-betting laws. Their clerks held up a small twelve-by-six-inch slate, or "splitter," in their hands, with prices posted on each horse. Each bettor got a receipt with a number identifying winning ticket holders.[69]

The press gave more coverage to the social aspects of the day than the races. The *Tribune*'s feature story, "Dazzling Colors Mark the Great Derby," provided detailed descriptions of elite women's colorful dresses, as well as their escorts' apparel. According to the *Tribune*: "Chicago fashionable society turned out en masse . . . to celebrate the revival. Washington Park . . . was brilliant with the pageantry which has always characterized this occasion. . . . The attendance was immense. The enthusiasm was unprecedented. The costumes never were more brilliant. The races—but the races are of little account. . . . It is the spectacle which frames the races that is of most note, and as a spectacle it was all that could be desired. Without the society display Derby day would be as tame and inconsequential as any ordinary horse race."[70]

The United States was at war when the Derby took place. The *Tribune* did not see race going as unpatriotic, but viewed it as of value to the home front: "People must be amused and entertained, though war is raging. Fortunately, the war is so young and its scene so remote that it did not sound a jarring note in the symphony played by society and the Jockey club." Derby Day gave society "a chance to show its smart rigs and its stunning gowns . . . [and] relieved the seriousness of these war-making days by some harmless entertainment."[71]

The event did have its critics, particularly John Hill Jr., chairman of the Board of Trade's Committee on Bucket Shops and the leader of the CF's Committee on Gambling. He reported to the CF that twelve poolrooms were operating wide open, that five detectives were seen there gambling, and that the poolrooms were taking in $12,000 every day. Hill regularly sent his findings to Superintendent Kipley and Mayor Harrison. His Honor warned President Wheeler of the WPR at the end of June that his race-meet permit did not authorize gambling. Harrison was willing to oblige the CF because he saw this matter as a "family affair": "As everyone knows, the membership of the Civic Federation is nearly identical with that of the Washington Park Club." A large delegation of WPR directors and officials called on the mayor a week later to assure him there was no gambling, there was no bookmaking, and no betting privileges had been granted. Harrison told them that if his order against gambling was disobeyed, he would close the track "as if it were a Clark street gambling resort." Wheeler responded by modifying the betting system, removing bookmakers' booths and their big upright slates. Consequently, the bookies and their clerks at future races sat on stools with cash boxes and satchels at their feet.[72]

Hill continued to badger the mayor, pointing out that there was no effort to halt gambling at the track by the same men that the CF and the police had previously driven out of downtown. Hill claimed the police were protecting gambling and had made no efforts to suppress it since the start of 1897, except when pushed by the CF. Harrison told the press that he had done as much as possible to bar gambling at Washington Park and urged Hill to send the grand jury his evidence. Harrison noted that since the elite track claimed it was not getting money for the betting privileges (which was not true), the WPR was in a strong position to keep its racing permit.[73]

WPC members who enjoyed racing and belonged to the Board of Trade, including Wheeler, put strong pressure on the board to fire Hill and protect the club's interests, which it did. Hill responded by telling the press that a Board of Trade director involved with the track had offered him $500 to halt his antigambling fight. Hill said he had an understanding with the CF to conduct its gambling crusade pro bono in connection with his job duties. The CF then was so financially strapped that over the prior eighteen months, it had contributed only moral support toward antigambling efforts. The CF would decide in 1899 to largely discontinue its antiracing fight and focus on other issues.[74]

Hill organized an independent antigambling league after leaving the CF to fight bucket shops and pool selling and secured indictments against twenty or so bookmakers just before the WPR meet closed. His efforts led to a grand-jury investigation and indictment of Wheeler and WPR secretary James Howard following the meet for keeping and maintaining a common gaming house at the track.[75]

THE HARLEM AND HAWTHORNE MEETS OF 1898

Before the 1898 season began, Corrigan seemed prepared to exit Hawthorne and leased his track to well-known bookmakers George Rose and Barney Schreiber (who was also a prominent horse owner) for $10,000. However, this amount was not enough to cover taxes and other fixed expenses, including a $100,000 mortgage that his partners were not helping to pay. Harlem planned to fight the new Hawthorne regime by replacing its old syndicate betting system with the more popular arrangement of open betting that allowed unaffiliated book-makers to take bets.[76]

Cicero's antiracing Reform League, mainly composed of Chicago businessmen who were local residents, led the attack on Hawthorne. The Reform League gathered incriminating information to send to the grand jury and asked town president H. A. Emerson not to grant Hawthorne a license. However, a majority of the eight-member town board seemed to favor the track, because, as one Chicago newspaper alleged, Corrigan had already bought their votes.[77]

The paper's prediction did not hold water, since on July 23 the town board voted unanimously to reject Corrigan's bid for a liquor permit instead of a more general amusement license, as was normally done. President Emerson admitted that townsfolk welcomed the money generated from license fees, but they felt that horse-race gambling drew unruly crowds and encouraged lawlessness. He was not personally opposed to the track and believed that only the local clergy and the track's immediate neighbors opposed racing. But one week later, Corrigan got his license, supposedly the old-fashioned way, by paying off a board member with a 50 percent interest in the bar privilege.[78]

In the meantime, Harlem and Hawthorne arranged a scheduling compromise by tossing a coin. Harlem won the toss and chose to open first. Thereafter, they alternated bimonthly racing dates. Harlem had twenty-three betting booths that operated more secretly than at Washington Park for fear of discovery by Hill's agents. On opening day, ten were arrested and indicted, including Kid Weller and James O'Leary, but Condon was not worried: "The public and the business people want racing at Chicago, as it brings a lot of money to the city, and the gambling . . . is simply incidental to racing everywhere."[79]

Hawthorne's first opening in three years on August 8 was threatened by minority partner John Brenock, who donated $200 to Cicero's town manager to cover police expenses in raiding the track. However, the authorities took no action. Brenock accused President Emerson of being financially involved in the track's bar concession and Cicero's police superintendent and other officers of being on the CRA's payroll. Emerson denied his own financial involvement, but did not rebuff allegations that some local men worked at the track, which he said was their own business. Emerson explained that the town could not afford a legal war with Corrigan and was also beholden to him because its sewage emptied into Corrigan's property at Mud Lake.[80]

Women constituted one-third of the opening-day audience. The betting ring was half full with fourteen bookmakers and two field books that each paid $121.75 a day to operate. The facilities were enhanced by a vastly upgraded paddock that Broad Church called the best in America. The CRA used a barrier to start races for the first time, which made a big improvement in getting races off on time.[81]

Four days later, Brenock's people drew up sixty-six warrants for alleged bookmakers and gamblers at Hawthorne, which Sheriff James Pease served once the races were over. A raid was staged the next day, Saturday, August 13, with six thousand people at the track, that resulted in a full-scale riot. Seventy-five men directed by the Mooney & Boland detective agency went to the track, accompanied by Brenock and John Burke. Corrigan was alerted in advance and was ready, with four Pinkertons, normally working as ticket takers, guarding the main entrance, backed up by Chief E. T. Vallens and eleven uniformed Cicero officers. The invaders, mostly former policemen acting as constables, were refused admission unless they bought a ticket. So, the constables reconvened about a hundred feet away along a fence, took out clubs the size of baseball bats, and began battering down the barrier.[82]

Corrigan summoned his "rough riders," more than a hundred rugged stable hands and track followers, to the scene to protect the fence, carrying fence pickets and stones wrapped in handkerchiefs. Corrigan left the paddock for the riot scene, where he encountered John Burke just outside the track, armed with a pistol. Corrigan grabbed Burke around the neck, and they fought on the railroad track just outside the course. Meanwhile, the constables were blocked by brawny men inside the track with staves and clubs, who paid no attention to the intruders waving revolvers. The defenders were backed by scores of patrons who rushed to the scene and began hurling stones at the constables, battering twelve into submission, and the rest fled. Following the races, Deputy Sheriff Porter arrested Corrigan, George Rose, and two other men.[83]

The authorities prepared for serious trouble the following Monday. Mooney & Boland, embarrassed by their defeat, were determined to return with vigor, warning they would send men armed with shotguns, ready to shoot. Corrigan promised to protect his patrons: "We will meet force with force." Fortunately, cooler heads prevailed, and Corrigan and Brenock agreed to have their lawyers patch up their differences.[84]

The metropolitan season ended with a third meet at Harlem in October and then two weeks of racing at Lakeside. Condon and O'Leary introduced syndicate betting at Lakeside, and the track owners reputedly made $100,000 during the short meet. Stable owner Kid Weller, one of the lessees of the Lakeside betting privileges, who ranked among the most successful western bookies, served as the bellwether for syndicate bookies that copied the odds he drew up. *Spirit* described him as "an odd little fellow, smiling and pleasant, with anything but the tact and close-fistedness attaching to the average Hebrew." One of his "outside men" who placed bets with other bookies to "round out" Weller's book was a young Jewish kid named John Hertz, who later owned the Yellow Cab Company and Hertz Rent-a-Car.[85]

The *Spirit*'s Broad Church rated the 1898 season as a mixed bag. The Chicago tracks drew nearly one million paid admissions, and four world records were set at Harlem. However, the twenty-plus bookmakers working each track struggled financially, and W. H. Laudeman, a Kentucky bookie, reported his colleagues all lost money, around $250,000 since the close of the Washington Park meet. Jim

O'Leary, for instance, was down $40,000, and Marcus Cartwright was out $25,000.[86]

The four Chicago-area tracks spent about $750,000 in purses, stakes, and incidental expenses. Harlem led with $320,000 in purses, followed by Hawthorne ($180,000), Washington Park ($155,000), and Lakeside (nearly $110,000). The WPR was a financial and racing success, while Hawthorne suffered a net loss because of expensive litigation and the costs associated with the pitched battle at the track. Harlem had a more complicated situation, losing a little money in the spring with light attendance and syndicate betting, yet did quite well in the summer with good crowds with free and open betting by twenty-five bookmakers. It remained profitable during the early fall, but October rains put the track in a quagmire and hurt attendance. The track was also hindered by competition from Hawthorne and the economic impact of the Spanish-American War. Nonetheless, Broad Church believed that overall, Harlem enjoyed moderate profits, less whatever Condon spent "to head off the interference." A fair amount of "grease" was needed, "or otherwise the machine could not be kept in running order."[87]

In November, Judge Richard S. Tuthill, a future pioneering juvenile-court judge, placed Hawthorne under receivership in response to stockholder complaints that the CRA was operating in the red and that management was trying to close the track because of its complicated litigation. The property was ostensibly sold for $200,000 to superintendent Richard Fitzgerald of the Chicago Terminal Company, who had recently gotten involved in the track as a mediator between Corrigan and Brenock. Fitzgerald became track president, and Corrigan and Brenock each gave him a 2.5 percent interest in Hawthorne. Fitzgerald was seldom seen at the track, devoting himself to his railroading career, and relied on Corrigan's advice to run the track's affairs, siding on every issue that came up with Corrigan.[88]

The Second Closing of Washington Park

Racing supporters in the legislature tried again in 1899 to legitimize the sport. The most impressive proposal was Albert J. Kettering's

(R–Chicago) bill to regulate racing and pool selling, based on the Fitzgerald plan and New York's 1893 Saxton Act that made pool selling a felony. Kettering's proposal limited tracks to a sixty-day meeting from May to November, banned night racing, and permitted books and pools only inside tracks. It assessed a 5 percent fee on the gross of tracks located within twenty-fives miles of cities with more than one hundred thousand inhabitants, 3 percent for tracks within fifteen miles of a city with fewer than one hundred thousand residents, and 2 percent for rural tracks.[89]

The *Spirit* claimed that Kettering's bill had wide support among turfmen and prominent businessmen, but the *Tribune* disagreed. Republican governor John R. Tanner promised to veto it because he thought the result would be six months of continuous racing, and he preferred just a three- or four-week meet at Washington Park. Illinois House Speaker Lawrence Y. Sherman (R–Macomb) opposed state-sanctioned gambling and was against any proracing bill, although he did not believe legislation could halt gambling. He blocked passage by refusing to recognize anyone who tried to call up the bill. The house's actions were considered crucial because the senate seemed to favor the track bills. National turf leaders were disappointed by the outcome that would have ensconced Chicago as the nation's center of racing west of the Hudson River and enhanced the local breeding industry, while boosters saw a lost opportunity to bolster Chicago's economic development.[90]

The legislative failure increased the uncertainty about racing in 1899. The WPR was so upset by the petty nuisances created by racing foes, and the humiliation of President Wheeler by grand-jury indictments the year before, that its directors were afraid of repeated harassment and felt no reason to carry on. Once it was apparent no racing bill would be passed, the WPR decided to again close.[91]

As it turned out, there was little interference by the authorities with thoroughbred racing in 1899. As the *Tribune* reported at the end of the season, county officials let the track managers know that they were not opposed to the sport as long as it was "conducted within certain limitations." The only problems came early in the racing calendar, the long-standing conflicts between Hawthorne's own managers.[92]

The Harlem Scene

The 1899 racing season began at Lakeside where middle- and lower-quality horses competed for purses suitable for higher-grade thoroughbreds. The track still employed the syndicate betting system that included O'Leary, head of Chicago's Bookmakers' Association. The Harlem meet followed, with high expectations and without syndicate betting. Management made many improvements, including laying a new racing surface and significantly improving the connections between the elevated and surface electric cars that previously made for long delays and tedious journeys. A new three-quarter-mile track was laid that enabled special trains from the Loop to run right into the grounds.[93]

However, Harlem also started the season with serious concerns, beginning with the declining health of John Condon, rumored to be retiring because of failing eyesight. Then there was a big fire on the racetrack on May 22, likely springing from arson. Just two weeks earlier, O'Leary's Roby poolrooms were set afire, one day before the Lakeside track opened, which suggested that foes of the O'Leary-Condon alliance were responsible. The Harlem fire caused an $80,000 loss, of which the jockey club's share was $10,000. The Harlem club built an improvised structure to complete the season that accommodated five to six thousand people. By late June, attendance nearly surpassed the entire previous season because of perfect racing weather, the fast condition of the track, and interest in watching first-rate horses compete.[94]

Condon remained in charge of his track despite losing his eyesight and enjoyed widespread public support. Fans considered him a stand-up guy, which, along with his political clout, helped him get the backing of village and county officials who did not interfere with the track. Condon tried to force Fitzgerald to introduce the syndicate system at Hawthorne, arguing it would make for big profits, but was unsuccessful. Ironically, Condon himself gave up syndicate betting at Harlem, recognizing that bettors preferred the greater flexibility they had at Hawthorne. A few days after Condon leased out the betting privilege, four big downtown poolrooms, apparently connected to Condon, began operating wide open, drawing business from his track.[95]

The Hawthorne Meet

The CRA was renamed the Chicago Jockey Club in May. Hawthorne's management was optimistic about the future because the site was going to be annexed into the new township of Stickney, making the CJC "exempt from the blackmailing force of Cicero" and because they thought a truce with Harlem was possible since Corrigan's bête noire, John Condon, was expected to retire.[96]

Racing went on well early in the meet, although Cicero president John Lewis harassed the management and sought to close the track. Lewis wanted to get CJC president Fitzgerald arrested and worked with Police Chief Vallens to amass evidence of gambling at the track. A number of Hawthorne bookmakers were indicted, purportedly the work of Condon, but he pulled back for fear his track would be similarly harassed, which it was by his poolroom rivals.[97]

The metropolitan racing season lasted 133 days, including 71 days at Harlem and 30 at Lakeside, with purses of $173,400 and $72,500, respectively (averaging from $400–$500 per race). Purses were enhanced by charging horse owners entrance fees that came to $11,150 and $4,455, respectively. Journalists believed that providing valuable purses was the means to attract first-class horses, whose presence was the only way to draw in new fans. The *Tribune* considered the attendance good "and showed that the sport is always bound to pay in this city, but it has at no time aroused the interest of the general public, there having been no event that has attracted the attention of those not ordinarily interested in racing." Still, according to the *Spirit*, both Harlem and Hawthorne made money.[98]

COMPARING NEW YORK AND CHICAGO RACING

Even with the loss of Washington Park, the *Tribune* estimated that racing in 1899 put $2 million into the local economy. Harlem racing secretary Martin Nathanson pointed out that Chicago "turfmen and patrons of the sport are free spenders, [and] the necessities of the sport divide a large sum of money for stable equipment, feed, care of hundreds of trainers, jockeys and stable boys and stimulate breeding interests."[99]

Still, Chicago continued to lag far behind metropolitan New York, especially after the closure of Washington Park, when measured by attendance, purses, and amounts wagered at the tracks, as well as more subjective variables like the social composition of the crowds; the quality of facilities, such as space in the betting rings; and the class of horses and jockeys. Other important differences were the leadership exercised by turfmen and the comparative legal situation of racing. In New York State, the government backed the sport with the state's Racing Commission set up in 1895 in conjunction with The Jockey Club, while in Illinois the legal status of racing was uncertain at best. For that matter, the legal standing of racing was pretty questionable nearly everywhere outside of New York. As the *Tribune* pointed out, in New York "the sport is legalized, it is largely in the hands of men known in the community and business world, who makes of it a sport and not a business, thereby making the vital distinction upon which rests the right of horse-racing to a claim to respectability."[100]

The *Tribune* also applauded New York tracks for being stricter in giving out free passes, which did get more people into the track to bet, but resulted "in filling the [betting] ring with idlers and 'sure thing' men," a most undesirable outcome. Chicago racing topped New York only in setting lower admission prices by about 67 percent.[101]

Despite Chicago racing's ups and downs, particularly the closing of Washington Park and the absence of strong legal backing for on-track gambling, the ever-optimistic *Spirit* thought that Chicago's racing future was secure. The weekly argued, in the finest tradition of disingenuous sportswriting, that the turf's clean and wholesome character, combined with a tolerant public sentiment, enabled the authorities to wink at the sport's gambling problem. More concretely, the *Spirit* attributed a lot of the success to "Mayor Carter Harrison [who] is a liberal, tolerant, sport-loving individual, and likely enough other officials do not feel like running counter to the exactions of public sentiment. The situation suggests a case of elastic toleration for conditions under an unsatisfactory racing law, with the hope and expectation that desirable legislation may be secured in the sweet by-and-by."[102] Ironically, Harrison in 1904, driven by ambitions for national office, would probably become the single most important person in the closing of Chicago racing.

THOROUGHBRED RACING AND NORTH AMERICAN TRACKS, 1882–1909

Given the small number of major racetracks that operated in Illinois and the entire United States in the late nineteenth and early twentieth centuries, it is surprising to discover that an average of 153 courses operated each year between 1882 and 1908, although the great majority were obscure facilities. There were 188.5 courses on average from 1882 through 1889 (23 in Canada), rising to 207.5 in the 1890s (32 in Canada). The number of courses was quite stable from 1882 through 1888, but this stability was followed by wide swings. There was a 49.1 percent drop from 1888 to 1889, followed one year later by a nearly 100 percent increase. There was another huge increase from 137 tracks in 1896 to 306 one year later, an increase of 223 percent as the depression was coming to an end. Shortly thereafter, another sharp drop occurred in the early 1900s when there were no more than 61 racetracks in operation. By 1908 the number went down to just 22 as the more obscure tracks quickly disappeared, owing to costs, competition from harness racing, and antigambling pressure in small towns (see table 8).[103]

The overwhelming majority of courses in this era were obscure minor facilities in small communities, often employed for county fairs. In 1892, for instance, 80.9 percent of the tracks were minor meets that lasted four or fewer days, rising to 93.4 percent in 1898 (computed from table 8). Those tracks' stages were small fields composed of nondescript local horses and even pony races. Purses were as little as $25, and there were heat races for distances as short as two furlongs. In 1897 when Illinois had only two major meets at Harlem and Joliet, there was sufficient interest in racing for the promotion of twenty-six minor meets in towns off the beaten path such as Camargo, Griggsville, Pana, and Rushville.

Table 8
Racetracks and Major Courses in North America, 1882–1909

	ALL RACECOURSES		MAJOR MEETS	
	United States	*Canada*	*United States*	*Canada*
1882	181	12	n.d.	n.d.
1883	200	12	17	0
1884	197	27	24	0
1885	211	20	16	0
1886	201	32	17	0
1887	196	32	17	0
1888	210	22	20	0
1889	112	28	21	0
1890	220	32	18	1
1891	235	38	19	1
1892	110	39	21	1
1893	154	28	21	1
1894	188	39	23	1
1895	166	25	25	3
1896	137	26	24	3
1897	306	41	22	1
1898	300	35	20	1
1899	259	39	22	3
1900	93	24	22	4
1901	146	30	25	4
1902	57 3	1	23	3
1903	60	24	30	3
1904	34	4	27	3
1905	61	5	18	1
1906	42 4	25	4	
1907	28	6	23	3
1908	22	5	22	5
1909	NA	NA	13	5

Source: Adapted from *Goodwin's Annual Official Turf Guide [1882–1908]*.

Racetracks then were the most notable facility at county fairs. The racing of horses under saddle, largely forgotten today, or drawn by harness, attracted the biggest crowds and were the most profitable ventures. Not much is known about the county- and state-fair meets. A number of them built decent-size grandstands, like the $10,000 structure at the Alabama State Fair. Historian Ted Ownby argues that its meets seemed more like urban mass-spectator operations than the old-time small races (like the various Illinois county fairs), complete with substantial gambling and a "debauched, disreputable crowd."[104]

From 1890 through 1908, there were just an average of 23 major tracks in operation in the United States. Canada had merely 1.3 from 1890 through 1899 and in the early 1900s, as the number of American courses were sharply dropping, rose to 3.5. Small meets pretty much disappeared in the United States by 1907, while there were just a handful in Canada. The major American tracks barely survived at the end of the 1900s, falling to a low of 13. Canada always had just a small number of major tracks (2.9 from 1899 through 1909), peaking in 1909 with 5. That year it had 27.7 percent of the major North American tracks, by far its largest proportion. The Windsor and Fort Erie tracks were able to pick up a lot of trade because major American cities were in close proximity.

CONCLUSION

The last few years of the nineteenth century were tough years for racing. Racing's problems were in part because of the panic of 1893 that led to a dreadful economic depression that lasted for four years in the United States. It also contributed to a political realignment in 1894 centered around such social and cultural issues as Prohibition, gambling, assimilation and acculturation, and ultimately, social control.[105] The changing economic and political conditions created a problematic environment for the racing industry, since its appeal was based on wagering. While racing was popular in Chicago in the early 1890s, its connections to immorality, political corruption, and the crime world put it in a vulnerable position. Racing temporarily died at the Chicago racetracks in the mid-1890s, as it did in New Jersey, and almost did in New York. However, the appeal to bet on horses remained strong, and Chicago racing was set up for a huge, albeit temporary, revival at the turn of the century.

6

From Glory Days to Collapse, 1900–1905

Chicago thoroughbred racing made a huge turnaround at the end of the century and regained its status as the second-leading turf center in the United States. Washington Park reopened for the third time in a handful of years, and a fourth track opened one year later. The renewed American Derby regained its stature as one of the preeminent events in North American sports, attracting the finest horses and drawing record crowds that included people from all walks of life, but most notably the crème de la crème of Chicago society, wearing the most stylish clothes and arriving in the most fashionable carriages. The legal status of on-track gambling was still shaky, but few fans or journalists considered it a problem. If there was a quandary, it was the ever-growing menace of offtrack gambling that the authorities could not, or would not, resolve.

Chicago in the early 1900s was the nation's second most important center of professional sport and equally important as the site of amateur athletics. The city had Major League franchises in both the American and the National Leagues. The Cubs were a powerhouse, winning pennants from 1906 to 1908 and in 1910 and the World Series in 1907 and 1908. The 1906 team went 116–36, the most wins by any team, and the highest winning percentage, .763, in history and led Major League Baseball (MLB) in attendance (654,300). Yet the Cubs were upset in the Series by their crosstown rival, the White Sox, who were second in attendance (585,202). The Cubs were third overall in MLB attendance in the 1900s with 4,329,678, surpassed only by the White Sox (4,470,955 in nine seasons) and the New York Giants (5,167,211).[1]

Working-class sports were extremely popular, especially prize-fighting, but it was not legal. It survived in the early 1900s by circumventing the law at neighborhood gymnasiums and indoor arenas. However, in 1904 big-time bouts open to the public were completely banned. Unlike pugilism, professional wrestling was legal. In 1908 American Frank Gotch defeated unbeaten world champion Estonian George Hackenschmidt, at the Dexter Park Pavilion, and on September 4, 1911, successfully defended his title against the "Russian Lion" at Comiskey Park before 30,000 spectators.[2]

Indoor amateur working-class sports programs were sponsored by settlement houses such as Hull House, religious groups like the YMCA and the Chicago Hebrew Institute, and ethnic associations, including the German turner societies, Bohemian sokols, and Polish falcons. Soccer was heavily dominated by immigrants and was so popular that Charles Comiskey, owner of the Chicago White Sox, organized in 1901 a Midwest professional soccer league. Inner-city youth employed Chicago's nationally renowned parks programs for outdoor sports. African Americans were active in sports and supported outstanding all-black semiprofessional baseball teams, but encountered de facto segregation at YMCAs, public parks, and beaches.[3]

The city was well known nationally for its high school sports programs. The first American high school team was the Morgan Park boys who played a West Side YMCA team in 1893. Three years later, Austin HS women played an interscholastic game against Oak Park HS. Hyde Park HS had the finest overall sports program, highlighted by its victory in 1902 in the "mythical" national football championship, 105–0 against Brooklyn Poly. The following year, North Division HS defeated Boys' High of Brooklyn, 75–0. At this time, the University of Chicago sponsored national interscholastic championships in basketball, tennis, and track and field.[4]

The University of Chicago was then a major sports powerhouse whose athletic program was directly by Amos Alonzo Stagg. He recruited athletes from local high schools and teams that competed in its national tournaments. The Maroons won the 1904 Olympic Games collegiate championship meet, defeating Princeton, Illinois, Michigan State, and Colgate, and captured three straight intercollegiate championships in basketball (Helms Foundation, 1906–9), and the football team was named national champion in 1905 after defeating the University of Michigan's "Point a Minute" team, and again in 1913.[5]

The local population remained extremely ethnic. About 27.7 percent of the city's 1,698,575 residents were German, there were more Poles in Chicago than any Polish city other than Warsaw, and it was the third-largest Czech city in the world. In addition, it had the second-largest Jewish population and third most Italians and African Americans of any American city. European immigrants and their children largely lived free of the social control that old-stock Protestant evangelicals tried to impose elsewhere on urban residents, especially in the East and South. Sunday blue laws were lightly enforced, neighborhood taverns often stayed open well beyond legal closing hours, and prostitution and gambling flourished. Urban machine politicians protected—for a price—gambling halls and brothels, a blight that religious and moral reformers sought to close.[6]

The Progressive movement that sought to ameliorate some of the greatest urban problems of the day was strong in Chicago. Progressives pursued political democracy, economic opportunity, social justice, and efficiency in government. They particularly targeted the problems of immigrants living in the city's slums, but less so the needs of African Americans. Social reform leaders were mainly middle-class liberal Protestant ministers, journalists, temperance advocates, settlement-house workers, social scientists, and members of municipal reform organizations who tried to discover the underlying problems of urban life and then apply that research to come up with answers to solve those dilemmas. Their efforts to improve the quality of urban life included securing clean and safe streets, better education, and honest government, as well as the closure of vile amusements, replacing them with uplifting recreations.[7]

Progressives also sought to acculturate urban folk, particularly immigrant children, into law-abiding citizens, though they employed less heavy-handed methods than evangelical Protestants. The progressives believed their traditional moral values promoted good health, proper social conduct, and a strong sense of community, which they tried to inculcate through public education and fighting vice. Progressives supported the use of leisure time for clean sports like baseball that purportedly promoted morality, built character, and improved public health, and they advocated the building of inner-city parks for similar purposes. However, they disapproved of blood sports and pastimes that relied on gambling for their popularity. Progressives opposed gambling as a socially dysfunctional activity that promoted crime and machine politics and destroyed working-class families. The reformers' long-standing fight against prizefighting and horse racing reached fruition in Chicago in the mid-1900s.[8]

THE RETURN OF WASHINGTON PARK

Even without racing in 1899, the Washington Park Club was still one of the finest American men's clubs, reflected by a long waiting list for potential new members. The *Spirit* rated the Washington Park Racetrack clubhouse as the most attractive in America, even if New York's Morris Park was "far more expensively built and luxuriously furnished." There were rumors at the end of 1899 that the WPR would reopen, even if no new laws were passed to protect racing. Then on February 6, 1900, the WPR announced it would hold a race meet under Secretary James Howard, with fourteen stakes, virtually identical to the 1898 meet, with $100,000 in prizes. The club still had a big division between the golfing members, who mainly joined for its social activities, had little if any interest in racing, and did not like getting insulted by fans at the races, and the proracing members, who enjoyed going to the races dressed in their finery and watching the races from their carriages or the posh clubhouse. One month later, the WPR's stockholders voted unanimously to reduce the number of directors from an unwieldy twenty-four to seven. Shortly thereafter, WPC president C. D. Hamill, head of the Board of Trade, stepped down, replaced by thirty-year-old Lawrence A. Young of Louisville, a streetcar attorney, former Princeton baseball captain, and son-in-law of former WPC president George Wheeler. The new vice president was Watson J. Ferry, an attorney and former Kansas City legislator and police commissioner. This leadership put the club firmly in the hands of the proracing faction.[9]

Indiana's Lakeside Racetrack led off the racing season, followed by Harlem with an eleven-day spring meet and then a twelve-day meet at Hawthorne, and finally in June Washington Park reopened. However, the renewal's euphoria was taken aback on June 20 when Mayor Carter Harrison II, a former supporter of Washington Park racing, ordered the suppression of overt bookmaking at the American Derby. The mayor's action drew a very negative response from WPC members, and other prominent citizens sent him telegrams and letters in protest. They felt that betting at the track was an integral part of the enjoyment and rituals of racing. As Charles A. Mair, a member of the Board of Trade and former WPR director, noted, "Horse racing without betting is a situation of a somewhat incongruous character, especially on a day like Derby day, where immense crowds watch the races." Chicago Republicans criticized Harrison for threatening raids for political purposes and urged him to close all late-evening saloons and gambling places before going after some of the city's leading businessmen who ran Washington Park.[10]

Harrison backed down, claiming he had ordered only that state laws be enforced and that open bookmaking be prevented. "Of course," he admitted, "it would be impossible in a crowd of 25,000 people for any number of policemen to prevent all betting, but it is possible to prevent bookmakers holding forth in stands displaying their odds and publicly recording bets, and that is what the law which I have ordered enforced prohibits." Police Superintendent Joseph Kipley washed his hands of the on-track gambling problem and left responsibility to Inspector Nicholas Hunt, well known to be a close friend of bookmaker Jim O'Leary.[11]

A glorious crowd of forty thousand attended the Derby, with ten thousand turned away. As the *Tribune* recounted, "Business-men locked their offices and places of business earlier than for years. Bank president and bootblack, clubman and newsboy joined the throng. Staid and dignified capitalists who did not know a paddock from the quarter-stretch jostled elbows with the street gamin who could 'tip' the winner. There were women and men, old and young, rich and poor, but all were going to the track." Politicians came out in droves, including the county commissioner, commissioner of public works, and five aldermen, including John Coughlin. For the first time ever, a few wealthy race goers arrived in automobiles. The race was won by Sidney Lucas, a long shot at 20–1 who defeated Kentucky Derby winner Lieutenant Gibson by six lengths on a slow, muddy track.[12]

Superintendent Joseph Kipley was a notable absentee. He had previously announced no expectation of gambling at the track and did not assign a large force to nab bookmakers. There were forty-four bookmakers present, including Barney Schreiber, Harry Perry, Kid Weller, James O'Leary, and Max Blumenthal, who each operated a "club" to take bets. Reportedly, $100,000 changed hands on the Derby alone, plus another $180,000 on the other four races. Unlike earlier derbies, there were no betting rings with blackboards and chalking up of the odds before each race: "Soap boxes firmly placed on chairs, rolls of bills in a tin box, two men with tally sheets betting 'tickets' of the old days style—these constituted the essentials of each 'club.' The odds were not posted, but men stood at the front and rear of each booth-like enclosure waving about 'official programs,' with the ratio at which money would be accepted, penciled in figures an inch deep after the name of each horse."[13]

The *Spirit* praised Washington Park, ruing it had ever been shuttered, "for the club, with its great social prestige, the best representative of what is clean, wholesome and high toned in racing deserves the utmost latitude in the way of practical encouragement." A few plunger-level bets were made by William A. Pinkerton, of the world-renowned security firm, who wagered more than $1,000, and the "picturesque" Steve L'Hommedieu, who had reputedly won $300,000 betting on races in 1899, bet $8,000.[14]

Hawthorne's summer meet came off well, highlighted by Saturday, July 28, that drew sixteen thousand spectators and thirty-four bookmakers. However, the track suffered from a scarcity of good stakes horses in late summer that resulted in fields of just three or four horses in events worth $1,000–$1,500 to the winner. The odds-on favorites were often so unattractive that there was little betting. Consequently, the track decided to drop such races and instead employed the money for overnight events in which horses could be entered twenty-four hours before post time, with lower purses ranging from $400–$750, to attract and support smaller stable owners.[15]

Harlem underwent a $40,000 renovation to refurbish the large and roomy grandstand, built an ideal betting enclosure, and laid a new asphalt pavement between the grandstand and track. However, management did not resolve spectators' discomfort on hot days because the poorly shaded grandstand faced the sun. Harlem set an attendance record in the fall when the more moderate climate made watching races more comfortable. Entrance fees for most races was doubled to $20, and admission fees for spectators were also doubled.[16]

Harlem encountered pressure from the bookies of the Western Turf Association that had recently dropped its annual membership fee to $100 and increased its membership from fifty-four to seventy-six. The WTA wanted Harlem to further reduce members' daily fee from $100 for the usual five races (plus an additional fee for extra races) to $75, which the WPR charged for six races. The WTA also complained that Harlem made its members buy supplies from the track at exorbitant prices. Owners who stabled horses at Harlem had a similar complaint because they had to buy their provisions from the track's feed store at well above market prices.[17]

Late in August the Oak Park Citizens' Federation reopened the antiracetrack movement, alleging that there was wide-open gambling at Hawthorne and Harlem and that the bookies at Hawthorne even put up the purses. Oak Park was then a middle-class part of Cicero that boasted of its twenty-five homes built by renowned architect Frank Lloyd Wright, a local resident. Oak Park split away in 1902 from the largely working-class community and quickly banned the sale of liquor. The CF claimed that the fifteen to twenty-five bookmakers at each track had expenses of $50 a day plus their $100 fee to operate. Their average daily take was $267–$400 per bookie (totaling between $4,000 and $6,000). The CF estimated that if one added to those expenses the $3,000 that spectators daily paid for admission and car fare, then $1 million was spent at the two tracks for gambling, mainly "from a source where its loss means privations and defalcations." The CF subsequently charged that Cicero president John Jones and members of the town board had received money to permit racing and gambling to continue at the Hawthorne track and urged townsfolk to elect new officials and license the track to regulate its business.[18]

All three tracks set financial records in 1900, and the quality of racing was high, with eighteen new records. Hawthorne and Harlem averaged five thousand spectators during the week and nearly twelve thousand on Saturdays. The average daily attendance surpassed that of the big eastern tracks, as well as the Chicago Orphans, as the Cubs were known then.[19]

Chicago Tracks and the Western Jockey Club

The Chicago jockey clubs were not strong supporters of the American Turf Congress, which was divided into two factions: the "Little Seven," comprising smaller, mostly southern tracks (Latonia [Covington, Kentucky], Louisville, Newport, Little Rock, Memphis, Nashville, and Highland Park [a Detroit suburb]) and the metropolitan "Big Five" (the three Chicago tracks, the St. Louis Fairgrounds, and the New Orleans Fair Grounds). Chicago was closely allied to the Gateway City since most Chicago horses wintered there. The ATC at its annual Chicago meeting rejected Lakeside's membership bid and that of the soon-to-open Worth course, twenty-two miles south of downtown Chicago (111th Street and Ridgeland Avenue).[20]

Circuit-court judge George G. Perkins of Covington, Kentucky, the owner of Latonia, was mainly responsible for determining ATC racing dates. He favored southern tracks, even though their purses and lesser facilities were insufficient to attract top stables. His time table cut about seven weeks from Chicago's racing scene, leaving Washington Park its usual twenty-five days and Hawthorne and Harlem splitting the rest, with none for Lakeside. The Chicago tracks felt the new schedule was unfair, especially given their liberal purses. Harlem and Hawthorne agreed with the St. Louis tracks to disregard the ATC's division of dates.[21]

The governance of western racing changed significantly on February 4, 1901, when representatives of several high-level southern and western jockey clubs met in Chicago to organize the new Western Jockey Club. They included Chicago's three tracks and the New Louisville, New Memphis, St. Louis, Crescent City, and Latonia Jockey Clubs. They were dissatisfied with the ATC's decisions and the influence of the Cella-Adler-Tilles (CAT) crowd that owned most of the St. Louis tracks. The WJC officers, mainly Chicagoans, were chairman Lawrence A. Young, vice chairman Robert Aull (former president of the prestigious St. Louis Fairgrounds track), secretary George Kuhl, Hawthorne's racing secretary (1891–95, 1898–1901), and treasurer James Howard of the WPR. The WJC promised to treat all turf groups fairly and strengthen common interests. The initiation fee was $1,000 and annual dues $100. The WJC's stewards were empowered to draw up a racing calendar; investigate fraud; appoint handicappers, the clerk of scales, starters, and judges; and supervise the licensing of tracks, trainers, and jockeys.[22]

The 1901 Season

Chicago's new racing season started in the spring at Lakeside. The *Tribune* printed a photo of the "so-called" grandstand, followed by Worth's grand opening on May 2, 1901, drawing some nine thousand fans. One year earlier, Aldermen Johnny Powers and William J. O'Brien signed a ten-year lease to build a track at the old Piper farm in the town of Worth, thirty-one minutes from Dearborn Station via the Wabash Railroad. Powers was the club president, and O'Brien, recently defeated for reelection, was the treasurer, supported by bookmakers Samuel Wagner, vice president, and E. J. Wagner, track manager.[23]

The Worth track was modeled from an old trotting course with good drainage and had a capacity of about ten thousand. The new

12. Worth Racetrack, located in the town of Worth in suburban Will County. Worth (1904) was operated by prominent Chicago politicians and bookmakers. Reproduced by permission from Robert O'Shaughnessy, director of parks and recreation, Worth, Illinois.

two-story twenty-six-hundred-seat grandstand, modeled after Harlem, had a roof supported by a single span of steel trusses so there were few posts to obstruct spectators. The stand faced south so everyone could see the head of the stretch.[24]

The racing season shifted in late May to Hawthorne. On May 31, Powers sent private constables hired by the Dean Detective Agency (also known as the Chicago Constabulary), recently established by Dickie Dean and John Ryan, con men who once worked for Mike McDonald, to Hawthorne to arrest bookmakers. The private security force did not have the best reputation. This move was reportedly in revenge for the Chicago Jockey Club trying to deny Worth certain desired racing dates. The constables arrived with warrants to arrest bookmakers George Carroll and Marcus Cartwright of Oregon, but agreed to wait until after the races when the crowd dispersed. Then a fight broke out between the constables and Pinkertons policing the track. Revolvers were drawn, and Captain W. T. Forsee of the Pinkertons was hit by a pistol butt. Hawthorne ended its season with a forty-seven-day fall meet with 293 contests, nearly half of which (44.4 percent) were a mile or more, and distributed $203,735 in purses. Profits were lower than the prior season.[25]

On June 18, poolroom keepers with a grudge against John Condon because he and his friends tried to monopolize the poolroom trade secured a temporary injunction to halt bookmaking at Harlem. The instigators included the Cella-Adler-Tilles syndicate, irate at Condon for using his clout in Springfield to force them out of business at their Madison poolroom, and because of his role in Chicagoan H. A. Perry getting a one-year lease and a three-year option of St. Louis's Kinloch Park Racetrack. The St. Louis triumvirate enlisted attorney Fred Rowe, Governor Richard Yates's private secretary, to fight the Chicago crowd. Rowe hired Colonel W. D. Washburn, an attorney on the governor's staff, to close the Cook County tracks, but he was unsuccessful.[26]

The 1901 Washington Park season was highly anticipated following the prior year's successful meet, and the track reportedly made one of its biggest profits ever. Few purses were less than $600, and stakes were doubled in value, with overnight handicaps worth at least $1,000, sufficient to attract top stables. The Derby drew an enormous crowd, estimated at fifty-six thousand, but its size was never accepted as a record. It was a gala affair according to the *Spirit* reporter, reminiscent of "an English or French race course," who never saw "so smartly gowned women and a better class assemblage in general in the clubhouse and on the lawn . . . ever . . . at any American racecourse."[27]

The race was won in a big upset by Colonel Edward R. "Pa" Bradley's Robert Waddell, who went off at 15–1, having been originally quoted in the future books at 150–1. Bradley made his money as a bookmaker and real-estate investor. He was just starting a brilliant career in horse racing and went on to win nine Triple Crown races. Bradley claimed he did not bet on the race on Derby Day, but had made an advance bet with Jim O'Leary's outfit in Hot Springs, Arkansas, that made him $15,000. O'Leary could stand the loss because he had booked more than $120,000 on the Derby.[28]

On July 2, Dickie Dean led five constables, mostly men with criminal records, to Washington Park to halt gambling there. He was working with state representative Walter A. Lantz (D–LaGrange), recently indicted for malfeasance as a member of the Civil Service Commission.

Warrants were secured, leading to the arrests of President Young, Secretary Howard, and five bookmakers. The court freed the WPR officials, who argued that the constables' real aim was extorting $25 from Young and Howard, as they had previously done at the Worth track and had tried to extract from downtown bookies.[29]

About a month later, the fifty-member Business Men's League was organized to stop racetrack gambling because it seemed that whenever their clerks went to the races, their accounts were coming up short. The BML wanted a writ of mandamus to compel Sheriff Ernest J. Magerstadt to serve bench warrants on alleged malefactors at Harlem. The recent fiasco at Washington Park when constables failed to shut down bookmaking convinced the BML that if the sheriff failed to carry out his duties, he should be charged with malfeasance. Condon hired Pinkerton detectives to investigate the BML, which he thought, correctly, was a front for the CAT syndicate and certain of his poolroom foes, all trying to hinder his operations.[30]

The Chicago season ended on October 1 with a near riot at Worth. The judges in the last race agreed that Gonfalon won by a very narrow margin, but spectators seated at the finish line believed it was a bad call. They called the judges thieves and robbers and talked about slugging and lynching them. The crowd followed the judges to their train, and they were lucky to escape.[31]

The regional racing season actually lasted well into November at Lakeside, which reportedly made a substantial $90,000, though there was growing dissatisfaction against its use of syndicate betting. Overall, observers considered the season a success from the point of attendance and quality of competition, although the tracks did not earn as much in 1900 owing to larger purses and stakes and the revised division of the racing calendar.[32]

THE 1902 SEASON

The 1902 racing calendar started at Lakeside and Worth and moved on to Hawthorne, which on May 30 drew nearly ten thousand spectators. But that evening the racetrack burned to the ground from a suspicious

13. Crowd at the Washington Park Racetrack, ca. 1900. This photograph of fans in front of the grandstand depicts an upper-middle-class crowd of men wearing summer suits and hats and women clad in their stylish dresses and hats. Reprinted from *Chicago* (Portland, ME: L. H. Nelson, 1906), 40. Digital Collections, University of Illinois at Urbana-Champaign.

fire. Two men were seen leaving the cupola where the fire originated shortly after the fourth race. Management claimed that criminals had started the fire to cover for a big robbery. Most spectators escaped before the fire broke through the roof of the pavilion after the final race, though unpaid winning bettors rushed into the betting ring to get their money before the flames got there. The fire was exacerbated by the track's nearly bare water cistern and the lack of essential equipment to fight the blaze. There was little Cicero and Chicago firemen could do. Everything was destroyed except the stables and cottages occupied by track officials. The CJC suffered a $100,000 loss not covered by insurance and moved the rest of the meet to Harlem. Chicago gamblers blamed Jim O'Leary for the fire because of his involvement with the rival Lakeside course and his opposition to the Smith-Perry-White syndicate that took bets at Hawthorne.[33]

Corrigan, largely absent for two years, announced the track would be rebuilt in time for the August meet with a steel and cement seven-thousand-seat grandstand in place of the original wooden structure. Safety concerns led to the edifice getting its own waterworks and access to Berwyn's water mains. The problem of fire safety in semi-public buildings was of great concern to Chicago-area residents, especially because of the Great Chicago Fire of 1871. One year after the Hawthorne blaze, on December 30, 1903, Chicago suffered its deadliest conflagration ever when more than six hundred people died in the Iroquois Theater fire. This tragedy led to the rewriting of the city's building codes in 1909 that included specific regulations for future fire-resistant baseball stands.[34]

Derby Day

The 1902 American Derby attracted enormous national attention and drew about five thousand tourists to downtown hotels, including 20 percent just at the Palmer House. Rich people not only rented carriages for $50 to get to the track, but were now thinking about driving cars there, encouraged by the new Chicago Automobile Club. Chicago was an early center of automobile interest, reflected by the *Times-Herald* car race (the first in North America, in 1895), the twelve local automobile manufacturers, and the first national auto show at the Coliseum in 1901. An average car then cost $840 ($25,418 in 2020).[35]

The Derby was a spectacle attended by a reported record sixty-eight thousand people and viewed by more fans watching from buildings two blocks away. City hall caught Derby fever, as only two local aldermen appeared at a subcommittee meeting to consider a building ordinance. Track security was largely in the hands of three hundred uniformed private detectives, many of them policemen on furlough. The only trouble all day was at the entrance bolstered by twenty-five detailed Chicago officers. There were sixty-seven bookmakers in the betting ring, plus sixteen field books that took $1 bets. But the throngs were so large that many people never had the chance to bet.[36]

Wyeth, a stallion owned by Chicago multimillionaire John A. Drake, won the 1902 Derby in an upset, earning the $20,125 purse, half of which went as a bonus to his trainer. Drake, the son of a former Iowa governor, was a legendary bettor who often wagered secretly through agents at poolrooms all over the country to keep ahead of gamblers who followed his every step. Drake had been so confident in Wyeth that he placed $100 bets with several bookies at 9–1, earning him an additional $50,000. The huge crowd bet about $500,000 on the race. Several bookmakers laid off their bets with O'Leary, the day's big loser, who paid out $123,000 on Wyeth just from his winter book that took advance bets on major races staged across the country.[37]

Drake was a boon companion of John W. Gates and had two years earlier taken a racing stable to England. While overseas he bought an over-the-hill six-year-old Irish stallion, Royal Flush, who his trainer thought still had great potential. Royal Flush was entered in the Steward's Cup at Goodwood, at 40–1, although Gates and Drake bet on him so heavily that the odds dropped to 5 1/2 to 1 by post time. Gates alone won more than $600,000 on the race. Gates made out even better in 1902 when he won $650,000 on Savable, Drake's two-year-old, who captured the Futurity at Sheepshead Bay.[38]

Considerable prerace attention was given to spectator fashion. The *Tribune* featured a story about women's gowns a few days before the race, because "a marvelous show of dresses is expected, for Derby day was made for clothes no less than for horses." Green was the season's color, and store windows featured Irish point lace, silk coats, French high heels, and parasols to match the gowns. The sports section published a large ad for A. Bishop's men's hats, headlined "Derby Day Winners," with prices ranging from $2.50 to $5, including panamas, splits, and the top-priced milians.[39]

The Derby showed a surprisingly big shift in fashion, with gowns patterned after the styles at Epsom Downs. They were less bold, with somber colors, including white and black, along with soft tinted grays and cream colors. Many gowns were shorter than usual, better to

Table 9
Racing Days and Purses in Greater Chicago, 1902

COURSE	DAYS	PURSES
Harlem	43	$187,735
Hawthorne	47	189,580
Lakeside	30	78,400
Washington Park	25	192,725
Worth	44	137,875
Total	189	$786,315

Source: Chicago Tribune, November 21, 1902, 7-1.

accent the popular high French heels. Surprisingly, hats did not get much attention, although they were often wide brimmed and pretentious, decorated with flowers, so large they could block the view of spectators. At a time when people dressed up to go out in public to ball games, museums, or horse races, most men wore conventional summer suits of blue serge or homespun, caps if they were working class, panama hats if middle class. Upper-class men wore frock or cutaway coats and a top hat.[40]

The metropolitan area had 189 days of racing in 1902, led by Hawthorne (47), Worth (44), and Harlem (43). Total purses came to $786,315, or a daily average of $4,160 (see table 9). Washington Park offered the largest prize money by a narrow margin over Hawthorne and Harlem, even though its twenty-five-day meet was the shortest. The WPC's average daily purse was $7,709 ($192,725 for the meet), among the largest in the nation, while Lakeside offered the smallest daily prizes in Chicagoland ($2,610).[41]

Secretary Nathanson of Harlem asserted that the turf had a direct and positive impact on the local economy. He estimated there were about fourteen hundred racehorses in Chicago in 1902, costing owners $140,000 just for feed. The tracks employed some twenty-five hundred workers, largely menials, who earned about $50 a month, or $525,000 for the 4.2 months of racing. Nathanson estimated the employees spent $20 a month for food and clothes, putting another $210,000 into circulation.[42]

THE 1903 DERBY: A RACING LANDMARK

The quality of racing in Chicago in 1903 was quite high, and nine records were set that year. Lakeside opened the Chicago-area racing season in April, but closed after only thirteen days on April 28. This came after progressive Indiana governor Winfield T. Durbin, a Republican, had announced on April 17 that he would send in the national guard to close the track if the gambling was not halted, overriding both the local police and the Lake County sheriff. The track's operators, John Condon and Jim O'Leary, were on their second five-year lease, which was set to expire in February 1904. They later decided not to run a second meet in the fall. Worth opened on April 29, followed by Hawthorne.[43]

The big event of the year was the American Derby on June 20 that opened the Washington Park season. Some seventy thousand reportedly attended the Derby, and the WPR took in $125,000 at the gate. The reported attendance, which was probably exaggerated, would have been a record attendance for any American sporting contest staged in an enclosed sporting facility until 1911, when eighty thousand viewed the first Indianapolis 500. Bookies made out well when the Picket, a 10–1 underdog, won his maiden (initial victory), capturing the $25,000 first prize with a race record time of 2:33, besting the old mark by 0.8 seconds. J. C. Yeager, a Cincinnati plunger and bookie, won more than $30,000 on the race, which included a 60–1 wager with Kid Weller on a $3 bet. Racing fans that year were also excited by the setting of nine American records at local courses.[44]

Captain P. J. Carmody, the owner of the new St. Louis Union Jockey Club who was interested in investing in Chicago racing, published in St. Louis his estimations of the 1903 WPR season. However, he had a glaring error, reporting there were thirty racing dates in 1903, when Washington Park always had twenty-five days. I corrected the data based on the actual racing season. The adjusted data found that

Table 10
Washington Park Club Estimated Financial Records, 1903

Receipts

3,000 paid admissions per day	$75,000
20 bookmakers, $100 each	50,000
Field books	10,000
Bookmakers' fee for sixth race	12,500
Western Union telegraph service	12,500
Bar, restaurant, fruit, and lunch	7,500
Programs	2,500
Admission to paddock	2,500
Run-up money in selling races	2,500
Messengers in grand stand	1,250
Ring supplies for bookmakers	1,250
Total	$177,500

Expenditures, twenty-five-day meeting

Stakes, handicaps, and purses	$95,833
Operating expenses	12,500
Rent, taxes, and insurance	8,750
Expenses maintaining labor, etc.	5,000
Expense advertising	2,000
Total	$124,083

Source: *St. Louis Republic*, July 24, 1903, 8-1.

the WPR expended $124,083, while producing $177,500 in revenue. This figure came to a profit of $53,417 (see table 10). The *St. Louis Republic* credited the WPR with more than a 25 percent profit, but the return on out-of-pocket expenses was 30 percent. Still, the profit was far below the six-figure returns reported in the early 1890s.[45]

Washington Park relied heavily on the entrance fees from owners so it could end up distributing a Chicago-high $216,470 to race winners in 1903, compared to $192,725 the year before. The daily average purse was $8,659, up 11.0 percent from the year before. Elsewhere, both Hawthorne and Harlem also surpassed $200,000 in purses, followed by Worth at $145,611. Lakeside, which had just one meet, instead of its usual two, dropped from $78,000 to $31,000. These figures came to a grand total of $798,006, only about $12,000 more than 1902. There was no solid data on profits, but the Chicago tracks did well. Hawthorne, whose facility was worth $500,000, was believed to make around $100,000. The *Los Angeles Times* estimated a more positive return for Washington Park of around $400,000 between 1901 and 1903. Racing on both coasts did well in these years. The *New York Commercial* reported that New York's tracks, worth about $7.5 million, were returning a 25 percent profit.[46]

Racing Scandals and Unsavory Horsemen

Chicago tracks in 1903 were bedeviled by unscrupulous horsemen. Washington Park faced an ugly crusade in July, led by E. E. Farley and J. E. Glenn, horsemen recently barred by the WJC from member tracks for racing a horse with another's name in Detroit, earning the cabal around $50,000 in bets. Farley and Glenn sought revenge by hiring constables to deliver warrants against President Young and Secretary Howard as well as various bookmakers, but had a hard time since so many members of the Constables' Association worked for the local tracks. Eight constables returned the next day and arrested Young, Howard, and fifteen bookies. The track officials were taken to a justice of the peace in distant LaGrange and advised that no charges would be pressed if they hired or paid off the arresting constables. Young and Howard refused, but were released anyway. Farley and Glenn also instigated a major raid against Harlem on Saturday, August 8, when there were more than eight thousand spectators at the track, but their efforts soon petered out.[47]

Another racing disgrace drew front-page coverage on October 19, two months after Harlem and Hawthorne barred owner Daniel J. Lynch, trainer C. Lind, and jockey J. Treanor for doping the colt Bondage at Hawthorne. Lynch was well known in sporting circles, having managed heavyweight contender Tom Sharkey in his 1896 fight against future champion Bob Fitzsimmons. The favored Australian knocked Sharkey down in the eighth round with a stunning solar-plexus punch. However, referee Wyatt Earp, the former western lawman, disqualified Fitzsimmons for hitting his downed opponent with an illegal blow that no one else saw.[48]

The track came under considerable political pressure from eastern sources for punishing the alleged dopesters and reinstated Lynch, Lind, and Treanor. Rumors spread about protection money being paid. Local track managers reconsidered their prior lenient decision, which was hurting public confidence in racing and ruled all three men off the tracks. The revoked bans had become a cause célèbre, elevating public ire against the involvement of politicians in racing's integrity that lessened any chance of a new proracing state law and raised fears about the sport's possible closure in 1904. The *Tribune* was elated because the turn of events showed the public how badly racing was run and that it should be banned.[49]

THE END OF PRIZEFIGHTING IN CHICAGO

Boxing in Chicago was a minor social problem compared to horse-race gambling, but the ending of prizefighting in 1904 provided momentum for the war on horse racing. Boxing was a means for lower-class men to prove their manliness, gain fame, and make money. Formal prizefights were banned in Chicago, as in most of the United States, because of its violence, gambling, and lowlife crowds it attracted, though informal matches were held surreptitiously in saloons and barns. In the 1880s, Parson Davies successfully staged matches at racetracks, saloons, and armories with the backing of Mike McDonald and later on relied on Aldermen Bathhouse John Coughlin or Hinky Dink Mike Kenna to get his bouts staged.[50]

Louisiana in 1890 became the first state to legalize boxing, enabling wide-open New Orleans to hold bouts in buildings owned by established athletic clubs. Local politicians were prominent in running the sport there. Commissioner of public works John Fitzpatrick refereed both the John L. Sullivan–Paddy Ryan (1882) and Sullivan–Jake Kilrain (1889) championship fights, staged near New Orleans. Fitzpatrick was the dominant figure in the "Ring," the city's political machine, and served as mayor in 1892 when the Olympic Athletic Club staged three world championship bouts, including the Sullivan–Jim Corbett heavyweight-title fight.[51]

In 1896 New York's Horton Act legalized boxing, mainly thanks to Big Tim Sullivan, the number-two man in Tammany Hall, who became Greater New York's leading boxing promoter. Coney Island hosted a number of world championships in the next few years, but in 1900 upstate Republicans repealed the Horton Act because of the sport's brutality, unruly crowds, the prevalence of gambling, and Tammany Hall's extensive influence in the sport. The sport managed to survive in the early 1900s through a "boxing trust" led by Sullivan and other leading Tammanyites via "membership clubs." Fights then were limited to a few rounds, were not heavily advertised, and admitted only "members" of the clubs sponsoring the bouts.

Boxing's legal status in New York was reversed in 1911 under the Frawley Act, passed when the Democrats took control of both branches of the legislature and elected John A. Dix as governor. The legality of prizefighting continued its roller-coaster ride, when the sport was banned again in 1917. Finally in 1920, the Walker Act permanently legitimized proboxing.[52]

Chicago at the turn of the century hosted brief "scientific sparring matches" between lighter-weight combatants at about a hundred small member clubs, but there were also bouts at larger arenas such as Tattersall's and McGurn's Handball Court, operated by politically connected promoters who paid off Aldermen Coughlin or Kenna to evade proscriptive laws.[53]

On December 13, 1900, Tattersall's staged a rare major match between world featherweight champion "Terrible" Terry McGovern and African American lightweight Joe Gans, a gifted fighter who had a hard time getting fights because of his race. The fight, scheduled for six rounds, was an obvious fix, with Gans "knocked out" in round two by a phantom punch. Four days later, the city council passed a bill banning prizefights by a vote of 53–14, but it was not signed by Mayor Harrison. Minor bouts still occurred over the next couple of years, but Harrison did not license any major matches. Gans went on to hold the world lightweight championship from 1902 until 1908. He is rated by experts as the top lightweight of all time.[54]

In 1904 new complaints about fixed fights, corrupt referees, and rough crowds led Mayor Harrison to change his mind. He announced no more approvals of any matches and called for the closing of boxing arenas. The final straw for Harrison came on November 14 in a welterweight bout when Chicagoan "Buddy" Ryan knocked out Billy "Honey" Mellody in the first round. Chaos ensued, leading to a "Thieves' Carnival" as pickpockets and holdup men worked the crowd. One month later, Harrison enforced an old Chicago antiprizefight law that made public professional boxing a felony. This act killed professional boxing in Chicago, which was not resumed until 1926.[55]

THE END OF THE WASHINGTON PARK CLUB

When the 1904 racing season began, the local turf faced serious problems, surprising given the recent success of thoroughbred racing in Chicagoland. However, relations between the area tracks were still quite poor because of conflicts over racing days and lack of support for racing bills in Springfield. There was concern about repercussions from the Farley and Lynch episodes and the CAT's strong bid for midwestern racing supremacy, which included the sponsorship of a $50,000 World's Fair Handicap in conjunction with the upcoming Louisiana Purchase Exposition that commentators thought might lead to the demise of local racing and gambling. The WPR continued to come under mounting disapproval despite its superbly run meets. The complaints mainly came from religious reformers, many of whom were residents of the nearby University of Chicago community in Hyde Park, concerned about the morality of racing, and from property owners living near the track, worried about local land values. The possibility loomed that the WPR would close for a third time.[56]

Neighborhood residents concerned about protecting their property values formed the fifty-member Washington Park Improvement Association, which asserted that the track was a public nuisance with lowlifes coming and going and that there were better uses for the site. The WPIA drew up petitions against the racetrack and initiated condemnation proceedings to cut streets through the racecourse. Racing foes believed that if they halted gambling at the track, racing would become unprofitable, the WPR would close, and the vacated land could be used for better usages, like new homes or even a park, an idea supported by the *Inter Ocean*.[57]

Newly appointed assistant superintendent of police Herman Schuettler was a prime WPIA alley. He already had nearly twenty years on the force and in 1917 rose to head the department. He had a great reputation as a detective who solved dramatic crimes, notably the 1889 murder of Dr. Patrick Cronin. Cronin was a critical supporter of the secret Clan-na-Gael, an Irish Republican political organization, who was killed by four fellow members to shut him up and prevent the exposure of substantial corruption in the organization. Cronin's funeral was the most heavily attended in Chicago since the death of Abraham Lincoln.[58]

Schuettler organized a "flying squadron" of elite detectives to quickly fight the gambling menace. The special squad had a citywide jurisdiction that enabled it to avoid the influence of aldermen who normally had a big impact on police actions in their wards, as well as politically powerful gamblers. Schuettler believed he could end gambling at Washington Park Racetrack and nearly everywhere else in the city. He declared, "Where there is gambling in Chicago, we will stop it. There is no reason to believe that we will permit gambling at Washington Park when we have stopped it elsewhere." The *Tribune* supported the crusade, hoping to not just end offtrack bookmaking but close the tracks as well. The editors denied that such draconian measures would, as track partisans alleged, result in a backlash, opening the city more than ever to the rule of vice.[59]

Schuettler's boss, Superintendent Francis O'Neill, received appeals to halt racing from critics who classified horse racing with "handbook betting and all other common forms of gambling" and demanded no distinction be made among them. The *Chicago Tribune* pointed out that this argument was, ironically, the same one made by local owners of handbooks and gambling dives: "The gamblers believe a crusade carried to the extent of closing all racing will result in a reaction of public sentiment such as is credited with having overthrown Mayor [Seth] Lowe [*sic*] and his so-called 'blue laws' administration in New York, and thereby give them an opportunity sooner or later to carry on their trade in Chicago unrestrictedly."[60]

The 1904 racing season began on April 30 at the Worth course on a beautiful day before eight thousand fans. The management made $177,000 in 1903 and expected similar results in the following year. Shortly after the opening, Western Union announced it would close its racing bureau and stop transmitting racing news (although private interests could still send data over the wires). Track managers welcomed this news, believing it would curtail offtrack betting and encourage more racing fans to attend races and bet there.[61]

The Worth meet was followed by Hawthorne on May 21. Opening day was attended by ten thousand devotees with more than a hundred uniformed Pinkerton guards and twenty-six constables at the track for security. The feature race was the Chicago Derby, won by English Lad, a 6–5 favorite in 2:06, just three-fifths of a second off the course record for a mile and a quarter. Track workers removed all telegraph wires and phones from the grounds, and even lines direct to newspapers, to deprive offtrack bookmakers of racing results. This move cost Hawthorne about $800 a day in lost revenue from Western Union, but the jockey club expected to make up the loss with a higher anticipated gate and the presence of eight to ten more bookmakers each paying $100 for the privilege. Harlem immediately announced it would adopt the same plan. Sheriff Thomas E. Barrett welcomed the news and announced he would not order any raids that summer. As far as he was concerned, "Horse races have become a permanent institution."[62]

The Washington Park Season

On June 10, Washington Park sent the city collector an application for an amusement license with a check for $1,250 for twenty-five days of racing. Mayor Harrison, who had his eye on the Democratic presidential nomination, took the opportunity to present himself as a moral crusader by instructing the police superintendent to bar bookmaking within the city limits and to suppress racetrack gambling. Critics justifiably derided Harrison, an old-time bettor and friend of racing, as quite the hypocrite. He focused on Washington Park because it was the standard-bearer of local racing and the leading track in the Midwest and also because the area's three suburban tracks were beyond his jurisdiction. He said Washington Park could get a license and have races if it conformed to the law: "There is no law forbidding the running of horses. . . . There is a law against betting, however, and that law will be enforced. It would appear foolish to stop handbook gambling inside the city and then allow bookmaking on a big scale to be carried on."[63]

Harrison sent a sharp note to Superintendent Francis O'Neill, instructing him to suppress handbooks and racetrack gambling at Washington Park. The message included a copy of the *Daily Racing Form* with ads offering quotations from winter books operated by Weller, O'Leary, and Jacob "Mont" Tennes as evidence of gambling. Harrison told the press, "There will be no bookmaking inside of the city limits of Chicago if I can prevent it." On June 11 the big "future books" were raided, some arrests were made, and betting literature was confiscated. Four days later, the mayor announced, "I will take away the license of those millionaires as quickly as I would that of a saloonkeeper." Of course, Harrison's sudden conversion was somewhat disingenuous, since he was closely tied to political bosses like Bathhouse John Coughlin who thrived on gambling revenues.[64]

The mayor's speech elated the WPIA, which announced that the closing of Washington Park would "purify the moral atmosphere in the neighborhood of the racetrack." City hall considered halting gambling inside Washington Park and the rest of the city a joint duty of the police and the Cook County sheriff. The responsibility of halting gambling at the three suburban courses, along with fighting the illegal poolrooms and the handbooks, belonged to Sheriff Thomas E. Barrett. Reform-minded journalist and respected sociologist Josiah Flynt did not expect much action by Barrett, who was elected "by the racing and poolroom interests" and was not a Harrison political ally. The sheriff was uninterested in fighting gambling at Washington Park, which he considered the city's responsibility.[65]

The *Daily News* backed the mayor: "As a breeding ground for vice, under the patronage of fashion, the Washington park racetrack has worked incalculable evil in the past. Chicago . . . must cease to give itself up, for a gambling orgy on Derby Day. The pretense that this kind of debauch is delightful and fashionable and generally refined and soulful is a wicked pretense." The Republican *Inter Ocean* was pretty skeptical: "The moral effect on the community may be eliminated, since nobody believes for a moment that there is any genuine element of reform in the attitude of the 'business' administration. Politics, revenge, personal spite, playing to the galleries, and racetrack jealousies are in the situation. The action would hurt small businesses who rely on the trade of tourists, and endanger the breeding industry of the state."[66]

The tracks still believed they were protected under the Gibbs Act of 1887. However, an attorney interviewed by the *Inter Ocean* claimed that the police could arrest anyone making bets and even club members wagering with one another, although it was difficult to gather the evidence needed for such a conviction. Corporation counsel William H. Sexton referred to Section 127 of the criminal code that prohibited all gambling and pointed out that the Gibbs Act had been overturned by the *Swigert* case in 1895.[67]

WPR officials feared their track would be shut down, but thought that preventing race reports leaking out to poolrooms and handbooks would help the sport's public image. Jockey-club managers were certain that handbook men were responsible for the antigambling crusade and tried to work with secular reformers, but the situation was becoming untenable. Gambling was essential for Washington Park to stay in operation because gambling brought in the paying crowds, Western Union payments of $700–$1,500 a day, and fees from bookmakers. The WPR, without gambling, would pay out five times in purses what it made at the gate and have a harder time meeting daily overhead expenses. Management anticipated the meet would have fifty bookmakers a day for twenty-four days, at $1,000 a day ($120,000), one field book at $1,000 a day, plus the extra revenue for Derby Day with a hundred bookies at $100 a day ($10,000) and $2,650 for the field book, which came to $156,650 for the entire season.[68]

The 1904 American Derby

Harrison's pronouncements did not impress the leading on-track bookies, who publicized their intent to take bets on and prior to Derby Day. They insisted their customers had nothing to worry about from the police or private constables that offtrack bookmakers were rumored to be hiring. One big bone of contention was the field book, which provided betting opportunities for the long shots, because the jockey club had no direct control over it. Blind John Condon and partners Hinky Dink Kenna and bookmaker-saloonkeeper Tom McGinnis threatened to use their clout with Harrison to bar gambling at the track unless the WPR accepted an offer of $100,000 for the field book (estimated to make $400,000 from "piker" bets) and the betting ring for an unnamed amount. They were rebuffed by WPR treasurer John R. Walsh, president of the Chicago National Bank. He was part of a syndicate that controlled the field book the year before and made $160,000.[69]

Schuettler announced extensive plans to curtail gambling at Washington Park just prior to its opening. He assigned multiple officers to guard every bookmaker and scattered officers throughout the crowd to arrest anyone who tried to bet, even by mere nods or signals. The principal bookies took seriously his intentions and announced they were closing operations. The WPR bowed to police pressure and the mayor's threat to revoke its amusement license and agreed to open without gambling. However, the club made it clear that without paying people coming out to watch the races, the meet could not continue. The police also announced that telegraph transmissions would be banned and the wires cut and warned they would put out of commission any phone used at Washington Park to send out racing news.[70]

On opening day, Saturday, June 18, as forewarned, 216 patrolmen and 90 plainclothesmen were assigned to Washington Park, with 200 police officers placed on reserve at the Englewood Station. Schuettler's flying squadron scattered about the track, abetted by many detectives unknown to the bookmakers. The track itself hired 362 Pinkerton detectives to help suppress bookmaking. The police raided ten downtown handbooks during the races, putting a damper on the harvest anticipated by bookmakers who expected the flying squadron would be busy at the track. Kid Weller said the police vigilance cost him $35,000, although his poolroom in Hammond had heavy wagering. O'Leary paid out $260,000 to his winning clients, largely people who had bet in advance, leaving him with a loss of $40,000.[71]

Approximately 40,000 people turned out for the Derby on opening day. While significantly fewer than the record-breaking crowd of 1903, it was still one of the largest crowds that year at any sporting event. The audience included several US senators and other prominent politicians in town for the Republican National Convention. The Derby got six pages of coverage in the *Tribune* and similar coverage in other papers with Sunday editions, which excluded the *Daily News*. The race was won in record time by Highball, the second favorite, at 4–1, earning a purse of $26,325 for owner W. S. Sheftel, a young stockbroker. The betting ring was closed for the race, which meant a lot of the excitement normally observed with money on the line was missing, though bets were taken unobtrusively in the paddock and infield.[72]

The large Derby attendance produced a gate of $80,000. The track made good money that day, albeit $60,000 less than the year before. Observers felt this reduced figure indicated financial trouble for the WPR, since Derby Day profits were not only a major source of annual profits, but a good measuring stick for the entire meet. The *Tribune* predicted the meet would run a $150,000 deficit, and another authority estimated it could reach $250,000 if it continued without the betting ring.[73]

President Young said his track's future was up to the public, implying its destiny was in doubt unless there were sufficient attendees to pay expenses. He was optimistic that betting would resume, claiming that the hundreds of officers and detectives did not completely halt gambling at the Derby. But the truth was that the authorities had pretty much halted the bookmakers, who did not appear the next racing day, Monday, June 20. Even though ticket prices were down to $1, the attendance was below a thousand, a devastating drop-off from the Derby on Saturday and also compared to the second day of the 1903 meet when attendance was reported at twenty thousand. The evidence was strong that racing fanatics were unwilling to buy tickets to watch races without any betting and pretty conclusive that Washington Park could not operate without bookmaking. Conditions looked so bleak that the suburban tracks, worried about their own prospects if the flagship track went under, offered their facilities to the WPR to finish the meet.[74]

Day three of the meet was highlighted by the popular Lakeside Stakes, but gate receipts were merely around $500, the smallest in track history. It was a tiny fraction of what was needed to keep the track running, with such daily operating costs as $4,100 in purses and $2,000 for various fixed expenses. While there was some dispute whether the police could totally suppress gambling, especially off the track, their efforts at Washington Park were strangling the sport. Officials kept the screws tightened until the jockey-club directors decided to discontinue all racing, with no plans of reopening. The board of directors relinquished the remaining dates to Harlem (seven), Hawthorne (seven), and Worth (six), which helped protect horsemen who had twenty-five hundred racing horses in the metropolitan area. The *Record-Herald* saw the closing of Washington Park as evidence that racing, even at elite tracks, was not just for the love of the turf: "It now shows itself, however, to have been neither more nor less than a huge gambling enterprise, falsely masking itself under the flag of sportsmanship."[75]

Harrison on Horse-Race Gambling

Following the closing of Washington Park, Carter Harrison promised, "As long as I am mayor of Chicago there will be no bookmaking out there." He recommended that if Chicagoans felt that racetrack gambling was a legitimate recreation, then they should go to the state legislature and copy states like New York that legalized gambling inside the enclosures. In early July, when Mayor Harrison was trying to develop a progressive reputation for a possible run at national office, he published "The Dope Sheet" in the popular *Saturday Evening Post*, asserting that horse-race gambling injured the American work ethic. Harrison recommended the federal government halt interstate transmission of racing news:

> Race-track gambling destroys one's ideas of political economy. . . .
> It breaks down the "sweat-of-the brow" theory. It takes from one
> the desire to live by honest work. The clerk whose ideas of advancement had embraced a schedule of work and thrift substitutes for this
> a programme of luck and hazard. . . . If congress will take the same
> cognizance of racetrack gambling that it did of the Louisiana Lottery, it will be possible to exterminate the former as the latter was
> exterminated. The use of the mails must be forbidden to race-track
> gamblers. It must be made illegal to transit race-track information
> from one state to another.[76]

One year later, Harrison gave a valedictory address at the conclusion of his fourth term as mayor. He spoke proudly about his attack on horse-race gambling that sought equal treatment for everyone under the law:

> [A] community may not safely have one law for the rich and another
> for the poor. If it be unlawful for the saloonkeeper or the cigar dealer
> to make a handbook, or to permit the making of a handbook in his
> place of business, it is equally unlawful for the directors of a great
> social organization like the Washington Park club to farm out gambling privileges within its enclosure. The charge, indeed, has been

made that some of the directors of this great club personally operated the so-called "dollar-book." Whether this be true or not, the
immediate closing up of the Washington Park club track, as soon as
it was definitely understood the police were in earnest in prohibiting
the making of bets within the enclosure, shows it was largely to the
financial interest of the club to farm out gambling privileges.[77]

The WPIA gloated at the outcome of its fight against racing and
promptly petitioned the Board of Local Improvements to cut streets
through the track site. Attorney P. S. Brown claimed the track hurt
nearby property values by twenty-five to fifty dollars per frontage foot
and that the neighborhood was less safe than in pretrack days. Developer
H. H. Gross agreed: "We have suffered from this track long enough.
Thieves, hangers on for the races, and touts have infested the neighborhood, preying on the people. It should be permitted no longer."[78]

Chicago Racing after the Demise of Washington Park

The antiracing fight shifted out of the city to Hawthorne, which
opened for racing on June 24, knowing that Sheriff Thomas Barrett
would not interfere without a court order. Barrett recognized that racing had been going on at Hawthorne since 1891 and saw no reason to
contradict his predecessors. The Citizens' Association sent the sheriff a letter criticizing his prior inaction, especially given the results
of Harrison's fight against horse-race gambling. The CA suggested
that if he just emulated Harrison and "determinedly expressed official disapproval," the tracks would close. Barrett ignored the letter.
Republican state's attorney Charles S. Deneen advised the CA to seek
convictions of bookmakers rather than harass the sheriff, noting legal
precedents that did not require Barrett to arrest the bookmakers.[79]
    A grand-jury meeting on July 1 returned forty-two indictments
against alleged Hawthorne bookmakers and hoped to compel Barrett
to arrest the accused or get them to appear in court. In the past, true
bills were voted against bookmakers as inmates of gambling houses,

but this grand jury was the first to employ a section of the penal code that enabled it to indict bookmakers for keeping gambling apparatus.[80]

Three weeks later, the grand jury began a broader investigation of on-track gambling. The jury first focused on the need to suppress racing information, the lifeblood of gambling, including dope sheets that published entry names, weights, and odds and gave advice to bettors. The jury's aim was to prove that newspaper publication of racing forms and track ads was nearly as responsible for betting as failures to enforce the law. Publisher Victor F. Lawson of the *Daily News* and editor Frank B. Noyes of the *Herald* responded as spokesmen for a free press, asserting the legitimacy of any publication to accept racing ads. Lawson's position was a bit of a surprise, since he was a leading racetrack opponent. The grand jury ended up censuring newspapers that published betting odds and other racing information and passed a resolution asking the press to desist from publishing racing news.[81]

The grand jury summoned the sheriff, who seemed remarkably ignorant about racetrack gambling, explaining he had not been to Hawthorne for two years and had no memory of betting at a race. Nonetheless, he pledged to enforce the new rulings against gambling. The sheriff offered legal opinions that he was required to suppress crime only following formal complaints. However, assistant state's attorney Frank Blair pointed out that the law provided that the sheriff should make arrests with or without warrants when he had reasonable grounds the law was being violated. The *Tribune* predicted such actions would shut the Harlem and Hawthorne parks as surely as they had closed Washington Park.[82]

On July 26, the grand jury took major steps toward killing racing, calling for the suppression of all bookmaking, and indicted twenty-five bookmakers. The jury also sent Barrett an ultimatum to do his duty and halt on-track betting: "It is in the interest of public morals and good order that tracks where such gambling is carried on should be closed, and kept closed, and we hereby request the sheriff of this county to proceed to such tracks with sufficient force and to arrest on view all persons who may be engaged in gambling . . . , or who may be aiding, abetting, or assisting in the same, or may be operating said track and allowing and permitting gambling to be carried on."[83]

The Citizens' Association of Harlem, which included a hundred local property owners, continued its crusade against gambling at the local track's summer meet. The CA planned to summon the sheriff as a private citizen to join a constable's posse to raid Harlem's bookies and serve warrants on village officials, including village president Henry Mohr, police captain Charles Schwass, and police magistrate O. H. Gerke, who had previously ignored gambling at the track. Former Harlem police captain Chris Lange, considered the most active member of the association, declared, "It is an open secret that town officials are receiving a 'rakeoff' from the race-track authorities." The CA got support from state's attorney Deneen, who changed his mind about the sheriff's duties. He now claimed the law expressly empowered Sheriff Barrett to fight gambling and that his inaction made him guilty of negligence of duties.[84]

The "inglorious season" played out with Harlem closing in late September, followed by Worth, which had a thirty-one-day meet at the end of October. The Worth meet was rated as the most crooked local meet in years. According to the *Tribune*, "1904 has been a black eye for the turf in Chicago." The *Tribune* asserted that Washington Park's closing, "attended by general denunciation of racing as a sport, alienated a large element that recently had become interested in the pastime," leaving patronage mainly to "regulars." The public attacks on racing "disgusted many of the better class of racing men and racing followers, making them lukewarm in their support, and this naturally gave the dishonest element the better opportunity to come to the front." The paper argued that while the sport had been consistently improving for several years, it was definitely on the downswing at the proprietary tracks, with a decline in the quality of horses, jockeys, and stables and an increase in fraudulent races, attributed to younger and less experienced jockeys.[85]

The *Tribune*'s review of the season concluded that it was a bad year for racing despite the presence of excellent facilities. The paper asserted, "However true it may be that horse racing always will thrive to a certain degree, whether under a legal ban or not, it is certain that no sport will gain the sympathy of a great mass of Americans where it is officially and emphatically pronounced lawless by those in authority."[86]

Chicago racing in 1904 had its lowest attendance in more than a decade, with Hawthorne the only bright spot. Its five meetings lasted fifty-three days with 327 races and an average daily purse of $4,659 ($755 per race), for a grand total of $246,917.50, 30.2 percent higher than in 1902 ($189,580). Hawthorne's prizes that year would have been the tenth highest in the United States in 1905, though well behind the leader, the Coney Island Jockey Club, whose purses came to $571,300 ($3,174 per race) over thirty dates.[87]

Despite the decline in attendance, the financials still looked good. A St. Louis bookmaker estimated the average racing crowd in Chicago paid $5,000 for admissions, spent an additional $2,000 at the track, and bet $200,000, 2.7 times as much as was bet at the St. Louis Fairgrounds and four times much as Kansas City's Elm Ridge track. The average Windy City track spent $400 on employees and $300 on maintenance, offered purses of $3,500, and netted $5,800, more than ten times Elm Ridge, the free-admission fairgrounds, and the St. Louis Union track, which all lost money. Chicago bookies made collectively $3,000, while paying $1,500 to their clerks. These bookies took home 20 percent more than their colleagues at the fairgrounds and twice the amount of the other two Missouri tracks.[88]

THE END OF CHICAGO RACING

The racing community was concerned that the antitrack crusade would eliminate all racing in Cook County in 1905, given what happened to Washington Park and the prevailing nationwide efforts against racing. Furthermore, newly elected state's attorney John J. Healy announced in December in no uncertain terms his intent to close racetracks in Cook County that permitted gambling.[89]

The new season was anticipated with less excitement than any in memory, since racing followers expected the authorities would bar on-track gambling. The Chicago Racing Club (Hawthorne) was the only track to announce its upcoming stakes events, though few experts expected them to take place. They did not anticipate Sheriff Barrett interfering, but there was concern about the ongoing conflict between Corrigan and Condon. Corrigan could no longer compete with Condon's fortune of more than $1 million, his political pull, and his connections with the underworld. Aficionados expected Condon to open Lakeside, but not Harlem, and foresaw him using his influence to halt racing in Cook County.[90]

Chicago's racing future was seen as tied to the results of the April mayoralty election between reformers Republican John M. Harlan, who had previously run for mayor in 1897, and Democratic circuit-court judge Edward F. Dunne, although the primary issue was not racing, but municipal ownership of public transportation. Harlan enjoyed a good horse race and had no objection to occasional racing under the proper environment, but the conventional wisdom was that he would continue to bar racing at Washington Park in deference to the wishes of certain leading supporters, while Dunne would be more supportive of the turf. Dunne won with 49.7 percent of the vote to Harlan's 42.2 percent. Mayor Dunne turned out to be an ineffective administrator, was indecisive and impractical, and failed to produce on his electoral promises, alienating both reformers and bosses. Horse racing ended up a nonissue in his two-year term.[91]

The Swift Demise in 1905

In early April, and again two weeks later, the new Republican state's attorney John J. Healy reiterated his intent to stamp out pool selling and handbooks and close the remaining racetracks. Healy proclaimed, "I understand that three or four race tracks will start up in Cook County within the next month or two. I also understand that pools or handbooks will be run in connection with these tracks. The laws prohibit gambling, and pools and handbooks are a form of gambling. I will therefore, see that the laws are enforced." He pledged to bring to justice anyone who "commits, aids, abets, or connives in any way" with gamblers. Healy's announcement came as no surprise and had been rumored since the 1904 elections. Track managers held off their plans until Healy finally made his position clear.[92]

The press applauded Healy's decision. The *Tribune* admired high-class racing as a wonderful sport as carried out at places like Washington Park that had real racing admirers who could afford to lose a small sum staked upon the results. However, "racing as . . . carried on at other resorts is an abomination, a scandal, and a disgrace, and ought to be stopped. . . . Chicago will do infinitely better without any racing."[93]

The *Tribune* blamed racing men for the coming demise, criticizing the argument of turf proponents that racing brought increased trade to the city. Any new capital that tourists spent at saloons, barbershops, hotels, and similar enterprises "do not equal the losses directly or indirectly caused by the 'industry.'" Any small or sporadic benefit was negated by "the losses to business and especially the impairment of character among employees of commercial houses, owing to the practice of 'following the races.'" The *Tribune* concluded, "All honor to state's Attorney Healy. He has declared his intention to enforce the law as he knows it, and the community will applaud his efforts."[94]

Worth failed to open as scheduled on April 29, its many problems only exacerbated four days earlier when dynamiters threw two bombs over the fence at one thirty in the morning. One device landed on the roof of a row of empty stalls, tearing a one-foot hole, and another exploded when it struck the top of the fence. A similar bomb had demolished part of a stall's roof a week earlier, but the event had been hushed up. The racing crowd was frightened by the violence, which some attributed to the conflict between the WJC and the new rival, the American Turf Association. There had also been recent questionable fires at Hawthorne and Harlem and an attempted arson at Lakeside.[95]

None of the tracks reopened. One year before Worth's property was said to be worth $300,000, Hawthorne $350,000–$500,000, and Harlem $500,000. Their management recognized they had no hopes of making money without gambling, which Healy was not going to allow. Chicago became only the second of the world's fifteen largest cities, joining Philadelphia, to ban thoroughbred racing. Even the staid *Tribune* was uncomfortable being placed in the same category as the City of Brotherly Love, given its reputation for enforcing strict blue laws. The paper interpreted the ending of racing less as a problem with the sport than with Chicago's local practices, where there was no longer an elite course, but just profit-oriented facilities.[96]

There was also no more racing at Lakeside either, as the Indiana General Assembly forbade betting on horse races. In addition, there was also a campaign well under way to close St. Louis racing, vigorously promoted by the *Post-Dispatch*, which sought repeal of the Breeders' Law to fight political corruption, moral depravity, the corruption of youth, and the breaking up of families. The paper claimed that the gambling syndicate running Delmar Racetrack had certain powerful Democratic bosses on its payroll supporting lobbyists in Jefferson City to challenge laws that sought to raise their taxes or their gambling monopoly.[97]

Civic and religious reform groups established the Citizens Organization for the Suppression of Racetrack Gambling on January 28, 1905, to fight the sport. They got help from progressive governor Joseph Falk, who got the legislature to repeal the Breeders' Act that permitted bookmaking to ostensibly promote the breed and enacted a new antigambling law that made all pool selling a felony. Missouri's tracks closed permanently on July 29.[98]

Comparing the Canadian and American Racing Scenes

As American racing collapsed, the Canadian thoroughbred racing business took advantage and grew significantly. In 1905 Canada had just five courses, including prestigious facilities in Hamilton, Montreal, and Toronto and proprietary tracks in Fort Erie and Windsor. They staged eighty-seven days of racing for $228,868 in purses. In 1909 $22 million was bet offtrack on thoroughbred races in the Dominion, and Windsor alone made $150,000 under American managers. One year later, Parliament banned bookmaking, which led to tracks instituting pari-mutuel betting. By 1914 there were eight major tracks in Canada.[99]

The Canadian expansion of thoroughbred racing at a time when the American turf was near collapse seems incongruous, since Canada was extremely similar to the United States in nearly every way. Canadians were relatively prosperous, spoke the same language as Americans (outside of Quebec), were heavily Protestant, and had the same British-based culture. The dominant anglophone Canadians supported a similar strict moral code in the nineteenth century as Americans, which included strict Sunday blue laws. Canada banned working and playing sports on the Lord's Day in 1845, and in Toronto streetcars were closed on Sundays until 1897. In regards to horse-race gambling, the confederation in 1878 passed the Blake Act that banned the recording of bets. Bookmakers were forced underground and consequently employed various schemes to evade the antibetting laws, such as selling betters lithographs of the horse they wagered on after the races.[100]

There were, however, important differences between the United States and its northern neighbor. Canada had a whiter bicultural population that was primarily Francophone and Catholic in Quebec, less open to immigration, and far more rural. Second, Canada was still part of the British Empire, which had a notable impact upon its social and moral values. Racing was well regarded as a sporting pastime, but not when run for commercial purposes. And third, while both countries had democratic federal governments, the Canadian central government, like its British model (the Westminster system), controlled the police power and set standards of decency, whereas in the United States the police power and the regulation of morality were reserved to the states. The Canadian government in the early 1900s also had certain elements that reflected an aristocratic social structure with a royal sovereign (King George V) and a Senate modeled after the House of Lords, appointed by the governor-general. Such institutions helped make thoroughbred racing in Canada indeed "the sport of kings."[101]

American moral reformers mainly devoted their attention to fighting gambling with governments on the local and state levels where most moral legislation was framed and where the reformers had more influence. A recent study of the influence of Christian lobbyists on moral legislation considered in Congress found that nearly 20 percent of the proposed moral legislation submitted to Congress between 1877 and 1891 dealt with gambling, but just 11 percent between 1891 and 1907 when Christian and secular reformers had success in halting racetrack gambling on the state and local levels.[102]

The federal government had limited authority to regulate public morality, like the Comstock Laws, applied through its control over the mail, and the Page Act of 1875 that banned the admission to the United States of Asian women brought in for prostitution. The next major development was the Mann Act, enacted in 1910 in response to the public outcry over the white slave trade, which banned men from taking a woman across state lines to engage in prostitution or for other immoral purposes. The first prominent conviction came in 1913 against world boxing heavyweight champion Jack Johnson for taking prostitute Belle Schreiber across state lines.[103]

Congress passed only a handful of antigambling bills, none of which dealt with comprehensive antigambling laws. Those bills enacted into law employed existing federal powers to deal with gambling and interstate commerce, like the Louisiana Lottery, banned in 1894, or gambling in the District of Columbia, where Congress had direct jurisdiction. It passed in 1890 a bill banning bookmaking and pool selling except on racecourses, but President Benjamin Harrison vetoed the measure since it effectively licensed gambling, which it was supposed to have prohibited. One year later, the federal government banned all bookmaking and pool selling within the capital area and one mile beyond its boundaries. This prohibition contributed to the closing of the suburban Ivy City and Benning tracks. Benning reopened in 1896 with betting, though payoffs were collected off the track, but closed in 1908 after the Senate and then the House of Representatives passed antigambling bills, the latter unanimously. One year later, and again in 1911 and 1916, Congress tried unsuccessfully to halt the interstate transmission of racing information through its control over interstate commerce.[104]

Canadian legal behavior at the turn of the century was encoded in the nation's Criminal Code of 1892. This distinction facilitated

Canada's continuance of racing since, as the solicitor general asserted during the debate on the Criminal Code, "the law has always allowed betting on horses." Parliament subsequently added the McCarthy Amendment that legitimized any racecourse conducted by a registered corporation, largely following the model of racing in Great Britain.[105]

In 1905 Canadian courts further supported racing when a ruling declared that track managers were not directly involved in betting, contrary to the legal position in several American states, and thus did not violate the antigambling laws. The courts additionally bolstered horse-race betting one year later in the *Moyett* case, which involved a bookmaker and his assistants at Toronto's Woodbine case who took bets, but did not do business on a fixed spot. The court ruled as long as they continuously walked around the betting ring, they were not violating the law. The proracing view was supported by the popular weekly *Saturday Night* that thought moderate betting was a "legitimate and time-honored institution . . . that should not be done away with a process of the law . . . endeavoring to manufacture morality by acts of Parliament instead of by education and home and church influences." In 1908 the Canadian Racing Association was organized.[106]

Canada, like the United States, and unlike Great Britain, had no national antiracing organization. The opposition to gambling and racing mainly came from anglophone pietists in groups like the Moral and Social Reform Council of Canada (MSRCC) and the Women's Christian Temperance Union that considered gambling a sin and by secular progressives who hoped to end all horse-race gambling because of its negative impact on gamblers' families and urban politics. The MSRCC included Baptists, Methodists, Presbyterians (collectively 38.6 percent of the national population), and Anglicans, as well as members of the Salvation Army, labor unions, and farmer organizations. They were opposed by a broad coalition that included working-class bettors, Roman Catholics (41.4 percent of the population) who were heavily concentrated in francophone Quebec, and elite Canadians who owned breeding farms, racing stables, and racetracks, similar to racing's supporters in Great Britain and the United States.

Canadians recognized the need to curtail gambling, but backed the interests of horse owners and elite jockey clubs that wanted to promote the sport and the right of elite and upper-middle-class Canadians to gamble at the tracks since they could control themselves, unlike the working class, who could not. This stance was similar to Canadian attitudes toward liquor consumption.[107]

The issue of racetrack gambling came to a head in December 1909 when Liberal member of Parliament H. H. Miller introduced Bill No. 6 to criminalize bookmaking at the tracks, a measure strongly supported by Canadian pietists. Miller argued that it was hypocritical to ban gambling across the board, except inside racetracks. His proposal, prepared by the MSRCC as a private member's bill, was opposed by turf leaders who had considerable clout in the Commons and the Senate and by Sir Wilfred Laurier's Liberal government.[108]

The discussion in the House of Commons openly recognized that there were different laws for gentlemen and the working class. "Speculation" was fine for men with sufficient income, but not for crass gambling by punters with limited resources. The debaters were heavily divided by religious affiliation, with pietists and several Anglicans in favor of the Miller bill. Historian Douglas Brown argues that Anglican foes of horse-race gambling were often nationalists seeking independence from British law and culture and negative American influences. They felt the worst attributes of horse-race gambling was owing to American sportsmen trying to take over the Canadian turf.[109]

The Miller bill was heavily opposed by an unusual coalition of legislators from Catholic and working-class districts and Anglican politicians seeking to preserve traditional values, social behavior tied to British imperialism, and the right of the people to decide moral issues for themselves. They backed a sport whose leading stables were owned by prominent industrialists and whose elite racetracks were run by highly respected citizens. The horsey set, who was well represented in Parliament, was seen to embody the finest traits of amateur sport and an upper-class lifestyle that epitomized the finest values of British civilization. Historian Greg Waters argues that business-minded supporters of racing wanted "to insulate capital invested in the respectable tracks from moral censure and possible destruction" that they blamed on lower-status racing associations, individual promoters, Jewish entrepreneurs and gamblers, and such American-based influences as proprietary tracks, short meets, and syndicate betting. The gambling advocates thought that racing was necessary to test the breed and that the sport could be sustained only with professional gambling. Betting was fine when conducted among people who could afford to lose a friendly wager, but not by the working class. Brown also felt this position reflected a romantic perspective that overemphasized agriculture's importance to the nation's economy.[110]

The Miller bill was approved in committee, but lost in an early procedural vote, 77–78, on April 7, 1910. Eight days later, the Laurier administration helped pass a heavily amended bill that protected the racing crowd's financial interests while curtailing the sport's profit-minded entrepreneurs. Each track was limited to two seven-day meets with bookmaking; new tracks were not allowed in communities with fewer than fifteen thousand residents; tipsters, poolrooms, and handbooks were barred; and no racing data could be transmitted for gambling purposes.[111]

Racing flourished under the Miller Act, especially once pari-mutuel machines were introduced in 1911. In Windsor, for instance, after the Jockey Club spent about $70,000 on thirty-two pari-mutuel machines following the 1914 fall meet, betting revenue more than doubled to $196,650 in 1915 and then rose by more than 50 percent to $300,332 the following year. Profits more than doubled from $54,627 in 1914 to $120,766 a year later and then $179,177 in 1916.[112]

What Happened to the Chicago Tracks?

Washington Park was dismantled in 1906, and by 1910 apartment buildings were under construction there. The Worth track was demolished in 1910 and was used for the militia and occasional auto races before becoming a cemetery in 1923. The Harlem course hosted a twenty-four-hour automobile endurance race and was a golf course until 1918. John Condon claimed that shutting down racetracks in the 1900s cost him $1,178,500. His losses in Chicago alone included $500,000 from Harlem that he fully owned (though he anticipated future gains when he sold the property) and $75,000 of the $300,000 Worth track. Condon also had sizable holdings in California racecourses. He had invested $100,000 in California tracks, losing his entire stake in the New California Jockey Club and 35 percent of Tanforan in 1909 when the Walker-Otis Act ended racing in California. He was also heavily invested in the Oaklawn racetrack in Hot Springs, Arkansas; New Orleans's Crescent City JC; the Denver JC; the New Douglas JC of Louisville, Latonia; and two Canadian courses. Nonetheless, he still died a millionaire.[113]

Ed Corrigan remained active in racing after Hawthorne closed. At one time, his track holdings were said to be worth between $750,000 and $1 million. Corrigan had established Kansas City's Elm Ridge track in 1904, but Missouri halted racing one year later. His final racing endeavor was New Orleans's City Park, opened in 1905, but Louisiana halted racing three years later. Corrigan was so bad off he had to sell his $48,000 investment in New Orleans's City Park for $2,000. Then in 1909, his big investment in Tanforan in California became worthless.[114]

On May 19, 1909, the bankrupted Ed Corrigan, with $101,936 in unsecured liabilities, sold Hawthorne to Democratic Committee chairman Thomas Carey, a racing stable owner, for a mere $2,000 in cash and $26,000 toward notes Carey had previously endorsed for Corrigan. Carey was born in Brookfield, Massachusetts, in 1860 and moved to Chicago in 1881. He became an attorney, but he made his fortune manufacturing bricks. The Irish American was elected to the city council from the working-class Back of the Yards district and sought his party's mayoralty nomination in 1919. The family still owns the racetrack.[115]

The banning of on-track gambling killed racing in metropolitan Chicago, but it did not kill public interest. Carey was determined to bring racing back to Chicago, but had no idea how long it would take. He hosted occasional races at Hawthorne beginning in 1909 to motivate support for legalization of the sport. His first event was staged on

Labor Day with the support of the executive committee of the Carpenters' Executive Council, led by secretary-treasurer John J. Britain of the Chicago Business Agents Association, and other labor leaders. The advertised program consisted of five horse races, including the Stockyard Derby, for horses working at the Union Stockyards, and also motorcycle races, automobile races, and three boxing matches. Upwards of 20,000 spectators attended, largely drawn by the expectation of gambling. The police assigned to the track made little effort to halt the gambling. The event was so popular that it was repeated in 1910, 1911, and 1912. He was supported by the Chicago Letter Carriers' Association, which put up $3,650 in purses for the three-day 1911 meet. One year later, the Chicago Business Agents Association put up $3,600. Sheriff Michael Zimmer was there with 125 deputies, but the *Tribune* reported that "there was gambling in plenty." There were no races in 1913, but Democrats in Springfield began trying to pass legislation legalizing on-track betting.[116]

In 1916 Hawthorne reopened in cooperation with the new Illinois Jockey Club (IJC). Its feature event was the first renewal of the American Derby since 1904, which drew 20,000 spectators. There was no racing during World War I, resuming in August 1919 at Aurora's Kane County Fairgrounds, a lengthy train ride from Chicago, but it drew poorly and was closed after eight days, losing at least $14,000. The Hawthorne experiment returned in 1922, sponsored by the IJC, mostly gentlemen of property and standing.[117]

A new Washington Park track opened in 1923 in south suburban Homewood, and a test case was initiated at Hawthorne to assess the legal standing of gambling at the track. Bookmaker Jacob Lipsitz and a client were arrested for making a bet and were found guilty of violating the law. Then on April 19, 1924, criminal-court judge William L. Lindsay issued a pivotal decision, declaring that "oral betting" did not violate state antibetting laws. This ruling opened the floodgates for on-track betting, and by 1926 there were four tracks in the metropolitan area and two elsewhere in Illinois. One year later, the state legislature passed the Lager Act that licensed thoroughbred racing and legalized pari-mutuel racing. This passage led directly to the opening of the elite Arlington Park racetrack that became the featured course in the Chicago area.[118]

CONCLUSION

Thoroughbred racing flourished in Chicago at the turn of the century. The three established courses were all back in business, there was a new suburban track in Worth, and Chicagoans were running thoroughbreds at nearby Lakeside in Indiana. The future of Chicago racing in the early 1900s seemed bright, drawing record crowds, offering large purses, and attracting heavy betting. Washington Park was without question one of the most prestigious courses in the United States, a popular elite resort whose feature event, the American Derby, drew a greater audience than any sporting event in North America. Yet the track was in an unsteady position, having been closed from 1895 to 1897 and again in 1899. The Chicago courses were among the most successful tracks in the United States, though they did not have as much betting or make as much money as the California Jockey Club in Emeryville, near Oakland, open nearly half the year, until California closed it down in 1909, or New York State's preeminent facilities, closed by the state in 1910.

Chicago's glorious era in racing proved short, and the end came stunningly quickly. The WPR quit within days of forty thousand fans attending the Derby, caving under strong pressure from Mayor Harrison that encouraged the betting public to stay home. The suburban proprietary tracks carried on, since Harrison's authority stopped at the city limits, but each had its own mounting problems. Then in 1905, the tracks closed shortly after the season began, faced with memories of the closed courses in the mid-1890s, vigorous opposition from antigambling reformers, weak support from political allies, and Cook County state's attorney Healy's strong commitment to block gambling at the tracks.

The end of racing in Chicago was hardly unique, but it was a major part of the virtual collapse of thoroughbred racing in the United States. The downfall was the product of an unusual coalition between conservative religious evangelicals and progressive reformers to fight vice in America. While tracks had always come and gone because of economic factors, the main reason for the sport's failure in the early 1900s was reform pressure on local and state governments to fight wagering at thoroughbred courses legitimized by favorable court rulings or legislation. Between 1904 and 1914, local governments closed tracks in such racing states as Missouri (1905), Tennessee (1906), Louisiana (1908), and New York (1910). The actions in northern states by Republican-dominated legislatures reflected their antigambling positions, opposed by Democratic legislators whose constituents were heavily Catholic and Jewish immigrants who had little problem with gambling. But Democrats in single-party southern states, who opposed the legalization of gambling, represented conservative white pietists who considered betting sinful. This point of view directly countered the long southern support of horse racing in the nineteenth century.

By 1911 the only notable tracks legally in business were in the breeding centers of Kentucky and Maryland, which both still had strong racing traditions, yet they barely kept alive. Maryland's only important racetrack in the late nineteenth century was Pimlico, site of the Preakness, but it was closed from 1889 to 1904.[119]

Even Kentucky nearly lost racing in 1908 when an antigambling coalition took over control of the Louisville government and passed a law banning bookmaking, which threatened the survival of the local course. Former Louisville mayor Charles Grainger (1901–5), the president of Churchill Downs (1902–18), and track vice president Matt Winn, a past member of the Board of Public Safety, remembered an old act from 1878 act that exempted pari-mutuel machines from municipal interference. They replaced the bookmakers who took bets at Churchill Downs with pari-mutuel machines and thus remained in business. Their reintroduction of betting machines was backed up by the state court in *Grimstead v. Kirby* (1908).[120]

Nationally, the statistics for thoroughbred racing in 1910 were dismal. The number of yearlings dropped from 3,990 in 1904 to 325 in 1910. The number of races dropped from 8,594 in 1906 to 1,063 four years later. Purse distributions in that period dropped from $5.4

million to $2.9 million, and the average purses declined from $779 to $453.[121]

The reformers won the battle against racing in Chicago, but the war on gambling was another story. Ending racing in Chicagoland hurt the pocketbooks of track operators, on-track bookmakers, and businesses that relied on racing aficionados, like hotels and restaurants. However, Mont Tennes and other illegal entrepreneurs who ran poolrooms and handbooks still enjoyed enormous action on out-of-town races and enjoyed substantial profits. Many racing devotees who used to go to the tracks now turned to downtown poolrooms (said to cover $30,000 daily on foreign races in 1905) and neighborhood bookmakers to test their racing acumen.[122]

7

James O'Leary, Mont Tennes, and Offtrack Gambling in Chicago, 1895–1911

Chicago in 1900 was the second most important offtrack betting center in the United States, surpassed only by New York in the number of poolrooms and handbooks. Reformers considered poolrooms and bookmakers a scourge on American life that broke up families, led to crimes like embezzlement, and strengthened the connections between syndicate crime, corrupt policemen, and duplicitous politicians. However, bettors who visited poolrooms or handbooks, as well as a considerable portion of the general public, did not see offtrack gambling as a social menace, but viewed it as a victimless crime since no one compelled clients to make wagers. It was an accessible form of popular recreation, a means to display manliness by backing one's judgment with wagers, and, as far as many speculators were concerned, a rational means to make money fast by investing in their expertise and successfully handicapping races.[1]

In 1905 when the Harlem, Hawthorne, and Worth tracks closed, Americans bet an estimated $110 million at racetracks and, in all likelihood, considerably more off the tracks. Two years later, the poolroom menace achieved considerable national attention when Josiah Flynt wrote a major five-part investigation of the poolroom problem for *Cosmopolitan*. His editor prefaced the series by decrying poolrooms as a "canker on our national life . . . [that] . . . reputedly wrecked more homes than Wall Street." He asserted that poolrooms counted more victims than bucket shops and were conducted by a cluster of trusts "more viciously, more rapaciously, and more absolute, than the Standard Oil Company." *Cosmopolitan*'s editor attributed the poolroom's success to men who "have built up around themselves and their vile dens a barrier composed of political 'pull' and a fat corruption fund."[2] Flynt himself asserted, "No crime in America equals in despicability this racing game," particularly the poolroom: "It has been said that the pool-room may be likened unto a spider's web. The spider catches the fly; the poolroom catches the Sucker." He conservatively estimated that track bookmakers in 1905 grossed $15.5 million, while entrepreneurs running illegal poolrooms and handbooks grossed at least $20.5 million because they shaved the odds and had political protection. Chicago alone in 1905 reportedly had forty on-track bookmakers and a remarkable seventy-five hundred people working off the track as bookmakers, as their staff, or as touts.[3]

The Chicago-Area Poolrooms

The poolroom business was very quiet in the summer of 1895. Two of the most notable downtown bookies then were "Big John," who took bets of $5 up to $1,000 at Chapin & Gore's Saloon, where he had access to a Western Union wire, and "Snow," an old Ullman employee, who ran a handbook in a downtown room owned by former alderman Louis I. Epstean behind Chapin & Gore's. By the fall, when all the Chicago-area racetracks were out of business, the *Daily News* reported that the authorities had shuttered the old-time poolrooms. Yet this was not completely true. On November 8, Police Chief John J. Badenoch, who had been very lax in fighting the poolrooms, orchestrated a big raid on downtown poolrooms. Three poolrooms closed in advance, and raids on the others resulted in 108 midday arrests.[4]

As the summer of 1896 approached, and the local tracks remained closed, the press and moral reformers gave a lot of attention to fighting the poolroom menace, which may have been down but was not out. The reformers up to then had focused their attention mainly on the racetracks, which they had closed, temporarily. This shuttering indirectly hurt the city's poolrooms because it likely cut back on local interest in horse-race gambling among the less serious fans, though not completely since there was still a lot of interest in out-of-town events.

The police in early 1896 gave negligible attention to the few open poolrooms, but on June 13 the *Tribune* ran a front-page story titled "Bold Sale of Pools," subtitled "Rooms Run Wide Open," which claimed that pool selling was rampant and that poolrooms were nearly as accessible as they had been when racetracks still operated. The paper investigated a few of the downtown Chicago poolrooms that were open all day, particularly Smith & Perry's, reportedly backed by Blind John Condon, situated over poolroom keeper George Gale's saloon; the betting parlor located inside Alderman Bathhouse John Coughlin's Silver Dollar Saloon; and the Powers & O'Brien's poolroom over their Madison Street saloon.[5]

Bathhouse John Coughlin's saloon openly sold pools on the first floor, probably the only downtown Chicago gambling emporium where such a thing took place. No potential customer was ever challenged by guards or doorkeepers. Entries and odds on foreign races were posted on the wall in a room nearest the bar on small sheets of white paper. Women bettors did not enter the saloon but met a messenger at an outdoor beer garden where they placed their wagers.[6]

A reporter investigating the poolroom business entered Smith & Perry's through two glass doors guarded by a sentry. He was "knocked in," and a second guard admitted him up the stairs where a third guard peeped through a slide to admit people into the betting room. A single bookmaker was present, with his staff of assistants. News on races at such courses as the Fairgrounds (St. Louis), Gravesend (Brooklyn), and Oakley (Cincinnati) were posted on cards placed on a wall that could easily be removed if there was a raid. The room serviced three to four hundred patrons a day who bet $3,000–$4,000.[7]

The journalist found that Powers & O'Brien was operating at full blast most every afternoon, just like the infamous House of David poolroom. When Powers & O'Brien first opened up, they limited admission to vouched-for clients, a policy still employed at the House of David. But in due course, Powers & O'Brien admitted anyone who was not a journalist or police officer.[8]

14. James O'Leary and Mont Tennes, Chicago's leading bookmakers in the early 1900s. O'Leary was the preeminent gambler on the South Side. Tennes became Chicago's leading offtrack gambler in the mid-1900s and a few years later also ran the national racing wire. Reprinted from Hugh S. Fullerton, "American Gambling and Gamblers," 36, 38.

Police Superintendent John J. Badenoch claimed he had the gambling problem well under control since his twelve best men detected no violations at downtown saloons. He claimed that only "hand bets" were made, which he considered impossible to suppress. However, the *Tribune*'s investigation convinced him that poolrooms were operating, and he promised to close them, even "if we have to close up the saloons attached and revoke their licenses." Badenoch excused the police's prior poor performance, claiming his detectives were too well known to gather evidence. He then ordered Police Inspector J. E. Fitzgerald to stop pool selling inside the city and Inspector Nicholas Hunt to watch O'Leary's resort near the stockyards (4183 South Halsted), said to be the busiest in Chicago, with up to $10,000 a day exchanging hands. This move was certainly not astute, since Hunt and O'Leary were good friends. The *Tribune* had low expectations for solid police work on this matter because the "department is too feeble," though poolroom operators had become more cautious than in the recent past.[9]

The Poolrooms Move to Suburbia

Reform pressure in 1896 persuaded pool operators to leave the Loop for the less convenient, but safer, southern Cook County suburbs where they could function more freely. One of the more successful establishments already running in the suburbs since 1895 was the Harlem Club, owned and operated by Sid McHie and Barney Zacharias at a former restaurant across the road from the Harlem Racetrack. Pools were sold there in 1896 to as many as three hundred men at a time, or fifteen hundred for the day, while the second floor was reserved for faro, roulette, and stud poker. George Hankins and other Harlem racetrack folk owned the building and provided political protection. The *Tribune* ran a front-page story about the "dinner pail game" there that catered to the working class. It was a "piker's" resort, with most bets at $1 and $2. The Harlem village board favored the poolroom in large measure because its owners operated the Harlem racetrack, which helped finance the local government. The town reportedly charged the Harlem Club $100 a day to do business, though village president John Gorke denied that story and claimed the only revenue the city got from it came from fining the managers $150 a week for operating an illegal gambling hall.[10]

In 1896 Powers & O'Brien moved to the hamlet of Le Moyne and O'Leary moved to Worth, where he already had a saloon. They built large resorts with room for three hundred to fifteen hundred patrons. The Grand Trunk ran special trains for the gambling crowd to Worth and the Santa Fe to Le Moyne. The Civic Federation, the press, and various antigambling reformers claimed these new poolrooms harmed the financial and moral health of their new locations.[11]

O'Leary's poolroom in Worth was the area's most important suburban gambling facility, purportedly pulling in up to $10,000 a day. Worth was attractive because it was on a railroad line, fifteen miles from the Loop, and had no police department to interfere with

O'Leary's business. The bookie started out in early August with a tent opposite the Mount Olivet Cemetery, near Worth's railroad station, where former prizefighters and other toughs provided security. Magistrate J. D. Cunningham sympathized with the poolroom and rejected early efforts to block it by the CF and residents of the nearby middle-class Chicago community of Morgan Park, particularly Catholics who resented its location near their cemetery. O'Leary's room had modest expenses, including a $25 daily fee to Western Union for racing information and $10 for the telegraph operator.[12]

Republican president Daniel Healy of the Cook County Board of Commissioners said he could not take action against the suburban gambling halls unless someone swore out warrants and followed up in the courts. The CF resolved to do so and asked Sheriff James Pease for the same support he gave when the Harlem Racetrack was closed. Pease ordered every county poolroom closed and on August 29 sent deputies to resorts in Harlem, Worth, and LeMoyne who warned proprietors to shut down. That afternoon O'Leary's five hundred patrons in Worth found a sign on the blackboard: "This room will be closed until further notice," though betting continued until five thirty. The crowd was smaller there than usual because of competition from Kenosha's Ideal Race Track.[13]

Reopening Chicago's Poolrooms

Despite Sheriff Pease's posturing, Chicago's poolrooms reopened in early September, most notably O'Leary's, which may explain why he readily complied with the authorities in Worth. On September 10, there were at least five hundred men at his South Side room, with bets beginning at one dollar, all recorded by the bettor's initials.[14]

Nonetheless, most metropolitan poolrooms did remain closed until early December. Attorneys advised their clients to set themselves up as commission operations that "telegraphed" money bet on New Orleans races to confederates at the Milwaukee track where foreign bookmaking took place. Bert Thompson, chief of the police telephone operators, went undercover and got a job working in a poolroom. He discovered that the commission system was a scam. The telegraph instruments at his workplace were not connected to Western Union, and all bets were actually covered inside the poolroom.[15]

On December 12, after a week of large profits and open defiance of the law, seven downtown rooms were raided and three hundred prisoners taken, many having their bonds signed by Alderman Johnny Powers. Some operators subsequently moved to new locations, including across state lines. Condon and O'Leary both went to northwestern Indiana, a ten-cent train ride from Chicago, where Hammond's city council had recently rescinded its rules against pool selling.[16]

In the winter of 1896–97, about twelve downtown rooms operated profitably, taking bets on out-of-town races. The owners expected that if Carter H. Harrison II was elected mayor in April 1897, gambling would expand, as it had under his father, which was precisely what happened. The local racetracks reopened, energizing interest in horse-race betting, which was good for poolrooms even if they lost their monopoly over thoroughbred wagering. In the past, each jockey club had leased the rights to its information to an individual who negotiated directly with the poolrooms, charging them for information on entries, betting odds, and results. Poolrooms paid more than $500 a day for Harlem's racing news, a substantial savings from past fees that were as high as more than $800 a day. This system changed in the late 1890s when Western Union took over the task of transmitting racing news and negotiated directly with the tracks, sharing 20 percent of their fees with them. The *Spirit* claimed that the telegraph company became "virtually the lessee of the poolroom privilege."[17]

THE DOWNTOWN POOLROOMS

The numerous well-connected poolrooms of Chicago and the surrounding suburbs received a lot of press attention because they operated illegally and overtly, made a lot of money, and purportedly ruined the families of many of their clients. Poolrooms had no outside signage to attract street traffic, yet were widely known to clients and reporters who had no trouble finding them, even if the police could not. The downtown rooms mainly catered to white-collar workers and other men who had discretionary income to wager. The rooms were typically large facilities with space for hundreds of customers (often on the second floor of saloons), had guards posted outside and inside, and offered the best offtrack odds. The finest poolrooms were elegant, well-appointed facilities with soft, comfortable chairs to encourage clients to sit and stay for a while. Tuxedoed waiters brought them free roast beef and drinks while they considered their bets. Poolrooms would continue to operate into the 1920s and 1930s when the most stylish rooms limited patrons to "members" and required higher minimum bets than at the more modest rooms. The high-end betting parlors provided a model for the Chicago poolroom depicted in the 1973 Academy Award–winning movie *The Sting*.[18]

Poolrooms located outside downtown were more modestly furnished, took bets as low as fifty cents, and charged clients for refreshments. All poolroom walls were plastered with information about the day's races. They received excellent and speedy information about current races from across the country, usually transmitted by the racing wire to a betting syndicate's headquarters, then forwarded, usually by ticker and later by phone, to affiliated rooms. Clerks seated behind barriers took the bets. Prior to each race, an announcer would read over a loudspeaker the names of horses running in the event, their jockeys, the betting odds, and the track conditions. Then once betting was closed and the races were under way, the broadcaster re-created the race, reading the data sent by the ticker and using his imagination to add some flavor to the call, bringing some of the excitement of the track into the betting parlor. Winning wagers were paid off immediately. As late as 1940, the reputedly nine hundred poolrooms in Chicago reportedly handled 75 percent of the city' illegal bets.[19]

The authorities throughout the nation had little success in quashing the poolrooms, despite their visibility. As the *Spirit of the Times* noted in 1897: "The average pool-room has more lives than a cat. You may squelch it for a time, but it opens up again in due time, and anon it flourishes. . . . There is no secrecy or concealment at all, and everything is as free and easy as the operations in the . . . Board of Trade."

Police cooperation with poolrooms was normative in American cities, especially New York, where it became a major topic in 1895 of the Lexow Commission's investigation into police corruption. Louisville, Kentucky, poolrooms operated so openly that a grand jury indicted the Board of Administration and other city officials for failing to enforce the antigambling laws. In Chicago, as elsewhere, police raids were often orchestrated by a major betting ring to force out competitors. If an independent room opened up, a syndicate leader would call an unlisted number at police headquarters, and within twenty minutes there would be a raid.[20]

The CF rebuked the Chicago police in early 1898 for shirking their duty with lackadaisical efforts against poolrooms. The department was considered so ineffective that Senator Orville F. Berry (R–Hancock) initiated an investigation into its practices, including the alleged inaction against poolrooms. However, the press at this time applauded Cook County sheriff James Pease, although he was actually ineffective, for shutting gambling houses and prosecuting proprietors. His deputies often encountered policemen at raided rooms working the counters, including Officer Henry Kipley, the police superintendent's brother.[21]

In May, CF investigator John Hill Jr. reported that poolrooms were making from $10,000 to $12,000 a day and were always forewarned when a police raid was imminent. Hill claimed his investigations led to some one hundred convictions and that he was working on another two hundred cases. Two months later, Hill's house was bombed. He blamed the gambling interests, who he claimed raised $100,000 to do him in. Hill claimed that his fight "has caused a greater loss of prospective profits to the police of Chicago than to any combination in the gambling fraternity."[22]

Women and the Poolrooms

The public presumed that offtrack betting was an exclusively male pursuit, a vile pastime that no respectable woman would enjoy. Consequently, Chicagoans were surprised to learn that on September 28,

1896, fifteen women, along with a Western Union inspector, were arrested following a raid on a poolroom at 351 Thirty-Third Street, a two-story brownstone with a large basement that neighbors presumed belonged to a well-to-do family. Gussie McKee ran the business that had all the paraphernalia of a well-operated poolroom.[23]

Neighbors noticed several women visiting in the morning, and when more arrived in the evening in a dozen private equipages, residents informed the police of their suspicions. The police found a wire strung along a post of a nearby railway structure that they traced to the brownstone. They moved in and found eighteen women in the attic seated around five tables, awaiting racing news from a ticker. The room was sumptuously furnished and carpeted, with cards and books. One woman sat behind a small desk, accepting bets on local or foreign races. The clients were described as well dressed and from prosperous homes. They veiled themselves when the police arrived, and all gave aliases at the police station.[24]

Such reports certainly startled many Chicagoans who grew up in the Victorian era when women's primary sphere was still domesticity and they were expected to maintain a high level of morality. However, the McKee raid was hardly unique. On October 8, a *Tribune* reporter uncovered a poolroom on the fourth floor of a downtown building, ostensibly a furnished flat rented by the week, entirely patronized by women. Clients ran the gamut from young women to grandmothers, ranging from the ordinary looking and poorly clad to others wearing expensive, fashionable dresses. The room was protected by an electric device on the lower tread of stairs leading down from the third floor that activated an alarm.[25]

One week later, another raid occurred at a women's poolroom across the street at the Ricardo Hotel (168 Clark Street) in its third day of operation, having moved from another nearby site. Proprietor Charles Roby, who ran the poolroom, and eighteen unfashionably dressed women were arrested. They were described as middle class, probably married to shopkeepers and artisans, and included two policemen's wives. The authorities learned about the operation from Millie McGuire, a mulatto woman who had laid bets there but was barred from returning and sought revenge. When the raid began, Roby tried to tear up the betting sheets and papers, while his clients cried and tried to escape.[26]

Jim O'Leary, the Poolroom King

At the turn of the century, "Big" Jim O'Leary was the preeminent professional gambler in Chicago, residing in a $100,000 mansion on West Garfield Boulevard. His philosophy of life was pretty harsh, not surprising given his background: "There are three classes of people in the world—gamblers, burglars, and beggars. Nearly everybody gambles. Sometimes it's with money, sometimes it's with time, sometime it's with jobs. . . . A fellow that won't gamble or steal is a beggar."[27]

Jim used his Back of the Yards saloon as a clearinghouse for South Side bookies connected to his headquarters by a telephone exchange. In 1907 Josiah Flynt described O'Leary as "the meanest man, because he is the biggest, of the Chicago poolroom crowd." O'Leary controlled South Side gambling through police payoffs and his close connections to downtown Democratic ward leaders, particularly First Ward aldermen Hinky Dink Kenna and Bathhouse John Coughlin, as well as his own Twenty-Ninth Ward alderman, Tom Carey, a significant figure himself in South Side gambling.[28]

O'Leary's strong police connections were largely through his friend Inspector Nicholas Hunt, of the Hyde Park precinct, which at one time included the stockyards district. Hunt had a checkered career and would be suspended in 1906 as chief of detectives after thirty-five years of service, but got reinstated as inspector in 1907. Hunt was thought to be the richest policeman in Chicago, his wealth amassed through payoffs from brothel keepers and gamblers and from $400,000 in real estate. O'Leary also got protection from his son's father-in-law, Inspector William P. Clancy, longtime chief of the Back of the Yards precinct. O'Leary's rooms were frequently raided, but his managers were usually forewarned. O'Leary himself was not convicted of a serious gambling violation until 1921.[29]

In 1899 O'Leary owned two major downtown poolrooms that serviced businessmen and clerks. Three other key poolrooms were operated by Ed Wagner, Bud White, and Smith & Perry, none of whom made any effort to conceal their betting parlors. They did not even post a lookout. Pedestrians could hear the cry "They're off" from one hundred feet away.[30]

The police took significant actions in late 1899 against the rooms, following lengthy press reports that led to a grand-jury investigation. Superintendent Joseph Kipley testified that he knew nothing about poolrooms, angering the jurors who pressed him for information. A few days later, on December 21, the police suddenly discovered many rooms in operation and staged raids, but only after Central Station detectives warned protected poolrooms of the upcoming forced entries. The police closed more than thirty poolrooms and twenty handbooks, including O'Leary's in the Back of the Yards, the House of David, and Power & O'Brien's, the latter two located downtown.[31]

Following this "show of force," O'Leary opened a big poolroom in Romeoville, a small town just inside suburban Will County. O'Leary's competitors expected he would soon use his clout to close their downtown rooms. His syndicate's main man at city hall was Tom McGinnis, a saloonkeeper and close friend of Kenna and Coughlin, who reputedly had a big share in the Condon-O'Leary poolrooms and racetracks. The police turned up the heat on O'Leary's rivals, employing twenty special detectives at a cost of $80 a day to keep handbooks off the streets.[32]

O'Leary briefly tried to become a big player on the national racing scene. In the summer of 1903, he helped finance Ullman, B. J. Weller, and Maxie Blumenthal's "Big Store" to handle the heavy action of Drake and Gates at Saratoga, taking bets as high as $100,000 before moving to the lucrative New York City market. Gates later lost $200,000 on one race at Sheepshead Bay to the Big Store. Ullman and Weller made 40 percent of a reputed $300,000–$500,000 profit, and their backers got the rest. O'Leary subsequently put up $3,000 to buy a membership in the Metropolitan Turf Association that ran the books at New York City tracks, but was blackballed with 3 negative votes out of 230 because of his association with the Big Store. Ullman was also unpopular back east, and in 1905 a couple of Saratoga betting rooms, including his, were dynamited.[33]

The Poolroom Syndicates

By spring 1900 the quarreling among poolroom owners and gamblers reached a boiling point, and the police had a hard time following the revolving alliances. The city had three powerful, heavily Irish gambling combinations that competed for territory, often retaliating against each other by hiring constables to secure warrants against their rivals and then staging raids. However, they were not long lasting, and members would shift from year to year. The leading group was originally the Condon-O'Leary syndicate. In 1900 they ran a club house in Hot Springs, Arkansas, already well known as a resort and center for gambling, that reputedly made them $250,000. Their syndicate then included Tom McGinnis, who had a lot of political clout through Aldermen Coughlin and Kenna and also Smith and Perry, who later broke with O'Leary in 1900, but not for long. A second group was the old McDonald group, now led by Mike's former associates pool seller Frank McWhorter, bookkeeper Harry Holland, safe blower "Paddy" Guerin, and former burglar John Ryan, who controlled a faction of Cook County constables that "made life a burden for the gamblers until Ryan organized them and took them into partnership." The third, and dominant, group was the Gambling Trust composed of Bud White, Kid Weller, Charles "Social" Smith, and Harry Perry, a suave, well-dressed, and hard-partying man, a model of the stereotypical bookmaker. A couple of years later, they added Tom McGinnis, formerly with the Condon-O'Leary group.[34]

Mayor Harrison came into office in 1897 and stayed out of the anti-offtrack-betting movement for a number of years. At this time, horse-race gambling became the dominant portion of the gambling category. The number of vice arrests was triple gambling detentions until 1899, but three years later, when horse-race gambling flourished, gambling arrests outdid vice arrests for the first time (2,259 to 1,727) and continued to lead until 1909. Harrison started out with a very low index of 19 in 1897 and 1899. In June 1900, when new poolrooms opened, he denied their existence until shown a list in the *Tribune*. He called at the time for the suppression of gambling at the Washington Park Club, yet said nothing about the poolrooms. As far as city hall was concerned, handbooks were said to be "all right." Superintendent Kipley's response to the press reports was "What? Poolrooms open in Chicago?" Thereafter, he became slowly more involved in fighting gambling, and thereafter his index rose to 53 in 1902 and topped out at 102 in 1904.[35]

Shortly after the fall 1900 election, O'Leary opened the Santa Fe Turf Exchange with Smith and Perry, and their partners, in Richton, a village about thirty miles southwest of Chicago. It was the bleakest spot along any railroad line in Will County, a mile from any house and thirty miles from Joliet, the county seat, which made interference by the authorities unlikely. The exchange leased adjoining lots and built a stockade to keep away troublesome neighbors. It promoted good community relations by purchasing its lumber from local dealers and hiring farm boys as watchmen.[36]

Chicago Poolrooms in 1901

On April 13, 1901, shortly after Mayor Harrison was elected to his third term, and went on vacation, the O'Leary-Condon syndicate closed its Richton facility, intent on reopening in Chicago. The *Tribune* expected that Harrison would become more receptive to the poolroom interests since poolrooms operators White, Smith, Perry, O'Leary, McGinnis, Powers, O'Brien, Alderman John Coughlin, Senator John Broderick, and former alderman Rogers of the Eighteenth Ward had all helped him in his reelection campaign. That summer the handbooks operated without interference.[37]

Meanwhile, Chicago gamblers also opened up poolrooms and saloons along the Indiana lakeshore, at sites near the Lake Shore Railroad. They included John Condon and F. T. "Bud" White's Long Beach Turf Exchange, a gambling venue and poolroom located east of Whiting, daily patronized by nearly a thousand people, advertised with space for five thousand, who bet on out-of-town races. The management was security conscious, with double walls of heavy timbers that prevented access or egress except through gates opened only on the arrival of special trains, abetted by the presence of mastiffs and Great Danes. However, the exchange closed on August 27, with its advertising riling opposition from the local community and rival interests in racing. Condon's rival Edward Corrigan of the Hawthorne track used his influence to block the reporting of its results to the poolrooms, and the local authorities stepped up and closed the facility.[38]

The African American Poolroom Experience

In the 1880s, blacks were not barred from poolrooms in Gamblers' Alley, but the distance from their homes, and the high costs of dollar bets with a bookie, and five-dollar wagers with an auction pool, discouraged their participation. Yet they could afford pari-mutuels and combinations that cost as little as ten cents. A poolroom catering to African Americans opened in 1887 at 1321 South State Street, known as the Turf Exchange. Outside on most afternoons, especially from two to four thirty, there would be a small crowd of black men and youth hanging around the area. A *Tribune* reporter investigating the operation found about fifty customers in a twenty-by-ten-foot room. He reported, "Inside—if one has the temerity to go inside—one will find a small apartment . . . filled with a noisy gathering of colored men and boys and a noisome smell, of one knows not what. An analysis of that smell would probably indicate a high percentage of perspiration, a scarcity of ventilation, an abundance of bad tobacco, and a flavor of onions." A white man nicknamed "Mr. Whiskers" ran the operation, charging as little as five cents to bet, but most bets were ten, twenty-five, or fifty cents. He offered the same odds as downtown rooms. The owner got racing results by phone at a corner drugstore. The information came from a Clark Street saloon that got the news from Dowling's poolroom in Gamblers' Alley.[39]

By the 1890s, black clients were no longer welcome at the downtown poolrooms. This discouragement provided an opportunity for black entrepreneurs who catered to fellow African Americans. Mark Haller, the preeminent historian of American crime, found that "blacks never broke into bookmaking," though there were a few prominent black gamblers. The most pretentious African American gambling saloon was John Weston "Poney" Moore's Turf Exchange at Twenty-Second Street on the South Side, in a mainly African Americans neighborhood. The exchange opened in the late 1890s and had an interracial clientele, including whites, blacks, Chinese, and Japanese. According to historian Thomas Bauman, Moore used his political connections to keep his operations open, but in 1899 Detective Clifton Wooldridge ran a successful raid. Afterward, Moore stopped making book and focused more on late-night craps games for local waiters and piano players and later ran a roulette wheel. Moore enjoyed going to the tracks at Churchill Downs and Saratoga with "an entourage of thoroughbred fanciers." Robert Motts was another major African American gambler who took bets on races. However, he grew tired of the raids and politics of the gambling business (probably instigated by white competitors) and in 1904 turned his resort into a grand cultural center, the Pekin Theater (Twenty-Seventh and State Streets).[40]

The Poolrooms of Madison, Illinois

The small town of Madison in southern Illinois was well known for notorious offtrack gambling. The local poolroom in 1901 was run by the Cella-Adler-Tilles syndicate, especially busy following the recent closing of St. Louis's poolrooms. It was daily patronized by some two thousand St. Louisans, mainly mechanics, laborers, and clerks. The parlor took bets as small as twenty-five cents, offered poor odds, and had a reputation for welshing, yet the local authorities did not interfere. Condon, Smith, Perry, and some other Chicago gamblers opposed the St. Louis syndicate coming into their state and pressured Springfield to close them. Illinois attorney general H. J. Hamlin personally inspected the poolroom, which he described as "a den of infamy where the poor were robbed" and in March temporarily closed it as a public nuisance.[41]

THE POOLROOM WAR

In 1901 O'Leary signed an "ironclad" ten-year agreement with other leading gamblers who promised not to operate a winter handbook or poolroom in Chicago, to limit themselves to one suburban room, and to build their headquarters outside the city. They agreed to allow summer handbooks as long as no one tried to dominate and to close several rooms in Indiana and suburban Chicago. According to O'Leary, "The idea was to remove the chance of continual crusades against gambling. Business would increase and everything would be peaceful. . . . I started in to keep to the letter and spirit of the agreement, but in less than a year the other fellows had poolrooms going downtown and handbooks in every corner they could get them in. Of course, I came back at them and closed them all. . . . Let them raid me every day if they want to. Raids don't hurt me."[42]

The ironclad agreement collapsed in the summer of 1903, following Washington Park's meet. O'Leary responded by initiating raids against handbooks, breaking the pact. He used his clout to halt Western Union service to fifty-eight poolrooms operated by the Gambling Trust. Shortly thereafter, on August 24, the Gamblers' War, which may have actually begun back in 1902 with the fires set at the Hawthorne Racetrack, broke out full blast when Albert Hollie, said to represent the Gambling Trust, swore out warrants against thirty handbook men and twenty saloonkeepers who worked for O'Leary. The trust's goal was to push him out business for refusing to compromise or divide up territory. O'Leary retaliated with warrants against Smith & Perry, whose agents worked in twenty-five saloons.[43]

Smith & Perry relied heavily on the Chicago constabulary during the war to counter O'Leary's clout with the police, employing such aggressive tactics as driving spikes into cables carrying poolroom phone lines. On August 26, Dickie Dean's men, armed with fifty warrants, axes, and shotguns, raided O'Leary's stockyards headquarters and other saloons and went after the Richton stockade the next day.[44]

O'Leary's agents retaliated on August 28 by breaking into Tom McGinnis's North Clark Street resort. Dean's constables then went after the up-and-coming Mont Tennes's downtown headquarters, while another raid attacked his clearinghouse. Police Superintendent O'Neill was pleased at the internecine conflict among the poolrooms because "the result . . . is less gambling in Chicago than there has been for a long time." A couple of days later, the war escalated when arsonists set fire to a can of oil under the Washington Park grandstand. The *Daily News* reported that Inspector Hunt just stood by and watched.[45]

The conflict came to a resolution in late October 1903, when the gamblers agreed to form a new trust that included the Smith-Perry-White-McGinnis crowd and Mont Tennes. O'Leary took a backseat in this development. The trust reapportioned the city handbook and poolroom privileges and combined the downtown clearinghouses. The syndicate within a few months purportedly amassed a war fund of $200,000. It was reported to pay out $10,000–$20,000 a month for protection.[46]

THE RISE OF MONT TENNES

In 1904 there were some three to five hundred handbooks in Chicago, estimated to be pulling in $100,000 a day in bets. Gambling was dominated by O'Leary on the South Side; Alderman Johnnie Rogers on the West Side; Kenna, Coughlin, Tom McGinnis, Pat O'Malley, and John F. O'Malley in the Loop; and Jacob "Mont" Tennes on the North Side. Tennes was born in Chicago on January 16, 1874, to an immigrant German family whose breadwinner was a clerk. Mont was a successful gambler as a teenager and ran a handbook by the time he was twenty. He opened a billiard hall in 1898 and two years later began operating saloons. His name first appeared in the *Tribune* in 1902, by which time he was already a prominent poolroom operator.[47]

By late 1903, Tennes and three of his five brothers were part of the reorganized gambling combine and on their way to running the biggest handbook syndicate in Chicago. The Tennes boys, in conjunction with James O'Leary, opened a clearinghouse on the Northwest Side at a little cottage in the Dunning neighborhood (near O'Hare Airport today) to service themselves and their associates with national racing information transmitted by Western Union wires to the syndicate's downtown headquarters. Operators there phoned the data to various North Side gambling resorts and to handbooks throughout the city. Mont broke up with O'Leary around 1906, irate with his involvement with the *City of Traverse*, a boat that operated as a gambling hall on Lake Michigan from 1905 to 1907.[48]

Tennes reputedly made, within a year or two, $90,000, which constituted half of Chicago's handbook profits, plus he collected nearly half the gross of the city's faro and roulette games. Besides his North Side ventures, Tennes had a subordinate gambling ring on the West Side, composed of the powerful Aldermen Johnnie Rogers and John Gazzolo, along with Patsy King, the man who helped introduced policy betting to Chicago. Policy bettors picked three numbers between one and seventy-eight and made bets as small as five cents. Winning numbers were selected from a tumbling drum ("wheel").[49]

Mont maintained good relations with the police by letting supportive officers bet for free and by using payoffs to encourage the police to raid his rivals and not interfere with his business. In addition, he was heavily involved in politics with Democrats like his mentor, "Hot Stove" Jimmie Quinn, boss of the Twenty-First Ward machine and onetime city sealer, who was influential in North Side gambling. Tennes regularly donated $2,500 to the infamous December First Ward Ball sponsored by Aldermen Kenna and Coughlin, their well-known fund-raiser that drew slumming elites, politicians, ranking policemen, gamblers, and prostitutes.[50]

Josiah Flynt attributed part of Mont's success to the "determination with which Tennes defied the police. . . . [T]he care he has taken to provide immediate release for customers arrested in his place have endeared him to the Suckers." Noted sports columnist Hugh Fullerton explained that "Tennes's strength seemed to lie in a huge and mysterious 'pull' and an ability to organize." It certainly did not seem to be his rooms' ambience. A veteran journalist reminiscing about visiting a Tennes room around 1910 with a buddy just hired as a sheet writer wrote in 1953, "It was a dingy place, and for the life of me, I couldn't see why people would crowd about, waiting for the results of

15. Mayor Carter H. Harrison of Chicago (1897–1905,
1911–15). Harrison originally supported betting on racing, but in 1904 he joined racing's critics to promote his
national political ambitions. Library of Congress Prints
and Photographs Division, Washington, DC, LC-
USZ62-123214. Photographed by Moffatt, Chicago.

a horse race." Clients could barely hear the results, "and no one was
sure they were right." Tennes fortified his position by organizing a
distributing agency for news, with a telephone system reaching the
handbooks from clearinghouses. By 1911 he monopolized the news
service and cut out bookies not meeting his prices. He became quite
rich and in 1934, during the heart of the Depression, was reportedly
worth $5 million.[51]

CARTER HARRISON AND THE POOLROOMS

Mayor Carter Harrison was not originally in the forefront of the war against poolrooms. He seemed to join the movement on February 5, 1903, when he declared war on O'Leary's syndicate, warning he would cancel its liquor licenses if they did not stop making book, but nothing happened. Later that year, once the poolroom men had settled their differences, Harrison announced he would fight poolrooms by stopping tickers from sending racing information, while continuing to revoke liquor licenses of offending saloons tied to poolrooms or harboring handbook makers. The mayor also announced his intent to immediately halt winter books, which he thought would prevent (or at least greatly hinder) betting at Washington Park in the upcoming 1904 season. Harrison's pronouncements were met with considerable cynicism, especially since Superintendent Francis O'Neill told a grand jury investigating gambling: "Handbooks are one of the most elusive things. . . . There is hardly a case that could be successfully prosecuted if an attorney appears and makes a defense." His testimony convinced critics that he was blind and lethargic in implementing his duties.[52]

On November 9, Harrison started a new handbook war when he revoked Tennes's saloon license near city hall at 123 North Clark (soon to be the nation's most frequently raided betting parlor). The mayor had recently reported that police lieutenant Andy Rohan's son was handling money there and that policemen were frequent customers. Harrison also canceled the license for J. K. Sebree's bar at the Hotel Saratoga and the Siebens wine company, all for allegedly operating handbooks.[53]

Harrison's proposal to require permits for tickers used as gambling apparatus was considered by the city council on November 23, 1903. The opposition was led by Aldermen Coughlin, Kenna, and Carey, then an adviser to the mayor, chairman of the Democratic Party's county central committee, and a racehorse owner. He reminded his colleagues that many of them were big racing fans who would be calling upon him the next summer for racing tips. The measure's critics complained that the major gambling cliques would not be harmed by

the new law since they could afford to equip their facilities with telegraph wires but not the smaller gamblers. Nonetheless, the bill passed
30–23. Thereafter, companies that had tickers had to secure a permit
and give a $1,000 bond. They were barred from receiving or transmit-
ting any information that could be used in gambling.[54]

Displeased bookmakers responded by taking bets at extremely low
odds. Barney Zacharias, for example, paid off on a Siddons victory
in New Orleans at 7–10, compared to ticker odds that were 16–10.
Yet Chicago players kept on betting, and bookmakers kept on making
money. On December 8, President Robert Clowry of Western Union
agreed to obey the ordinance and announced his company would halt
the delivery of racing news. This closure led poolrooms to seek alternate sources of racing information, primarily by telephone. However,
his promise was not worth the paper it was printed on, and Western
Union continued to sell racing news to gambling syndicates.[55]

Harrison's turn to reform became stronger in 1904, when Chicago
poolrooms were taking in an estimated $200,000 a day in bets. That
year there were five times as many arrests for gambling compared to
prostitution. As we have seen, by then he was eyeing national office and
came out as a strong reformer to bolster his case by first ending prizefighting in Chicago and then gambling at Washington Park. He also
intended to halt offtrack gambling by increasing police involvement.[56]

The main policeman in the antipoolroom fight was Assistant
Superintendent Herman Schuettler. His flying squad did whatever
necessary to investigate and arrest malefactors, sometimes disguis-
ing themselves as teamsters, peddlers, or telephone linemen to gain
entrance into poolrooms. In one daring attack against Tennes's Central Exchange, some operatives climbed a telephone pole and entered
the building through its second-floor windows. Once poolroom workers found Schuettler's men making bets to gather information for
arrests, operators created a secret code to communicate with their
headquarters. The code included the track's name, designated by a
bird; the particular race by a state; the horse by a cipher based on its
initials; and then the betting odds.[57]

Schuettler and his men worked hard, but found it difficult to shut the poolrooms. As in the past, any poolroom operator or employees arrested would rely on their boss's clout with local politicians and pay-offs to the police to escape serious problems. Magistrates or police-court juries regularly acquitted people involved in gambling cases because they were paid off, were spellbound by the defense attorney, felt the offense was an insignificant victimless crime that harmed no one, or believed that petty gambling was an inherent human frailty that should be minimally punished.[58]

TELEPHONY AND POOLROOMS

The telephone was invented by Alexander Graham Bell in 1876, and by 1904 there were 3,317,000 in use in the United States. The phone was originally primarily a commercial device, and thus it should not be surprising that by the early 1900s they were employed to trans-mit essential information to poolrooms and handbook operators. In March 1904, the *Tribune* had chastised the Chicago Telephone Com-pany (CTC) for servicing gamblers who ran illegal businesses and also rebuked the police for permitting phones to remain in raided pool-rooms. The paper agreed with New York mayor George B. McClellan Jr. that phone company executives should be held to a higher standard than average people and take responsibility for their firm's misdeeds. Josiah Flynt estimated in 1907 that the CTC made $3,000 a day from offtrack racing and the New York Telephone Company $1 million a year. Bettors in New York wagered $40 million over the phone with their bookies.[59]

Despite the flying squad's earnest efforts, Superintendent O'Neill ended Schuettler's gambling detail on March 13, probably because it was *too* successful and was stepping on important toes. Headquarters announced that instead of the gambling detail being responsible for gambling matters, the department's three district inspectors would handle that problem. Schuettler still insisted on a special force and two days later organized a unit of sixteen plainclothesmen from outlying precincts to investigate poolrooms. The corps became known as the "pony ballet" because it focused on poolrooms, whose clients referred to a racehorse as a "pony." Schuettler told his staff to disconnect all phones found in poolrooms that were not party lines. He also recommended that arrested bookies be tried in criminal courts instead of police courts, where penalties were such small fines that gamblers dismissed the levy as a cheap "tax" on their business.[60]

Corporation counsel Edgar Tolman advised Mayor Harrison that the best way to fight poolrooms was to enjoin the CTC from furnishing phone service to poolrooms that abetted gambling and to order police raids to cut down on phone connections. On March 17, St. Patrick's Day, Schuettler's team, in conjunction with Tolman, seriously impaired the poolroom men by securing seventy arrests and confiscating betting paraphernalia. This mass arrest convinced the CTC to capitulate and promise to remove phones from gambling sites. Many poolrooms then decided to close, fearing raids, prosecutions, and a drop-off of clients worried about arrests. Poolroom business dropped by half. However, as one syndicate member pointed out, the raids were mainly nuisances, resolved by paying moderate fines. Then, if need be, the poolrooms could be reestablished elsewhere. The poolroom men and the bookmakers were more concerned about the loss of communications that could cripple their enterprises. Schuettler decided that the key to beating the gamblers was to shut off their source of information, which meant finding their clearinghouses.[61]

The CTC was in no hurry to disconnect phones in suspicious sites or terminate contracts with known bookies. Phone company president Arthur D. Wheeler pointed out that it was illegal to interfere with the apparatus of telephone or telegraph companies or for its workers to divulge transmitted information. He argued that the municipality was prohibited from interfering unless it proved the actual transmittal of gambling news, which Western Union and the CTC both denied they were doing.[62]

In mid-April, several raids took place, among them saloons belonging to pool owners O'Leary, Tennes, and William Skidmore, a Democratic committeeman who was a partner in the top West Side handbook syndicate and the city's leading policy wheel. Skidmore in 1912 served as sergeant at arms at the National Democratic Convention and later became a prominent bail bondsman and junk dealer. Historian Mark Haller indicates that "it would be impossible to unravel Skidmore's diverse careers to determine whether he was saloon keeper, gambler, politician, or businessman."[63]

O'Leary, Tennes, and Skidmore all lost their liquor licenses, despite their clout, though they kept selling pools. O'Leary turned for help to South Sider Edward Brennan, the Seventh Ward Democratic committeeman, who had saloons with thirty-six handbooks in Hyde Park and Woodlawn. Brennan was a loyal Harrison man who got O'Leary's suspended liquor license restored in return for a $40,000 gift to the party's war chest.[64]

If anything serious was to be done about the poolrooms, it had to include Western Union. As President William T. Baker of the Chicago Board of Trade pointed out in 1897: "Bucket shops and poolrooms are twin outlaws in nearly every State. . . . Their united corruption fund has enabled them to baffle justice . . . but they could not continue in existence a day but for their alliance with the Western Union Telegraph Company."[65]

Mayor George McClellan (New York City's forward-looking chief executive), various progressive reformers, and, most important, several major Western Union stockholders and directors called for the firm to close the racing bureau because of its connections to illegal enterprises. Those directors included US senator Chauncey Depew, former president of the New York Central Railroad; Jacob Schiff, the renowned investment banker and philanthropist; and three children of robber baron Jay Gould, its former principal owner, including daughter Helen, his most ardent critic, who spent much of her life as a philanthropist trying to redress her father's transgressions.[66]

On May 18, bookmakers and poolroom operators received a seemingly crushing blow when Western Union announced the closure of its lucrative racing bureau. The company's total reported income from all sporting events was nearly half its total ticker return of more than $17 million from 1893 through 1904. More than 90 percent of that sports income came from racing. The racing business in those years brought in an average of $644,875 a year, or a total of $7,738,503 (see table 11). In 1903 Western Union made $1,033,928 from racing, nearly as much as from stock quotations ($1,104,214), and its total sports operation ($1,106,000) surpassed the revenues from market data. From 1893 through 1904, racing profits were 73.6 percent of its stock data service. Historian David Hochfelder found an internal AT&T memo that identified the racing business as actually even more profitable than publicly reported, making about $2 million in income annually (including returns from circuits leased to betting groups), which in 1904 generated a $216,000 profit.[67]

Western Union's planned closing stunned Chicago gamblers, who were "thrown into a panic." According to the *New York Tribune*, "Throngs of men and boys crowded into the poolrooms, only to find that the telegraph service was entirely discontinued and operations were suspended for the day, or that books were being made with the understanding that the bookmakers would pay off according to the racing from odds to-morrow."[68]

The pronouncement left antigambling forces in city hall ecstatic, though Schuettler claimed his squad had already forced a decline from fifty to sixty poolrooms to four or less. A prominent bookie confirmed that Schuettler had killed 80 percent of the action. While this pronouncement was an exaggeration, the pony ballet was so busy confiscating phones that Schuettler's office resembled an electric repair shop. At the end of June, they raided exchanges run by Tennes, Weller, and O'Leary. Charley Choppy, manager of a Tennes room, kissed his confiscated phone and said, "Farewell, old pal. We've made $10,000 together, and I hate to lose you."[69]

Corporation counsel Tolman credited Harrison for the antiticker ordinance and the fight against telephonic distribution of racing information. Carter immodestly told the press, "I am proud of being the originator of the plan to halt the bookmaking evil abruptly by cutting the wires that fed it. The summary measures tried with such success in Chicago will accomplish untold good for the whole country in the abatement of gambling."[70]

Table 11
Western Union Income from Ticker Service, 1893–1905

Year	Quots.	Races	Baseball	Boxing	Football	Misc.	Total
1893	$587,733	$729,263	$30,702	$8,804	$122	$2,857	$1,359,481
1894	623,098	463,355	33,129	11,866	270	1,598	1,133,313
1895	699,114	425,966	42,355	12,698	319	712	1,181,164
1896	774,210	514,811	48,052	4,360	367	258	1,342,059
1897	873,092	646,649	52,103	27,591	849	165	1,600,449
1898	887,050	509,245	43,348	7,629	746	5	1,448,023
1899	891,626	646,399	39,935	32,719	1,109	1	1,611,789
1900	887,584	669,565	40,886	28,447	1,031	15	1,627,528
1901	928,294	694,908	38,350	4,109	669	56	1,666,386
1902	1,027,414	906,072		(all sports)	49,988	⋯	1,983,474
1903	1,104,214	1,033,928		(" ")	71,588	⋯	2,209,733
1904	1,237,911	498,342		(" ")	71,293	⋯	1,807,546
1905	1,314,488	⋯⋯		(" ")	85,190	⋯	1,399,678
T=	$11,835,828	$7,738,503		(all sports)	$790,624	$5,667	$20,370,623

Source: Adapted from "Commercial News Department: Revenue" (1908). Adapted from Statistical Notebooks, Western Union Telegraph Company, Lemelson Center, Smithsonian Institution, Washington, DC, courtesy of David Hochfelder. See also David Hochfelder, *The Telegraph in America, 1832–1920,* 115.

The press was also delighted and expected the gambling chiefs would soon retire because of room closures, pending indictments, and the absence of the racing wire. However, the press was wrong. The poolroom trust was still well represented in the Harlem and Hawthorne betting rings. More to the point, Western Union still allowed the transmission of racing data over its lines by a second party that provided a lifeline for the poolrooms. John Payne of Cincinnati, a former Western Union telegraph operator, set up a company to deliver racing data straight to poolrooms and leased a network of circuits to transmit data to his clients. After every race, a confederate at the track would use a mirror and flash back a coded report to a telegrapher in a nearby building who relayed the results to bookmakers throughout Cincinnati. By late July, poolroom men were back at their old stands, often with plans to move to the suburbs. O'Leary was bound for Blue Island, Frank McWhorter to Richland, and Bud White to the village of Evason in Lyons Township, on the Chicago and Alton Railroad.[71]

Harrison summarized his antipoolroom campaign for the *Saturday Evening Post*, explaining to a national audience that the local press was responsible for spreading the racing mania. Consequently, he sought new powers from the state to ban publication of racetrack information mainly used for betting purposes. His investigators "discovered the big downtown buildings were so saturated with the craze for gambling that agents of poolrooms made it a practice to visit office after office to obtain commissions for bets." The criminals were so enterprising that they "worked the elevated trains and surface cars just as a baggage collector does a through train, not only the cars to the races, but the cars carrying people to and from their work. Hardly anyone escaped the gambling fever."[72]

The Poolroom Grift

For more than 140 years, and probably for many years before then, professional gamblers and their clients were targeted by scammers or confidence men because they had a lot of cash on hand, and when the scam was uncovered, it was hard for them to get redress. Who were they going to complain to—the police? One reason many gamblers joined crime syndicates was for protection against scam artists. As early as 1880, swindlers were trying to cheat poolroom operators by fixing races or sending false reports to poolrooms about results of a race so their associates could place and collect winning bets on the purported winners before the correct results were reported. These attacks might be aimed at a particular poolroom, betting parlors in a certain city, or, as in 1883, a nationwide effort that included Chicago, Brooklyn, and Baltimore poolrooms.[73]

Poolrooms, by the turn of the century, if not earlier, were employed as the site of "confidence games." The term emerged in the mid-nineteenth century to describe a well-plotted scam in which a victim is defrauded by a confidence man who induces the victim (mark) to trust him with his money by convincing deceptions, often including compelling bogus or confusing assurances. A successful scam was known as a "sting."[74]

Chicago was a major scene of con games aimed at ingenuous travelers, but also astute, larcenous-minded businessmen, preferably out-of-towners, looking for a quick, large score. The con could be small or large. The small con, like three-card monte, was a modest operation that took just a minute and produced a small profit. The big con was a complex deception involving several participants that can extend over several days or longer, involving carefully prepared scripts, sets, and props. In a successful sting, the grifter (swindler) in charge obtained a large sum of money or valuable property from the mark who would ideally not discover the scam before returning home and then be either too embarrassed or afraid of self-incrimination by his own participation in a crime to seek police assistance against the defrauders. If he did return to the scene of the crime, it was probably vacant when he got there.[75]

Joseph "Yellow Kid" Weil was one of the great Chicago con men, who purportedly made $8 million from his cons. Weil was very familiar with the turf as a horse owner and tipster and used his expertise to arrange big cons involving offtrack poolrooms. His escapades and the exploits of other renowned con men like New York's Charley

Gondorff provided the inspiration for the Academy Award–winning movie *The Sting* (1973).[76]

Weil recounted in his autobiography a big poolroom con when he scammed "Marcus Macallister," a well-known Chicago plunger and downtown theater owner. Weil met him after placing an ad in an evening newspaper looking for a man to invest $2,500 in a project. Weil, operating under his own name, visited Macallister at his office and found him ready for a big score even if it meant pushing the letter of the law. He gained the mark's confidence by telling him that his brother-in-law, a Western Union employee, needed a $2,500 loan to pay off a loan shark and in return would provide a route to a fortune. The hook was that his in-law could use his position to provide race results before poolrooms got the news. The inside man was actually an actor who met Weil and Macallister at Western Union's downtown headquarters. Wall agreed to hold back the results wired from the company's New York headquarters for two minutes. The next day, Weil and his mark went to a downtown poolroom to place a bet. It was actually a betting parlor Weil's confederates decorated to look like a real poolroom, filled with some one hundred actors.

In the next stage, called in the trade "giving him the convincer," the mark got the advance information at a telephone booth across the street from the poolroom to test out the scam. Macallister was informed that Colorado had won the chosen race at Saratoga at 4–1. He raced to the betting cage, but a scuffle took place ahead of him, and he was too late to make his bet. Macallister heard a clerk report that Colorado had won the race, and he was hooked.

The final problem was collecting on the mark and finishing up the con. In *The Sting*, after crime boss Doyle Lonnegan (Robert Shaw) makes his successful bet, a "murder" takes place inside the poolroom. Before the police can arrive, Lonnegan is led away to safety by Henry Gondorff (Paul Newman), but in the rush leaves his winning wager behind. Cons were usually concluded in a more prosaic manner after the mark is fed inaccurate information and makes a losing bet at the poolroom. For example, in one con, Weil told his mark, a Mr. Fetterman, that his inside man at Western Union would hold back the result of the fifth race that day. Fetterman got a written message to bet on Lightning, with "3" written on the reverse side. Fetterman thought this meant the odds were 3–1, and bet Lightning to win. But the note meant the horse was coming in third. Fetterman lost but begged for another chance. This time the mark got a phone message: "Place your money on Humming Bird." Fetterman misunderstood the instructions and bet on the horse to win, but Humming Bird placed, coming in second. Fetterman got one more chance. The inside man called him and instructed the mark just to bet on the winner and that "Twenty won." So, he bet on horse 21, but the horse running from the "20" position won. The Fetterman con made Weil and his friends $28,000 after expenses.[77]

A New Racing Wire

Western Union revoked its pledge to close its racing business in 1904 and resumed operations at a greatly reduced level. Then there was pretty much no service in 1905. In September that year, director Jacob Schiff got a resolution approved by its board that resulted in the company permanently closing its racing service. However, messages written by customers that included racing information were still distributed over company's wires, as required of a common carrier.[78]

New companies were formed to fill the void, notably the St. Louis's Metropolitan News Company, which began in 1906 and made between $800,000 and $1,000,000. The old Western Union service was split up into two new companies that divided the market between a northern firm, the National News Company (NNC), popularly known as Payne's Telegraph Service, and a southern organization, the Cumberland Telephone Company (CTC). The NNC became the prime distributor of racing news under Payne, the biggest poolroom keeper in vice-riddled Covington, Kentucky, just across the Ohio River from Cincinnati. He brought to the firm his years of expertise in transmitting racetrack news over the Western Union wires. Payne's financial backers were reportedly John Condon, Ed Corrigan, several bookmakers, and an Indiana bucket-shop owner. One could imagine that if such long-term enemies as Condon and Corrigan would invest in the same company, it would have to be a sure thing. The firm serviced betting rooms in fourteen states and Canada using Western Union wires or long-distance telephone lines. The NNC sent race results to poolrooms in Chicago, Hot Springs, and San Francisco, while the CTC provided data to Atlanta, Los Angeles, Memphis, Nashville, and New Orleans. Journalists estimated that Payne's wire in 1907 grossed between $7 million and $15 million, netting a profit of $500,000. In addition, handbook men began relying more heavily on telephone messages sent by news gatherers operating from various racetracks via long-distance phone lines.[79]

O'LEARY'S STOCKADE

Shortly after the end of the 1904 racing season, Jim O'Leary established the Chicago Turf Exchange, a poolroom involving twenty-eight bookmakers, near Burnsville (currently Palisades), a small DuPage County village west of Chicago. Patrons got to the poolroom via the Santa Fe Railroad, which ran three eight- to ten-car daily "Gamblers' Specials" for a 25-cent round-trip ticket. O'Leary was concerned that public pressure was moving toward suppressing Chicago's poolrooms, so he sought a new safe outlet. His building was surrounded by two sixteen-foot-high solid wooden fences about four feet apart, patrolled by vicious dogs. A deputy sheriff declared that a successful raid "would take a regiment of Japanese infantry with siege guns."[80]

O'Leary's protectors included Democratic committeeman Edward Brennan and Sheriff Thomas E. Barrett. Gamblers in 1905 spent 20 percent of their gross profits, an estimated $15,000–$20,000 a month, for protection. O'Leary spent heavily not only for protection but also for public relations, employing a press agent, particularly for his winter book.[81]

Reformers mounted a crusade against the stockade, abetted by track managers who had lost business to O'Leary and jealous political opponents, irate they had not gotten a big payoff. Trustee Thomas A. Smyth of the Drainage Board urged the authorities to suppress O'Leary's poolroom and got the DuPage grand jury to investigate the operation. The Sanitary Police were instructed to look into all poolrooms and racetracks within one and a half miles of the Sanitary Canal, which included Worth and Hawthorne.[82]

On March 4, state's attorney Healy determined that the campaign against O'Leary's Stockade was involved in a blackmail scheme tied to a lot of forged anti-Stockade correspondence sent to Governor Deneen and DuPage sheriff Joseph M. Heiser. Nonetheless, the antipoolroom campaign generated sufficient pressure to prod Deneen and Healy to convince the Santa Fe Railroad to halt its special trains and Western Union to cut down its wires to the Stockade. Daily patronage dropped from about fifteen hundred to seven hundred and led to the indictment of O'Leary and seventeen employees. O'Leary copped a plea and was fined $750 for keeping a gaming room and $200 for selling liquor without a license.[83]

The grand-jury investigation into the Stockade, plus O'Leary's arrogant statement that "there would be more gambling in Chicago than ever," persuaded Assistant Police Superintendent Schuettler to initiate the city's first important attack on handbooks since the police initially removed telephones from poolrooms. His efforts were abetted by corporation counsel Tolman's legal opinion that building owners of handbook sites were as liable to punishment as the bookmakers, and the police began going after the real-estate agents.[84]

Democrat Edward Dunne took over as mayor in April 1905, after defeating distinguished politician and lawyer John M. Harlan, pushing a program of municipal ownership of the streetcar lines. Dunne became involved in fighting gambling, as the number of gambling arrests was four times as many as vice arrests. He appointed political ally John C. Collins, a Haymarket-era veteran of the police force, as superintendent. The press considered him a quality appointee who would vigorously fight crime. Collins told the press that "gambling in this town is a disgrace" and promised, like every other new chief, to drive it out. Collins set up flying squads and orchestrated spectacular raids on his first day on the job, including one at Tennes's cigar shop. John Binder argues that Dunne had a well-earned reputation for fighting organized crime. His gambling index was 110 that year and rose to a historic high (140) the following year, when there were 7,774 arrests, the most until 1929. However, most scholars believe his numbers were mainly for show because those arrests were merely inconveniences that cost a poolroom owner a $100 fine and patrons a $1 penalty. The handbooks and poolrooms immediately reopened and flourished during Dunne's tenure. By 1910 Mayor Fred Busse had a dismal gambling index of just 25.[85]

Betting on the Lake

In 1905 the O'Leary and the Smith & Perry syndicate expanded their gambling operations by spending $40,000 to outfit the thirty-six-year-old steamer *City of Traverse* for off-shore horse-race gambling, buying the essential racing data from the DeForest Wireless Telegraph Company for $100 a day. The vessel made its inaugural voyage on June 29 from the Sixty-Eighth Street pier, sailing outside the three-mile limit that put it beyond state or federal authority. Race results were received by an on-board operator, who telephoned the data in code to the bookmaking stands on the lower deck.[86]

Detectives from the gambling squad were aboard for the initial run, but could do nothing once the boat moved outside the state's three-mile jurisdiction. The gamblers posted pasteboards with the names of horses running at a Buffalo racetrack, took bets, and paid off on winning wagers. Management burned the betting slips before the boat landed at six o'clock at the South Water Street pier. The offshore gambling continued into August. It resumed one year later, when the syndicate paid Alderman Kenna $1,700 a week for protection. Business was so good that Mont Tennes bought his own $75,000 gambling boat, the *John R. Sterling*, to emulate Smith and Perry.[87]

The Profits of Bookmaking

In 1907, muckraking journalist George Kibbe Turner published an article in the popular *McClure's Magazine*, examining immorality in Chicago. He studied liquor (a $100 million business in 1906), prostitution ($20 million), and gambling ($15 million in receipts). Turner reported that bookmaking comprising 80 percent of the betting, producing a profit of $5.6 million. Turner estimated that two-thirds of the action occurred downtown in the First Ward and the nearby Eighteenth Ward (Chicago River west to Clinton Ave. Lake Street south to Van Buren St.). He reported that one former police chief claimed to have made $187,000 in payoffs.[88]

Mayor Fred Busse and the Poolrooms

The 1907 mayoralty campaign, between Mayor Dunne and Chicago postmaster Fred Busse, was the first ever for a four-year term. Busse had briefly served in the state legislature and was primarily a businessman. Mayor Dunne turned out to be an ineffective administrator, indecisive and impractical, and had failed to produce on his electoral promises to establish municipal ownership of the streetcar lines and alienated both reformers and bosses. The main issues in the campaign were mass transit, public education, and more centralized government, key elements of a proposed new city charter. It was a nasty campaign, with conservative journalists attacking Dunne as boss connected and applauding Busse for his business experience, conveniently forgetting his ties to the Republican machine. Busse won a hotly contested campaign by about thirteen thousand votes. He was not a particularly effective mayor, and crime flourished during his tenure. Nonetheless, Dunne went on to become the only mayor of Chicago elected governor (1913–17).[89]

Horse racing was a nonissue in the campaign. However, muckraker Charles Russell uncovered an important deal between Tennes and the First Ward Democratic bosses who promised to deliver twelve thousand votes for Busse, the approximate winning margin. The purported payoff would be no police interference in Coughlin and Kenna's ward and for Tennes a free hand for his syndicate, the closing of his rivals' *City of Traverse*, and the reinstatement of two police allies suspended in 1906, inspectors Nicholas Hunt and Patrick Lavin, worth reportedly about $500,000.[90]

Busse hired Inspector George Shippy as police superintendent. Shippy, an experienced and brave policeman and detective, was a strict disciplinarian. He maintained the same bravado as his predecessors about running the gamblers out of town. Shippy abandoned the special gambling detail and made each precinct's officers responsible for combating local gambling. The *Tribune* supported this idea: "Wherever a gambling resort is maintained it will be proof positive that the precinct sergeants and lieutenant are not doing their duty.[91]

Shippy at first seemed to turn up the heat on downtown poolrooms, with a big foray against Tennes's downtown headquarters and then weekly raids against his four North Side saloons. But these incursions were largely shams, and the rooms reopened immediately. Renowned sportswriter Hugh Fullerton reported that when Busse took office, "'the word' went out to open up," and gamblers swarmed into Chicago. Poolrooms ran on a larger scale, although less overtly than before, with open bookmaking everywhere, plus the return of faro and roulette, barred since 1893. Fullerton believed that the Tennes crowd got special treatment mainly "because of their better organization and more careful management than from political influence."[92]

The administration failed to pass an ordinance to penalize the publication and circulation of racing data, but did take action against the *City of Traverse*. On May 25, when the betting season opened for the vessel, policemen made their first arrests ever against the boat. The *City of Traverse* departed at two thirty with four hundred passengers aboard, and when it returned two hours later dozens of clients were taken off by tugboat a half mile from shore and promised a shortcut home. Plainclothes police nabbed them as they alit on shore and arrested seventy-two for disorderly conduct. The *City of Traverse* was closed until a trial ended with acquittals. Still, the betting public had learned a lesson. When the boat sailed again on June 6, there were fewer than one hundred patrons, and the owners decided to temporarily close.[93]

On June 18, Mayor Busse wrote Congressman James R. Mann (R–Chicago) for help in revoking the boat's license. The congressman is mostly remembered today for the Mann Act that made it illegal to transport women across state lines for immoral purposes. Mann took Busse's concern to the White House, and President Theodore Roosevelt agreed to investigate the matter. On July 10, the government canceled the *City of Traverse*'s license, ending its tenure as a gambling vessel because the boat was approved only for coastal trade and not gambling. It was an important precedent for maritime law, since the federal government previously limited itself to issues of safety on American waterways.[94]

Mont Tennes and the Bombing Wars

Mont Tennes at the end of spring 1907 was the second most powerful offtrack gambler in Chicago after O'Leary, with hundreds of small handbooks under his control. That summer he surpassed O'Leary, earning a share of profits from nearly all the city's handbooks and poolrooms. Mont achieved his status by financing raids by constables against his rivals, shutting down winter betting at the O'Leary-Smith-White-Perry-run Dearborn Park poolroom in Indiana, and purchasing for $300 a day exclusive rights from Payne for racing data transmitted in Illinois, rights that previously belonged to the Smith-Perry organization. Tennes's syndicate received the data at a switchboard in the newly named town of Forest Park (formerly Harlem) train station, the starting point of a trunk line with forty to forty-five wires that sent the information in code to several hundred handbooks and poolrooms. Handbooks paid $25–$50, and poolrooms $50–$100, plus half their net receipts for information, protection, and assumption of half of their losses. Soon no gambling room in the city could gather racing results by telephone or wire without paying Tennes, making him the offtrack gambling chief of Chicago.[95]

Tennes's growing success led to a violent bombing war over territories and spoils. The starting point for the viciousness may have been on June 18, 1907, when he was beaten up walking with his wife, supposedly by a client who called him a welsher. It was the same day that his rivals sold the *City of Traverse*. Three weeks later, a bombing war broke out, with O'Leary, Wagner, White, Smith, and Perry out to destroy the Tennes-Condon-O'Malley-McGinnis crowd. The first bomb exploded on July 8 on a first-floor windowsill in the back of Blind John Condon's fashionable home at 2623 South Michigan Avenue. The press reported it had apparently been set to kill Condon and his family. Ten days later, another bomb exploded in the basement of John O'Malley's downtown saloon, followed five days later when Tennes's garage behind his home was blasted.[96]

Tennes's men retaliated by bombing O'Leary's saloon at 4183 South Halsted on August 12. Then five days later, Tennes's front yard was hit by a bomb made of "safeblower's soup" (nitroglycerin and TNT). Thereafter, Tennes reportedly began paying $1,500 a week for protection to a crime syndicate that shook down rival Chicago gamblers. In all, there were thirteen gambling-related bombings in 1907. The gambling continued despite the bombings, and nearly $60,000 a day was bet at the city's poolrooms that summer.[97]

Superintendent George M. Shippy assigned Assistant Chief of Police Herman Schuettler to investigate the bombings by using the seldom-enforced vagrancy law to make arrests. The squad broke the gamblers' secret code used to send race results, but had little success ferreting out the bombers.[98]

There were fifteen bombing attacks in 1908. Democratic committeeman Edward F. Brennan, an independent handbook operator, was hit twice, as were two rooms belonging to Johnnie Rogers. O'Leary was the target of three attacks. The *Daily News* charged that someone in the police department knew the identity of the men behind the bombings but did not want to arrest them, worried that the inside story of police protection of horse-race gambling would become public. The *Examiner* blamed Tennes's efforts to create a monopoly as the cause of the bombings, leading to his rivals' retaliation.[99]

One of the worst bombings occurred on June 27, 1909, when a twenty-five-pound bomb exploded at Tennes's Clark Street poolroom in the heart of downtown, injuring twenty-seven, with property damage to fifteen buildings estimated at $200,000. The extensive damage may have discouraged the warfare because there were no more bombings until October 31, when for the first time two bombs were detonated on the same day. One was aimed at "Big Ed" Wagner, who had recently taken over a downtown poolroom from the old Smith & Perry outfit, and the second blast went off thirty minutes later at a downtown building recently sold by Second Ward Republican alderman George F. Harding, a member of Chicago high society and one of the biggest real-estate agents in the city. The first-floor saloon was owned by former state senator Billy O'Brien, former president of the Worth Jockey Club. Ed Wagner, his old racing partner, sublet a third-floor room in the same building from Alderman Johnny Powers.[100]

The thirty-fifth bomb exploded on February 17, 1910. In the next two years, fifteen more bombs were set off, though only a few seemed directed at the poolroom crowds. The police never found out who did the bombings—only two arrests were ever made, and there was just one conviction—or why they stopped. One Tennes associate claimed the bombers were extortionists, who stopped once paid off, while Harry Brolaski, a former bookmaker arrested nearly eighty times, turned public lecturer on gambling issues, claimed that Hinky Dink Kenna mediated an end to the war and received $40,000 for his efforts. One unintended result of the bombing wars was that gamblers invented new ways to advance their businesses, such as using handbooks written in Hebrew, whose owners claimed were religious books. At this time, even without any local racing, the typical bookie covered $300 a day in bets and earned about a 10 percent gross profit. Binder estimates a $4.1 million return among Chicago's gamblers.[101]

TENNES AND THE RACING WIRE

Tennes's growing control of the bookmaking business was connected to his growing influence in the local and national distribution of racing information. He told the press that he first got interested in the business of disseminating racing news in 1907 when a telegraph strike enabled certain gamblers to wage a great scam tampering with the Payne racing wire. The system reported only the highest odds on a winning horse at Fort Erie, Ontario, at 20–1, although track odds had dropped to 6–1. Poolrooms lost a fortune by paying off at the higher odds. This error showed him the power of controlling the wire.[102]

Tennes probably got into the business of distributing racing news around November 1909 when he and his associate Horace Argo formed a partnership with Tim Murphy and the Murphy Brothers News Service in Cleveland. Tim Murphy had once worked ten years for Western Union and then for Payne from 1905 to 1907. He and his three brothers, financed by Kentucky Derby executive Matt Winn, sent racing news across the country on their own wires because Western Union refused them access to their system.[103]

Murphy sold Tennes the right to sell his betting news in Chicago for $300 a day. Shortly thereafter, Tennes demanded an ownership stake in the business, warning Murphy to agree or the police would run him out of the business. This threat put Murphy in a tenuous position because of Tennes's control over the invaluable offtrack betting business in Chicago. Tennes paid him $4,500 for a 33 percent share of the firm and soon invested $5,000 more. By then he owned 50 percent of Murphy's company, renamed the General News Bureau (GNB). Tennes subsequently squeezed Murphy down to just a salary and 10 percent of the profits. Murphy retaliated in August 1911, suing Tennes for defamation of character and a financial accounting of the firm, charging that Tennes owed him $35,000. They settled out of court.[104]

Tennes left no stone unturned in the GNB's drive to push the Payne News Service out of Chicago and then to monopolize the wire service, such as stealing news sent from Canadian tracks into the United States, a violation of Canada's Miller Act. Tennes's men harassed the competition and tipped off their police friends to close Payne's outlets. Finally, the GNB employed violence to annihilate the competition. Mont's agents destroyed Payne's $12,000 home in Crystal, Kentucky, and bombed his affiliated poolrooms in Columbus (Ohio), Hanover (Indiana), and St. Louis that had refused to switch to Tennes. The Chicagoan's agents also burned down H. I. Brown's Jacksonville, Florida, racetrack three times. Tennes wore down Payne, and in a secret meeting on May 1, 1910, in Hammond, Indiana, Payne agreed to sell his company to Tennes for $300 a day and a 5 percent interest.[105]

Table 12
Mont Tennes's Betting Service Fees, 1911

City	Poolrooms	Daily Tribute	Weekly Tribute
Albany, NY	4	$25–$40	$ 1,000
Buffalo	4	5–10	180
Chicago	90	6–20	3,600
Cincinnati	10	5	300
Cleveland	1	5	30
Dayton, OH	1	20	180
Detroit	2	5–20	210
French Lick, IN	1	15	50
Indianapolis	1	15	50
Memphis	1	40	240
Muskogee, OK	1	30	180
Nashville	1	40	240
New Albany, IN	2	—	50
New York	70	8–25	3,000
Oklahoma City	1	35	210
Pittsburgh	4	10	240
South Bend, IN	2	15	90
St. Louis	6	10–15	480
Toledo	1	25	180
Toronto	3	15–30	300
Total	206	$356–$415	$10,810

Source: *Chicago Examiner*, August 9, 1911, 8.

By 1911 Tennes was the king of Chicago bookmakers and controlled the racing wire throughout North America. Former partner Tim Murphy claimed that by then, Tennes's syndicate had 300 gambling rooms, including poolrooms, and halls that featured faro and roulette. The syndicate had a viselike grip on the horse-race gambling business, operating openly as a racing-news distributing service that sold racing news to at least 206 poolrooms (of which 43.7 percent were in Chicago and 30 percent in New York), while also operating, less overtly, as a handbook consortium (see table 12). An investigation by three state attorneys general estimated the racing wire annually made more than $500,000, employing eighteen telephone and telegraph companies. Mont had 90 poolrooms in Chicago, paying $3,600 a week (averaging $40 a week), including business rivals like O'Leary, whom he charged $60 a week; Rogers, $90; and White, $100. He had seventy customers in New York paying a total of $4,000 a week, along with rooms in San Francisco, Salt Lake City, San Antonio, New Orleans, and Baltimore.[106]

HARRY BROLASKI AND THE NATIONAL FIGHT AGAINST POOLROOMS

The growing prominence of offtrack betting in 1909 in Chicago, in New York, and across the country led the Senate Judiciary Committee to investigate horse-race gambling because of the use of federally regulated communication systems to distribute valuable information. The committee also considered a bill by Senator E. J. Burkett (R–NE) to prohibit the transmission of racetrack news over telegraph or phone lines, which never passed. Racing then was permitted in just California, Kentucky, Maryland, New York, and Nevada. Harry Brolaski, the noted former bookmaker and Juarez track owner, was the primary witness. He had become a popular spokesman for the International Reform Bureau and other antigambling organizations and two years later wrote *Easy Money: Being the Experiences of a Reformed Gambler*, which publicized the extent of illegal gambling in the United States. Brolaski provided the committee with considerable statistical evidence on racetracks and offtrack betting, but he was not the most reliable witness, since he frequently changed his statistics from one public lecture to another. Brolaski estimated that a bookie operating out of a saloon spent $10–$50 a day to operate and took in $100–$5,000 in bets.[107]

Brolaski testified two years later at the Interstate Commerce Commission's investigation of racehorse gambling and the national distribution of racing information. He identified Mont Tennes as the head of a handbook trust that included Condon, Kenna, O'Leary, McGinnis, politician and gambler Billy O'Brien, and superintendent of streets Frank Solon. Brolaski claimed that Tennes was paying $10,000 a month in payoffs to the police to destroy anyone who dared go into the handbook business without his syndicate's consent, usually by getting the police to raid and arrest them. The commission decided that the transmission of race results was not necessarily uplifting but was legal.[108]

Harrison and the Poolrooms

In 1911 Carter H. Harrison came out of retirement and won his fifth term as mayor after a difficult campaign over his formidable Republican opponent, reform alderman Charles Merriam. Harrison got 48.4 percent of the total vote, beating his chief rival by 17,132 votes. Merriam taught political science at the University of Chicago (1900–1940), chairing the department for thirty years. He was a prominent progressive and founder of the behavioral approach to political science. Harrison ran with the support of the gambling, saloon, and vice elements who anticipated he would permit the good times to roll. Tennes was one of his biggest financial supporters, reportedly donating $20,000 to the campaign.[109]

After the April election, several gamblers moved to Chicago in anticipation of the return of the frolicking and rollicking good old days. However, Harrison made another about-face, responding to a public clamor to close the infamous Levee District, with its prostitution and gambling, which had begun in 1910. Harrison set up the Chicago Vice Commission, which together with the Women's Christian Temperance Union helped publicize the evils of the vice district. The government made a big push against the Levee District in October, closing saloons, gambling dens, and brothels, including the notorious Everleigh House. By 1912 the police had the area pretty well shut down. Police Superintendent John McWeeney pledged to close the Chicago poolrooms, but put Inspector Hunt, an old bookmaker ally, in charge. The promised restrictions on bookmaking soon faded, and the gambling situation returned to normal, if not worse. Many pool-rooms were remade into complete betting parlors with dice, cards, and roulette. The reformers felt double-crossed by the mayor, and the poolroom menace remained a feature of Chicago's sporting subculture for more than thirty years.[110]

Conclusion

At the end of the nineteenth century, offtrack gambling was one of the most successful illicit enterprises in the United States. Despite gambling's universal illegality, the criminal justice system and the general public considered it a victimless crime and thus a low priority for the police or the judiciary. It was primarily an urban business that flourished in a number of American cities and existed in many more whether the city had horse racing or not, although having racing helped substantially. Americans liked to gamble, whether it was legal or not. Betting on horse racing gave wagerers a chance to demonstrate their expertise, and while attending a race was part of the fun, it was not essential. What was crucial were the men prepared to engage in an illegal enterprise, which required their own organization to secure financing, rapid racing news, and protection from the authorities. Syndicate crime in Chicago enabled the city to rank just behind New York in the number and quality of its poolrooms and handbooks and place it far ahead of any other city in this illegal business.

Handbooks were modest operations, mainly found in working-class neighborhoods where bookies catered to blue-collar ethnic customers like themselves. Irishmen serviced Irish customers (among others), Jewish bookies took bets from Jewish patrons, and African American bookies had African American clients. Handbooks offered ready accessibility to racing information, and personal attention, taking small bets and offering credit. The handbook operators were commonly clients of syndicates that provided them with essential services similar to poolrooms, such as financing, protection, and a chance to lay off large bets.

Poolrooms were far more substantial operations, typically located downtown. These betting parlors catered to workers in the central business district who had discretionary money to gamble, plying them with food and drink in a pleasant atmosphere, where they could hear reenactments of important races, all intended to keep them in the room, betting. When the authorities clamped down on these betting parlors, the owners relocated, often to suburbs near accessible train routes. Poolrooms that lasted were typically associated with gambling syndicates that had the political clout and the financial resources to get the authorities to avoid interfering with them, while harassing and stifling their competition.

The illegal enterprise engaged in violence, including setting fires at racetracks; bombing racecourses, rival poolrooms, and homes of prominent gamblers; fights among gangsters; and brawls initiated by private security agents, all while encouraging violent raids on poolrooms by policemen. However, there were rarely killings of major business rivals. Some news dealers who ran handbooks on the side were beaten or murdered in the ferocious "Circulation Wars." The violence began in 1910 when the circulation managers of the *Examiner*, the *Record-Herald*, and the *Chicago Tribune* hired street toughs to bolster their papers' sales by intimidating news dealers. The thugs employed blackjacks, brass knuckles, firebombs, and guns to beat and murder uncooperative newspaper retailers. The most famous gangland murder of an American bookmaker in the early 1900s occurred in 1912 in New York when bookmaker Herman Rosenthal was assassinated by hoodlums hired by Police Lieutenant Charles Becker. The officer had been shaking down the bookie who was intending to report Becker's misdeeds to the district attorney.[111]

Gamblers' clients were not usually subject to physical intimidation. Poolroom customers mainly paid in cash. Handbooks were more likely to give credit, albeit in small amounts. Like loan sharks at the time, they mainly relied on nonviolent methods to enforce collection, such as cutting off a line of credit, embarrassing the client by telling his family (a major blow to the welsher's manliness), or threatening to report the debt to the client's employer, who would fire him as untrustworthy. The underworld's use of violence like threats to break legs did not come into vogue for another generation.[112]

Mike McDonald in the 1870s formed the first crime syndicate to nearly monopolize the offtrack gambling business by financing operations, limiting entry into the occupation, providing essential information about races via telegraphy, and supplying protection, legal representation, and bonds if their associates and employees were arrested. This system continued in the 1890s after McDonald retired. The McDonald system was largely replicated in New York City by the Tammany-run Gambling Trust that nearly monopolized offtrack betting at the turn of the century. The trust's leading figure was state senator Tim Sullivan, the number-two man in Tammany Hall, abetted by Mayor Robert Van Wyck, Police Chief William Devery, and Frank Farrell, the city's leading gambler. The trust reportedly made $3,095,000 in a single year, including $1,440,000 in fees from four hundred poolroom operators.[113]

This gambling was a cornerstone for the rise of syndicate crime and a major source of income. Horseracing was a crucial element in the alliance between the underworld and urban political machines as big-city crime syndicates worked in close cooperation with machine politicians and local police to protect this illegal business.[114]

By the early 1900s, the business in Chicago was divided among three major poolroom syndicates that divided up the city by geography and shared the business in the CBD. Each confederation of gamblers was led by a well-known gambler with important political clout that protected his colleagues' interests. However, by the end of the decade, Mont Tennes had created a citywide gambling organization through his growing control over the supply of racing information, political connections, and intimidation. Mont achieved a near monopoly over the city's poolrooms and handbooks and, once he took over the race wire, created a national cartel over the supply of racing information. Tennes became the single most important figure in offtrack betting, making Chicago in the future the center of illegal offtrack betting in the United States.

8

Conclusion

Equine sports had a long history in Chicago. The preeminent antebellum sport in the instant city was harness racing, contested at modest proprietary tracks operated by politically prominent businessmen.
The popularity of racing was overwhelmingly based on the opportunity to make bets, giving gamblers a chance to display their racing acumen and their manliness by putting themselves on the line
through their wagers. Harness-track operators relied on the reticence
of the authorities to interfere with wagering between individual bettors, along with their own power and connections to protect an enterprise reliant on illegal gambling to survive. After the Civil War, when
Chicago continued to boom economically, despite the setbacks created
by the disastrous Chicago Fire, the harness-racing business grew, with
bigger courses, larger purses, and modest profits.

A big change occurred in the early 1880s when harness racing was
supplanted by the more expensive and prestigious sport of thoroughbred racing, employing expensive horses bred for racing, with powerful, strong bodies that produced great speed. These horses were no
longer bred and trained for long-distance heat racing of up to four
miles, but were prepped for shorter distances that facilitated more
races and more betting. The major urban racing markets preferred flat
racing at tracks of one mile or less, with ample numbers of stables and
large seating capacities. Betting formats were also geared at increasing the action. The antebellum emphasis on bets between individuals
was first supplanted by auction pools that offered a big advantage to
wealthy bettors, but became more democratic with the populariza-
tion of bookmaking, further enhanced with the rise of pari-mutuel

machines that gave bettors more confidence in the integrity of the betting and the races.

Harness racing and thoroughbred racing coexisted after the Civil War, but the former quickly took over under the leadership of the fabulously new wealthy elite class who made their fortunes in the rebuilt post-fire city. Well-off Chicagoans joined the new and costly Washington Park Club, an elite men's club with strict standards for admission. Members not only had wealth but were also employed at prestigious occupations, married well, lived in the best neighborhoods, and attended the most prestigious churches. Admission to the WPC certified members' social status and enabled them to make valuable social and business contacts. The club did not identify itself as a jockey club by name, but its major project was to establish and operate the Washington Park Racetrack that became the most prestigious racecourse west of the Hudson River.

Only a small number of members were themselves horsemen who invested heavily in costly breeding or built major stables, but they did further enhance their personal status by their attendance at the track, arriving by expensive carriages and socializing at the park's clubhouse, embellishing their own lifestyle as "conspicuous consumers."

The track drew huge crowds, among the largest, if not the largest, in any American sport. The audience came from all social classes, men and women attracted by nationally renowned horses and jockeys who competed for glory and lucrative purses, participation in the rituals of the track, a chance to be in the presence of the rich and fashionable of Chicago society, and an opportunity to bet legally. The Washington Park Racetrack was instrumental in setting the tone for making Chicago the western center of thoroughbred racing, but was also abetted by local proprietary tracks owned by profit-oriented businessmen and prominent politicians using political connections to enhance their business interests and make money. Most American tracks were built with the intention of making money. The West Side Racetrack in the 1880s moved from being primarily a trotting and pacing facility to a thoroughbred track. The relations between the track operators was never close, but they did combine to help secure the passage of the Gibbs Act in 1887 that declared on-track gambling legal in Illinois.

However, the prestige of Chicago racing was soon marred in 1891 by politically connected bookmakers, including Mike McDonald, known as the first founder of an American crime syndicate, who established the city's gambling organization that virtually monopolized the illegal poolroom business. He and his associates used their political clout to force the closure of the West Side Track that moved to the town of Hawthorne and replaced it with the new Garfield Park track. Their outlaw enterprise was extremely profitable in its short life. However, management ran roughshod over the neighborhood, which lobbied Mayor Washburne, who got the track closed, despite their strong connections on the city council.

The political connections of Chicago racing men were hardly unique but in fact were commonplace in professional sports, particularly baseball and prizefighting. In the late nineteenth century, it was commonplace for track operators to be politicians, or at least politically connected businessmen. In New Jersey and New York, racing doyens were frequently professional politicians or well-linked businessmen, like financier August Belmont Sr., who from 1860 to 1872 was head of the national Democratic Party. Then there were entrepreneurs like the Dwyer brothers, who owned Brooklyn's Gravesend racetrack, raced horses, and took bets, who were closely associated with Tammany boss Richard Croker, himself a prominent horseman who won the Epsom Derby in 1907.

Political connections, primarily with northern Democratic politicians, whose urban, ethnic working-class constituents supported gambling, helped track owners. Track owners got essential information about where to build their track, secured the necessary licenses, kept taxes and fees as low as possible, and utilized city hall to fight rival racetracks and offtrack bookmakers who took away considerable betting action. Political contacts in the state legislature helped them secure new laws, like the Gibbs Act that legalized on-track racing, and also fight negative court decisions that weakened their right to sponsor on-track betting. It was difficult to secure legalization of on-track gambling and preserve that hard-won right against adverse court rulings. New Jersey Democrats passed the Parker Acts in 1893 that legalized on-track racing, but just one year later the acts were overturned by a political realignment in New Jersey, a historically strongly Democratic state. The election brought in a new Republican legislature who helped outlaw thoroughbred racing in their state. Horsemen's political clout in Illinois was far below the influence of New York State's racing men, who in 1895 circumvented the new state constitution that directly banned horse racing by getting the legislature to pass the Percy-Gray Act that protected on-track wagering by setting up the state's Racing Commission to supervise the sport in coordination with the new elite Jockey Club, a completely private organization. Yet even the enormous political clout of the New York racing set was not enough to block the state from banning racetrack gambling in 1910.

Racing men needed political clout at the turn of the century to fight off antigambling groups that had a lot of influence throughout the United States. The sport had long been under attack by small-town and rural evangelical Christians motivated by their religious beliefs that gambling was a sin and that it was their duty to protect their fellow men from immoral behavior. In the late nineteenth century, the antigambling movement gained support from progressive reformers, many of whom were ardent Christians, but their enthusiasm was mainly based on social research by journalists, social workers, and scholars who found that horse-race gambling led to the ruin of families whose breadwinners were driven to crime to pay their gambling debts. Secular reformers also claimed that the syndicates involved in horse-race gambling used their profits to corrupt local governments to advance their illegal enterprises and to expand into other sectors of organized crime.

In Illinois, like many other states, the legislature was a political minefield for racing. Across the country, first in the mid-1890s, and a decade later in the mid- to late 1900s, antibetting lobbyists had great success in halting racing. Furthermore, a number of conservative lawyers in the early 1890s got judges to overturn proracing laws like the Gibbs Act. The Illinois General Assembly, like in many other midwestern states, was dominated by the Republican Party, aided by gerrymandered districting and bullet voting. The Republicans were highly receptive to constituents with conservative social values, including opposition to gambling, namely, small-town and rural evangelical Christians.

In Illinois the Democrats did not implement an enhanced proracing bill in 1893–94 when they had rare control over the general assembly and the governorship. Then they lost control of the general assembly in late 1894. They entered the next legislative session with high expectations of a new act in 1895, but did not have the votes.

While northern Democrats supported horse-race gambling, the story was different in the South, where conservative Democrats dominated post-Reconstruction politics in one-party states. States like Kentucky, Louisiana, Maryland, and Virginia had strong racing traditions that went back for two hundred years, but politicians were also committed to the points of view of devout Protestants who considered gambling a sin. Consequently, racing was banned in most of the South, and even Kentucky barely managed to keep Churchill Downs in operation.

The number of American racecourses dropped from 306 in 1897 to just 25 in 1908, mainly because of political opposition, but also because many courses were not profitable. By 1910, after New York's tracks closed, only six states had racing: Kentucky, Maryland, Montana, Oklahoma, Utah, and Virginia. New York City resumed thoroughbred racing in 1913 because of court rulings in *People ex Rel. Shane v. Gittens* (1912) that found that track directors were liable for criminal activities only if they had prior knowledge of professional bookmaking taking place. Chicago would be the next major city to regain horse racing, when in 1924 the local courts legalized oral betting, and three years later the state legalized pari-mutuel betting.[1]

The legal problems American tracks had with state governments was quite different from foreign courses that operated without interference by their national legislature that was responsible for moral issues like gambling. Members of each country's racing set were well represented in their nation's legislature and had powerful friends in the government. The interests of the horsey set in Great Britain were especially well set up to defend themselves in the House of Lords, as well as the House of Commons. Furthermore, many voters across the globe still had a great deal of respect for upper-class candidates, people who commonly were identified with elite sports like thoroughbred racing, which was, after all, "the sport of kings."

Religion did not play a big role in horse racing overseas. The European and Latin American countries that supported racing were mainly Catholic and did not see gambling as sinful. Asian nations were also more accepting of wagering than Protestant America. Great Britain and its predominantly white colonies and dominions with large Protestant populations like Canada and Australia shared an old sporting and gambling tradition that carried a lot of weight in countering evangelical opposition to horse-race betting.

Thoroughbred racing's involvement with American politics in the nineteenth century was hardly a unique phenomenon. Baseball and boxing, the two other major professional sports, were even more dominated by professional politicians and businessmen closely connected to major local political figures, who employed that clout to protect or advance their commercial interests. Major League Baseball was the only major professional sport then that was always legal. Americans had a pristine image of the national pastime that did not have a gambling image and was a minor factor in the sport's popularity. Yet fans did wager at ball games, mainly with other fans. They bet on the outcomes of ball games and statistical accomplishments, such as numbers of hits or even the call of a pitch. The owners placed signs inside the ballpark warning against making bets, but no one cared. Baseball's immaculate image was forever destroyed in late 1920 by the news that the "Black Sox" had fixed the 1919 World Series on behalf of such prominent bettors as Arnold Rothstein.[2]

Baseball franchises used their clout in several ways. They employed their political influence to deter possible rival teams from moving into their territory. Teams also used their political power to legalize

Sunday baseball, as midwestern teams had done in the late nineteenth century (including the Chicago Colts, formerly the White Stockings, in 1893). However, New York's teams did not get Sunday ball until 1920 and Philadelphia and Pittsburgh until 1934. MLB franchises also used their clout to obtain inside information on land-use and mass-transit plans to help them site their ballparks and to secure preferential municipal treatment when it came to taxes, license fees, policing, and building codes.[3]

The business of racing was much more similar to boxing than baseball because they both operated with a highly tenuous legal status. Horse racing was widely banned and under constant opposition because of the gambling issue. Prizefighting was universally banned because of the gambling, but also for its violence and corruption. Matches for most of the nineteenth century had to be staged secretly in saloon backrooms, barns, or obscure out-of-town locations. In 1890 the sport was legalized in Louisiana for prizefighting in New Orleans. Six years later, New York State legitimized pugilism under state supervision. However, New York's boxing laws were reversed four times in the next twenty-five years, and prizefighting was not permanently legitimized there until 1920. American promoters had a hard time finding sites for world championship fights in the early 1900s because of widespread opposition. A number of bouts were staged in San Francisco, but their locations had to be sanctioned by its political boss, attorney Abe Ruef. Other major bouts were held in such out-of-the-way places as Gold-field and Reno, Nevada; Fort Erie, Canada; Sydney, Australia; and Havana, Cuba. The sport began to regain its legal status in the 1920s, following the passage of the Walker Act in New York in 1920. However, the sport was soon heavily dominated by the underworld.[4]

The closing of nearly all American racetracks in the 1900s was a big victory for religious and moral reformers that largely paralleled their simultaneous efforts to eliminate prizefighting. However, the reformers' victory over horse-race gambling was incomplete. While the track owners did not have the influence or the wherewithal to legitimize racing, offtrack gambling went on largely uninterrupted. Chicago was the second-leading city for unlawful off-course gambling after New York. The crime syndicates that ran the illegal enterprise effectively employed violence and their connections in the criminal justice system to protect their interests from competition and prevent persecution, arrests, and prosecutions. If anything, Chicago's influence in offtrack gambling only expanded when Mont Tennes took over the racing wire in 1911.[5]

The pressure groups that fought the racetracks had limited success against the visible poolrooms in the mid-1890s, despite repeated raids sponsored by the Civic Federation and other reform organizations, and no success at all against the largely invisible handbooks. The closure of local racing had limited impact on the illegal entrepreneurs, and efforts on the local and national level to restrict the business by regulating the transmission of racing news went nowhere.

How did the effort to clean up offtrack gambling compare to other moral movements? Prostitution was illegal in every state nearly always. There was a virtually universal consensus that prostitution needed to be banned for health and moral reasons and because women were thought to need the state's protection from abusive men. Yet at the same time, red-light districts operated with little interference because of payoffs to local authorities.[6]

The temperance and Prohibition movements, on the other hand, encountered far-greater opposition than gambling. A national temperance movement dated back to the 1820s, led by evangelicals in organizations like the Washingtonians in the 1840s, the YMCA in 1851, and the Women's Christian Temperance Union in 1873. Then in 1893 the Anti-Saloon League was founded, focusing on urban drinking. The reformers encountered strong opposition because men were heavy drinkers and enjoyed the ambience and sociability of public drinking. There were thousands of saloons in working-class neighborhoods across the country. These establishments were major social centers for ethnic men and were intimately tied to urban political machines. Furthermore, the production of alcoholic beverages and the sale of those products were a huge business. Liquor manufacturers had enormous political clout, like the "Whiskey Ring" of the early 1870s, and German brewers were major leaders in their communities. The result was that as late as 1905, only six states had ever passed Prohibition acts, and three subsequently suspended those laws. The fight for Prohibition did manage to get liquor banned in nineteen states by 1917. That year the reformers recognized they needed to move to the national scene to secure their goal, which led to the passage of the Eighteenth Amendment, passed in 1919, that prohibited the manufacture, sale, and distribution of alcoholic beverages in the United States.[7]

Thoroughbred racing did not regain its national luster until the golden age of sport in the 1920s, when Americans enjoyed their highest standard of living until then, with higher wages and shorter working hours. Many Americans used their free time and increased discretionary income to enjoy such commercialized amusements as movies, vaudeville, and sports. In the 1920s, thoroughbred racing was no longer seen as immoral or criminal, once on-track gambling was legalized, plus the tracks were considered valuable sources of public revenue for state coffers. In Chicago boxing and horse racing both became legitimized in the mid-1920s, highlighted by the 1927 Jack Dempsey–Gene Tunney heavyweight championship "long-count" bout, won by Tunney. State endorsement of these sports contributed markedly to the national revival of both activities. Ironically, in the mid-1930s, when Chicago tried to regulate bookmaking, the plan was well received by social reformers like urban sociologist Ernest Burgess of the University of Chicago, who argued that the failure to ban off-track gambling called for a radical new approach to the problem. The concepts of legalization and regulation were popular with the city's powerful Democratic machine, which was closely tied to local bookmakers, and justified it as a means to raise revenue for the cash-starved city's coffers. The bill passed the legislature but was vetoed by Democratic governor Henry Horner. But that's a story for another book.[8]

APPENDIX

NOTES

BIBLIOGRAPHY

INDEX

APPENDIX

Determining Racetrack Profits

Baseball historians have long benefited from the extensive financial records reported in the daily press; scattered financial records preserved at the National Baseball Hall of Fame Library in Cooperstown, New York; and congressional investigations of baseball, especially the famous *Organized Baseball* report of 1951. In addition, scholars studying the recent business history of Major League Baseball, the National Football League, the National Basketball Association, or the National Hockey League have benefited from the superb research of these sports by *Forbes* journalists, who have mined public records since 1998.[1]

Students of horse racing and other commercialized sports are not so fortunate. Newspapers and sporting weeklies provided far less coverage about the financial status of those sports, nor is there much data in archives or congressional investigations. Historian Melvin Adelman circumvented that problem in his study of early-nineteenth-century New York thoroughbred racing by pulling together Cadwallader Colden's expenditures on his Union Course in the 1820s that included purses, rent, improvements on the physical plant, and daily expenditures on a ten-day meet that came to less than $20,000. He needed to sell four thousand tickets a day at 50 cents to break even, which did not happen.[2]

In my previous study of New York racing at the turn of the century, I had some success inferring profits because the state began regulating the sport in 1895 and charged tracks 5 percent of their gross. This information created a reliable database. I could thereby determine each track's gross and employ data on ticket prices, gates, purses (not all of which were provided by the track), and daily expenditures to determine profits (or losses).[3]

Press reports of attendance, gate receipts, and track expenses as well as profits (or losses) are rare, and often, even when it comes to attendance, were just estimates, not turnstile accounts. Other essential statistics were

Table 13
San Francisco Racetrack Profits, 1909

Daily Receipts

Gate 3,000 @ $1	$3,000
Bookmakers 30	3,000
Revenue—poolrooms 150 @ $10	1,500
Programs @ 10 cents	300
Field and combination books	250
Grandstand messengers (betting commissioners) for women	100
Fines and run-up money in selling races	100
Admission to paddock @ 50 cents	100
Boarding kitchens and stables	50
Feed privilege (for horses)	25
Sale of box seats	25
Selling of tips (to the suckers)	25
Restaurant	20
Candy, fruits, nuts	15
Lunch stand	15
Sandwich stand	10
Checkroom	10
Bookmakers' supply room	10
Opera glasses	5
Barbershop	5
Harness and saddle maker	5
Laundry delivery	5
Bootblack	3
Total receipts	$ 8,578

Daily Expenses

Purses, 4 @400 per purse	$1,600
Purse, 1 @$800	800

Table 13 (Con't.)
San Francisco Racetrack Profits, 1909

Advertising and printing	150
25 police and gate men @$6	150
Mortgage interest on $250,000 @ 6%, and insurance	41
Secretary	50
Judge and assistant	50
Starter and assistant	50
Treasurer	25
Two detectives @$10 each	20
Labor	20
Clerk of the scales	20
Paddock judge	15
Patrol judge	15
Official announcer	15
Track superintendent	15
Official timers	10
Entry clerk	10
Assistant clerk of scales	10
Bookkeeper	5
Two teams	5
Jockey-room attendant	5
Veterinary doctor	5
Total Expenses	$3,086
Income (daily)	$8,578
Expense (daily)	$3,086
Net gain	$ 5,492
100 days' racing, at $5,492	$ 549,200
Taxes and other expenses	
Maintenance in off season $	20,000
1 percent of all mutual bets per days, allowing mutuals to handle $10,000 per day	100

Table 13 (Con't.)
San Francisco Racetrack Profits, 1909

License	100
License, special	25
Daily Tax	$225
Daily tax @$225	
100 days	22,500
To the city of Juarez, yearly	5,000
Total yearly taxes	$27,500
After maintenance and tax profit	$501,700

Source: US Senate, *Prevention of Transmission of Race-Gambling Bets before the Subcommittee of the Committee on Interstate Commerce*, 92–93.
Note: This is my corrected accounting of Brolaski's chart.

usually never mentioned. In 1906 the *Los Angeles Times* published a detailed report on the Ascot Racetrack's finances. It reported explained its expenditures in 1905 at $275,000, including purses ($250,000) and expenses for advertising and wages for track employees ($25,000). However, unmentioned were expenditures for maintenance, insurance, security, or mortgages; it also failed to point out that purses for stakes events included entry fees or money contributed by race sponsors. When it came to receipts, there was only scant mention of about $192,400 from the fees of professional gamblers, but no data on revenue from the gate, fees from poolrooms for news reports, or payments from concessionaires.[4]

In 1909 retired bookmaker and racing promoter turned reformer Harry Brolaski provided the US Senate's Judiciary Committee investigating the interstate transmission of racing results an extremely detail accounting of the New California Jockey Club (NCJC)'s meet at Emeryville racetrack, located just outside Oakland. His report thoroughly indicated the legitimate sources of revenue and expenditure for one of the busiest tracks in the United States, but must be used cautiously because he had a reputation for being loose with his figures. I have not discovered why the city of Juarez, the site of racing impresario Matt Winn's soon-to-be-completed track, merited an annual $5,000 payment. Brolaski helped manage the track, but it was not completed until months after California banned racing in April 1909.[5]

The NCJC was one of the busiest tracks in the United States. In 1905 the NCJC was second nationally in purses ($450,145) to the Coney Island Jockey Club, leading the nation with 150 racing dates and 907 races. However, its average purse of $496 was far below the national average ($788). In 1909 the NCJC operated for ninety-six days. The press reported earnings of about $400,000, well below the $537,700 estimated by Brolaski (see table 13).[6]

Finally, another problem is that even when data is reported in full, nineteenth-century newspapers may have printed illegible numbers. Furthermore, data may not have been accurately counted. For instance, Brolaski's detailed report of the NCJC's finances were not corrected toted, ending up overestimating the profit by $36,000.

Notes

ABBREVIATIONS

BE	*Brooklyn Daily Eagle*
CDN	*Chicago Daily News*
CE	*Chicago Examiner*
CEJ	*Chicago Evening Journal*
CEP	*Chicago Evening Post*
ChT	*Chicago Times*
CIO	*Chicago Inter Ocean*
Clipper	*New York Clipper*
CRH	*Chicago Record Herald*
CT	*Chicago Daily Tribune*
DRF	*Daily Racing Form*
EC	*The Encyclopedia of Chicago*, edited by James Grossman, Ann Keating, and Janice Reiff
NPG	*National Police Gazette*
NYDT	*New York Daily Tribune*
NYMT	*New York Morning Telegraph*
NYT	*New York Times*
Spirit	*Spirit of the Times*
TFF	*Turf, Field, and Farm*

PREFACE

1. Haller, "Organized Crime in Urban Society," 230n13. Journalist Edward Ho-taling helped bring attention to the subject with *They're Off* and *Great Black Jockeys*.

On recent scholarly studies, see Wall, *How Kentucky Became Southern*; Riess, *Sport of Kings*; Nicholson, *Kentucky Derby*; McDaniels, *Prince of Jockeys*; and Mooney, *Race Horse Men*.

2. Findlay, *People of Chance*; Lears, *Something for Nothing*, 1–95; Davies and Abram, *Betting the Line*, 9–17; Breen, "Horses and Gentlemen"; Adelman, *Sporting Time*, 35–78, which includes an essential analysis on the rise of harness racing.

3. Grant and Jaher, "Chicago Business Elite," 288; Szuberla, "City Comes of Age," 1099; Barrett, *Work and Community in the Jungle*, 87.

4. "Hot-Blooded Horses." For a brief survey of American thoroughbred racing, see Riess, "Cyclical History of Horse Racing."

5. Riess, *Sport of Kings*.

1. Harness Racing, Politics, Gambling, and the Origins of Syndicate Crime in Chicago, 1837–1883

1. Thale, "Gambling"; Fabian, *Card Sharps and Bucket Shops*, 161; *CT*, Feb. 7, 1887, 1-4.

2. *CT*, Sept. 23, 1866, 4-2, Sept. 24, 1866, 2-2 (quote), 4-2, Sept. 25, 1866, 4-2, Dec. 14, 1866, 3-4; Gocher, *Wet Sundays*, 15–18.

3. Breen, "Horses and Gentlemen"; Gill, "Sport Only for Gentlemen"; Riess, *Sport of Kings*, 2.

4. Gill, "Sport Only for Gentlemen"; Riess, *Sport of Kings*, 1–6.

5. Riess, *Sport of Kings*, 5–6.

6. Riess, *Sport of Kings*, 6–8.

7. Robertson, *History of Thoroughbred Racing*, 16; Struna, "North–South Races"; Adelman, *Sporting Time*, 27–28, 31, 32, 38, 41, 44–46, 51, 240; Eisenberg, *Great Match Race*.

8. Cohen, "'Entreaties and Perswasions of Our Acquaintance'"; Mooney, *Race Horse Men*, 79, 84–85; Kupfer, "Presidential Patron of the Sport of Kings," 243–53; Meyer, "Henry Clay's Legacy"; Remini, *Life of Andrew Jackson*; Heidler and Heidler, *Henry Clay*.

9. Sullivan, *Harness Racing*, 13–19; Adelman, *Sporting Time*, 62.

10. Block, "Organized Crime." On the emergence of urban crime syndicates, see Haller, "Rise of Urban Crime."

11. Miller, *City of the Century*, 48–121; Pacyga, *Chicago: A Biography*, 7–34; Mayer and Wade, *Chicago*, 18; Barth, *Instant Cities*, xxi, 4.

12. Mayer and Wade, *Chicago*, 3–117; Cronon, *Nature's Metropolis*; Miller, *City of the Century*, 66–121; Wade, "Meatpacking"; Bensman and Wilson, "Iron and Steel."

13. G. D. Smith, "Gambling in Illinois," 24–25; Riess, "Leisure."

14. Adelman, *Sporting Time*, 56–58.

15. Petersen, "Absorption of French-Indian Chicago," 41; Pierce, *A History of Chicago*, 1:20, 206–8; Riess, "Leisure"; Marie Fisher, "Horse Racing in Old Chicago," unpublished ms., box 83, Federal Writers Project, Abraham Lincoln Presidential Library, Springfield, IL, 2, 4.

16. Thale, "Gambling."

17. Adelman, *Sporting Time*, 41–51, 55–73; Fisher, "Horse Racing in Old Chicago," 4–5; Pierce, *A History of Chicago*, 1:207.

18. Cross, *Burned-Over District*.

19. Fenich, "(Legal) Gaming," 67; Somers, *Rise of Sports in New Orleans*, 24–34.

20. Pierce, *A History of Chicago*, 1:207; Harpster, *Railroad Tycoon*; Rinker, *Chicago's Horse Racing Venues*, 7; *American Turf Register and Racing & Trotting Calendar* 16 (1845–48): 25, 59, 65, 66, 96.

21. *CT*, June 28, 1864, 4-4; *NYT*, Apr. 18, 1903, 2-6; Pierce, *A History of Chicago*, 1:207; Dutson, *Horse Breeds of North America*, 212–13.

22. Pierce, *A History of Chicago*, 2:92; *American Turf Register and Sporting Magazine* 11 (Oct. 1840): 237, 555; Fisher, "Horse Racing in Old Chicago"; Hervey, *Racing in America, 1922–1936*, 238; Asbury, *Gem of the Prairie*, 31–32, 36. Robertson, *History of Thoroughbred Racing*, 80, has a slightly different chronology.

23. Adelman, *Sporting Time*, 60–63; "Lady Suffolk," Hall of Fame, https://harnessmuseum.com/content/lady-suffolk.

24. Adelman, *Sporting Time*, 66–68; *NYT*, Apr. 22, 1888, 2-2.

25. Adelman, *Sporting Time*, 55–56, 71–73. In 1876 at least eight Illinois cities belonged to the NTA. See *CT*, Feb. 13, 1876, 12-5.

26. *CIO*, Sept. 3, 1907, 6. Another source claims that Garden City was at the current site of Fifty-Fifth and Cottage Grove. "Garden City Racetrack," *Illinois Trotting Chronicles* (June 18, 2020): 1. The periodical's home page (https://theillinoistrottingchronicles.weebly.com/#stayhere) has a map of eleven nineteenth-century trotting sites. On the controversial history of the Graves bequest, see Borzo, *Chicago's Fabulous Fountains*, 154.

27. *Spirit* 96 (Oct. 19, 1878): 295; *Clipper* (Aug. 22, 1863): 150; Vosburgh, *Racing in America*, 59; Rinker, *Chicago's Horse Racing Venues*, 7; Pierce, *A History of Chicago*, 2:467; Chafetz, *Play the Devil*, 214; Levy, *To Die in Chicago*, 216; *CT*, Apr. 12, 1889, 6-6, Nov. 9, 1991, 41. On Civil War–era racing, see Suttle, "Horse Racing," 11–12.

28. Suttle, "Horse Racing," 5–9.

29. Akers, *Drivers Up*, 155.

30. Riess, *Sport of Kings*, 18–21; Suttle, "Horse Racing," 16–43.

31. Lindberg, *Gambler King*, 23–24; Asbury, *Sucker's Progress*, 211.

32. CT, Oct. 30, 1869, 3-4, Apr. 12, 1889, 2-6; Riess, Touching Base, 60.

33. *CT*, Aug. 25, 1863, 4-3, Aug. 26, 1863, 4-2, Aug. 6, 1863, 1-8; Karamanski, "Civil War." Most of the track was on John Wentworth's property. See W. L. Flower

and J. Van Vechten, *Davie's Atlas with the Latest Recorded Subdivisions* (1863), cited in "Early Chicago Racetracks," https://chicagology.com/racetracks.

34. *CT*, Aug. 25, 1863, 4-3.

35. *CT*, Aug. 25, 1863, 4-3, Aug. 26, 1863, 4-2, Aug. 6, 1863, 1-8.

36. Suttle, "Horse Racing," 51–52.

37. Akers, *Drivers Up*, 85–86; Fisher, "Horse Racing in Old Chicago"; Suttle, "Horse Racing"; "Headlines," *Illinois Trotting Chronicles* 17 (Oct. 2020): 1–2; "The Sporting Fraternity," *CT*, Sept. 25, 1866, 2-2 (quote), Oct. 30, 1869, 3-4, Apr. 12, 1889, 6-6, Nov. 3, 1878, 12-1.

38. Lindberg, *Gambler King*, 16–17; Asbury, *Gem of the Prairie*, 71, 73–74, 75–76; "1866—Hairtrigger Block and Gambler's Row," https://chicagology.com/notorious -chicago/hairtriggerblock.

39. *CT*, Sept. 5, 1866, 4-3; *NYT*, Apr. 22, 1888, 2-2; Adelman, *Sporting Time*, 66–69; Akers, *Drivers Up*, 85–86.

40. *CT*, June 26, 1867, 3-2, Aug. 27, 1873, 4-5, Oct. 17, 1867, 4-3; Lindberg, *Gambler King*, 18.

41. Funchion, "Irish Chicago," 58-59; *NYT*, 30 April 1922, 1-1; Riess. Sport of Kings, 152–55.

42. Funchion, "Irish Chicago," 58-59; Pierce, *A History of Chicago*, 2: 432; Asbury, *Sucker's Progress*, 290; Johnson, "Sinful Business," 20, 22–24, 37.

43. Haller, "Illegal Enterprise," 219, 236 (quotes), 221–42. The first usage of the term *organized crime* as employed today was in Frank M. White, "The Increasing Menace of the Black Hand," *NYT*, Mar. 29, 1906, SM1.

44. Haller, "Changing Structure of American Gambling," 88.

45. Haller, "Illegal Enterprise," 223–24. On the relationship between sport and nineteenth-century crime syndicates, see Lindberg, Gambler King; Johnson, "Sinful Business," 17–47; Johnson, *Policing the Urban Underworld*, 148–81; Griffin, "Big Jim O'Leary," 214–16; Riess, *Touching Base*, 87–96; Riess, *City Games*, 181–87; Riess, "In the Ring and Out"; and Daniel Czitrom, "Underworld and Underdogs."

46. *CT*, Feb. 19, 1867, 4-1, Apr. 26, 1867, 4-3, July 7, 1867, 4-2, Oct. 15, 1867, 3-2, Apr. 26, 1874, 16-1, Feb. 26, 1902, 9-6; *TFF* 16 (Mar. 28, 1873): 201; Wade, *Chicago's Pride*, 52, 55, 56; Krout, *Annals of American Sport*, 35.

47. *CT*, June 16, 1867, 1-5, July 4, 1867, 4-4, July 7, 1867, 4-2, Oct. 15, 1867, 3-2, Mar. 15, 1873, 2-6, June 20, 1873, 8-1; *Spirit* 28 (Sept. 12, 1873): 363, 373; *TFF* 16 (Mar. 28, 1873): 201.

48. *Spirit* 18 (July 11, 1868): 372; 18 (July 18, 1868): 392.

49. *CT*, Sept. 19, 1869, 3-1; *Spirit* 22 (July 9, 1870): 326; 22 (July 16, 1870): 339.

50. Robertson and Robertson, *Our American Tour*, 59; Akers, *Drivers Up*, 137.

51. *CT*, Mar. 15, 1873, 2-6, June 20, 1873, 8-1; *Spirit* 28 (Sept. 12, 1873): 363, 373; *TFF* 16 (Mar. 28, 1873): 201.

52. *CT*, Apr. 26, 1974, 16-1, Aug. 26, 1874, 16-1, Aug. 11, 1874, 8; *Spirit* 87 (May 16, 1874): 333; 88 (Dec. 26, 1874): 469 (quote).

53. *Spirit* 91 (Apr. 15, 1876): 234; *CT*, Dec. 2, 1877, 7-1.

54. *Spirit* 89 (July 31, 1875): 641; *TFF* 21 (Sept. 1875): 241; *CT*, Jan. 7, 1877, 7-2.

55. *CT*, June 13, 1877, 2-5, July 5, 1877, 5-2, July 21, 1877, 7-3, July 22, 1877, 16-1 (quote), Mar. 31, 1878, 7-3, May 5, 1878, 7-3; Wade, *Chicago's Pride*, 56, 181.

56. *Spirit* 95 (Feb. 2, 1878): 63; 96 (Oct. 19, 1878): 295.

57. "A Good Idea," *CT*, Apr. 14, 1878, 7-3, Apr. 21, 1878 (quote).

58. *NYT*, Mar. 7, 1906, 2-5; Cook, *Bygone Days in Chicago*, 154.

59. *CT*, Aug. 11, 1878, 7-1, Dec. 8, 1931, 12-5; Andreas, *History of Chicago*, 3:695–96; Adelman, "Quantification and Sport," 51–75. *American Field* was founded in 1874 as *Field and Stream*. It focused on hunting, fishing, firearms, and conservation. In 1879 *Field and Stream* exposed the tragic slaughter of passenger pigeons killed by market hunters, which led to their eradication in 1914. See Biscotta, *American Sporting Periodicals*, xv.

60. *CT*, Apr. 21, 1878, 7-2; *Spirit* 96 (Oct. 12, 1878): 260; 97 (Oct. 19, 1878): 295; 98 (Oct. 25, 1879): 291; Marquis, *Marquis' Hand-Book of Chicago*, 244. The track was preceded by a shorter gentlemen's course south of the park. See Greta Polites, "Ghosts of Garfield/West Side/Chicago Driving Park," https://www.flickr.com /photos/glpolites/9304665226.

61. *CT*, May 26, 1878, 7-1, July 21, 1878, 7-5, Aug. 2, 1878, 5-4, Oct. 9, 1878, 1-2, Oct. 11, 1878, 5-1; *Spirit* 96 (Sept. 2, 1878): 182; 99 (Nov. 6, 1880): 367.

62. *CT*, July 7, 1878, 7-4, July 21, 1878, 7-5, Aug. 11, 1878, 7-1; *Spirit* 97 (June 28, 1879): 505; Sennett, *Families against the City*, 16.

63. *CIO*, Oct. 7, 1878, 2-6; Erickson, "Newspapers and Social Values," 132.

64. *CT*, Oct. 9, 1878, 5-2.

65. *Spirit* 96 (Oct. 19, 1878): 286 (quote), 295; *CIO*, Oct. 11, 1878, 5-1 (quote); *CT*, Oct. 10, 1878, 7-1, Oct. 11, 1878, 5-1, Oct. 12, 1878, 12-1, "The Race," Oct. 13, 1878, 4-4; *Washington Evening Star*, Oct. 11, 1878, 1-5; *New York Sun*, Oct. 12, 1878, 4-1; *Washington Post*, Oct. 11, 1878, 1-5; Wade, *Chicago's Pride*, 181.

66. *CT*, 20 Nov. 1878, 5-5, Dec. 2, 1883, 4-3; *Spirit* 96 (Sept. 2, 1878): 182; 101 (Feb. 5, 1881): 12; (Apr. 30, 1881): 320; (July 30, 1881): 712 (quote); 103 (Feb. 4, 1882): 14; *CDN*, July 25, 1881, 6-3; Longstreet, *Chicago, 1860–1919*, 236; Erickson, "Newspapers and Social Values," 133.

67. *Spirit* 97 (Feb. 15, 1879): 37; (July 5, 1879): 533; 99 (June 19, 1880): 506; 106 (Jan. 12, 1884): 721; *CT*, June 21, 1879, 5-1, June 26, 1879, 5-1, June 27, 1879, 5-1.

68. *CT*, Dec. 7, 1879, 19-1.

69. *Spirit* 98 (Oct. 25, 1879): 291; *TFF* 65 (Dec. 24, 1897): 809; Cook, *Bygone Days in Chicago*, 155–56. Haverly's obituary claimed the purchase price was $150,000. See *CT*, Sept. 29, 1901, 9-1.

70. *Spirit* 99 (Mar. 20, 1880): 156; (Mar. 27, 1880): 180; 100 (Jan. 15, 1881): 608.

71. *Spirit* 99 (Mar. 20, 1880): 156; *CDN*, July 19, 1880, 1-7; *CT*, June 20, 1880, 3-6 (quote).

72. *Spirit* 99 (July 3, 1880): 562; 100 (Nov. 6, 1880): 366 (quote); *CDN*, June 28, 1880, 1-4, Sept. 27, 1880, 1-5, Oct. 7, 1880, 1-3, Oct. 8, 1880, 1-6, Nov. 12, 1880, 1-4.

73. *Spirit* 97 (July 5, 1879): 533; *CDN*, Sept. 27, 1880, 1-5; *CT*, Nov. 28, 1880, 13-1, Jan. 2, 1881, 6-1.

74. *NYT*, Dec. 15, 1874, 11-7; Riess, *Sport of Kings*, 18; Hotaling, *They're Off*, 44–45. The first time the term *poolroom* was used was reportedly in 1861. See http: /www.merriam-webster.com/dictionary/poolroom. In the twentieth century, billiard parlors were normally known as pool halls, though often called poolrooms because of the betting. For an example of how the auction operated, see "Selling the Pools," *CIO*, July 25, 1881, 8.

75. *CT*, July 20, 1879, 16-1. On New York poolrooms, see Riess, *Sport of Kings*, 175–213, 264–301.

76. Riess, *Sport of Kings*, 38.

77. *CT*, Dec. 2, 1883, 14-5; Riess, *Sport of Kings*, 18, 35–37.

78. *CT*, Oct. 31, 1880, 11-1, Jan. 2, 1881, 6-1.

79. *CT*, July 18, 1880, 13-1, July 22, 1880, 8-3, July 23, 1880, 3-1; *Wallace's Monthly Review* 15 (Dec. 1889): 808; *Spirit* 99 (Nov. 6, 1880): 367; 100 (Jan. 15, 1881): 608; 101 (Feb. 5, 1881): 12; 103 (July 29, 1882): 752; 104 (Nov. 18, 1882): 456–57; *CDN*, Sept. 27, 1880, 1-5, Oct. 7, 1-3, Oct. 8, 1880, 1-6, Nov. 12, 1880, 1-4.

80. *CT*, Oct. 31, 1980, 11-1.

81. *CIO*, Sept. 15, 1880, 5-5 (quote); *CT*, Sept. 17, 1880, 5-2, Sept. 19, 1880, 3-1; *NYT*, Oct. 2, 1880, 8-2; Hatton, *To-Day in America*, 1:97–110.

82. *CT*, Jan. 2, 1881, 6-1, July 18, 1881, 5-7, Dec. 4, 1881, 15-1, Dec. 2, 1883, 14-5; *Spirit* 103 (July 19, 1882): 172; 104 (Nov. 18, 1882): 456, 457; 103 (July 19, 1882): 172; 104 (Nov. 18, 1882): 456, 457; *American Millionaires*, 13–15.

83. *Spirit* 101 (Feb. 5, 1881): 12; (Apr. 30, 1881): 320; (July 30, 1881): 712 (quote); 103 (Feb. 4, 1882): 14; *CDN*, Sept. 27, 1880, 1-5, Oct. 7, 1880, 1-3, Oct. 8, 1880, 1-6, Nov. 12, 1880, 1-4, May 14, 1881, 1-4, July 25, 1881, 6-3; Longstreet, *Chicago*, 236; Erickson, "Newspapers," 133.

84. *CT*, Dec. 2, 1883, 14-5; *CDN*, Dec. 4, 1883, 2-1; Andreas, *History of Chicago*, 3:676.

85. Lindberg, *Gambler King*, 40–41.

86. *CT*, Oct. 29, 1882, 10-6; Johnson, "Sinful Business," 24–26; Green, "Chicago Democratic Party," 39.

87. Johnson, "Sinful Business," 25 (quote), 27, 37; "Tom Foley's Great Billiard Room," https://chicagology.com/rebuilding/rebuilding090/.

88. Johnson, "Sinful Business," 27, 37.

89. Asbury, *Gem of the Prairie*, 146; *CT*, May 26, 1878, 7-3; *Spirit* 96 (Sept. 2, 1878): 182; 97 (Feb. 22, 1879): 61; (June 28, 1879): 505; Vosburgh, *Racing in America*, 59; Lindberg, *Chicago by Gaslight*, 40, 47; Lindberg, *Gambler King*, 70, 110–11; Lindberg, *To Serve and Collect*, 40; Lindberg, *Gangland Chicago*, 42; *CRH*, Aug. 8, 1907, quoted in Asbury, *Gem of the Prairie*, 142; Johnson, "Sinful Business," 25, 27; Ginger, *Altgeld's America*, 99.

90. *CT*, Sept. 13, 1898, 10-3; Lindberg, *Gambler King*, 129–30; Dowling, *City Hospitals*, 39.

91. Johnson, "Sinful Business," 25, 26 (quote); Asbury, *Gem of the Prairie*, 145, 148; Lindberg, *Gambler King*, 66; *CT*, Oct. 22, 1894, 1-3, Aug. 30, 1897, 8-6, Sept. 13, 1898, 10-3; *NYT*, Oct. 12, 1888, 3-3; A. Smith, *Syndicate City*, 22.

92. *Spirit* 115 (Feb. 11, 1888): 77; 116 (Nov. 17, 1888): 605; 119 (July 5, 1890): 1045; 120 (Aug. 16, 1890): 132; (Sept. 27, 1890): 382; *CT*, Sept. 6, 1888, 9-4, Oct. 11, 1888, 2-7, Oct. 12, 1888, 6-2, July 23, 1890, 8-1, Aug. 13, 1890, 6-1, Oct. 7, 1890, 7-1; *CEP*, July 13, 1890, 3-4; *Daily Alta California*, June 22, 1890, 5. On McLaughlin, see W. S. Vosbourgh, "Famous American Jockeys," *DRF*, Feb. 22, 1920; and Barnes and Wright, *Butcher Boys*, 170.

93. Johnson, "Sinful Business," 25, 26; Asbury, *Gem of the Prairie*, 145, 148, 160; Lindberg, *Gambler King*, 66; Lindberg, *Chicago by Gaslight*, 48; CT, Oct. 22, 1894, 1-3, Aug. 30, 1897, 8-6; CIO, February 2, 1905, 4; NYT, Oct. 12, 1888, 3-3, March 29, 1906, 22-2; Spirit 134 (Oct. 30, 1897): 423.

94. Johnson, "Sinful Business," 26–27.

95. Lindberg, *Gambler King*, 80–81, 98 (quote), 101–10; Johnson, C. *Carter H. Harrison I*, 186–87, 286; *CDN*, Mar. 25, 1883, 1; Asbury, *Gem of the Prairie*, 154; *CIO*, Mar. 28, 1893, 2; *CT*, Oct. 2, 1893, 2-3.

96. Dunn, *Chicago Politics*, 24–25, 43–44; Lindberg, *Gambler King*, 104, 110–11, 121, 128–35; Lindberg, *To Serve and Collect*, 40; Mitchell P. Roth, "William J. Mc-Garigle," in *Historical Dictionary of Law Enforcement*, ed. Roth and Olson, 208.

97. *CT*, Mar. 24, 1893, 4-7.

98. The Gambling and Vice Indexes were developed by business professor John J. Binder, standardized to equal 100 in base year 1920. Binder employed the number of number of offenses multiplied by the percentage of offenses that led to an arrest, and the current population. By keeping the number of offenses per capita constant, he felt he could explore how enforcement over time changed. Harrison later had an index of 31 in 1893. See Binder, *Capone's Beer Wars*, 20–23.

99. Nicholson, *Notorious John Morrissey*; "The Chicago Democratic Boss," *CT*, Aug. 29, 1880, 4-4 (quote).

100. On McDonald's alleged hold over Harrison, see *CDN*, Apr. 1, 3, 4; and *CRH*, Aug. 10, 1907, 8-1. McDonald's power was exaggerated by Pierce, *A History of Chicago*, 3:305; Asbury, *Gem of the Prairie*, 142; and Wendt and Kogan, *Lords of the Levee*, 27. For

a conservative assessment of McDonald's power, see Miller, *City of the Century*, 450. Carter Harrison II claims in *Growing Up with Chicago*, 261, that his father broke with the machine by 1880. On Harrison's bad relations with McDonald, see *CIO*, Mar. 28, 1893, 2; *CT*, Oct. 2, 1893, 2–3; Green, "Chicago Democratic Party," 39, 42; Johnson, "Sinful Business," 27; and Johnson, *Carter Henry Harrison I*, 186–87, 286.

101. Johnson, *Harrison*, 186–87, 286; *CDN*, Mar. 25, 1883, 1; *CIO*, Mar. 28, 1893, 2; *CT*, Oct. 2, 1893, 2–3; Asbury, *Gem of the Prairie*, 154; Abbot, *Carter Henry Harrison*, 112–13; Ginger, *Altgeld's America*, 71–72.

102. Longstreet, *Chicago, 1860–1919*, 202 (quote); Lindberg, *Gambler King*, 62; Dunn, *Chicago Politics*.

103. *CT*, Nov. 3, 1877, 3-3; Thorn et al., *Total Baseball*, 2, 489–94; *St. Louis Globe Democrat*, Nov. 1, 1877, cited in Cash, *Before They Were Cardinals*, 41. On early baseball fixes, see Seymour, *Baseball: The Early Years*, 52–54, 87–88, 200–201.

104. *St. Louis Globe-Democrat*, Nov. 1, 1877. On reports that McDonald had an impact on an earlier game, said to be the first fixed game in Chicago, see *CT*, 6 August 1874, 8-2; *NYT*, 5 August 1874, 5-4, described as resulting from glaring by the Mutuals "which gave color to the supposition that the game was sold." See Ryczek, *Blackguards*, 173-74.

105. *CIO*, Aug. 10, 1907, 2–3; *CRH*, Aug. 16, 1907, 1-1; Lindberg, *Chicago Ragtime*, 52–54; Lindberg, *Gambler King*, 139, 159–64, 176–77; Asbury, *Gem of the Prairie*, 152; Asbury, *Sucker's Progress*, 296–302.

106. *CT*, Aug. 10, 1907, 7-5, Aug. 13, 1907, 4-1, Aug. 14, 1907, 5-1; Lindberg, *Gambler King*, 144–51, 190–202.

2. The Chicago Elite and the Rise
of the Washington Park Club, 1883–1889

1. Meyer and Wade, *Chicago*; Miller, *City of the Century*, 258, 272, 288–92, 318.

2. Jaher, *Urban Establishment*, 582; Riess, *Touching Base*, 135–38.

3. Riess, *City Games*, 24–26, 54–60; Riess, *Sport of Kings*; Mooney, *Race Horse Men*; Veblen, *Theory of the Leisure Class*, 18–47, 142–43.

4. *CT*, Jan. 19, 1883, 8-5; Sparks, "Gentleman's Sport"; Somers, *Rise of Sports in New Orleans*, 91–114.

5. Andreas, *History of Chicago*, 3:674 (quote); *Chicago Commerce*, 61–67; *Hyde Park Herald*, Jan. 19, 1884, 10; *CT*, June 28, 1884, 12-3, June 10, 1888, 11-3; *Spirit* 107 (May 17, 1884): 489; 115 (June 23, 1888): 814; (June 30, 1888): 846–47 (quote); 116 (Sept. 22, 1888): 326.

6. *Spirit* 106 (Dec. 22, 1883): 625.

7. *Spirit* 106 (Dec. 22, 1883): 625; 107 (May 17, 1884): 489; (June 28, 1884): 684; 126 (Oct. 14, 1893): 393; 127 (Feb. 10, 1894): 125; *CT*, Sept. 20, 1896, 39-4, Mar.

28, 1903, 4-5; Gems, "Sport and Culture Formation," 82; Tarr, "John R. Walsh of Chicago," 455–59, 462, 466; Moses, *Biographical Dictionary*, 2:585–86; Andreas, *History of Chicago*, 3:674–76.

8. *Spirit* 106 (Dec. 22, 1883): 625; 107 (May 17, 1884): 489; (June 28, 1884): 684; 126 (Oct. 14, 1893): 393; 127 (Feb. 10, 1894): 125; *CT*, June 28, 1884, 12-3; Gems, "Sport and Culture Formation," 82–83.

9. Jaher, *Urban Establishment*, 536–37; *American Millionaires*; *Lakeside Annual Directory [1875–1917]*; *Chicago Blue Book [1890–1914]*.

10. *Spirit* 106 (Dec. 22, 1883): 625; 107 (May 17, 1884): 489; (June 28, 1884): 684; 126 (Oct. 14, 1893): 393; 127 (Feb. 10, 1894): 125; *CT*, June 28, 1884, 12-3; Gems, "Sport and Culture Formation," 82–83; Jaher, *Urban Establishment*, 536–37; *Chicago Blue Book*. Memberships computed from study data.

11. Melvin Adelman uncovered extensive data on the social origins of the American Jockey Club's original 862 members in 1866 and 1867, including social characteristics, occupational mobility, social affiliations, and the higher standing of the life time members, who ran the club's affairs. Members were not solely "the richest of the rich," though 60 percent were rich or super rich, working in commerce or finance. They were not all of high social status, since its membership included Tammany Boss William M. Tweed. The AJC's main function, according to Adelman was to sustain upper class hegemony. Adelman, "Quantification and Sport, 54-63, 72-75. Study data; Chicago Board of Trade, *Annual Report [1880–90]*; Hoyt, *Land Values in Chicago*, 185in.

12. "Washington Park Club, Chicago, 1886," http://data.genealogytoday.com/search/Washington_Park_Club_Chicago_1886.html; *Chicago Clubs, Illustrated*, 71–73; *CT*, June 2, 1887, 3-1.

13. *CT*, Mar. 7, 1884, 8-2, Mar. 8, 1884, 7-5 (quote), Mar. 11, 1884, 8-4, Sept. 14, 1886, 3-1. Belmont had strayed from the faith, marrying the daughter of Commodore Oliver Hazard Perry. He raised his children Episcopalian and was disowned by his family and the American Jewish community. His biographer did not find evidence he ever converted, and he certainly encountered considerable anti-Semitism. See Black, *King of Fifth Avenue*. Recently, evidence of his conversion was found in the *American Israelite*, Aug. 7, 1874, 4; and *Jewish Exponent*, Dec. 19, 1924.

14. *American National Biography*, s.v. "Seligman, Joseph."

15. *CT*, Apr. 14, 1878, 7-3, Apr. 21, 1878, 7-2; Andreas, *History of Chicago*, 675; *Spirit* 119 (July 19, 1890): 1132.

16. *CT*, June 8, 1884, 16-3, June 28, 1884, 12-3, July 9, 1916, C4-1; *Spirit* 106 (Dec. 22, 1883): 625; (Jan. 5, 1884): 689; (Jan. 12, 1884): 720; 107 (June 28, 1884): 680; Riess, *Touching Base*, 103.

17. *CT*, Feb. 17, 1884, 9-6, June 29, 1884, 13-1.

18. *CT*, June 29, 1884, 13-1 (quote), July 9, 1916, C4-1.

19. *CT*, June 29, 1884, 13-1.

20. *Spirit* 106 (Jan. 12, 1884): 720; 107 (June 8, 1884): 107; (June 28, 1884): 680; (July 5, 1884): 710, 711; (July 12, 1884): 736; 108 (Jan. 3, 1885): 713; Clark, *Elegant Eighties*, 205; Gems, "Sport and Culture Formation," 83; *CEP*, June 21, 1890, 1-3; *CDN*, July 25, 1893, 2-1; Wiggins, *Glory Bound*, 21–33. On Corrigan and Murphy, see McDaniels, *Prince of Jockeys*, 276–79, 273–76, 288, 289, 292–96, 337–38.

21. *CT*, July 5, 1884, 3-2, July 13, 1884, 6-4, 14-1; *Spirit* 109 (July 11, 1885): 744, 746.

22. Marquis, *Marquis' Hand-Book of Chicago*, 244; *CT*, May 13, 1884, 9-1; *CDN*, May 15, 1884, 4-3, Nov. 18, 1884, 8-3.

23. Steven A. Riess, "Leisure," *EC*, 467–74. On ritualists and liturgicals, see Jensen, *Winning of the Midwest*, 58–88; and Kleppner, *Cross of Culture*, 73–74. For the Sabbath and baseball, see Riess, *Touching Base*, 13–15, 33, 38–41, 134–55; and Bevis, *Sunday Baseball*. On the positive attitudes of Roman Catholic leaders to gambling on horse racing, see O'Hare, *Socio-economic Aspects of Horse Racing*, 108–11.

24. *CT*, May 13, 1884, 9; *Los Angeles Herald*, Dec. 19, 1897, 1-6.

25. *CT*, May 14, 1884, 5-4; *CDN*, June 20, 1884, 5-5; "Chicago Foreign Language Press Survey," *Chicago Abendpost*, Dec. 20, 1897.

26. *CDN*, June 15, 1884, 4-3.

27. *Spirit* 107 (June 28, 1884): 680; *Clipper* 32 (Jan. 31, 1885): 733. See also *CT*, May 27, 1884, 11-2, June 2, 1884, 6-1, June 6, 1884, 9-4, June 16, 1884, 8-2, June 21, 1885, 4.

28. *CDN*, May 15, 1884, 4-3 (quote); *CT*, Feb. 9, 1884, 2-6.

29. *CDN*, May 15, 1884, 4-3, May 18, 1884, 4-6, May 20, 1884, 2-2, 4-1; *CT*, Jan. 25, 1885, 16-2.

30. *CDN*, May 15, 1884, 4-3, May 18, 1884, 4-6, 20 May 18 1884, 4-1, 2-2 (quote), Aug. 18, 1884, 4-6, Aug. 23, 1884, 3-7, Oct. 11, 1884, 2-5, Dec. 8, 1884, 4-4, Jan. 24, 1885, 6-1, June 20, 1885, 5-5; *Spirit* 113 (Feb. 12, 1887): 91.

31. *CT*, Jan. 24, 1885, 8-4, Jan. 25, 1885, 16-2, June 20, 1885, 13-6; *Clipper* 32 (Jan. 31, 1885): 733; *CDN*, Jan. 24, 1885, 6-1; *Spirit* 109 (June 27, 1885): 688.

32. *CT*, June 20, 1885, 13-6, July 10, 1885, 2-1, July 11, 1885, 2-4; *Clipper* 32 (Jan. 31, 1885): 733; *Spirit* 109 (June 27, 1885): 675, 688; (July 4, 1885): 721; *CDN*, Jan. 24, 1885, 6-1, June 15, 1885, 4-3, June 18, 1885, 1-7, June 20, 1885, 1-2, 5-5.

33. *CT*, July 9, 1894, 4-1, July 5, 1924, 9-8; *Day Book* (Chicago), Aug. 8, 1912, 11; "Death of Edward Corrigan," 17; Wall, *How Kentucky Became Southern*, 143 (quote), 145–46; "An Incorrigible Character," 2225; "History Challenge: Hawthorne," *DRF*, Sept. 24, 2010.

34. *CT*, July 9, 1894, 4-1, July 5, 1924, 9-8; Robertson, *History of Thoroughbred Racing*, 198.

35. *CT*, July 5, 1924, 9-8.

36. *Spirit* 113 (Jan. 29, 1887): 2.

37. *CT*, July 1, 1885, 10-2; *Spirit* 109 (June 27, 1885): 675, 688; (July 4, 1885): 721; (July 11, 1885): 744; 113 (Jan. 29, 1887): 2; Lindberg, *Chicago by Gaslight*, 1–3, 2 (quote). *CIO*, June 28, 1885, 4, estimated the crowd at twenty thousand.

38. *CT*, June 20, 1886, 9-1.

39. *CT*, July 5, 1885, 2-1, July 10, 1885, 2-1, July 11, 1885, 2-4; *Spirit* 109 (July 11, 1885): 744, 746; *Cincinnati Enquirer*, June 27, 1897, courtesy of Howard Rosenberg; Lindberg, *Chicago by Gaslight*, 5; *NYT*, Mar. 2, 1909, 9-1.

40. *CT*, June 24, 1886, 1-5, June 25, 1886, 1-5, June 27, 1886, 9-1, June 28, 1886, 4-3, July 4, 1886, 1-7, July 6, 1886, 1-7, Feb. 6, 1887, 20-4; McDaniels, *Prince of Jockeys*, 303; Mrs. B. F. Ayers, "Old Hyde Park," 188–89.

41. *CDN*, Aug. 1886, 1-7; *CT*, Aug. 14, 1886, 1-4.

42. McDaniels, *Prince of Jockeys*, 305; *NYT*, Aug. 17, 1886, 5-6.

43. *Spirit* 112 (Jan. 4, 1887): 704. On doping, see Gleaves, "Enhancing the Odds."

44. *CT*, July 22, 1887, 3, July 30, 1887, 5-2, Feb. 22, 1890, 12-4, July 31, 1890, 1-3, Oct. 10, 1910, 1-3; Lindberg, *Gambler King*, 165.

45. *CT*, Feb. 7, 1887, 1-4, June 28, 1887, 1-2; *NYT*, July 19, 1958, 15-6 (quote). On the history of bucket shops, see Hochfelder, "'Where the Common People Could Speculate.'"

46. *CT*, Feb. 6, 1887, 20-3, Feb. 7, 1887, 1-4, June 28, 1887, 1-2.

47. *CT*, June 29, 1879, 4-4, Feb. 7, 1887, 1-4.

48. *CT*, June 29, 1879, 4-4 (quote), Feb. 6, 1887, 20-3 (quote).

49. *CT*, June 29, 1879, 4-4.

50. Harrison, *Growing Up with Chicago*, 70–76.

51. *CT*, June 6, 1885, 3-5, July 16, 1885, 4-2, July 26, 1889, 3-1.

52. *CDN*, July 24, 1885, 1-4; *CT*, Apr. 16, 1887, 1-5.

53. *CT*, June 6, 1885, 13-1, Feb. 6, 1887, 20-3, Apr. 16, 1887, 1-5; *Spirit* 116 (Nov. 17, 1888): 605; 117 (Feb. 2, 1889): 66; *ChT*, Dec. 5, 1888, June 24, 1889, 3-1. Riley was reputedly worth at least $200,000 in 1888, but died penniless. See *Pittsburgh Press*, July 31, 1913, 17; and *Milwaukee Journal*, July 31, 1913, 13.

54. "Chicago Mayors, 1837–2007"; *ChT*, Nov. 3, 1889, 12-1, Nov. 11, 1889, 3-5.

55. *ANB*, s.v. "Comstock, Anthony"; *NYT*, Sept. 9, 1933, 13-1; Riess, *Sport of Kings*, 69–70, 183–84; Dixon, *From Prohibition to Regulation*, 48–49.

56. Lears, *Something for Nothing*, 173, 175, 177; *CT*, July 17, 1886, 1-6. On Herbert Spencer's views, see Dixon, *From Prohibition to Regulation*, 48–49.

57. *CT*, Apr. 16, 1887, 1-5; *CEJ*, Apr. 16, 1887, 12-2.

58. Jensen, *Winning of the Midwest*, xii.

59. In 1885–86 the Democrats and Republicans each had seventy-six assembly seats, but an independent aligned with the former, enabling the Democrats to elect the house Speaker. See "Political Party Strength in Illinois," https://en.wikipedia

.org/wiki/Political_party_strength_in_Illinois#Table; Jensen, *Winning of the Midwest*, 58–88; David Kenney, "No Cumulative Voting," http://www.lib.niu.edu/1976/ii761112.html; and Argersinger, *Representation and Inequality*, 233–68.

60. "Political Party Strength in Illinois"; Citizens' Association of Chicago Records, MSCAC_66, http://www.uic.edu/depts/lib/findingaids/MSCAC_66.html; *CT*, Apr. 1, 1887, 3-4, Apr. 16, 1887, 1-5.

61. *CT*, Apr. 14, 1887, 4.

62. *CT*, Apr. 16, 1887, 1-5, Apr. 21, 1887, 2-3, May 1, 1887, 4-4; *CEJ*, Apr. 16, 1887, 12-3.

63. *CEJ*, May 1, 1887, 4-4; *CIO*, May 13, 1887; *Spirit* 113 (May 14, 1887): 514; 114 (Dec. 25, 1897): 688; *CDN*, July 24, 1887, 1-4. On the Ives Act, see Riess, *Sport of Kings*, 81–87.

64. *CEJ*, May 31, 1887, 1-7; *CT*, May 26, 1887, 7, May 27, 1887, 2-5, June 4, 1887, 4-3, Mar. 9, 1889, 9-3, Aug. 2, 1890, 7-1. The *Tribune*, *Daily News*, *Evening Journal*, and *Inter Ocean* offered no explanation for the passage of the amended Chase Act.

65. *CT*, June 1, 1887, 1-6, June 2, 1887, 2-1.

66. *CT*, June 1, 1887, 1-6.

67. "Illinois and New York Pool Acts," *CT*, May 30, 1887, 4-4, June 4, 1887, 4-3, "Pool-Rooms and Pool-Yards," June 5, 1887, 4-4.

68. "Pool-Rooms and Pool-Yards."

69. *CT*, Mar. 24, 1887, 1-7, 4-2, Apr. 5, 1887, 1-7, June 16, 1887, 1-5, June 28, 1887, 1-6, July 1, 1887, 1-1, Feb. 5, 1988, 1-4, July 26, 1889, 3-1, Sept. 7, 1889, 4-3, Aug. 1, 1890, 4-3; *NYT*, June 28, 1887, 5-3.

70. *CEJ*, June 6, 1887, 5-1; *Spirit* 115 (June 23, 1888): 814; 113 (June 25, 1887): 747 (quote).

71. Johnson, "Sinful Business," 41, 47; *CDN*, June 25, 1887, 2-2; *CT*, June 26, 1887, 9-3; *Spirit* 113 (July 2, 1887): 766–67, 782; *ChT*, June 29, 1887, 2-2; *NYT*, June 28, 1887, 5-3, Sept. 13, 1914, 21-1.

72. *CT*, July 8, 1888, 25-1.

73. *CT*, July 8, 1888, 25-1, June 26, 1887, 9-3 (quote). On crowds, see *CDN*, June 25, 1887, 2-1; *ChT*, June 29, 1887, 2-2; and *Spirit* 113 (July 2, 1887): 766–67; 115 (June 23, 1888): 814.

74. *CT*, July 8, 1888, 25-1 (quotes), June 24, 1888, 12-3 (quote). See also "Seen by a Woman," *CT*, June 26, 1892, 3-7.

75. *ChT*, June 28, 1887, 2-3.

76. *ChT*, June 29, 1887, 2-2.

77. *ChT*, July 17, 1887; *Spirit* 113 (July 23, 1887): 869.

78. *CT*, July 22, 1887, 3-5, July 30, 1887, 5-2, July 31, 1887, 5-4, Aug. 7, 1887, 5-4, July 31, 1890, 1-3, Jan. 24, 1891, 6-3; *Spirit* 114 (Sept. 24, 1887): 297; Lindberg, *Gambler King*, 165.

79. *NYT*, Sept. 9, 1887, 1-1, July 16, 1888, 3-5; *CT*, Sept. 18, 1887, 13-5, July 16, 1888, 3-5, July 1, 1890, 1-3; Jaher, *Urban Establishment*, 510.

80. *ChT*, Oct. 14, 1888, 6-3; Dec. 12, 1905, 9-4. On racing honesty, see *CT*, July 23, 1890, 8-1.

81. *Spirit* 115 (June 23, 1888): 797; (June 30, 1888): 850; 116 (Sept. 15, 1888): 280; (Sept. 22, 1888): 326; *CT*, Aug. 24, 1888, 6-1.

82. *CT*, May 18, 1888, 6-6, July 23, 1890, 8-1; *Spirit* 115 (Feb. 4, 1888): 53; (June 23, 1888): 797–98; (June 30, 1888): 836, 846–47, 850.

83. *CT*, June 10, 1888, 11-3, June 24, 1888, 12-3, June 29, 1888, 3-3, July 17, 1888, 3-3, Aug. 4, 1888, 3-4 (quote).

84. Hotaling, *Great Black Jockeys*, 209–11; "Anthony Hamilton," https://www.racingmuseum.org/hall-of-fame/anthony-hamilton.

85. *CT*, Feb. 22, 1888, 3-5; *ChT*, July 17, 1888, 3-1, July 18, 1888, 3-3; *Spirit* 113 (July 9, 1887): 802; 114 (Nov. 5, 1887): 493.

86. *ChT*, July 2, 1888, 6-5 (quote), Dec. 5, 1888, 2-6; *CT*, July 16, 1888, 3-5; *Spirit* 116 (July 28, 1888): 88; (Sept. 15, 1888): 280; (July 21, 1888): 942; (Nov. 17, 1888): 605.

87. *ChT*, July 20, 1887, 2-2; *CT*, July 17, 1888, 3-3; *Spirit* 115 (July 21, 1888): 942; 118 (Sept. 15, 1888): 280; (Sept. 22, 1888): 326.

88. *CT*, July 17, 1888, 3-3 (quote); *ChT*, July 17, 1888, 3-1, July 18, 1888, 3-3.

89. *ChT*, July 17, 1888, 3-1, July 18, 1888, 3-3, Mar. 31, 1889, 6-3, Aug. 4, 1889, 12-5, Oct. 13, 1889, 12-6; *CT*, Sept. 28, 1888, 2-6.

90. On ballpark fires, see Riess, *Touching Base*, 103, 113, 115–16.

91. Clarke, "American Horse-Racing."

92. *CT*, Mar. 2, 1889, 9-3, 3, Mar. 20, 1889, 9-5, Mar. 21, 1889, 9-7, Mar. 29, 1893, 7-3, Apr. 21, 1893, 8-3.

93. *CT*, Mar. 9, 1889, 9-3.

94. *ChT*, Mar. 31, 1889, 6-3, Aug. 4, 1889, 12-5, Oct. 13, 1889, 12-6, Oct. 23, 1889, 7-3, Nov. 3, 1889, 12-2; *CT*, June 23, 1889, 4-3 (quote); *Spirit* 118 (Aug. 3, 1889): 42; (Aug. 10, 1889): 86.

95. *CT*, June 23, 1880, 9-1, June 24, 1889, 1-3; *Spirit* 117 (June 29, 1889): 909; (July 6, 1889): 989.

96. *ChT*, July 17, 1888, 3-1, July 18, 1888, 3-3; *CT*, July 25, 1890, 2-4 (quote), July 31, 1890, 1-3, Jan. 24, 1891, 6-3; *CEP*, Aug. 16, 1890, 1-5; *Spirit* 117 (May 25, 1889): 709.

97. *Spirit* 117 (May 25, 1889): 709; *ChT*, Oct. 20, 1889, 11-2 (quote).

3. Politics, Gambling, Syndicate Crime, and the Chicago Turf, 1890–1892

1. Reiff, "Chicago's Social Geography"; S. Hirsch, "Economic Geography"; Hirsch, *Urban Revolt*.

2. Mayer and Wade, *Chicago*, 119–21, 128–35.

3. Miller, *City of the Century*, 176–554; Pacyga, *Chicago: A Biography*, 69–109.

4. *CT*, Oct. 20, 1903, 6-1.

5. Miller, *City of the Century*, 435–55, 482–87; Wendt and Kogan, *Lords of the Levee*. The political composition of the city council is drawn from *Chicago Daily News National Almanac [1890–1900]*.

6. Lindberg, *Gambler King*, 153–54; *CT*, Apr. 3, 1891, 1-7, "City Hall and the Gamblers," Aug. 13, 1890, 4-1.

7. *CT*, Apr. 3, 1891, 1-7; Lindberg, *Gambler King*, 154.

8. *CT*, Apr. 3, 1891, 1-7.

9. *CT*, July 25, 1889, 2-1; "Poolrooms and Gambling Houses," *CT*, Sept. 7, 1889, 4-5.

10. *CT*, July 26, 1889, 3-1, May 4, 1890, 12-3.

11. *CEP*, July 21, 1890, 3-4; *CT*, July 31, 1890, 1-3, Aug. 1, 1890, 1-3, 4-3.

12. *CT*, July 26, 1889, 3-1, May 4, 1890, 12-3.

13. John Flynn, "Smart Money," 54; *CDN*, Sept. 19, 1895, 2-4.

14. *CEP*, July 21, 1890, 3-4, July 24, 1890, 3-3, Aug. 13, 1890, 1-4; *Spirit* 118 (May 31, 1890): 830; (June 7, 1890): 865; (July 19, 1890): 1132.

15. *CT*, July 31, 1890, 1-3; *CEP*, Aug. 13, 1890, 1-4.

16. *CEP*, July 21, 1890, 3-4.

17. *NYT*, Nov. 13, 1887, 2-5, June 27, 1894, 2-2, Oct. 2, 1896, 1-3; *CT*, Aug. 1, 1890, 1-3, Aug. 2, 1890, 7-1, Nov. 11, 1891, 10-1, Nov. 17, 1891, 3-5, "Ullman's Universal Fair Swindle," Nov. 18, 1891, 4-4, Feb. 24, 1893, 7-1, Aug. 22, 1902, 6-5, Jan. 23, 1908, 6-1; *CEP*, July 22, 1890, 3-3; Carver, *Making Tracks*, 92–100; Weeks, *American Turf*, 448; Wilson, *Alice Nielsen*, 379–80; Ullman, *What's the Odds?*

18. *CT*, July 23, 1890, 1-3, July 24, 1890, 3-1, July 25, 1890, 2-4 (quote).

19. *Chicago Mail*, July 29, 1890, 1-5; *CT*, July 31, 1890, 1-3, 4-2, Aug. 1, 1890, 1-3, 4-3.

20. "Pleading the Baby Act," *CT*, Aug. 1, 1890, 4-3, Aug. 3, 1890, 2-5, June 16, 1887, 1-5; *CEP*, Aug. 4, 1890, 3-7, Aug. 5, 1890, 1-1.

21. *CT*, Aug. 9, 1890, 1-3, "The Methods of Three Mayors," Aug. 10, 1890, 1-5, 12-2.

22. *CT*, Aug. 12, 1890, 2-7, Aug. 14, 1890, 8-1, Aug. 15, 1890, 7-5; *CEP*, Aug. 13, 1890, 1-4.

23. *CT*, Oct. 31, 1890, 8-1; *CDN*, Oct. 30, 1890, 1-4; *Spirit* 118 (May 31, 1890): 830; (June 7, 1890): 865.

24. *CEP*, Oct. 30, 1890, 1-1; *CT*, Oct. 31, 1890, 8-1 (quote).

25. *CDN*, Oct. 30, 1890, 1-4, "Judge Tully's Pool-Selling Decision," *CT*, Nov. 1, 1890, 4-3.

26. *Spirit* 119 (July 12, 1890): 1083.

27. *CEP*, June 21, 1890, 1-3, July 24, 1890, 3-3 (quote).

28. *CT*, June 22, 1890, 2-1, Aug. 27, 1903, 4-3; *CEP*, July 19, 1890, 2-4; *Spirit* 119 (July 5, 1890): 1045; (July 19, 1890): 1132; 132 (Aug. 15, 1896): 125; (Nov. 28, 1896): 598. Racine's record lasted three years. In 1900 Orimar at Washington Park ran the mile in a new record 1:38. See Parmer, *For Gold and Glory*, 145.

29. *CT*, July 23, 1890, 8-1 (quote), July 25, 1890, 2-4, July 31, 1890, 1-3, Aug. 1, 1890, 1-3; *CEP*, June 21, 1890, 1-3, July 16, 1890, 3-1, July 19, 1890, 2-4; *NYDT*, Aug. 4, 1890, 3-4.

30. *CT*, July 16, 1890, 6-4.

31. *CT*, July 18, 1890, 3-3, July 23, 1890, 8-1; *CEP*, July 17, 1890, 1-7, 3-7, July 18, 1890, 3-3 (quote).

32. "Jiggled Races at Washington Park," *CT*, July 17, 1890, 4-4.

33. *CT*, July 23, 1890, 8-1.

34. *NYT*, Sept. 15, 1927, 19-2; *CT*, Feb. 13, 1891, 7-3, Apr. 11, 1891, 6-2, Jan. 27, 1893, 3-2, Mar. 6, 1893, 12-6, Mar. 9, 1893, 9-3, Apr. 20, 1893, 4-1, Apr. 21, 1893, 8-3.

35. *NYT*, Jan. 24, 1891, 6-3, July 27, 1892, 7-1; Lindberg, *Gambler King*, 165, 167.

36. *CDN*, Sept. 30, 1890, 1-2, Oct. 30, 1890, 1-2; *Spirit* 120 (Sept. 27, 1890): 381–82; (Oct. 25, 1890): 542; (Sept. 27, 1890): 381–82; (Oct. 25, 1890): 542; 121 (Feb. 7, 1891): 93; (May 23, 1891): 786; (May 30, 1891): 840; 122 (July 25, 1891): 2; *CT*, Jan. 24, 1891, 6-3, Sept. 8, 1891, 1-5, July 27, 1892, 7-1 (quote).

37. *CT*, Apr. 3, 1891, 1-7.

38. "Elmer Washburn," https://peoplepill.com/people/elmer-washburn; "Chicago Mayors, 1837–2007."

39. *CT*, Apr. 29, 1891, 1-1, Sept. 7, 1892, 5-4.

40. *CDN*, Sept. 30, 1890, 1-2, Oct. 30, 1890, 1-2, Apr. 16, 1894, 1-2; *Spirit* 121 (Feb. 7, 1891): 93; (May 23, 1891): 786; (May 30, 1891): 840; 122 (July 25, 1891): 2; (Oct. 10, 1891): 460; *CT*, June 19, 1891, 1-5, Aug. 14, 1898, 3-5; *CIO*, Aug. 3, 1891, 3-5; *NYDT*, Oct. 29, 1898, 3-1.

41. *CT*, June 19, 1891, 1-5, June 20, 1891, 2-2, June 21, 1891, 5-5.

42. *CT*, June 20, 1891, 2-2, Nov. 4, 1900, 8-7; Jack Sullivan, "'Those Pro-whiskey Men,' Chapin & Gore: Kings of the Chicago Saloon," http://pre-prowhiskeymen .blogspot.com/2013/07/chapin-and-gore-kings-of-chicago-saloon.html.

43. *CT*, June 21, 1891, 2-5; *Spirit* 121 (June 27, 1891): 1016; *CIO*, June 21, 1891, 2-2.

44. *Spirit* 122 (Aug. 1, 1891): 42; *ChT*, July 20, 1891, 3-5, 4-4, July 21, 1891, 1-1, 9-3, July 22, 1891, 5-5, July 27, 1891, 3-5; *NYT*, July 21, 1891, 2-4.

45. Hotaling, *Great Black Jockeys*, 279, 313; Hamburger, "Jimmy Wakefield," 11–14.

46. *CT*, Jan. 12, 1891, 3-1, Jan. 24, 1891, 6-3. For a less conspiratorial narrative, see *CT*, Oct. 22, 1894, 1-3; *Spirit* 122 (Sept. 19, 1891): 329; 134 (Oct. 30, 1897): 423; *ChT*, July 8, 1891, 9-4; *Clipper* (Mar. 14, 1896): 26.

47. *CT*, May 29, 1891, 6-6, June 5, 1891, 6-3, June 21, 1891, 5-5, June 27, 1891, 8-4, Sept. 15, 1892, 5, Aug. 10, 1915, 10-2; *ChT*, July 8, 1891, 9-4; *CIO*, Sept. 23, 1892, 1; Lindberg, *Gambler King*, 167, 188. Another accounting of the Garfield Park stock was McDonald ($20,000), George Hankins ($35,000), Al Hankins ($10,000), B. J. Johnson ($15,000), two eastern turf men ($20,000 each), and lesser amounts for others.

48. Lindberg, *To Serve and Collect*, 99; Flanagan, "Grey Wolves"; *CT*, May 20, 1930, 1-7.

49. Riordan, *Plunkitt of Tammany Hall*, 3.

50. Wendt and Kogan, *Lords of the Levee*, 28–29, 176, 349; *CT*, Nov. 12, 1938, 12-1, Apr. 7, 1939, 35-5.

51. *CT*, Aug. 10, 1915, 10-2.

52. *CT*, Aug. 10, 1915, 10-2.

53. *CT*, Aug. 10, 1915, 10-2; *Washington Times*, June 14, 1904, 8-1; *Washington Star*, Jan. 11, 1905.

54. *CT*, June 16, 1891, 1-3, June 21, 1891, 5-5, June 27, 1891, 8-4 (quote).

55. *CT*, June 5, 1891, 6-3.

56. *CT*, June 21, 1891, 5-5, June 27, 1891, 8-4 (quote), Sept. 29, 1892, 1-2, Sept. 30, 1892, 8-2; *ChT*, July 4, 1891, 4-2, July 8, 1891, 9-4 (quote), July 11, 1891, 5-4.

57. *ChT*, July 4, 1891, 4-2, July 8, 1891, 9-4, July 11, 1891, 5-4.

58. *CT*, May 29, 1891, 6-5, June 5, 1891, 6-3, June 21, 1891, 5-5, June 27, 1891, 8-4, Sept. 15, 1892, 3-4, Aug. 10, 1915, 10-2; *ChT*, July 8, 1891, 9-4, July 13, 1891, 3-5, July 14, 1891, 6-7; *CIO*, July 13, 1891, 3-3; Lindberg, *Gambler King*, 167; Riess, *Touching Base*, 39–41.

59. *ChT*, July 13, 1891, 3-5, July 14, 1891, 6-7, July 15, 1891, 6-7, July 17, 1891, 7-1, July 19, 1891, 5-3; *CIO*, July 17, 1891, 2-5; *Spirit* 122 (Sept. 9, 1891): 329–30.

60. *CT*, June 21, 1891, 5-5, June 27, 1891, 8-4, "Pecksniff on Pool-Selling," Apr. 16, 1892, 4-4, Sept. 18, 1892, 1-1.

61. *ChT*, July 4, 1891, 4-2, July 8, 1891, 9-4, July 11, 1891, 5-4.

62. *Spirit* 122 (Sept. 19, 1891): 330; (Oct. 10, 1891): 446; 124 (Sept. 3, 1892): 223 (quote); *ChT*, July 13, 1891, 3-5, July 14, 1891, 6-7, July 15, 1891, 6-7, July 17, 1891, 7-1, July 19, 1891, 5-3; *CIO*, July 24, 1891, 2-2, July 26, 1891, 3-2, Aug. 3, 1891, 3-5; *CT*, Aug. 23, 1891, 4-1.

63. *CT*, Sept. 8, 1891, 1-5; *Spirit* 122 (Oct. 10, 1891): 446; *CIO*, July 20, 1891, 3-2, Aug. 1, 1891, 3-3.

64. *Spirit* 122 (July 25, 1891): 2; *CT*, July 20, 1891, 1-6.

65. *ChT*, July 8, 1891, 8-1, Aug. 23, 1891, 1-5; *CIO*, July 8, 1891, 3-3; *Spirit* 122 (Sept. 19, 1891): 330; Lindberg, *Gambler King*, 168.

66. *CIO*, Sept. 8, 1891, 7-1; *CT*, Sept. 8, 1891, 1-5; *Spirit* 122 (Aug. 1, 1891): 42; (Sept. 19, 1891): 329–30. On attendance, see, for example, *CIO*, Aug. 4, 1891, 2-1, Aug. 5, 1891, 2-1, Aug. 9, 1891, 3-1.

67. *Spirit* 122 (Sept. 19, 1891): 329, 330 (quote).

68. *CIO*, Sept. 27, 1892, 1–3.

69. *CT*, July 24, 1891, 6-2, Oct. 2, 1891, 6-4, Oct. 5, 1891, 6-1; *Spirit* 122 (Sept. 19, 1891): 329; *CIO*, Oct. 4, 1891, 6-2.

70. *CIO*, Oct. 4, 1891, 6-2. Attendance estimated based on data in *CT*, October 31 to November 30, 1891.

71. *CT*, Nov. 16, 1891, 6-1, Nov. 21, 1891, 7-1, Nov. 22, 1891, 6-3, Nov. 25, 1891, 7-1.

72. *Spirit* 122 (Dec. 19, 1891): 818.

73. *CT*, Nov. 18, 1891, 7-3; *ChT*, July 8, 1891, 9-4.

74. Riess, *Sport of Kings*, 52, 110–14, 117, 125–26.

75. *CT*, Oct. 22, 1891, 6-3, Oct. 26, 1891, 6-1, Nov. 18, 1891, 7-3, Nov. 30, 1891, 6-3, Dec. 13, 1891, 5-1; *Spirit* 122 (Dec. 5, 1891): 718; (Dec. 12, 1891): 787; (Dec. 19, 1891): 818; (Dec. 26, 1891) 857; *NYT*, Dec. 23, 1891, 8-3, Dec. 28, 1891, 2-4, Dec. 28, 1891, 2-4.

76. *CT*, Nov. 30, 1891, Dec. 13, 1891, 5-1; *Spirit* 122 (Dec. 12, 1891): 787; (Dec. 19, 1891): 818; (Dec. 26, 1891): 857; Wendt and Kogan, *Lords of the Levee*, 29.

77. *CIO*, Oct. 13, 1891, 5-1; *CDN*, Oct. 16, 1891, 1-3; *CT*, Dec. 15, 1891, 2-2; *Spirit* 122 (Dec. 19, 1891): 818; (Dec. 26, 1891): 857; (Jan. 16, 1892): 996; 123 (Feb. 6, 1892): 88.

78. *CT*, Nov. 30, 1891, 6-3; *Spirit* 122 (Dec. 19, 1891): 818.

79. *CT*, Oct. 5, 1891, Nov. 30, 1891, 6-3; Asbury, *Sucker's Progress*, 296–302.

80. *CT*, Nov. 30, 1891, 6-3; *Spirit* 122 (Dec. 5, 1891): 717; *NYT*, Sept. 20, 1891, 8-6; Riess, *Sport of Kings*, 142; Asbury, *Sucker's Progress*, 296–302. I estimated the daily Western Union fees at $1,000, which is probably high.

81. Hochfelder, *Telegraph in America*, 77, 113 (quote).

82. Hochfelder, *Telegraph in America*, 113–14; *NYT*, Mar. 25, 1891, 5-5, Aug. 4, 1893, 8-5, May 18, 1904, 2-3; Linder and Zacharias, *Of Cabbages and Kings County*, 242; Riess, *Sport of Kings*, 70, 72–75.

83. *NYT*, May 30, 1891, 5-1; Riess, *Sport of Kings*, 194; Hochfelder, *Telegraph in America*, 113.

84. Carver, *Making Tracks*, 92, 94, 103, 111; *Spirit* 122 (Dec. 26, 1891): 857.

85. *Spirit* 122 (Dec. 5, 1891): 717; (Jan. 2, 1892): 912; 123 (Feb. 27, 1892): 230; (Mar. 26, 1892): 385; Carver, *Making Tracks*, 111–13.

86. Carver, *Making Tracks*, 73–75, 103, 113–14, 118, 120; *CT*, Oct. 29, 1892, 7-3.

87. Carver, *Making Tracks*, 118, 120; *CT*, Dec. 1, 1893, 11-1, Dec. 3, 1893, 5-4, Dec. 25, 1893, 4-5, Dec. 29, 1893, 11-1, Dec. 31, 1893, 6-2, Dec. 4, 1895, 10-1; *CDN*, Oct. 27, 1894, 6-1.

88. *CT*, Mar. 29, 1897, 5-3.

89. *Illinois Political Directory*, 257; A. Marquis, *Book of Chicagoans*, 679; *CT*, Dec. 13, 1933, 20-1; *Spirit* 123 (Mar. 26, 1892): 386; (July 9, 1892): 1039; 124 (July 30, 1892): 41–42.

90. *CT*, Apr. 15, 1892, 9-2.

91. Wendt and Kogan, *Lords of the Levee*, 30, 50 (quote); *Spirit* 122 (Jan. 9, 1892): 965; 123 (Feb. 6, 1892): 86; (Mar. 26, 1892): 386.

92. *Spirit* 123 (Apr. 23, 1892): 550; *CT*, May 21, 1892, 6-1, May 22, 1892, 6-3, May 24, 1892, 6-3, May 31, 1892, 6-1, Sept. 13, 1892, 3-3.

93. *CT*, June 18, 1892, 6-1, Aug. 27, 1903, 4-3. *Swigert v. The People* (1895), 150 Ill App. 287, claimed the race drew more than thirty thousand, and average attendance was about six thousand.

94. *Spirit* 122 (Jan. 9, 1892): 951; 123 (July 2, 1892): 995; *CT*, Mar. 2, 1892, 7-1, June 13, 1892, 9-1.

95. *CT*, Feb. 29, 1892, 7-1; *Spirit* 124 (Jan. 14, 1893): 958.

96. *CT*, Mar. 2, 1892, 7-1, June 13, 1892, 9-1, June 26, 1892, 2-6, 4-2; *Spirit* 123 (July 2, 1892): 995.

97. *CT*, June 26, 1892, 3-7; Riess, *Sport of Kings*, 145–46.

98. *BE*, May 7, 1893, 17; Hotaling, *They're Off*, 152–56; Joe Drape, "Horse Racing: Saratoga Opener Today Has History and Horses," *NYT*, July 24, 2002, D4-1.

99. *CT*, June 15, 11-3, June 21, 1892, 11-3, June 25, 1892, 10-1 (quote), July 16, 1892, 7-2, July 20, 1892, 7-3, July 24, 1892, 6-1, Sept. 3, 1892, 4-1, 1-7; *Spirit* 123 (Apr. 23, 1892): 550; Wendt and Kogan, *Lords of the Levee*, 50 (quote); *CT*, July 19, 1892; *BE*, July 19, 1892, 2-4.

100. *CT*, July 16, 1892, 7-2, July 20, 1892, 7-3, July 24, 1892, 6-1, July 25, 1892, 3-1, July 27, 3-7, 7-1, July 28, 1892, 7-4, Aug. 5, 1892, 7-3, Aug. 9, 1892, 6-3, Nov. 19, 1893, 1-1; *Spirit* 123 (Mar. 26, 1892): 386; 124 (July 30, 1892): 42; *BE*, July 25, 1892, 2-4.

101. "Can He Veto It?," *CT*, July 27, 1892, 4-4.

102. *CT*, July 27, 1892, 4-4, July 30, 1892, 8-1 (quote), Sept. 10, 1892, 6-1.

103. *CT*, July 25, 1892, 3-1, July 27, 1892, 3-7, 7-1, Aug. 1, 1892, 7-4, Aug. 3, 1892, 6-3, Aug. 4, 1892, 5-7, Aug. 5, 1892, 7-3, Aug. 9, 1892, 6-3; *Spirit* 124 (Aug. 27, 1892): 181; (Nov. 5, 1892): 569; *NYT*, Sept. 7, 1892, 1-5; Carver, *Making Tracks*, 101.

104. *CT*, Aug. 9, 1892, 6-3, Aug. 10, 1892, 1-5, Aug. 11, 1892, 1-5, Aug. 12, 1892, 7-3, Aug. 18, 1892, 6-3; *CDN*, Sept. 6, 1892, 1-3; *Spirit* 124 (Aug. 13, 1892): 124; (Aug. 27, 1892): 181.

105. *CT*, Sept. 3, 1892, 1-7, 9-1, Sept. 4, 1892, 28-2; *CDN*, Sept. 3, 1892, 1-7, 2-1, Sept. 12, 1892, 1-1; Wendt and Kogan, *Lords of the Levee*, 54.

106. *CT*, Sept. 4, 1892, 1-3; Wendt and Kogan, *Lords of the Levee*, 54.

107. *CT*, Sept. 4, 1894, 28-2.

108. *CT*, Sept. 6, 1892, 1-5; *NYT*, Sept. 6, 1892, 3-6.

109. *CT*, Sept. 7, 1892, 1-3.

110. *CT*, Sept. 7, 1892, 1-1, 5-3, Sept. 8, 1892, 3-3, "The Garfield Park Murders," Sept. 8, 1892, 4-4; *CDN*, Sept. 10, 1892, 3-1; Wendt and Kogan, *Lords of the Levee*,

54; John K. Brown Jr., "My Southern Roots: James Madison Brown," https://sites
.rootsweb.com/~opus/p2844.htm; Lindberg, *Gambler King*, 170.

111. *CT*, Sept. 7, 1892, 1-1; *CDN*, Sept. 17, 1892, 1-5; Wendt and Kogan, *Lords of
the Levee*, 54; *Spirit* 124 (Sept. 17, 1892): 302.

112. *NYT*, Sept. 7, 1892, 1-5 (quote); *NYDT*, Sept. 8, 1892, 12-1; *CDN*, Sept. 8,
1892, 1-1, Sept. 9, 1892, 1-3, Sept. 10, 1892, 3-1; *Spirit* 124 (July 17, 1892): 302 (quote);
Chicago Globe, Sept. 7, 1892, quoted in Lindberg, *Gambler King*, 171. On the inquest,
see *CT*, Sept. 10, 1892, 6-3, Sept. 11, 1892, 14-1.

113. *NYT*, Sept. 7, 1892, 1-5; *CT*, Sept. 8, 1892, 3-3, Sept. 12, 1892, 7-1 (quote),
Sept. 13, 1892, 3-3.

114. *CT*, Sept. 10, 1892, 6-1, Sept. 13, 1892, 1-1, 3-3.

115. *Spirit* 124 (Sept. 17, 1892): 302; *CT*, Sept. 30, 1892, 8-2; *CDN*, Sept. 29, 1892,
1-1.

116. *CDN*, Sept. 13, 1892, 1-7, Sept. 26, 1892, 1-1; *CT*, Sept. 28, 1892, 8-5, Sept.
29, 1892, 1-2, Sept. 30, 1892, 8-2, Oct. 6, 1892, 7-2, Oct. 12, 1892, 7-7, Nov. 2, 1892,
7-2, Nov. 3, 1892, 4-5; Wendt and Kogan, *Lords of the Levee*, 57; *Spirit* 124 (Nov. 12,
1892): 607.

117. *CT*, Sept. 13, 1892, 3-3; *CDN*, Sept. 19, 1892, 1-5.

118. *CDN*, Sept. 17, 1892, 1-5; *CT*, Sept. 18, 1892, 1-1, 1-4, 1-5, Sept. 23, 1892, 1-1.
On political repercussions, see Lindberg, *Gambler King*, 173–74.

119. *CDN*, Sept. 14, 1892, 1-3; *CT*, Nov. 14, 1892, 12-1, Nov. 20, 1892, 7-3.

120. *CDN*, Sept. 14, 1892, 1-3; *CT*, Sept. 30, 1892, 6-3; *Spirit* 124 (Nov. 5, 1892):
569.

121. *CT*, Dec. 17, 1892, 6-1, Dec. 18, 1892, 6-1, Jan. 3, 1893, 1-5, Oct. 11, 1932,
21-3; *NYT*, Dec. 17, 1892, 6-3; *Spirit* 124 (Nov. 5, 1892): 569; (Dec. 24, 1892): 845.

122. *NYT*, Feb. 13, 1893, 6-2 (quote).

123. *CT*, Aug. 1, 1892, 2-4, Aug. 7, 1892, 4-3, Sept. 22, 1892, 6-5; *Spirit* 124 (Sept.
1892): 6-5; (Dec. 10, 1892): 764–65; Hmurovic, "Horse Racing."

124. Hmurovic, "Horse Racing"; Indiana, General Assembly, House of Representatives, *Journal of the House during the Fifty-Eighth Session*, 716–17, 725.

125. "Roby: 'The Biggest Little City in America,'" http://www.whiting.lib.in.us
/files/Roby%20Part%201.pdf.

126. *CT*, Sept. 22, 1892, 6-5; *Spirit* 124 (Dec. 10, 1892): 764 (quote), 765.

127. *CT*, Aug. 1, 1892, 2-4, Aug. 7, 1892, 4-3, Sept. 15, 1892, 5-3, Sept. 22, 1892,
6-5, Dec. 25, 1892, 4-2; Hmurovic, "Horse Racing."

128. *CT*, Nov. 13, 1892, 2-1.

129. *CT*, Jan. 6, 1893, 8-1, Feb. 19, 1893, 4-4, Mar. 27, 1893, 11-4, Apr. 4, 1893,
7-3, Apr. 5, 1893, 7-1, June 24, 1893, 6-1, Dec. 17, 1894, 2-5, Feb. 3, 1900, 6-1; *BE*, Aug.
1, 1892, 2-4; *Spirit* 124 (Aug. 13, 1892): 113; (Dec. 10, 1892): 764–65; *CDN*, Jan. 12,
1893, 6-2, Jan. 13, 1893, 6-2, Feb. 10, 1893, 7-1, Mar. 31, 1894, 2-1; Indiana, General

Assembly, House of Representatives, *Journal of the House during the Fifty-Eighth Session*, 717–18, 721. On winter racing in St. Louis, see Carver, *Making Tracks*, 86–88.

130. *CT*, Nov. 20, 1892, 7-1.

131. *CT*, Sept. 15, 1892, 5-3, Oct. 3, 1892, 12-3, Nov. 20, 1892, 7-1; Riess, *Sport of Kings*, 172.

132. *CT*, Nov. 20, 1892, 7-1.

133. *CT*, Sept. 15, 1892, 5-3, Sept. 23, 1892, 3-3, Oct. 3, 1892, 12-3, Nov. 14, 1892, 7-3, Nov. 20, 1892, 7-3.

134. *CT*, Sept. 13, 1892, 3-3, Sept. 15, 1892, 5-3. This probably does not account for a secret contract made with three or four poolrooms for racing information from May 1892 to May 1893 that came to $124,000.

135. *CT*, Sept. 15, 1892, 5-3. Financial data from the *Tribune* given for the 1891 season, and reported in both 1891 and 1892, is difficult to reconcile. In 1891, the paper reported the foreign book brought in $600,000 but one year later wrote it was $500,000.

136. Riess, *Sport of Kings*, 119, 151.

4. WASHINGTON PARK AND THE TENUOUS STATUS
OF THE AMERICAN TURF, 1893–1894

1. Badger, *Great American Fair*; Gilbert, *Perfect Cities*.

2. Muccigrosso, *Celebrating the New World*; Larson, *Devil in the White City*; Gustaitis, *Chicago's Greatest Year, 1893*.

3. *CT*, June 20, 1893, 12-6, June 21, 1893, 6-6, June 24, 1893, 7-3; Frank G. Menke, *All-Sports Record Book*, 206–7.

4. Adapted from *Goodwin's Annual Turf Guide for [1882–1908]*.

5. *CDN*, Feb. 17, 1893, 7-1; *CT*, "A Plague o' Both Your Houses," Feb. 17, 1893, 4-3 (quote); Abbot, *Carter Henry Harrison*, 206 (quote); Green, "Chicago Democratic Party," 50–51.

6. *CDN*, Feb. 17, 1893, 8-1 (quote); Johnson, *Carter H. Harrison I*, 188, 257–58.

7. *ChT*, Mar. 30, 1893, 2-3.

8. *CT*, Mar. 16, 1893, 12-2, Mar. 26, 1893, 1-1, Mar. 28, 1893, 3-1, "Harrison's Weak Arguments," Mar. 29, 1893, 12-2; "Harrison's Disreputable Campaign," Apr. 1, 1893, 12-2; Abbot, *Carter Henry Harrison*, 213–15 (213 quotes); Wendt and Kogan, *Lords of the Levee*, 67; R. Morton, *Sullivan and the Making of the Chicago Democratic Machine*, 33–35.

9. *CT*, Apr. 21, 1893, 4-3, 7-3, Feb. 23, 1914, 1-3.

10. *CDN*, Feb. 24, 1893, 6-3 (quote); *CT*, Mar. 9, 1893, 6-1, 9-2 (quote), Mar. 30, 1893, 7-1, May 17, 1893, 7-1; *Spirit* 125 (Jan. 28, 1893): 46; (Feb. 4, 1893): 91; Riess, "Horse Racing in Chicago," 1–57.

11. *CIO*, Mar. 24, 1893, 1-3; *CT*, Apr. 20, 1893, 4-1; *Spirit* 125 (Apr. 8, 1893): 463; (Apr. 15, 1893): 514.

12. *Spirit* 125 (Apr. 29, 1893): 600; *CDN*, Apr. 20, 1893, 7-3; *CIO*, Mar. 24, 1893, 1-3; *CT*, Apr. 20, 1893, 4-1 (quote); Apr. 21, 1893, 4-1, 8-3, Apr. 24, 1893, 12-4, Apr. 25, 1893, 7-3; Crossley and Gary, *Courts and Lawyers of Illinois*, 2:758–59.

13. *CT*, Mar. 6, 1892, 1-2, May 29, 1893, 12-5, June 21, 1893, 6-6, June 22, 1893, 6-5, 12-5, June 24, 1893, 7-3, June 29, 1893, 6-2; *Spirit* 126 (Aug. 5, 1893): 70; (Oct. 14, 1893): 393; *CDN*, Feb. 14, 1893, 6-1, May 18, 1893, 6-1 (quote), May 22, 1893, 8-1, June 3, 1893, 6-2.

14. *CT*, June 20, 1893, 12-6, June 21, 1893, 6-6, June 24, 1893, 7-3, June 25, 1893, 2-4, 28-5; *Spirit* 134 (Jan. 1, 1898): 732.

15. *CT*, June 25, 1893, 1, 2, 3, 4, "Chicago's Derby," 28-5 (quote); Robertson, *History of Thoroughbred Racing*, 161. Racing historian Charles B. Parmer claimed that in the 1890s big-time tracks had a great opportunity for gigantic profits with revenues that far exceeded their $10,000–$12,000 daily expenses. See Parmer, *For Gold and Glory*, 167.

16. *CT*, June 25, 1893, 2-3, 3-4.

17. *Spirit* 126 (Aug. 5, 1893): 67 (quotes), 80; (Aug. 19, 1893): 146; *CDN*, June 26, 1893, 1-1, 4-2, June 28, 1893, 2-1, July 25, 1893, 2-1, Aug. 14, 1893, 3-1.

18. *CDN*, June 26, 1893, 1-1, 4-2.

19. *CDN*, June 26, 1893, 1-1, May 17, 1893, 9-1.

20. *CDN*, June 17, 1893, 1-1, June 28, 1893, 1-1 (quote), 6-3, June 29, 1893, 1-1, June 30, 1893, 1-1, July 3, 1893, 2-1, July 5, 1893, 1-1.

21. *CDN*, July 1, 1893, 1-1.

22. *CDN*, July 6, 1893, 3-1, July 18, 1893, 3-4, 8-2 (quote), July 25, 1893, 3-1, Jan. 6, 1894, 2-2 (quote).

23. *CDN*, July 19, 1893, 6-1, July 22, 1893, 3-1, July 25, 1893, 6-1, July 29, 1893, 2-2.

24. *CDN*, Feb. 16, 1893, 6-1, July 25, 1893, 6-1.

25. *CDN*, Nov. 17, 1893, 2-2, Nov. 21, 1893, 2-1 (quote), Jan. 6, 1894, 2-2.

26. *CDN*, July 19, 1893, 6-1, July 22, 1893, 3-1, July 25, 1893, 6-1, July 29, 1893, 2-2; *Spirit* 126 (Oct. 14, 1893): 393 (quote).

27. *CT*, July 23, 1893, 6-3, Nov. 27, 1893, 4-1, Nov. 30, 1893, 6-1; *Spirit* 126 (July 29, 1893): 36 (quote); *CDN*, July 19, 1893, 6-1. If the press report that only one Washington Park event drew more than 6,000 is correct, the largest possible attendance was 184,000, or an average of 7,360.

28. *CDN*, May 17, 1893, 9-1, June 29, 1893, 1-2, July 3, 1893, 2-1, July 19, 1893, 6-1, Jan. 6, 1894, 2-2. These figures differ from those numbers reported a year later that the club received $40,000 from dues, and cost $70,000 to operate. *CT*, Oct. 14, 1894, 1-1, 4-4; Robertson, *History of Thoroughbred Racing*, 160; *Spirit* 126 (Aug. 5, 1893): 70.

29. *CDN*, July 19, 1893, 6-2, 8-2, July 25, 1893, 6-1, Nov. 22, 1893, 2-2, Nov. 29, 1893, 2-1; *CT*, Apr. 4, 1893, 7-3, Apr. 5, 1893, 7-1, June 24, 1893, 6-1, Aug. 7, 1893, 6-5, Nov. 27, 1893, 4-1, Nov. 28, 1893, 11-1, Nov. 29, 1893, 11-1, Nov. 30, 1893, 6-1, Dec. 3, 1893, 5-3; *Spirit* 126 (July 22, 1893): 4; (July 29, 1893): 36; (Aug. 5, 1893): 70; (Dec. 9, 1893): 679.

30. *Spirit* 126 (Sept. 9, 1893): 231; (Sept. 16, 1893): 267; (Sept. 23, 1893): 298; (Oct. 14, 1893): 393; (Nov. 11, 1893): 537.

31. *CT*, June 9, 1895, 5-3; Brolaski, *Easy Money*, 192.

32. Griffin, "Big Jim O'Leary," 214.

33. *Spirit* 136 (Dec. 24, 1898): 564; *CT*, Apr. 25, 1896, 1-1; Griffin, "Big Jim O'Leary," 214 (quote); Flynt, "Men behind the Poolrooms," 643; Wade, *Chicago's Pride*, 156.

34. *CDN*, Dec. 18, 1893, 5-1, Feb. 7, 1894, 2-1 (quote), Feb. 17, 1894, 6-1, Feb. 19, 1894, 3-1, Feb. 27, 1894, 5-2, Mar. 7, 1894, 8-2; *Spirit* 128 (Nov. 3, 1894): 538.

35. *CDN*, Apr. 16, 1894, 1-1.

36. *CDN*, Dec. 18, 1893, 5-1; *CT*, Oct. 14, 1918, 13-3; "Chicago Mayors, 1837–2007."

37. *CT*, Apr. 16, 1894, 1-1, 6-2.

38. *CT*, Apr. 17, 1894, 1-1 (quote), 1-3, "No Gambling at Garfield Park," 6-2; "Martin B. Madden."

39. *CT*, Apr. 18, 1894, 1-7, Apr. 21, 1894, 9-7, Apr. 22, 1894, 1-3, *BE*, Apr. 22, 1894, 23-4; *Spirit* 127 (Apr. 28, 1894): 523, 530; Lindberg, *Gambler King*, 188.

40. *CT*, Apr. 16, 1894, 1-2.

41. *CT*, Chicago Civic Federation, *First Annual Report*, 84.

42. *CT*, May 11, 1894, 11-1, July 9, 1894, 4-1 (quote).

43. *CT*, May 1, 1894, 11-1.

44. *CT*, May 21, 1894, 11-7, May 29, 1894, 11-7.

45. *CT*, June 25, 1894, 4-7 (quote); *Spirit* 127 (June 30, 1894): 895; (July 7, 1894): 934.

46. *CT*, Feb. 27, 1893, 12-3, May 21, 1894, 11-7, May 29, 1894, 11-7, July 2, 1894, 4-1, July 9, 1894, 4-1; *Spirit* 127 (June 30, 1894): 895.

47. *Spirit* 127 (June 30, 1894): 895; (July 7, 1894): 934; *CT*, July 19, 1894, 11-3; *San Francisco Call*, Nov. 27, 1895, 1-1, Nov. 29, 1895, 10-1.

48. *Spirit* 127 (June 30, 1894): 895; (July 7, 1894): 934; Robertson, *History of Thoroughbred Racing*, 194.

49. *CT*, Mar. 11, 1894, 2-1; Stead, *If Christ Came to Chicago*; Eckley, *Maiden Tribute*; Schults, *Crusader in Babylon*.

50. *CT*, 19 June 1894, 1-3, Aug. 11, 1894, Sept. 1, 1894, 1-1; "Chicago's Anti-gambling Crusade," 697; "How Gambling Was Stopped in Chicago"; Stead, *If Christ*

Came to Chicago, 120, 124; Smith, *Search for Social Salvation*, 74–83; Chicago Civic Federation, *First Annual Report*, 86.

51. *CT*, Aug. 11, 1894, 7-4.

52. *CT*, July 3, 1893, 9-4, "All the Gambling Tracks Must Go," Apr. 18, 1894, 6-2, Apr. 30, 1894, 4-1, May 1, 1894, 1-1.

53. Riess, *Sport of Kings*, 122–36.

54. *CT*, Sept. 24, 1894, 2-2, Sept. 25, 1894, 5-5.

55. *CT*, Apr. 30, 1894, 4-1.

56. *CT*, May 8, 1894, 1-1.

57. *CDN*, May 8, 1894, 1-1, May 10, 1894, 1-3 (quote).

58. *CT*, May 11, 1894, 1-1.

59. *CT*, May 11, 1894, 1-1.

60. *CT*, May 11, 1894, 1-1.

61. *Spirit* 128 (Oct. 20, 1894): 466 (quote); *CDN*, May 26, 1894, 5-1, June 23, 1894, 5-2; *CT*, May 12, 1894, 4-1, June 23, 1894, 1-1.

62. *CT*, June 23, 1894, 1-1.

63. *CT*, June 24, 1894, 3-5, 28-3 (quote); Hertz, *Racing Memoirs of John Hertz*. Fannie met a bookie clerk at the track, far below her social status, and eventually married him (17).

64. *CT*, July 23, 1894, 11-2; *CDN*, June 23, 1894, 5-2; *NYT*, June 24, 1894, 11-3; Harrison, *Growing Up with Chicago*, 76.

65. *Spirit* 128 (Oct. 20, 1894): 466; *CDN*, May 26, 1894, 5-1, June 23, 1894, 5-2, June 26, 1894, 5-1 (quote), July 5, 1894, 2-2, July 23, 1894, 2-1 (quote); *BE*, June 23, 1894, 1-5, June 29, 1894, 11-1.

66. Ginger, *Eugene V. Debs*, 170.

67. *CDN*, July 23, 1894, 2-1; *CT*, July 23, 1894, 11-1, Nov. 12, 1894, 11-3; *Spirit* 128 (July 21, 1894): 6.

68. *CDN*, July 23, 1894, 2-1, 5-2, July 5, 1894, 2-2, July 23, 1894, 2-1; *CT*, July 23, 1894, 7-1; *BE*, June 23, 1894, 1-5, June 29, 1894, 11-1; *Spirit* 127 (July 7, 1894): 934; 128 (July 21, 1894): 6.

69. These numbers were reported in *CT*, Nov. 12, 1894, 11-3. For a more modest report, except for the CIJC netting $287,915, see Riess, *Sport of Kings*, 169–73. On baseball profits, see *CT*, Oct. 1, 1893, 4-3.

70. *Spirit* 124 (July 23, 1892): 10; 134 (Oct. 30, 1897): 423; 138 (Aug. 5, 1899): 80–81; *Maysville (KY) Evening Bulletin*, May 17, 1899, 1; *CT*, Oct. 22, 1894, 1-3.

71. *Spirit* 127 (Feb. 17, 1894): 157; *CDN*, Mar. 14, 1894, 2-1; *CT*, July 11, 1894, 11-2, July 16, 1894, 11-3.

72. *CDN*, July 30, 1894, 2-7; *Spirit* 127 (July 7, 1894): 934; 128 (July 21, 1894): 6; (Aug. 25, 1894): 186; (Sept. 1, 1894): 224.

73. *CT*, Aug. 10, 1894, 11-5; *CDN*, June 23, 1894, 5-2, July 5, 1894, 2-2, July 23, 1894, 2-1; *BE*, June 23, 1894, 1-5, June 29, 1894, 11-1; *Spirit* 127 (July 7, 1894): 934.

74. *CT*, June 4, 1894, 11-1; *Spirit* 128 (July 21, 1894): 6; (Aug. 4, 1894): 74; (Aug. 11, 1894): 116; (Sept. 1, 1894): 224; 143 (Feb. 1, 1902): 62; *CDN*, July 30, 1894 (quote), Aug. 1, 1894, 7-1 (quote), Aug. 2, 1894, 7-1, Nov. 13, 1894, 9-1.

75. *NYT*, Aug. 26, 1894, 1-2.

76. *CDN*, Nov. 2, 1894, 8-1, Nov. 3, 1894, 6-2; *Spirit* 128 (Nov. 3, 1894): 538.

77. *CDN*, Oct. 22, 1894, 2-1, Oct. 23, 1894, 2-1; *CT*, Oct. 22, 1894, 1-3.

78. *CT*, July 1, 1894, 12-5. Corrigan claimed that a grand-jury member offered to get the indictments dropped for $2,500.

79. *CT*, July 9, 1894, 4-1.

80. *CT*, Sept. 23, 1894, 4-6, Oct. 14, 1894, 1-3; *Spirit* 128 (Sept. 29, 1894): 358; Lindberg, *Gambler King*, 266n6.

81. *CT*, Sept. 23, 1894, 4-6, Sept. 29, 1894, 7-6; *CDN*, Sept. 28, 1894, 1-4.

82. *CT*, Sept. 24, 1894, 2-4.

83. *CT*, Sept. 25, 1894, 6-4.

84. *Spirit* 126 (Sept. 9, 1893): 231; (Sept. 16, 1893): 267; (Sept. 23, 1893): 298; (Oct. 14, 1893): 393; (Nov. 11, 1893): 537; *CT*, Oct. 4, 1894, 5-6; *CDN*, Sept. 29, 1894, 1-2 (quote).

85. *Spirit* 128 (Sept. 29, 1894): 358; 129 (Mar. 9, 1895): 249; *CT*, Oct. 14, 1894, 1-3; *CDN*, Oct. 2, 1894, 2-1.

86. *Spirit* 128 (Oct. 27, 1894): 505 (quote); (Nov. 3, 1894): 538.

87. *CT*, June 20, 1889, 5-2, Oct. 28, 1893, 3-3, Oct. 14, 1894, 1-1, 1-2, Oct. 15, 1894, 11-5, Jan. 17, 1895, 11-5; *CDN*, Oct. 15, 1894, 1-5; *NYDT*, Oct. 15, 1894, 4-2; *NYT*, Oct. 15, 1894, 1-5; *History of the City of Chicago*, 204. On the demise of racing in New Jersey, see Riess, *Sport of Kings*, 133–35.

88. *CT*, Oct. 14, 1894, 1-1.

89. *CDN*, Oct. 15, 1894, 1-5, Nov. 2, 1894, 8-1; *CT*, Oct. 14, 1894, 1-1; *Spirit* 128 (Oct. 20, 1894): 466, 480–81; *CT*, June 24, 1895, 5-3, Oct. 15, 1894, 1-2; *NYDT*, Oct. 15, 1894, 4-2.

90. *CDN*, Oct. 15, 1894, 1-5, Nov. 2, 1894, 8-1; *CT*, Oct. 14, 1894, 1-1, 11-5, Oct. 15, 1894, 11-5, June 24, 1895, 5-3 (quote); *Spirit* 128 (Oct. 20, 1894): 466, 480–81; *NYDT*, Oct. 15, 1894, 4-2.

91. *CT*, Oct. 15, 1894, 11-5.

92. *CT*, Oct. 14, 1894, 1-1, 1-2; *Spirit* 134 (Jan. 1, 1898): 732.

93. *CT*, Oct. 15, 1894, 11-1, 11-5.

94. Riess, *Sport of Kings*, 134, 140; *Washington Post*, Dec. 31, 1888, 1-2; Kelly, "At the Track," 509.

95. Whyte, *History of the British Turf*, 190; Vamplew, *Turf*, 199–212; Huggins, "Culture, Class and Respectability," 225.

96. Huggins, *Flat Racing*, 1–16.

97. Huggins, *Flat Racing*, 89, 93–112; Cunningham, *Leisure in the Industrial Revolution*, 90.

98. Huggins, *Flat Racing*, 80–91, 99, 240; Vamplew, *Turf*, 204–5.

99. Dixon, *From Prohibition to Regulation*, 82–108, 148–85; Clapson, "Bit of a Flutter," 40–41; Laybourn, *Working-Class Gambling in Britain*, 35–48, 82, 91–98, 109; Munting, *Economic and Social History*, 25; "Bookmaking and Bookmakers."

100. Longrigg, *History of Horse Racing*, 115–204, 249–74, 281; McReynolds, *Russia at Play*, 78–82; Deas, *Horse Racing in India*, 16–42; Beezley, *Judas at the Jockey Club*, 27; Hora, "El turf como arena de disputa social." The Australian state parliaments dealt with moral issues in the late nineteenth century as political power and cultural dominance shifted from the rural gentry to mercantile capitalists to the detriment of working-class gambling. In 1883 South Australia banned the totalizator and book-making that led to the dissolution of two leading racing clubs and a major track. The other tracks barely survived, until five years later, when the tote was legalized following a change in the parliament's composition. O'Hara, *Mug's Game*, 90–94, 97–98.

101. Jensen, *Winning of the Midwest*; Kleppner, *Cross of Culture*; McSeveney, *Politics of Depression*.

102. "1893 Chicago Colts," http://www.baseball-reference.com/teams/CHC /1893.shtml.

103. On the fight to save New York racing, see Riess, *Sport of Kings*, 214–34.

5. The Fall and Rebirth of Chicago Racing, 1895–1899

1. *CDN*, Jan. 17, 1895, 6-1; *CT*, Mar. 27, 1895, 11-1; *Joseph Swigert v. People of the State of Illinois*, 154 Ill. 284.

2. Riess, *Sport of Kings*, 101–74.

3. *Spirit* 129 (Mar. 3, 1895): 215; *CT*, Mar. 7, 1895, 7-1, Mar. 13, 1895, 5-1, Mar. 22, 1895, 1-7, 6-2; "Political Party Strength in Illinois," https://en.wikipedia .org/wiki/Political_party_strength_in_Illinois#Table.

4. *CDN*, Mar. 7, 1895, 7-1, Mar. 9, 1895, 4-2, Mar. 25, 1895, 1-7; *Spirit* 129 (Mar. 3, 1895): 215; *CT*, Apr. 8, 1885, 8-2, Mar. 13, 1895, 5-1, Mar. 25, 1895, 5-1.

5. *CT*, Nov. 8, 1894, 2-2, Mar. 22, 1895, 1-7 (quotes), Mar. 25, 1895, 6-2, Mar. 30, 1895, 12-3; *Spirit* 129 (May 18, 1895): 616.

6. *CT*, Mar. 22, 1895, 1-7 (quote), Mar. 27, 1895, 6-3, Mar. 30, 1895, 12-3; *Spirit* 129 (May 18, 1895): 616.

7. *CT*, Mar. 22, 1895, 2-2, Mar. 24, 1895, 5-3, Mar. 25, 1895, 1-7, 5-1, Mar. 26, 1895, 8, Mar. 27, 1895, 11-1, Mar. 29, 1895, 12-3, June 14, 1895, 1-1, 10-3.

8. *Spirit* 129 (May 18, 1895): 616; *NPG* (Apr. 13, 1895): 10; (Aug. 3, 1895): 10; *CT*, June 1, 1895, 1-1, June 14, 1895, 10-3, July 10, 1895, 7-1, July 14, 1895, 4-4.

9. *CT*, July 10, 1895, 7-1, July 14, 1895, 4-4, July 18, 1895, 4-5, July 19, 1895, 6-3; *NPG* (Aug. 3, 1895): 10.

10. *CDN*, July 25, 1895, 1-7; *CT*, July 26, 1895, 1-1, July 27, 1895, 9-1, Sept. 13, 1895, 4-5; *Spirit* 130 (July 20, 1895): 6.

11. *Spirit* 130 (July 20, 1895): 6. On municipal support of private sports to promote development, see, for example, Euchner, *Playing the Field*; and Rosentraub, *Major League Winners*.

12. *CDN*, Oct. 22, 1894, 2-1, Oct. 23, 1894, 2-1, Mar. 11, 1895, 5-1, May 5, 1895, 9-1; *CT*, Mar. 10, 1895, 5-3, May 7, 1895, 11-1; *NPG* (Mar. 23, 1895): 10.

13. *CT*, May 15, 1895, 11-7, May 26, 5-1, June 9, 1895, 5-3, June 9, 1895, 5-3; *Spirit* 129 (May 18, 1895): 615, 617; *NYDT*, May 5, 1897, 3-2. Hankins sold his one-nineteenth share in the Roby Fair Association to his partners for $3,500, making the estimated value of the RFA $66,500.

14. *CT*, Oct. 14, 1894, 1-2, Oct. 15, 1894, 11-1, 11-5, June 24, 1895, 5-3.

15. *CT*, May 2, 1895, 11-1, "Suppress the Gamblers' Roost," May 3, 1895, 6-3, May 5, 1895, 4-1, May 11, 1895, 1-1, May 16, 1895, 8-2, June 10, 1895, 6-4, June 12, 1895, 11-2, June 14, 1895, 10-3, May 31, 1902, 2-1; *CDN*, Mar. 7, 1895, 7-1, Mar. 15, 1895, 9-5, June 14, 1895, 1-4, May 31, 1902, 2-1; *Spirit* 129 (June 22, 1895): 812.

16. *CDN*, May 10, 1895, 1-1, May 11, 1895, 1-3, 3-1, "A Blow at the Race Track Gamblers," 12-4, May 13, 1895, 8-1, May 16, 1895, 1-3; *NYDT*, May 11, 1895, 3-2; *NPG* (June 1, 1895): 11; *Spirit* 129 (May 18, 1895): 615, 617; (May 25, 1895): 655–56; (June 8, 1892): 732; (June 15, 1895): 772; (June 22, 1895): 812; *CT*, May 11, 1895, 12-4, May 12, 1895, 2-3, June 5, 1895, 7-4, May 31, 1902, 2-1.

17. *CDN*, Mar. 7, 1895, 7-1, Mar. 15, 1895, 9-5, May 13, 1895, 8-1, May 16, 1895, 1-1; *NPG* (June 1, 1895): 11; *Spirit* 129 (June 8, 1892): 732; (June 15, 1895): 772; (June 22, 1895): 812.

18. *CDN*, May 16, 1895, 1-3, June 14, 1895, 1-4; *Spirit* 129 (May 25, 1895): 654; 129 (May 18, 1895): 616; *NYDT*, May 17, 1895, 4-1; *NYT*, Jan. 3, 1896.

19. *CDN*, June 5, 1895, 7-4; *NPG* (June 1, 1895): 11; *Spirit* 129 (June 8, 1892): 732; (June 15, 1895): 772; (June 22, 1895): 812; *CT*, June 5, 1895, 12-3 (quote).

20. *CT*, June 15, 1895, 7-3, June 25, 1897, 5-3; *CDN*, June 22, 1895, 1-7.

21. *CT*, June 14, 1895, 1-1, 10-3, June 15, 1895, 7-5, 7-3; *NYT*, June 17, 1910, 18-2; *Spirit* 130 (Sept. 7, 1895): 238.

22. *CT*, July 1, 1895, 4-3, July 8, 1895, 4-5, July 14, 1895, 4-4, July 27, 1895, 9-1, Sept. 13, 1895, 4-5, Aug. 1, 1896, 7-1, Aug. 29, 1896, 7-6, Aug. 30, 1896, 7-4, July 7, 1897, 4-1; *CDN*, July 25, 1895, 1-7; *NYDT*, May 5, 1897, 3-2; *Spirit* 130 (July 20, 1895): 6; 132 (Aug. 15, 1896): 127; (Aug. 29, 1896): 201; (Sept. 5, 1896): 227; 134 (Nov. 6, 1897): 456.

23. *BE*, Aug. 9, 1895, 5-6; *Spirit* 130 (Aug. 10, 1895): 102; (Aug. 31, 1895): 207. Washington Park in August hosted a brief trotting meet without bookmaking and lost about $12,000. *CT*, Aug. 1, 1896, 7-2.

24. *CDN*, Aug. 15, 1895, 1-1, Aug. 24, 1895, 1-1, Aug. 1, 1896, 7-2.

25. *Spirit* 130 (Sept. 7, 1895): 238; (Aug. 31, 1895): 207 (quote).

26. *CDN*, Nov. 21, 1895, 10-1.

27. *CT*, Aug. 30, 1891, 5-1, Apr. 9, 1892, 6, July 7, 1892, 7-4, Aug. 25, 1892, 7-2, Mar. 7, 1893, 7-2; *CDN*, Oct. 9, 1891, 2-1.

28. *NYT*, Sept. 2, 1895, 3-2 (quotes); *Spirit* 130 (Sept. 14, 1895): 270; *NPG* (Sept. 14, 1895): 10.

29. Pacyga, *Chicago: A Biography*, 155–57; Miller, *City of the Century*, 268–73.

30. *CT*, Sept. 13, 1895, 4-5, Sept. 17, 1895, 7-1; *Indiana ex rel. Claude Matthews v. Edward Roby et al.*, 142 Indiana 700.

31. *Spirit* 129 (June 1, 1895): 695; (June 8, 1895): 732, 130 (Sept. 14, 1895): 270; *TFF* 61 (Aug. 30, 1895): 293; *CT*, Sept. 6, 1895, 5-1, Sept. 30, 1895, 5-5.

32. *Spirit* 131 (May 9, 1896): 537; 132 (Aug. 1, 1896): 75; 134 (Oct. 30, 1897): 423; (Nov. 6, 1897): 456; *CT*, May 3, 1896, 4-4, May 5, 1896, 4-3, July 18, 1896, 7-5, Aug. 1, 1896, 7-1, June 24, 1897, 5-1, July 7, 1897, 4-1; *CDN*, Mar. 3, 1896, 6-1, Mar. 8, 1896, 8-1; *Indianapolis News*, May 22, 1896, 5-1; *NYDT*, May 7, 1896, 8-2, May 5, 1897, 3-2.

33. Schulman, "'Making the Magazine,'" 9, 23.

34. Chatfield-Taylor, "Country Club Life in Chicago," 761.

35. *CT*, Oct. 26, 1897, 4-5, Aug. 14, 1898, 3-5.

36. *CT*, Sept. 22, 1896, 1-3, Aug. 14, 1898, 3-5.

37. *CT*, Dec. 11, 1896, 8-1.

38. *Spirit* 133 (Jan. 30, 1897): 68; (Feb. 20, 1897): 162. On the connection between traction lines and spectator sports, see Riess, *City Games*, 171, 181, 194, 208–9, 214–16; and Riess, *Sport of Kings*, 117.

39. *Spirit* 133 (Feb. 20, 1897): 162.

40. *CEJ*, Jan. 7, 1897, 8-1; Geiger, *Joseph W. Folk*, 89; *NYT*, Jan. 7, 1905, 1-6, Feb. 22, 1905, 2-2; *St. Louis Republic*, Feb. 20, 1901, 5-5, 6-4.

41. *CT*, Mar. 11, 1897, 8-5, Mar. 19, 1897, 8-3, Apr. 14, 1897, 5-1; Raum, *Illinois Republicanism*, 488.

42. *CT*, May 7, 1897, 6-3, May 27, 1897, 5-3; *Spirit* 133 (Apr. 17, 1897): 398; (May 1, 1897): 472; (May 22, 1897): 577; (May 29, 1897): 606 (quote); (June 12, 1897): 656, 666.

43. *CEJ*, June 2, 1897, 7-1; *CT*, May 10, 1897, 4-4, May 27, 1897, 5-3, June 2, 1897, 5, June 3, 1897, 6-3; *Spirit* 133 (Apr. 17, 1897): 398; (May 29, 1897): 606; (June 12, 1897): 658, 666; (June 19, 1897): 697; (June 26, 1897): 718.

44. Finegold, *Experts and Politicians*, 127–30; S. Roberts, "Municipal Voters' League"; Flanagan, "Grey Wolves."

45. *Spirit* 134 (Dec. 25, 1897): 688.

46. *DAB*, s.v. "Carter H. Harrison II"; *CT*, Mar. 15, 1897, 4-7; Green, "Chicago Democratic Party," 77; Lindberg, *Gambler King*, 139.

47. *Spirit* 133 (Apr. 1, 1897): 398; "Chicago Mayors, 1837–2007."

48. *CT*, Aug. 1, 1897, 3-5, 25-1, May 10, 1911, 13-4, Aug. 20, 1912, 1-6; *Spirit* 132 (July 18, 1896): 6; (Aug. 15, 1896): 125; (Nov. 28, 1896): 598; 134 (Oct. 30, 1897): 423; 138 (Aug. 5, 1899): 80–81; 143 (May 17, 1902): 363; 144 (Nov. 29, 1902): 408; *BE*, Aug. 7, 1896, 7-3; *NYT*, Oct. 16, 1900, 1-3.

49. Lindberg, *Gambler King*, 175–87; *CT*, Aug. 14, 1907, 5-1.

50. *CT*, May 9, 1897, 7-1, May 14, 1897, 7-1, May 21, 1897, 7-1; Aaron Mercavith, "Oh What Fun We Had: A Look at Recreation in Rhode Island," http://www.marcavitch.com/research/ca/amparks/senior/sport.html.

51. *CT*, May 20, 1897, 5-1; *Spirit* 133 (May 29, 1897): 598; (June 19, 1897): 697.

52. *CT*, May 20, 1897, 5-1, June 24, 1897, 5-1, July 7, 1897, 4-1; *Spirit* 133 (May 29, 1897): 598; (June 19, 1897): 697; 134 (Nov. 6, 1897): 456.

53. *CT*, May 17, 1895, 8-3, July 7, 1897, 4-1, July 14, 1897, 4-4, June 26, 1900, 9-2, Aug. 8, 1901, 3-7, Aug. 10, 1901, 3-1, Aug. 27, 1903, 4-4; *Spirit* 133 (July 10, 1897): 774; (July 17, 1897): 799; 134 (Oct. 30, 1897): 423; (Nov. 13, 1897): 487; (Nov. 20, 1897): 534.

54. *CT*, July 12, 1897, 4-1, July 14, 1897, 4-4; *Spirit* 134 (July 31, 1897): 32–33. Cook County was divided into twenty-nine townships, governmental districts that provided certain public services like security or road maintenance.

55. *CT*, July 15, 1897, 4-4 (quote). The *Spirit* reported daily attendance at Harlem in the range of seven to eight thousand, which was much higher than local reports. *Spirit* 134 (July 31, 1897): 32–33.

56. *TFF* 65 (July 30, 1897): 143; *Spirit* 134 (July 31, 1897): 29 (quote); (Sept. 25, 1897): 255; (Nov. 6, 1897): 456; *CT*, July 23, 1897, 10-4, July 24, 1897, 6-3, Aug. 2, 1897, 4-5. Clark committed suicide two years later, fearful of ending up in poverty, having lost his wealth in the 1893 stock-market crash and then lost his family legacy at Churchill Downs. Sarah Pruitt, "The Man behind the Kentucky Derby," https://www.history.com/news/the-man-behind-the-kentucky-derby. Windsor mayors in the late nineteenth century were either on the local track's executive or held shares in the association. See Waters, "'Operating on the Border,'" 31.

57. *CEJ*, Aug. 12, 1897, 7-1.

58. *CT*, Aug. 2, 1897, 4-5; *CEJ*, Aug. 2, 1897, 7-1; *Spirit* 134 (Aug. 14, 1897): 90.

59. *Spirit* 134 (Sept. 25, 1897): 255 (quote); (Nov. 6, 1897): 456.

60. *Spirit* 134 (Oct. 30, 1897): 423 (quote); (Nov. 6, 1897): 456; (Dec. 25, 1897): 688; *CT*, Aug. 10, 1915, 10-2.

61. *Spirit* 134 (Dec. 25, 1897): 688.

62. *CT*, Jan. 7, 1898, 5-1, Jan. 20, 1898, 7-1, May 17, 1919, 5-1; *Spirit* 135 (Feb. 2, 1898): 130; (Feb. 26, 1898): 191.

63. *CT*, Mar. 26, 1898, 7-3, Apr. 8, 1898, 4-1, Apr. 14, 1898, 7-1.

64. *CT*, Apr. 14, 1898, 7-1; *Spirit* 135 (Apr. 23, 1898): 431 (quote); (May 21, 1898): 532.

65. *CT*, May 23, 1898, 9-3, Sept. 18, 1899, 10-3, Sept. 24, 1899, 18-2, Aug. 27, 1903, 4-2, Jan. 12, 1954, 14-2; Wendt and Kogan, *Bet-a-Million!*, 177–82, 241–43, 250–51, 329; Wall, *How Kentucky Became Southern*, 179.

66. *CT*, May 23, 1898, 9-3, May 24, 1898, 4-3, May 25, 1898, 4-5, June 15, 1898, 10-3; *Spirit* 135 (May 28, 1898): 560; (June 4, 1898): 588; "George Siler," http://boxrec.com/media/index.php/George_Siler.

67. *CT*, June 15, 1898, 10-3; *Spirit* 135 (May 28, 1898): 560; (June 25, 1898): 667.

68. *CT*, June 23, 1898, 4-3.

69. *CT*, June 26, 1898, 3-3, July 12, 1898, 5-4, July 26, 1898, 4-1; *Spirit* 136 (Nov. 12, 1898): 419.

70. *CT*, June 26, 1898, 1-3, 3-1.

71. *CT*, June 26, 1898, 28-3.

72. *CT*, May 7, 1898, 5-4, June 30, 1898, 5-3, July 1, 1898, 5-5 (quote), July 7, 1898, 4-6 (quote), July 12, 1898, 5-4; *Spirit* 135 (July 9, 1898): 722.

73. *CT*, July 12, 1898, 5-4.

74. *CT*, July 19, 1898, 12-1, July 26, 1898, 4-1, July 28, 1898, 12-4; *Spirit* 137 (July 8, 1899): 1255; 138 (Aug. 19, 1899): 128.

75. *CT*, July 26, 1898, 4-1; *Spirit* 136 (Nov. 12, 1898): 419.

76. *CT*, Oct. 26, 1897, 4-5, Apr. 8, 1898, 4-1; *Los Angeles Herald*, Nov. 4, 1904, 10.

77. *CT*, July 13, 1898, 4-5, July 22, 1898, 4-7, Aug. 5, 1898, 4-4, Aug. 12, 1898, 4-3, July 4, 1900, 6-6, July 9, 1900, 8-4, Dec. 23, 1900, 20-5, Dec. 13, 1933, 20-1; *Spirit* 135 (Apr. 23, 1898): 431; (May 12, 1898): 532; 136 (Aug. 20, 1898): 128.

78. *CT*, July 24, 1898, 3-5, July 25, 1898, 4-7 (quote), Aug. 5, 1898, 4-4, Sept. 14, 1898, 5-5.

79. *CT*, July 24, 1898, 6-3, July 25, 1898, 4, July 28, 1898; *Spirit* 136 (Aug. 6, 1898): 81 (quote).

80. *CT*, Sept. 2, 1898, 12-3.

81. *CT*, Aug. 9, 1898, 4-3, Aug. 12, 1898, 4-3; *Spirit* 136 (Aug. 13, 1898): 124; (Aug. 20, 1898): 128; (Sept. 17, 1898): 198.

82. *CT*, Aug. 14, 1898, 1-1.

83. *CT*, Aug. 14, 1898, 1-1; *Spirit* 136 (Aug. 20, 1898): 128.

84. *CT*, Aug. 5, 1898, 5-3, Aug. 16, 1898, 4-4.

85. *Spirit* 136 (Oct. 29, 1898): 367; (Nov. 5, 1898): 390; (Nov. 12, 1898): 419; 139 (June 9, 1900): 444; 140 (Sept. 29, 1900): 297–98; (Nov. 10, 1900): 417; *CT*, Oct. 25, 1898, 4-1, Nov. 16, 1898, 4-1, Nov. 19, 1899, 19-5, Apr. 21, 1903, 6-3; Martin, "Racetrack Plunger Riley Grannan"; Hertz, *Racing Memoirs of John Hertz*, 16.

86. *Spirit* 136 (Oct. 15, 1898): 323; (Oct. 22, 1898): 343.

87. *Spirit* 136 (July 30, 1898): 62; (Sept. 3, 1898): 172; (Oct. 15, 1898): 323; (Oct. 22, 1898): 343; (Oct. 29, 1898): 367; (Nov. 5, 1898): 390; (Nov. 19, 1898): 450; (Dec. 24, 1898): 564; 137 (Apr. 8, 1899): 936 (quote); *CT*, Mar. 1, 1899, 4-1.

88. *Spirit* 136 (Nov. 5, 1898): 390; *CT*, Aug. 27, 1903, 4-3, July 5, 1924, 8-9. Fitzgerald's name first came up in 1893 when he and two partners bought the 66.8 acres of the CRA's excess land for $267,200, a 175 percent profit. *CT*, Mar. 28, 1893, 1. Some question if he actually ever bought any of Corrigan's shares. *CT*, Mar. 12, 1904, 8-1. On Tuthill, see E. Clapp, *Mothers of All Children*, 179–80.

89. *CT*, Feb. 24, 1899, 7-3, Feb. 27, 1899, 4-1; Riess, *Sport of Kings*, 203–4.

90. *CT*, Feb. 27, 1899, 4-1, Mar. 24, 1899, 4-3, Apr. 8, 1899, 6-2, Apr. 9, 1899, 7-1; *Spirit* 137 (Apr. 15, 1899): 969.

91. *CT*, July 26, 1898, 4-1, July 28, 1898, 12-4, Dec. 11, 1898, 7-3; *NYT*, Feb. 19, 1899, 9-1; *Spirit* 137 (July 8, 1899): 1255; 138 (Aug. 19, 1899): 128.

92. *CT*, Nov. 16, 1899, 4-1.

93. *CT*, May 15, 1899, 4-3, Mar. 19, 1900, 19-5; *New York Sun*, May 19, 1899, 8-4; *Spirit* 137 (June 6, 1899): 1160; (July 8, 1899): 1255; 138 (Aug. 19, 1899): 128; (Nov. 4, 1899): 400.

94. *CT*, Mar. 1, 1899, 4-1, May 9, 1899, 3-4, May 23, 1899, 7-4, June 26, 1899, 4-3; *Spirit* 138 (Dec. 16, 1899): 539.

95. *NYT*, Sept. 17, 1898, 5-1; *CT*, Mar. 25, 1900, 19-5.

96. *Spirit* 136 (July 30, 1898): 62; (Aug. 6, 1898): 81; 138 (Aug. 19, 1899): 128; (Dec. 16, 1899): 539; *CT*, Feb. 27, 1899, 4-1 (quote), Mar. 1, 1899, 4-1, May 28, 1899, 15-1; Gurlace, "Cicero, IL."

97. *Spirit* 136 (July 30, 1898): 62; (Aug. 6, 1898): 81; 138 (Aug. 5, 1899): 81; (Aug. 12, 1899): 103; (Aug. 19, 1899): 128; (Dec. 16, 1899): 539; *CT*, Feb. 7, 1899, 4-1 (quote), Mar. 1, 1899, 4-1, May 28, 1899, 15-1, Mar. 25, 1900, 19-4.

98. *Spirit* 138 (Nov. 4, 1899): 399–400; *CT*, Oct. 29, 1899, 19-3, Nov. 16, 1899, 4-1 (quote), Nov. 19, 1899, 19-5.

99. *CT*, Nov. 19, 1899, 19-5.

100. *CT*, June 26, 1899, 4-3.

101. *CT*, Oct. 1, 1899, 20-3.

102. *Spirit* 138 (Dec. 16, 1899): 539.

103. Wills, "Eclipse of the Thoroughbred Industry in Tennessee," 167; Robertson, *History of Thoroughbred Racing*, 196; Riess, *Sport of Kings*, 122–36, 163–64, 214–24. My extremely detailed source included virtually all races run in the United States and Canada, including steeplechases, hurdles, and heats. The data includes purses and names of the top competitors. See *Goodwin's Annual Turf Book [1882–1908]*.

104. Rasmussen, *Carnival in the Countryside*, 45–49; Ownby, *Subduing Satan*, 191.

105. The importance of cultural and social issues is stressed in Jensen, *Winning of the Midwest*; Kleppner, *Cross of Culture*; and McSeveney, *Politics of Depression*.

6. From Glory Days to Collapse, 1900–1905

1. "1900 Major League Attendance & Team Age," https://www.baseball -reference.com/leagues/MLB/1900-misc.shtml; "1909 Major League Attendance & Team Age," https://www.baseball-reference.com/leagues/MLB/1909-misc.shtml.

2. Riess, "History of Sports in Chicago," 18–20, 22, 24; Chapman, *Frank Gotch*, 101–12.

3. Riess, "History of Sports in Chicago," 3–5, 10–17; Logan, "Soccer"; Lovell, *Century of Urban Life*, 132–33.

4. Riess, "History of Sports in Chicago," 17–18.

5. Riess, "History of Sports in Chicago," 10, 17–18; Mallon, *1904 Olympic Games*, 88.

6. Riess, *City Games*, 54–55, 70–71, 93, 184–86, 211; Riess, "History of Sports in Chicago," 18–20; Duis, *Saloon*; Riess, "Leisure"; Herzig, "Germans." On the police and early organized crime, see Lindberg, *To Serve and Collect*; and Mitrani, *Rise of the Chicago Police Department*.

7. McGerr, *Fierce Discontent*; Link and McCormick, *Progressivism*.

8. On progressivism and sports, see Riess, *City Games*, 132–34, 151–53, 158–68, 186–87. On social reform in Chicago, see Diner, *City and Its Universities* ; Flanagan, *Seeing with Their Hearts*; and Geti, *Juvenile Court*.

9. *Spirit* 141 (Dec. 14, 1901): 976 (quote); *CT*, Nov. 16, 1899, 4-1, Feb. 11, 1900, 18-7, Feb. 18, 1900, 18-4, Mar. 7, 1900, 6-1, Mar. 11, 1900, 17-3, Mar. 23, 1900, 9-1, Mar. 25, 1900, 19-1.

10. *NYMT*, Oct. 2, 1899, 5-1; *Spirit* 139 (June 16, 1900): 459; *CT*, June 21, 1900, 6-4 (quote), June 22, 1900, 6-4, June 23, 1900, 5-4; Chicago Board of Trade, *Annual Report, 1883*, 4.

11. *CT*, June 22, 1900, 6-4 (quote), 24-3.

12. *CT*, June 24, 1900, 1-1, 3-3, 3-7 (quote); *Spirit* 139 (June 30, 1900): 494.

13. *CT*, June 24, 1900, 3-3.

14. *Spirit* 139 (June 30, 1900): 494; *CT*, June 24, 1900, 3-4; *NYT*, June 24, 1900, 18-7, July 5, 1900, 8-7; Brolaski, *Easy Money*, 198 (quote).

15. *Spirit* 139 (June 16, 1900): 459; 140 (Aug. 4, 1900): 68; (Sept. 22, 1900): 284; (Oct. 13, 1900): 342.

16. *Spirit* 139 (June 16, 1900): 459; 140 (Aug. 4, 1900): 68; (Oct. 27, 1900): 377; *CT*, Aug. 6, 1900, 8-4, Aug. 13, 1900, 8-3.

17. *CT*, Aug. 18, 1900, 6-3; *Spirit* 140 (Aug. 25, 1900): 123.

18. *CT*, Aug. 25, 1900, 7-3 (quote), Oct. 5, 1900, 3-4; *Spirit* 140 (Nov. 17, 1900): 440; "Brief History of Oak Park."

19. *Spirit* 140 (Dec. 15, 1900): 517–18; (Sept. 29, 1900): 298.

20. *Spirit* 140 (Sept. 29, 1900): 297–98; (Nov. 10, 1900): 417; Somers, *Rise of Sports in New Orleans*, 103.

21. *Spirit* 140 (Sept. 29, 1900): 297–98; (Nov. 10, 1900): 417; (Dec. 15, 1900): 517–18; (Sept. 29, 1900): 298.

22. *Spirit* 141 (Feb. 9, 1901): 91; (Feb. 23, 1901): 122; *San Francisco Call*, Apr. 2, 1901, 4; *Spokane Press*, June 7, 1905, 4.

23. *Spirit* 140 (Sept. 29, 1900): 297–98; (Nov. 10, 1900): 417; 143 (May 6, 1902): 343. The *Tribune* reported that O'Brien bought the eighty-five-acre site in October 1900 for $28,899. *CT*, Oct. 24, 1900, 16-1.

24. *CT*, Mar. 25, 1900, 19-1, Nov. 11, 1900, 20-1, Nov. 28, 1900, 6-1, Jan. 27, 1901, 17-6, Apr. 14, 1901, 17-3, May 3, 1901, 7-1; *Spirit* 141 (May 1, 1901): 352.

25. *CT*, June 1, 1901, 6-5, June 2, 1901, 19-4, Sept. 30, 1901, 8-1, 6-4, Nov. 3, 1901, 17-1, Nov. 11, 1901, 6-3, 6-7, Aug. 27, 1903, 5-4, Aug. 28, 1903, 2-5, Feb. 8, 1919, 13-3. The state closed the Chicago Constabulary in 1906. See Lindberg, *To Serve and Collect*, 101.

26. *CT*, Mar. 1, 1901, 1-5, Mar. 2, 1901, 4-2, Apr. 14, 1901, 17-4, June 19, 1901, 17-6, June 29, 1901, 1-5; *Spirit* 141 (July 6, 1901): 508; Brolaski, *Easy Money*, 204, 206–10; Chafetz, *Play the Devil*, 379–80.

27. *Spirit* 141 (June 2, 1901): 467; (Dec. 14, 1901): 976 (quote); *CT*, June 23, 1901, 2-1, Nov. 11, 1901, 6-7.

28. *CT*, June 23, 1901, 2-3; *Spirit* 141 (June 2, 1901): 467; (Dec. 14, 1901): 976; "St. Edward of Lexington"; *NYT*, Aug. 16, 1946, 15-1.

29. *CT*, July 3, 1901, 1-5, July 5, 1901, 1-6, July 7, 1901, 2-5, July 20, 1901, 8-3.

30. *CT*, Aug. 8, 1901, 3-7, Aug. 9, 1901, 3-1, Aug. 10, 1901, 3-1, Aug. 11, 1901, 8-2.

31. *CT*, Oct. 17, 1901, 17-1.

32. *CT*, Nov. 11, 1901, 6-7, Dec. 2, 1901, 6-3.

33. *CT*, May 31, 1902, 1-7, 2-1; *Spirit* 143 (June 7, 1902): 428.

34. *Spirit* 143 (June 7, 1902): 428; *CT*, Aug. 10, 1902, 9-2, Aug. 18, 1902, 4-6; Lindberg, *Chicago by Gaslight*, 163–64; Brandt, *Chicago Death Trap*; Riess, *Touching Base*, 114–17.

35. *CT*, May 11, 1902, 9-6, June 20, 1902, 6-3, June 21, 1902, 1-7.

36. *CT*, June 22, 1902, 1-7, 2-1, 3-2, 4-7. The huge attendances reported at this time were not recognized as records by racing organizations. The *Daily Racing Form* claimed that the spectatorship included thirty-five to forty thousand in the grandstand, clubhouse, and betting ring, "and the lawn in front of the stand was one solid mass of humanity." *DRF*, June 24, 1902, 1.

37. *CT*, June 22, 1902, 1-7, Nov. 18, 1903, 6-2.

38. Wendt and Kogan, *Bet-a-Million!*, 133, 180, 181, 243; *NYT*, Aug. 31, 1901, 1-7; *CT*, Aug. 2, 1938, 18-8.

39. *CT*, May 11, 1902, 9-6, June 19, 1902, 5-4 (quote), June 20, 1902, 6-5.

40. *CT*, June 22, 1902, 3-4; Riess, *Touching Base*, 37.

41. *CT*, Nov. 21, 1902, 7-1.

42. *CT*, Nov. 21, 1902, 7-1.

43. *CT*, Apr. 18, 1903, 1-5, Apr. 29, 1903, 7-6, Dec. 27, 1903, 11-13.

44. *CT*, Apr. 29, 1903, 7-6, June 21, 1903, 1-7, 2-7, 4-1; Dec. 27, 1903, 11-3; *DRF*, June 21, 1903. When fifty thousand attended the Belmont Stakes in 1906, it was cited as the largest racing audience in American history. *NYT*, May 31, 1906, 8-2.

45. *St. Louis Republic*, Nov. 6, 1903, 1; *CT*, Dec. 27, 1903, 31-3.

46. *CT*, Jan. 25, 1903, 10-1, June 5, 1903, 8-5, Mar. 12, 1904, 8-1; "The Chicago Racing Field" [1903], in author's possession; "Who Wins at Racetracks?," *Los Angeles Times*, May 25, 1906, 11-8; *St. Louis Republic*, Nov. 6, 1903, 1.

47. *CT*, July 9, 1903, 1-4, July 10, 1903, 1-4, July 11, 1903, 5-3, July 12, 1903, 5-3, July 16, 1903, 3-7, July 30, 1903, 3-3, Aug. 9, 1903, 1-7, 9-2, Aug. 10, 1903, 11-5, Aug. 11, 1903, 4-1, Aug. 12, 1903, 3-7; *NYT*, Aug. 6, 1903, 3-3.

48. *CT*, Oct. 19, 1903, 1-3, Nov. 7, 1903, 6-4; *NYT*, Nov. 26, 1995, S9-2.

49. *CT*, Dec. 3, 1896, 1-7, Oct. 19, 1903, 1-3, Oct. 20, 1903, 6-1, 8-5, Oct. 25, 1903, 13-1, Nov. 7, 1903, 6-4.

50. *CT*, June 13, 1885, 10-4, Sept. 21, 1897, 4-5, Dec. 3, 1901, 3-4, Dec. 25, 1901, 6-1, Dec. 28, 1901, 6-1; Johnston and Curtin, *Chicago Boxing*, 1–2; Riess, "History of Sports in Chicago," 19; Dunn, *Chicago's Greatest Sportsman*, 73–76, 407.

51. On the history of boxing, see Gorn, *Manly Art*; Sammons, *Beyond the Ring*; Boddy, *Boxing: A Cultural History*; and Gems, *Boxing*. On boxing's legalization, see Somers, *Rise of Sports in New Orleans*, 174–78; and Ettinger, "John Fitzpatrick," 348.

52. Riess, *City Games*, 171–202; Riess, "Sports and Machine Politics"; Morrow and Wamsley, *Sport in Canada*, 164. On politics and boxing in San Francisco, see Thomas, *Debonair Scoundrel*, 173, 191–93; and Bean, *Boss Ruef's San Francisco*, 85–88.

53. Johnston and Curtin, *Chicago Boxing*, 1–2; Riess, "History of Sports in Chicago," 19; Dunn, *Chicago's Greatest Sportsman*, 73–76, 407.

54. *CT*, Dec. 14, 1900, 4-1, Dec. 18, 1900, 1-5, Dec. 23, 1900, 17-1, Dec. 28, 1901, 6-1, Feb. 25, 1906, sec. 2, 4-3; Aycock and Scott, *Joe Gans*, 63–81; "McGovern Stops Gans This Day in Boxing, Dec. 13, 1900," https://www.youtube.com/watch?v=96xYoeThSGs.

55. *CT*, July 17, 1904, 3-7, Oct. 7, 1904, 8-7, Oct. 9, 1904, 3-4, Nov. 15, 1904, 3-1, 1-7, Dec. 16, 1904, 5-4; *CRH*, Sept. 24, 1905, 2-7, Oct. 18, 1905, 6-1.

56. *CT*, Apr. 10, 1904, 4-2, 11-1, Aug. 10, 1915, 10-2; "Who Wins at Racetracks?"

57. *CT*, Apr. 5, 1904, 1-6, 3-1, Apr. 10, 1904, 11-1, 11-2, June 22, 1904, 9-1, June 23, 1904, 10-6.

58. "Herman Schuettler," in *Historical Dictionary of Law Enforcement*, ed. Roth and Olson, 312; O'Brien, *Blood Runs Green*.

59. Lindberg, *To Serve and Collect*, 102; *CT*, Apr. 20, 1904, 3-3 (quote), Apr. 22, 1904, 6-2, 11-1, Aug. 23, 1918, 1-2; "Herman Schuettler," 312. Chicago's first flying squads were introduced by Carter Harrison to fight street robberies and holdups in early December 1903. See *CT*, Dec. 2, 1903, 1-4.

60. *CT*, Apr. 24, 1904, 11-1.

61. *CT*, Apr. 11, 1904, 8-1, May 1, 1904, 9-7, May 21, 1904, 4-2; Riess, *City Games*, 186.

62. *CRH*, May 21, 1904, 2-5 (quote); *CT*, May 22, 1904, 9-7, May 23, 1904, 7-1.

63. *CT*, June 11, 1904, 1-4.

64. *CT*, June 11, 1904, 1-4 (quote), June 12, 1904, 3-1, June 15, 1904, 7-3, June 16, 1904, 1-4 (quote); *CRH*, June 11, 1904, 2-3.

65. *CT*, May 23, 1904, 7-1, June 11, 1904, 1-4, June 12, 1904, 3-2; Flynt, "Men behind the Poolroom Interests," 643.

66. *CDN*, June 14, 1904, 2-4; *CIO*, June 17, 1904, 6-3.

67. *CIO*, June 12, 1904, 1-3, June 16, 1904, 2-7, 3-1; *Joseph Swigert v. The People of the State of Illinois* (1895).

68. *CT*, June 14, 1904, 3-7.

69. *CE*, Apr. 11, 1904, 5-5; *CDN*, June 10, 1904, 2-2.

70. *CDN*, June 15, 1904, 7-3, June 16, 1904, 1-4.

71. *CT*, June 18, 1904, 1-7, June 19, 1904, 4-3; *CRH*, June 18, 1904, 2-3; *CIO*, June 19, 1904, 1-5.

72. *CT*, June 19, 1904, 1, 2, 4-6, June 20, 1904, 10-5, Aug. 6, 1931, 19; *CDN*, June 16, 1904, 3-1; Pike, "The American Derby."

73. *CT*, June 19, 1904, 1-7, June 20, 1904, 10-5.

74. *CT*, June 20, 1904, 10-5, June 21, 1904, 9-1, June 22, 1904, 10-4.

75. *CT*, June 16, 1904, 1-4, June 20, 1904, 10-5, June 22, 1904, 9-1, June 23, 1904, 10-5; *NYT*, June 22, 1904, 10-4; *CRH*, June 23, 1904, 9-1; *New York Evening World*, June 22, 1904, 10-7.

76. *CT*, June 23, 1904, 10-5 (quote); Harrison, "The Dope Sheet"; *CRH*, July 8, 1904, 16-1, 8-3.

77. *CT*, Apr. 9, 1905, 4-1.

78. *CT*, June 29, 1904, 3-1; *CRH*, June 29, 1904, 3-4.

79. *CT*, June 24, 1904, 16-1, June 26, 1904, June 29, 1904, 3-1; Citizens' Association of Chicago, *Annual Report*, 5-7.

80. *CT*, July 2, 1904, 1-4.

81. *CT*, July 22, 1904, 1-6, July 27, 1904, 1-3, 2-6, July 31, 1904, 8-1, Aug. 5, 1904, 3-1.

82. *CT*, July 22, 1904, 1-6, July 23, 1904, 3-6, July 24, 1904, 4-1.

83. *CT*, July 27, 1904, 1-3.

84. *CT*, Aug. 3, 1904, 6-7, Aug. 5, 1904, 3-1 (quote).

85. *CT*, Oct. 31, 1904, 8-5.

86. *CT*, Jan. 1, 1905, 9-7 (quote).

87. Riess, *Sport of Kings*, 243.

88. *St. Louis Post-Dispatch*, May 7, 1905, IV: 5-2.

89. *CT*, Dec. 22, 1904, 5-3, Jan. 1, 1905, 9-7.

90. *CT*, Feb. 19, 1905, 15-5, Mar. 16, 1905, 10-5, Mar. 28, 1905, 6-2; *CDN*, Mar. 14, 1905, 8-7, May 6, 1905, 10-4.

91. "Chicago Mayors, 1837–2007"; R. Morton, "Edward F. Dunne," 221–22; R. Morton, *Justice and Humanity*, 1.

92. *CT*, Apr. 4, 1905, 4-1, Apr. 20, 1905, 7-3 (quote), Apr. 27, 1905, 1-4 (quote), 6-1; *CDN*, Apr. 20, 1905, 1-7, Apr. 27, 1905, 4-1.

93. *CT*, Apr. 4, 1905, 5-1; *CDN*, Apr. 28, 1905, 8-2.

94. *CDN*, Apr. 28, 1905, 8-2; "The Biter Bit," *CT*, Apr. 28, 1905, 8-1.

95. *CT*, Apr. 26, 1905, 6-6, Apr. 29, 1905, 10-5. Worth anticipated spending $3,200 a day in purses and $1,500 for other expenses. *CRH*, Apr. 27, 1904, 1-4.

96. *CT*, Apr. 27, 1905, 6-1, Apr. 30, 1905, A1-6; *CRH*, Apr. 27, 1904, 1-4.

97. Hmurovic "Horse Racing"; Piott, *Holy Joe*, 94.

98. "Law Enforcement in Missouri"; Piott, *Holy Joe*, 96–97; Carver, *Making Tracks*, 263–80.

99. Mikkelsen, "Sport of Kings in Victorian Canada," 21; Waters, "'Operating on the Border,'" 50; Metcalfe, *Canada Learns to Play*, 150; J. Thomas West, "Thoroughbred Racing." As late as 1903, there were twenty-six minor courses in Canada, running meets of a day or two, but they virtually all closed up. See *Goodwin's Annual Turf Guide for 1903*.

100. Joyce, "Canadian Sport and Social Control," 22, 31; Armstrong and Nelles, *Revenge of the Methodist Bicycle Company*, 4, 156–68.

101. Stephen Azzi, "Federal Government"; Waters, "'Operating on the Border,'" 53.

102. Foster, *Moral Reconstruction*, 228, 231, 244.

103. Werbel, *Lust on Trial*; Abrams, "Polygamy, Prostitution, and the Federalization of Immigration Law."

104. *NYT*, May 12, 1908, 2-2; Otis, "Washington's Lost Racetracks," 149–51; Kent Boese, "Lost Washington: Benning Race Track," https://ggwash.org/view /4055/lost-washington2--benning-race-track. On March 13, 1894, commissioners from the district asked the Senate to tighten the 1883 act on gambling, and a bill passed the Senate, thirty-four to eleven, to ban bookmaking, but it was never enacted. *Washington Times*, Apr. 5, 1894, 4; "Gambling in the District of Columbia," 250; US Congress, Senate, *Reports of Committees of the Senate*; US Congress, Senate, Committee on the Judiciary, *Interstate Racing by Telegraph*; US Congress, Senate,

Committee on the Judiciary, *Interstate Race Gambling*; Blakey and Kurland "Development of the Federal Law of Gambling," 928.

105. Brown, "Thoroughbred Horse-Racing," 252; Waters, "'Operating on the Border,'" 42 (quote), 44–45.

106. Waters, "'Operating on the Border,'" 44–46; *Saturday Night* (Dec. 11, 1909): 1, quoted in Waters, "'Operating on the Border,'" 80.

107. Waters, "'Operating on the Border,'" 54, 55, 64, 72n, 150; Brown, "Thoroughbred Horse-Racing," 252, 255, 257; Morton, *At Odds*, 9–12; Metcalfe, *Canada Learns to Play*, 151; Martel, *Canada the Good*, 79.

108. Brown, "Thoroughbred Horse-Racing," 258–59, 264.

109. Brown, "Thoroughbred Horse-Racing," 252, 260; Waters, "'Operating on the Border,'" 23–24.

110. Brown, "Thoroughbred Horse-Racing," 256, 260, 262; Waters, "'Operating on the Border,'" 53, 72.

111. *CT*, Apr. 8, 1910, 6-6; *NYT*, Apr. 15, 1910, 11-3; Brown, "Thoroughbred Horse-Racing," 262; Waters, "'Operating on the Border,'" 73, 77–81; Metcalfe, *Canada Learns to Play*, 151.

112. Mikkelsen, "Sport of Kings," 21; Waters, "'Operating on the Border,'" 91.

113. *CT*, June 20, 1909, G2, July 7, 1910, 3-4, July 11, 1910, 2-4, 7, Aug. 14, 1910, B3-3, July 1912, 8-6, Apr. 1924, 21-7, June 5, 1932, 73-2; P. Roberts, Taylor, and Weatherly, "Looking Back."

114. *CRH*, May 8, 1909, 7-1, May 21, 1909, 7-3; *CT*, July 7, 1910, 3-4, July 11, 1910, 2-4, 7, Aug. 14, 1910, B3-3, July 1912, 8-6, Apr. 1924, 21-7, Sept. 2, 1925, 12-1; *Day Book* (Chicago), Aug. 8, 1912, 11; Neil Milbert, "New Century of Memories," *CT*, Mar. 6, 2009, 2-5. Corrigan reportedly owned stock in Saratoga Springs that he sold to the disreputable racing promoter Gotfried Walbaum. See *St. Louis Republic*, Aug. 25, 1901, 26. On his New Orleans losses, see "The Anti-racing Crusade Cost This Man $3,000,000," *CT*, June 20, 1909, G2-1.

115. Riess, "History of Sports in Chicago," 27–28; *CT*, Apr. 27, 1905, 6-1, May 20, 1909, 7-4, Nov. 17, 1909, 14-4, Sept. 8, 1912, C4-1, Feb. 18, 1917, A2-2, Mar. 6, 2009, 2-5; "Anti-racing Crusade."

116. *CT*, Sept. 7, 1909, 5-1, 19-5, Sept. 6, 1910, 1-7, 16-1, July 4, 1911, 1-4, 13-1, July 5, 1911, 7-3, July 8, 1911, 1-5, July 9, 1911, 3-2, Aug. 24, 1911, 1-5, Sept. 3, 1911, 1-5, 4-2 (quote), Sept. 3, 1912, 1-6, Apr. 16, 1915, 12-5, Apr. 17, 1915, 12-4; *CRH*, Sept. 3, 1911, 4-2; "Racing Statistics of the Year 1911."

117. *NYT*, July 6, 1916, 4-2, July 15, 1916, 7-2, July 16, 1916, sec. 7, 2-5; *CDN*, July 15, 1916, 1-5; *CT*, May 10, 1916, 14-1, July 16, 1916, B1-7, July 20, 1916, 1-3, July 7, 1917, 8-6, Aug. 12, 1919, 16-5, Aug. 14, 1919, 12-5, Aug. 15, 1919, 18-7, Aug. 17, 1919, A4-5, July 10, 1922, 16-1, July 12, 1922, 21-3, Aug. 9, 1922, 14-6, Aug. 13, 1922, 29-7, Sept. 27, 1922, 16-6.

118. *CT*, Aug. 26, 1923, A5-1, Apr. 20, 1924, A1-7, Mar. 30, 1927, 22-6, Apr. 27, 1927, 17-3, May 4, 1927, 21-5, May 18, 1927, 23-2, May 19, 1927, 15-7, June 11, 1927, 17-2; *CDN*, Mar. 22, 1927, 23-8; *NYT*, Apr. 20, 1924, S5-1; Kirschner, *City and Country*, 108–11.

119. "Pimlico," http://www.pimlico.com/about/history.

120. Nicholson, *Kentucky Derby*, 24, 28–31; *Encyclopedia of Louisville*, s.v. "Charles F. Grainger"; *Grainger v. Kirby*; S. Otis, "Gambling on Horse Races," 12; Hillenbrand, "The Derby," 98–107.

121. Devereux, *Gambling and the Social Structure*, 31.

122. *CT*, Apr. 27, 1905, 6-1.

7. James O'Leary, Mont Tennes, and Offtrack Gambling in Chicago, 1895–1911

1. McKibbin, "Working-Class Gambling in Britain," 147–78.

2. US Congress, Senate, Committee on Interstate Commerce, *Prevention of Transmission of Race-Gambling Bets*, 52; Flynt, "Pool-Room Vampire," 359 (quote); Flynt, "Pool-Room Spider"; Flynt, "Men behind the Pool-Rooms"; Flynt, "Telegraph and Telephone Companies; Flynt, "Partners of the Criminal Pool-Rooms."

3. Flynt, "Pool-Room Victim," 360 (quote), 368; Flynt, "Pool-Room Spider," 513 (quote); Flynt, "Men behind the Poolrooms," 643 (quote); Hugh S. Fullerton, "Millions Spent on Sport but Workers Get Little," *CT*, May 7, 1905, D1.

4. *CDN*, Sept. 19, 1895, 2-4; *CT*, Nov. 7, 1895.

5. *CT*, June 13, 1896, 1-1, June 16, 1896, 7-6.

6. *CT*, June 13, 1896, 1-1, June 14, 1896, 9-3.

7. *CT*, June 13, 1896, 1-1, June 14, 1896, 9-3 (quote), June 16, 1896, 7-6.

8. *CT*, June 14, 1896, 9-3.

9. *CT*, June 16, 1896, 7-6.

10. *CT*, Jan. 3, 1896, 1-5, Aug. 30, 1896, 1-3, 39-1 (quote).

11. *CT*, Aug. 30, 1896, 1-3, 39-1.

12. *CT*, 1-3, 39-1, 39-3.

13. *CT*, Aug. 30, 1896, 1-3 (quote), 39-1, 39-3, Oct. 14, 1896, 7-5, Oct. 16, 1896, 9-7; Goodspeed and Healy, *History of Cook County*, 1:741–42.

14. *CT*, Sept. 11, 1896, 12-3, Oct. 18, 1896, 8-6.

15. *CT*, Dec. 13, 1896, 1-3.

16. *CT*, Dec. 14, 1896, 2-7.

17. *Spirit* 134 (Nov. 27, 1897): 571; (Oct. 30, 1897): 423; 132 (Dec. 19, 1896): 670; 134 (Aug. 14, 1897): 90 (quote); (Sept. 16, 1897): 256; (Oct. 9, 1897): 324.

18. Flynt, "Pool-Room Vampire," 368–70; Flynt, "Pool-Room Spider"; Flynn, "Smart Money," 54.

19. Flynt, "Pool-Room Vampire," 368–70; Flynt, "Pool-Room Spider; Flynn, "Smart Money," 54; Ogden, *Legacy*, 96.

20. *CT*, Oct. 19, 1911, 1-7, 2-1; Flynt, "Pool-Room Vampire," 368–70; Flynt, "Pool-Room Spider"; Riess, *Sport of Kings*, 205–6; Landesco, *Organized Crime in Chicago*, 63–64.

21. *CT*, Jan. 1, 1898, 4-1, "Censuring the City Authorities," Jan. 2, 1898, 28-1, Jan. 7, 1898, 12-2, Jan. 8, 1898, 8-2, Jan. 12, 1898, 1-1, Feb. 10, 1898, 7-1. For the Berry report, see Illinois, General Assembly, Senate, *Journal of the Senate of the Fortieth General Assembly of the State of Illinois, December 7, 1897–February 24, 1898*, 143–44.

22. *CT*, May 7, 1898, 5-4, Aug. 18, 1898, 1-1, Aug. 29, 1898, 4-3 (quote), Sept. 7, 1898, 7-5, Sept. 30, 1898, 1-1.

23. *CT*, Sept. 29, 1896, 1-3.

24. *CT*, Sept. 29, 1896, 1-3.

25. *CT*, Oct. 9, 1896, 7-3.

26. *CT*, Oct. 16, 1896, 9-7.

27. Quoted in Guy Murchie Jr., "Linked to Chicago's Worst Two Fires: The Family of O'Leary," *CT*, Mar. 31, 1935, E10.

28. *Spirit* 136 (Dec. 24, 1898): 564; 137 (June 6, 1899): 1160; *CT*, Mar. 25, 1900, 19-5, Aug. 31, 1903, 7-2, Sept. 2, 1925, 12-1 (obituary), Mar. 31, 1935, 94-4; Griffin, "Big Jim O'Leary," 214–16; *Illinois Political Directory, 1899*, 331; Landesco, *Organized Crime*, 63; Green, "Chicago Democratic Party," 314–16.

29. Flynt, "Men behind the Poolrooms," 646; Russell, "Chaos and Bomb Throwing," esp. 318; *CT*, Aug. 10, 1907, 1-1, Aug. 26, 1912, 3-7, Mar. 26, 1922, 1-5, Mar. 31, 1935, 94-1, Dec. 7, 1941, 24-3; Lindberg, *Chicago Ragtime*, 189; Lindberg, *To Serve and Collect*, 77; Flanagan, "Silent Mayor," 51. O'Leary left only $10,200 at his death. *CT*, Jan. 31, 1925, 3-1.

30. *CT*, Mar. 21, 1899, 3.

31. *CT*, Dec. 22, 1899, 4-5, Dec. 23, 1899, 6-5.

32. *CT*, Mar. 25, 1900, 19-5.

33. *CT*, Aug. 10, 1901, 3-1, Sept. 2, 1902, 6-2, Sept. 8, 1902, 4-3, Jan. 23, 1908, 6-1, Aug. 2, 1938, 18-8; Lloyd Wendt and Kogan, *Bet-a-Million!*, 251–52; Chafetz, *Play the Devil*, 268–69.

34. *CT*, Dec. 9, 1896, 7-4, Mar. 25, 1900, 19-5, Aug. 31, 1903, 7-2, Sept. 1, 1903, 1-6, May 5, 1904, 4-5; Flynt, "Men behind the Pool-Rooms," 643–44; Lindberg, *Chicago Ragtime*, 179; Asbury, *Sucker's Progress*, 307.

35. *CT*, June 11, 1900, 3-3, June 21, 1900, 6-4, June 10, 1900, 1-5 (quote); Binder, *Al Capone's Beer Wars*, 21–22, 24.

36. *CT*, Nov. 28, 1900, 6-1, Dec. 2, 1900, 2-2, Jan. 27, 1901, 17-6, Mar. 1, 1901, 1-5, Mar. 2, 1901, 4-2, Apr. 14, 1901, 17-3, May 3, 1901, 7-1.

37. *CT*, Apr. 14, 1901, 3-6; Lindberg, *Chicago Ragtime*, 179.

38. *CT*, Aug. 8, 1901, 3-7, Aug. 28, 1901, 7-1, 7-5.

39. *CT*, May 2, 1887, 9-6.

40. *CT*, June 23, 1901, 1-7, 2-7; Haller, "Policy Gambling," 723; Woolridge, *Hands Up!*, 421–24; Heap, *Slumming*, 42; Lombardo, *Organized Crime in Chicago*, 61–62; Blair, *I've Got to Make My Livin'*, 140; Bauman, *Pekin Theater*, 9; Levitt, "'Evening at the Pekin Theatre.'"

41. *CT*, Mar. 1, 1901, 1-5, Mar. 2, 1901, 4-2.

42. Lindberg, *Chicago by Gaslight*, 163; *CT*, Aug. 28, 1903, 2-5 (quote).

43. *CT*, Aug. 25, 1903, 3-4, Aug. 27, 1903, 5-4; Lindberg, *Chicago Ragtime*, 167–71; Lindberg, "Evolution of an Evil Business."

44. *CT*, Aug. 27, 1903, 5-4, Aug. 28, 1903, 2-5, Feb. 8, 1919, 13-3; Lindberg, *Chicago by Gaslight*, 162.

45. *CT*, Aug. 29, 1903, 2-1 (quote); Lindberg, *Chicago by Gaslight*, 167.

46. *CT*, Oct. 21, 1903, 5-2, Jan. 16, 1904, 5-3, May 20, 1904, 4-5.

47. Landesco, *Organized Crime*, 46; Lindberg, *Chicago by Gaslight*, 164; *CT*, Mar. 18, 1902, 7-1, Mar. 19, 1902, 7-1, Aug. 7, 1941, 20-3; "Mont Tennes, King of Gamblers," http://chicagocrimescenes.blogspot.com/2009/04/mont-tennes-king-of-gamblers.html.

48. *CT*, Jan. 16, 1904, 5-3, Mar. 23, 1904, 3-1; *CRH*, Aug. 17, 1907, 2-4; "Mont Tennes"; Allan May, "The History of the Race Wire Service: Mont Tennes and the Birth of the Race Wire," http://www.allanrmay.com/Race_Wire_Service.html. Brother Charles Tennes in 1908 was one of the city's leading bettors on baseball. Four of them collectively lost $93,000, including Charles, down $25,000. Their clients were so successful betting on baseball that they got out of the business. *CT*, Aug. 4, 1908, 10-1.

49. Flynt, "Men behind the Poolrooms," 644.

50. Flynt, "Pool-Room Spider," 520; Lindberg, *Chicago by Gaslight*, 168; Fullerton, "American Gambling and Gamblers," 35; Landesco, *Organized Crime*, 47, 71.

51. Flynt, "Men behind the Poolrooms," 644; Fullerton, "American Gambling and Gamblers," 35; James Doherty, "King of the Gamblers," *CT*, Jan. 25, 1953, G6 (quote). Doherty incorrectly claimed that there were no elegant poolrooms until the 1920s.

52. *CT*, Feb. 6, 1903, 7-5, Oct. 22, 1903, 14-1, Nov. 4, 1903, 5-3 (quote), Nov. 10, 1903, 3-1; *NYT*, Nov. 3, 1903, 8-2, Nov. 4, 1903, 5-2.

53. *CT*, Nov. 3, 1903, 1-3, Nov. 10, 1903, 3-1.

54. *CT*, Nov. 11, 1903, 3-2, Nov. 18, 1903, 6-2, Nov. 24, 1903, 2-5.

55. *CT*, Dec. 9, 1903, 6-7, Dec. 11, 1903, 8-1, May 19, 1904, 3-7, May 2, 1951, 8-1.

56. "Poolrooms and Telephones," *CT*, Mar. 14, 1904, 6-2, Oct. 26, 1911, 1-4, Aug. 23, 1918, 22-2; Binder, *Al Capone's Beer Wars*, 22.

57. *CT*, Aug. 23, 1918, 1-2; Lindberg, *To Serve and Collect*, 102; Lindberg, *Chicago by Gaslight*, 172; *Chicago American*, Mar. 14, 1904, Herman Schuettler Scrapbooks; Lindberg, *Chicago Ragtime*, 192, 195.

58. *CT*, Mar. 27, 1904, 3-3.

59. "AT&T: A Brief History: Origins"; Flynt, "Telegraph and Telephone Companies," 52–53; *CT*, Mar. 14, 1904, 6.

60. *CT*, Mar. 14, 1904, 8-4, Mar. 16, 1904, 14-2, Mar. 17, 1904, 14-1, Mar. 26, 1904, 3-4.

61. *CT*, Mar. 23, 1904, 3-1, "Schuettler Keeps after Gambling," Apr. 13, 1904, 6-1, Apr. 26, 1904, 14-1, June 23, 1904, 10-5; *CDN*, June 10, 1904, 2-2; "Why Not a Park?," *CIO*, June 13, 1904, 4-2.

62. *CT*, Mar. 21, 1904, 4-5, Mar. 22, 1904, 5-1, Mar. 27, 1904, 3-3.

63. Haller, "Organized Crime in Urban Society," 213–15, 213 (quote).

64. *CT*, Mar. 29, 1904, 3-3, Apr. 13, 1904, 3-2, Apr. 14, 1904, 16-3, Apr. 26, 1904, 14-1; Lindberg, *To Serve and Collect*, 102, 113n31.

65. Chicago Board of Trade, *Annual Report of the Board of Trade of the City of Chicago* 39 (1897): 87 (quote); *NYDT*, May 19, 1904, 6-2; Hochfelder, "'Where the Common People Could Speculate.'"

66. Riess, *Sport of Kings*, 284–91.

67. Hochfelder, *Telegraph in America*, 114; David H. Hochfelder, "Partners in Crime: The Telegraph Industry, Finance Capitalism, and Organized Gambling, 1870–1920," http://ethw.org/w/images/5/5b/Hochfelder.pdf.

68. *NYDT*, May 19, 1904, 6-4.

69. *CRH*, May 21, 1904, 2-5; *CT*, May 19, 1904, 3-7, May 20, 1904, 4-5, July 1, 1904, 1-4, 5 (quote); Riess, *City Games*, 186.

70. *CT*, May 19, 1904, 3-7.

71. Allan May, "The History of the Racing Wire: Mont Tennes and the Birth of the Race Wire," http://www.allanrmay.com/Race_Wire_Service.html; Landesco, *Organized Crime*, 46; Griffin, "Big Jim O'Leary," 215; *CT*, Feb. 9, 1900, 14-4, May 23, 1904, 7-1, July 30, 1904, 2-5, 9-4.

72. Harrison, "Dope Sheet," 3, 22.

73. *NYT*, Oct. 15, 1883, 1-1.

74. Broacher and Broach, "Scamming"; Halttunen, *Confidence Men*.

75. Maurer, *Big Con*, 1–102; Weil and Brannon, *"Yellow Kid" Weil*, 1, 13.

76. "Fred Gondorf and Charley Gondorf Case File," http://archive.today/bT H9M. *The Sting* supposedly takes place in 1936, more than twenty years after the heyday of the big con.

77. Weil and Brannon, *"Yellow Kid" Weil*, 21–31, 33–39.

78. *NYT*, Sept. 15, 1905, 9-1; Riess, *Sport of Kings*, 291–92.

79. May, "Race Wire"; *CRH*, Nov. 18, 1904, 6-1; *CT*, Oct. 1, 1907, 1-3; *Los Angeles Herald*, Nov. 18, 1907, 5-1; Lindberg, *Chicago Ragtime*, 198; Hochfelder, *Telegraph in America*, 114; Flynt, "Telegraph and Telephone Companies," 53–54.

80. Griffin, "Big Jim O'Leary," 216–17 (quote); *CDN*, Mar. 2, 1905, 1-1; *CT*, Mar. 6, 1905, 3-1.

81. *CDN*, Mar. 2, 1905, 1-1; Griffin, "Big Jim O'Leary," 217.

82. *CT*, Mar. 3, 1905, 1-4, Mar. 4, 1905, 9-5, Mar. 5, 1905, 1-3, Mar. 6, 1905, 3-1, Mar. 7, 1905, 5-4; Griffin, "Big Jim O'Leary," 217.

83. *CT*, Mar. 5, 1905, 3-1, Mar. 6, 1905, 3-1, Mar. 14, 1905, 16-3; *CDN*, Mar. 6, 1905, 2-5; Griffin, "O'Leary," 217.

84. *CT*, Mar. 6, 1905, 1-6, Mar. 7, 1905, 5-4.

85. *CT*, July 27, 1905, 1-5; R. Morton, *Justice and Humanity*, 19–20; Landesco, *Organized Crime*, 46; Lindberg, *Chicago by Gaslight*, 166–67, 182–83 (quote); Binder, *Al Capone's Beer Wars*, 22, 25–26.

86. Lindberg, *Chicago Ragtime*, 186–87; Campbell, Martin, and Fabos, *Media and Culture*, 113; *CDN*, June 16, 1905, 3-3; *CT*, June 30, 1905, 6-3; "Mont Tennes."

87. Lindberg, *Chicago by Gaslight*, 168–69; Lindberg, *Chicago Ragtime*, 186; *CT*, June 30, 1905, 6-3; *CRH*, May 11, 1907, 6-3.

88. Turner, 'City of Chicago," 583-84, 587, 590.

89. *NYT*, July 10, 1914, 9-6; Flanagan, "Silent Mayor," 50–60; "Chicago Mayors, 1837–2007"; R. Morton, "Edward F. Dunne," 221–22; R. Morton, *Justice and Humanity*, 1.

90. Russell, "Chaos and Bomb Throwing," 317–18; *NYT*, July 10, 1914, 9-6; Lindberg, *Chicago Ragtime*, 189; Flanagan, "Silent Mayor," 51. For Busse's obituary, see *NYT*, July 10, 1914, 9-6. Hunt died after forty-one years of service, leaving $87,104 to his heirs. Probate #88,570, Docket 221, p. 198, Probate Court, City of Chicago.

91. *CRH*, Apr. 25, 1907, 8-1; "Shippy, George Marion," https://www.geni.com/people/George-Shippy/6000000033744668794; Landesco, *Organized Crime*, 46–47 (quote); Russell, "Chaos and Bomb Throwing," 317.

92. *CRH*, Apr. 25, 1907, 8-1; Fullerton, "American Gambling," 36; Landesco, *Organized Crime*, 47.

93. *CRH*, Apr. 27, 1907, 8-3; *CT*, May 26, 1907, 1-4, June 5, 1907, 6-1, June 7, 1907, 3-4.

94. *CT*, June 19, 1907, 6-1, July 9, 1907, 2-1, July 11, 1907, 4-4.

95. Lindberg, *Chicago by Gaslight*, 174; Lindberg, *Chicago Ragtime*, 198; Landesco, *Organized Crime*, 51, 52, 55; Ogden, *Legacy*, 98; May, "Race Wire"; *CRH*, Aug. 10, 1907, 10-1; *CT*, Oct. 1, 1907, 1-3.

96. *Lake County Times* (Hammond), June 19, 1907, 5-2; Landesco, *Organized Crime*, 48–49; *CT*, July 9, 1-7, July 10, 1907, 2-2, July 26, 1907, 1-5, Sept. 27, 1907, 1-3, Nov. 2, 1909, 1-7, Aug. 27, 1911, 1-3.

97. *CRH*, Aug. 7, 1907, 2-5; *CT*, Aug. 13, 1907, 4-3, Sept. 27, 1907, 1-2, July 4, 1909, 47-1, H1; Lindberg, *Chicago by Gaslight*, 171, 173; Lindberg, *Chicago Ragtime*, 195.

98. *CRH*, Aug. 7, 1907, 2-5; "Another Anti-gambling Order," *CRH*, Nov. 25, 1907, 8-1; *CT*, Aug. 13, 1907, 4-3, Sept. 27, 1907, 1-2, July 4, 1909, 47-1, H1, Nov. 1, 1908, 8-3; Lindberg, *Chicago by Gaslight*, 171, 173; Lindberg, *Chicago Ragtime*, 193–95.

99. *CT*, Oct. 31, 1908, 3-5, Nov. 22, 1908, 2-6, June 28, 1909, 1-7; Landesco, *Organized Crime*, 52–53; *CE*, June 30, 1909, 2-2.

100. *CT*, June 28, 1909, 1-7, Nov. 1, 1909, 1-7, Feb. 18, 1910, 3-5; Walter J. Karceski Jr., "George F. Harding, Jr. and His 'Castle,'" http://www.artic.edu/aic /collections/exhibitions/Arms-and-Armor/resource/1246.

101. *CT*, Nov. 1, 1909, 1-7, Nov. 2, 1909, 1-7, Feb. 18, 1910, 3-5, Jan. 24, 1911, 1-7, Aug. 27, 1911, 4-4, July 7, 1921, 10-2; *CE*, June 30, 1909, 2-2; *CRH*, Nov. 4, 1909, 6-1; Landesco, *Organized Crime*, 52–53, 56, 62–63; Lindberg, *Chicago Ragtime*, 200; Lindberg, *Chicago by Gaslight*, 175; Harland, *Vice Bondage of a Great City*, 167; Binder, *Al Capone's Beer War*, 305n101.

102. *CT*, July 10, 1907, 1-3; *CRH*, Aug. 17, 1907, 2-4; *CE*, Aug. 30, 1911, quoted in Landesco, *Organized Crime*, 61.

103. Landesco, *Organized Crime*, 57; Lindberg, *Chicago Ragtime*, 198; *CE*, Feb. 8, 1911, 7-2; *CT*, Aug. 27, 1911, 1-3.

104. Landesco, *Organized Crime*, 59–62; *CT*, Aug. 27, 1911, 1-3, Aug. 28, 1911, 1-7, Aug. 29, 1911, 1-5, 4-2 (first mention of the General News Bureau), Aug. 30, 1911, 3-5.

105. *CT*, Feb. 8, 1910, 9-4, Aug. 27, 1911, 1-3, Aug. 28, 1911, 1-3; Landesco, *Organized Crime*, 60; Lindberg, *Chicago by Gaslight*, 175.

106. Lindberg, *Chicago by Gaslight*, 174–75; *CRH*, Aug. 29, 1911, 3-1; *CT*, Aug. 27, 1911, 1-3; Landesco, *Organized Crime*, 57–59; Lindberg, *Chicago Ragtime*, 198; *CE*, Feb. 8, 1910, 4-2.

107. *CT*, Dec. 15, 1909, 4-1, Dec. 26, 1909, 7-1, Jan. 24, 1911, 1-7; *NYT*, Dec. 14, 1909, 9-4; *Montreal Gazette*, Dec. 15, 1909, 6; Brolaski, *Easy Money*, 126; US Congress, Senate, Committee on Interstate Commerce, *Prevention of Transmission of Race-Gambling Bets*, 24. Experts estimated that clients won just 5–15 percent of the time, which were pretty dismal odds.

108. *CT*, Nov. 18, 1911, 1-7, Nov. 19, 1911, 1-7; Landesco, *Organized Crime*, 57–58; Lindberg, *Chicago Ragtime*, 198.

109. *CT*, Apr. 5, 1911, 1-1, Jan. 9, 1953, 20-2.

110. Landesco, *Organized Crime*, 58; Lindberg, *Chicago Ragtime*, 189; Lindberg, *Chicago by Gaslight*, 139–40, 175; *CE*, Aug. 9, 1911, 8-2, Aug. 28, 1911, 1-3, Aug. 30, 1911, 1-7; *CRH*, Aug. 29, 1911, 3-1; *CT*, Nov. 3, 1939, 27-1; Lineham, "Vice Commissions."

111. Dash, *Satan's Circus*. Becker was the only police officer ever executed for murder in the United States until Frank Joseph Coppola in 1982. Riess, *Sport of Kings*, 298–99, 403n134. On the gambling wars, see, for example, Ogden, *Legacy*; and Stoltzfus, *Freedom from Advertising*, 19.

112. Haller and Alviti, "Loansharking in American Cities."

113. Riess, *Sport of Kings*, 272–82.

114. Haller, "Illegal Enterprise," 219, 221–36.

8. Conclusion

1. Chafetz, *Play the Devil*, 383; Riess, "Cyclical History of Horse Racing," 48–49.

2. Nathan, *Saying It's So*.

3. Vincent, *Rise and Fall of American Sport*, 98–110, 125–28, 173–74, 176–77, 206–7; Riess, *Touching Base*, 98–12, 138–50.

4. Riess, "In the Ring and Out," 95–124; Lang, *Nelson-Wolgast Fight*, 16–17.

5. Riess, "Sports and Machine Politics," 99–121; Riess, *City Games*, 171–87; *Chicago: An Instructive and Entertaining History*, 168.

6. Rosen, *Lost Sisterhood*; Gilfoyle, *City of Eros*. For exceptions, see Cole, "'Upon the Stage of Disorder'"; and Wunsch, "Protecting St. Louis Neighborhoods."

7. McGirr, *War on Alcohol*; "Dry State," en.wikipedia.org/wiki/Dry_state; West, *Saloon on the Rocky Mountain Frontier*; Duis, *Saloon*.

8. Burgess, *Open Letter to Governor Henry M. Horner*, 11–12.

Appendix

1. Ozanian, "Selective Accounting." On data for baseball's business history, see US Congress, House, Judiciary Committee, *Organized Baseball*. For secondary studies, see, for example, Burk, *Much More than a Game*; Burk, *Never Just a Game*; Riess, "Business of Baseball, 1920–1956"; and Michael J. Haupert, "The Economic History of Major League Baseball," https://eh.net/encyclopedia/the-economic-history-of-major-league-baseball.

2. Adelman, *Sporting Time*, 48–49, 304n62.

3. Riess, *Sport of Kings*, 157–60, 227–33, 238–40.

4. Riess, *Sport of Kings*, 251–52.

5. US Congress, Senate, Committee on Interstate Commerce, *Prevention of Transmission of Race Track Bets*, 92–93; Brolaski, *Easy Money*, 248.

6. *NYT*, March 4, 1906, 11; *DRF*, October 17, 2014, 1; *San Francisco Call*, April 18, 1909, 37.

Bibliography

Archives

Chicago Foreign Language Press Survey. Newberry Library. http://flps .newberry.org.

Citizens' Association of Chicago Records. Richard J. Daley Library Special Collections and University Archives, Univ. of Illinois, Chicago.

Horner, Henry. Papers. 1899–1940. Abraham Lincoln Library & Museum. Springfield, IL.

Keeneland Library. Lexington, KY.

Probate Records, Chicago Police Department. Clerk of Cook County, Chicago.

Schuettler, Herman. Scrapbooks. Chicago History Museum, Chicago, IL.

Government Documents

"Appellate Court Decision: Edward W. Stanwood v. Sterling Metal Co." *Chicago Law Journal Weekly* 18 (Jan. 2, 1903): 317.

Binmore, Henry, comp. *Laws and Ordinances Governing the City of Chicago: From April 2, 1890, to July 10, 1894.* Chicago: E. B. Myers, 1894.

"Gambling in the District of Columbia." *Journal of the Executive Proceedings of the Senate of the United States, March 13, 1894.* 53rd Cong. Washington, DC: GPO, 1895.

Grainger v. Kirby (Kentucky 1908), 110 S.W. 247.

Illinois. General Assembly. House of Representatives. *Journal of the House of Representatives of the General Assembly of the State of Illinois [1885–1898].* Springfield, IL, 1886–98.

Illinois. General Assembly. Senate. *Journal of the Senate of the General Assembly of the State of Illinois [1885–98].* Springfield, IL: 1886–98.

Indiana. General Assembly. House of Representatives. *Journal of the House of Representatives of the State of Indiana Being the 60th Session of the General Assembly*. Indianapolis: Wm. M. Burford, 1897.

———. *Journal of the House of Representatives of the State of Indiana during the Fifty-Eighth Session, Commencing Thursday, Jan. 5, 1893*. Indianapolis: Wm. M. Burford, 1893.

Indiana. General Assembly. Senate. *Journal of the Senate of the State of Indiana Being the 60th Session of the General Assembly*. Indianapolis: Wm. M. Burford, 1897.

Indiana ex rel. Claude Mathews v. Edward Roby et al., 142 Indiana 700.

Joseph Swigert v. The People of the State of Illinois (1895), 154 IL 284.

Schott v. Youree, 31 Northeastern Reporter, IL 591.

US Congress. House. Judiciary Committee. *Organized Baseball: Hearings before the Subcommittee on Study of Monopoly Power*. 82nd Cong., 1st sess., 1951, serial 1, pt. 6. Washington, DC: Government Printing Office, 1952.

US Congress. Senate. *Reports of Committees of the Senate of the United States for the Second Session of the Fifty-Third Congress, 1893–1894*. Washington, DC: Government Printing Office, 1895.

US Congress. Senate. Committee on Interstate Commerce. *Prevention of Transmission of Race-Gambling Bets before the Subcommittee of the Committee on Interstate Commerce*. 64th Cong. Washington, DC: Government Printing Office, 1916.

US Congress Senate. Committee on the Judiciary. *Interstate Race Gambling: Hearings before the United State Senate Committee on the Judiciary*. 61st Cong., 2nd sess., Dec. 14, 1909. Washington, DC: Government Printing Office, 1909.

———. *Interstate Racing by Telegraph: Hearings before the United State Senate Committee on the Judiciary*. 60th Cong., 2nd sess., Jan. 21, 1909. Washington, DC: Government Printing Office, 1909.

NEWSPAPERS AND SPORTS WEEKLIES

Brooklyn Eagle, 1893–1905

Chicago Abendpost, 1897

Chicago American, 1904

Chicago Daily American, 1840

Chicago Daily News, 1876–1911

Chicago Democrat, 1836

Chicago Evening Journal, 1896

Chicago Evening Post, 1890

Chicago Examiner, 1908–11

Chicago Inter Ocean, 1875–78, 1881, 1885, 1887, 1892–93, 1899, 1904–7

Chicago Mail, 1890

Chicago Record-Herald, 1904–12

Chicago Tribune, 1841–1911

Daily Alta California, 1890

Daily Racing Form (Chicago), 1902

Day Book (Chicago), 1912

Hyde Park Herald, 1884

Indianapolis News, 1896

Lake County Times (Hammond, IN), 1907

Los Angeles Herald, 1904, 1907

Los Angeles Times, 1904, 1906, 1907

Maysville (KY) Evening Bulletin, 1899

Milwaukee Journal, 1913

Montreal Gazette, 1909

National Police Gazette, 1905

New York Clipper, 1896

New York Daily Tribune, 1894–1906

New York Sun, 1878

New York Times, 1851–1911

Pittsburgh Press, 1913

San Francisco Call, 1901, 1907

Spirit of the Times, 1845–1902

Spokane Press, 1905

St. Louis Globe-Democrat, 1877

St. Louis Post-Dispatch, 1905

St. Louis Republic, 1901, 1903, 1905

Turf, Field, and Farm, 1875–97

Wallace's Monthly Review, 1889

Washington Post, 1878, 1888

Washington Star, 1888, 1904–5

Washington Times, 1894

REFERENCE WORKS

American Millionaires: The "Tribune"'s List of Persons Reputed to Be Worth a Million or More. Lines of Business in Which the Fortunes Were Made. Chicago: Chicago Tribune, 1892.

American National Biography. New York: Scribner's 1973–.

Chicago: An Instructive and Entertaining History of a Wonderful City, with a Useful Stranger's Guide. Chicago: Rhodes & McClure, 1888.

Chicago Daily News National Almanac [1890–1900]. Chicago: Chicago Daily News, 1890–1900.

"Chicago Mayors, 1837–2007." In *Encyclopedia of Chicago.* http://www .encyclopedia.chicagohistory.org/pages/1443.html.

Dictionary of American Biography. New York: Oxford Univ. Press, 1999–.

Encyclopaedia of Biography of Illinois. Chicago: Century, 1892.

Goodwin's Annual Official Turf Guide. New York: Goodwin Bros., 1882–1908.

Grossman, James, Ann D. Keating, and Janice L. Reiff, eds. *The Encyclopedia of Chicago.* Chicago: Univ. of Chicago Press, 2004.

Illinois Political Directory, 1899: With Portraits and Biographical Sketches of Party Leaders. Chicago: W. L. Bodine, 1899.

Kleber, John E., ed. *Encyclopedia of Louisville.* Lexington: Univ. Press of Kentucky, 2001.

Marquis, Albert N. *Marquis' Hand-Book of Chicago: A Complete History, Reference Book, and Guide to the City.* Chicago: A. N. Marquis 1885.

Menke, Frank G. *All-Sports Record Book, 1932.* New York: All-Sports Record Book, 1932.

"Racing Statistics of the Year 1911." *Morning Telegraph's Racing Chart Book* 27, no. 2 (1912): 205.

CONTEMPORARY SOURCES

Abbot, Willis John. *Carter Henry Harrison: A Memoir.* New York: Dodd, Mead, 1895.

Ayers, Mrs. B. F. "Old Hyde Park." In *A Sheaf of Reminiscences, Garnered by Caroline Kirkland,* edited by Caroline Kirkland. Chicago: Daughaday, 1919.

Beaty, John F. *Ninth Annual Statement of the Trade and Commerce of Chicago for the Year Ending March 31, 1867.* Chicago: Horton and Leonard, 1867.

Brolaski, Harry. *Easy Money: Being the Experiences of a Reformed Gambler.* Cleveland, OH: Searchlight Press, 1911.

Burgess, Ernest W. *Open Letter to Governor Henry M. Horner and Report to Him, Entitled: "The Next Step in the War on Crime—Legalize Gambling."* Chicago: H. G. Adair, 1935.

Chatfield-Taylor, H. C. "Country Club Life in Chicago." *Harper's Weekly,* Aug. 1, 1896, 761.

Chicago Civic Federation. *Civic Federation of Chicago: Synopsis of Annual Report Covering the Period from Organization of the Federation to the First Annual Meeting, in April, 1895.* Chicago: Wm. C. Hollister & Bro., 1895.

———. *First Annual Report of the Central Council, May 1895.* Chicago: R. R. Donnelly, 1895.

———. *First Annual Report of the Chicago Civic Federation.* Chicago: Civic Federation of Chicago, 1894.

Chicago Clubs, Illustrated. Chicago: Leeward, 1888.

Chicago Commerce, Manufactures, Banking and Transportation Facilities. Chicago: S. Fred Howe, 1884.

"Chicago's Anti-gambling Crusade." *Literary Digest* 9 (Oct. 13, 1894): 697.

Citizens' Association of Chicago. *Annual Report of the Citizens' Association of Chicago, 1904.* Chicago: Hazlitt & Reed, 1904.

"Clubs of Chicago." *Cosmopolitan*, July 1889, 212–24.

Flynt, Josiah. "The Men behind the Pool-Rooms." *Cosmopolitan*, Apr. 1907, 636–45.

———. "Partners of the Criminal Pool-Rooms." *Cosmopolitan*, June 1907, 161–68.

———. "Pool-Room Spider, and the Gambling Fly." *Cosmopolitan*, Mar. 1907, 513–21.

———. "The Pool-Room Vampire and Its Money-Mad Victims." *Cosmopolitan*, Feb. 1907, 359–71.

———. "The Telegraph and Telephone Companies as Allies of the Criminal Pool-Rooms." *Cosmopolitan*, May 1907, 50–57.

Fullerton, Hugh. "American Gambling and Gamblers." *American Magazine*, Feb. 1914, 33–38.

Harland, Robert O. *The Vice Bondage of a Great City.* Chicago: Young People's Civic League, 1912.

"Harness and Saddle Races Chicago, 1845." *American Turf Register and Racing & Trotting Calendar* 16 (1845–48): 29–104.

Harrison, Carter H., Jr. "The Dope Sheet: An Account of the Effort to Stamp Out Race-Track Betting." *Saturday Evening Post*, July 9, 1904, 3–22.

———. *Growing Up with Chicago: Sequel to "Stormy Years."* Chicago: R. F. Seymour, 1944.

Hatton, Joseph. *To-Day in America: Studies for the Old World and the New.* London: Chapman and Hall, 1881.

Hertz, John. *The Racing Memoirs of John Hertz, as Told to Evan Shipman.* Chicago: n.p., 1954.

"How Gambling Was Stopped in Chicago." *Literary Digest*, Nov. 3, 1894, 7.

"Law Enforcement in Missouri." *Outlook*, Aug. 12, 1905, 895.

Pike, C. S. "The American Derby." *Town and Country*, June 25, 1904, 16.

Riordan, William L. *Plunkitt of Tammany Hall: A Series of Very Plain Talks on Very Practical Politics.* New York: Dutton, 1963.

Robertson, William, and W. F. Robertson. *Our American Tour: Being a Run of Ten Thousand Miles from the Atlantic to the Golden Gate in the Autumn of 1869.* Edinburgh: W. Burgess, 1871.

Russell, Charles Edward. "Chaos and Bomb Throwing in Chicago." *Hampton's Magazine*, Mar. 1910, 307–20.

Stead, William T. *If Christ Came to Chicago: A Plea for the Union of All Who Love in the Service of All Who Suffer.* Chicago: Laird & Lee, 1894.

Turner, George Kibbe. "The City of Chicago: A Study of the Great Immoralities," McClure's Magazine 28 (April 1907): 575-92.

Ullman, Joseph. *What's the Odds? Funny, True and Clean Stories of the Turf.* New York: Metropolitan, 1903.

Veblen, Thorstein. *The Theory of the Leisure Class: An Economic Study in the Evolution of Institutions.* New York: Macmillan, 1899.

Weil, Joseph, and W. T. Brannon. *"Yellow Kid" Weil: The Autobiography of America's Master Swindler.* Chicago: Ziff-Davis, 1948.

Woolridge, Clifton Rodman. *Hands Up! In the World of Crime; or, 12 Years a Detective.* Chicago: Thompson and Thomas, 1901.

WASHINGTON PARK MEMBERS' BIOGRAPHICAL SOURCES

A. N. Marquis & Co.'s Handy Business Directory of Chicago. Chicago: A. N. Marquis, 1889.

Album of Genealogy and Biography, Cook County, Illinois: With Portraits. Chicago: La Salle Book, 1900.

American Blue Book of Biography: Men of 1912. New York: American Publishers' Association, 1914.

Artistic Guide to Chicago and the World's Columbian Exposition. Chicago: R. S. Peake, 1892.

Bateman, Newton, and Paul Selby, eds. *Biographical and Memorial Edition of the Historical Encyclopedia of Illinois.* Chicago: Munsell, 1915.

Biographical Dictionary and Portrait Gallery of Men of Chicago, St. Louis and the Columbian Exposition. Chicago: American Biographical, 1892.

"Breese, J. B." *Economist* 19 (Apr. 9, 1898): 417.

Brownell, J. J. *The American Tyler-Keystone: Devoted to Freemasonry and Its Concordant Orders.* Detroit: J. H. Brownell, 1903-4.

Chicago Blue Book of Selected Names of Chicago and Suburban Towns [1880–1915]. Chicago: Chicago Directory, 1880–1915.

Chicago Board of Trade. *Annual Report of the Trade and Commerce of Chicago for the Year Ended December 31 [1880–1900].* Chicago: Knight and Leonard, 1880–1900.

Chicago Independent: A Monthly Journal for Life Insurance Agents 1 (Jan. 1889): 13.

"Chicago's Newest Millinery Salon." *Millinery Trade Review* 46 (Apr. 1921): 75.

Clapp, O. W. "Ozro W. Clapp." *Journal of the Illinois State Historical Society* 11 (Apr. 1918): 88–90.

Club Men of New York: Their Clubs, College Alumni Associations, Occupations, and Business and Home Addresses, with Historical Sketches of Many Prominent New York Organizations. New York: Republic Press, 1892.

Contemporary American Biography: Biographical Sketches of Representative Men of the Day. New York: Atlantic, 1895.

"Death of C. H. Besly." *Iron Trade Review* (Jan. 28, 1909): 224.

Elite Directory and Club List of Chicago. Chicago: Elite Directory, 1884–88.

Engelhardt, George Washington. *Chicago: The Book of Its Board of Trade and Other Public Bodies.* Chicago: n.p., 1900.

Flinn, John J., ed. *The Hand-Book of Chicago Biography: A Compendium of Useful Biographical Information for Research and Study.* Chicago: Standard Guide, 1893.

"George Bullen." *Brewers Journal* 33 (1907): 471–72.

"Good News from Chicago." *Our Dumb Animals* 13 (June 1880): 3.

"Grain Trade News." *Grain Dealers Journal* 36 (Mar. 10, 1916): 396.

Half-Century's Progress of the City of Chicago: The City's Leading Manufacturers and Merchants. Chicago: International, 1887.

Hall, Henry. *America's Successful Men of Affairs: The United States at Large.* New York: New York Tribune, 1895–96.

A History of the City of Chicago: Its Men and Institutions. Chicago: Inter Ocean, 1900.

Hotchkiss, George W. *Industrial Chicago: The Lumber Interests.* Vol. 6. Chicago: Goodspeed, 1894.

"Illinois." *Railway Age* 43 (Mar. 22, 1907): 425.

Kirkland, Joseph. *History of Chicago.* Chicago: Munsell, 1895.

Lakeside Annual Directory of the City of Chicago. Chicago: Chicago Directory, 1875–1917.

"The Late Vincent C. Price." *Coffee and Tea Industries and the Flavor Field* 37 (Aug. 1919): 834.

Leonard, Albert N., and Albert Nelson Marquis. *The Book of Chicagoans: A Biographical Dictionary of Leading Living Men and Women of the City of Chicago.* Chicago: A. N. Marquis, 1911.

Leonard, John William. *Who's Who in Finance, Banking, and Insurance.* Brooklyn: Who's Who in Finance, 1911.

Marquis, Albert N., ed. *The Book of Chicagoans: A Biographical Dictionary of Leading Living Men of Chicago.* Chicago: A. N. Marquis, 1911.

———. *Marquis' Hand-Book of Chicago: A Complete History, Reference Book, and Guide to the City.* Chicago: A. N. Marquis, 1885.

Maugham, C. B. "Carpet Business in Chicago and the West Continues Brisk." *American Carpet and Upholstery Journal* 27 (Feb. 10, 1909): 78.

Morris, Charles. *Men of the Century, an Historical Work: Giving Portraits and Sketches of Eminent Citizens of the United States.* Philadelphia: I. R. Hamersly, 1896.

Moses, John. *Biographical Dictionary and Portrait Gallery of the Representative Men of the United States: Illinois.* Chicago: Lewis, 1896.

Newton, Bateman, et al. *Historical Encyclopedia of Illinois: Biographical, Memorial.* Chicago: Munsell, 1920.

"Oliver D. Peck." *Economist: A Weekly Financial, Commercial, and Real-Estate,* Dec. 31, 1898, 804.

"Oliver D. Peck." *Plumbers Trade Journal* (Mar. 1, 1919): 300.

"Peck Brothers Company." *Engineering Review* (Sept. 12, 1902): xxiv–xxv.

Rothermel, Charles. T. *Portraits and Biographies of the Fire Underwriters of the City of Chicago.* Chicago: Compiler, 1895.

"Thomas Baxter: Well-Known Western Grain Broker." *Successful American* 3 (Nov. 1901): 606.

United States Brewers' Association. *Proceedings of the 36th Annual Convention.* New York: Economical, 1896.

Unrivaled Chicago: Containing an Historical Narrative of the Great City's Development, and Descriptions of Points of Interest . . . with Biographical Sketches of Representative Men in Their Several Lines. Chicago: Rand McNally, 1896.

Waterman, Arba Nelson, ed. *Historical Review of Chicago and Cook County and Selected Biography.* Chicago: Lewis, 1908.

SECONDARY SOURCES

Abrams, Kerry. "Polygamy, Prostitution, and the Federalization of Immigration Law." *Columbia Law Review* 105 (Apr. 2005): 641–716.

Adelman, Melvin L. "Quantification and Sport: The American Jockey Club, 1866–1867, a Collective Biography." In *Sport in America: New Historical*

Perspectives, edited by Donald Spivey, 51–75. Westport, CT: Greenwood Press, 1985.

———. *A Sporting Time: New York City and the Rise of Modern Athletics, 1820–70*. Urbana: Univ. of Illinois Press, 1986.

Akers, Dwight. *Drivers Up: The Story of American Harness Racing*. New York: G. P. Putnam's Sons, 1947.

Andreas, Alfred T. *History of Chicago: From the Earliest Period to the Present Time in Three Volumes*. Chicago: A. T. Andreas, 1886.

Argersinger, Peter H. *Representation and Inequality in Late Nineteenth-Century America: The Politics of Apportionment*. Cambridge: Cambridge Univ. Press, 2012.

Armstrong, Christopher, and H. V. Nelles. *The Revenge of the Methodist Bicycle Company: Sunday Streetcars and Municipal Reform in Toronto, 1888–1897*. Toronto: Peter Martin, 1997.

Asbury, Herbert. *Gem of the Prairie: An Informal History of the Chicago Underworld*. New York: Alfred A. Knopf, 1940.

———. *Sucker's Progress: An Informal History of Gambling in America from the Colonies to Canfield*. New York: Dodd, Mead, 1938.

Aycock, Colleen, and Mark Scott. *Joe Gans: A Biography of the First African American World Boxing Champion*. Jefferson, NC: McFarland, 2008.

Azzi, Stephen. "Federal Government." In *The Canadian Encyclopedia*. https://www.thecanadianencyclopedia.ca/en/article/federal-government.

Badger, Reid. *The Great American Fair: The World's Columbian Exposition & American Culture*. Chicago: N. Hall, 1979.

Barnes, Amanda, and Julia Wright. *The Butcher Boys, Part Two: The Breaking of the Brooklyn Stable*. Morrisville, NC: Lulu Press, 2019.

Barrett, James R. *Work and Community in the Jungle: Chicago's Packing House Workers, 1890–1922*. Urbana: Univ. of Illinois Press, 1987.

Barth, Gunther. *Instant Cities: Urbanization and the Rise of San Francisco and Denver*. New York: Oxford Univ. Press, 1975.

Bauman, Thomas. *The Pekin Theater: The Rise and Fall of Chicago's First Black-Owned Theater*. Urbana: Univ. of Illinois Press, 2014.

Bean, Walton. *Boss Ruef's San Francisco: The Story of the Union Labor Party, Big Business, and the Graft Prosecution*. Berkeley: Univ. of California Press, 1968.

Beezley, William H. *Judas at the Jockey Club and Other Episodes of Porfirian Mexico*. Lincoln: Univ. of Nebraska Press, 1987.

Bensman, David, and Mark Wilson. "Iron and Steel." In *EC*, 425–27.

Bevis, Charlie. *Sunday Baseball: The Major Leagues' Struggle to Play Baseball on the Lord's Day, 1876–1934*. Jefferson, NC: McFarland, 2003.

Binder, John J. *Al Capone's Beer Wars: A Complete History of Organized Crime in Chicago during Prohibition*. Amherst, NY: Prometheus Books, 2017.

Biscotta, M. L. *American Sporting Periodicals: An Annotated Bibliography*. Lanham: MD: Rowland & Littlefield, 2019.

Black, David. *The King of Fifth Avenue: The Fortunes of August Belmont*. New York: Dial Press, 1981.

Blair, Cynthia. *I've Got to Make My Livin': Black Women's Sex Work in Turn-of-the-Century*. Chicago: Univ. of Chicago Press, 2010.

Blair, Edward Tyler. *A History of the Chicago Club*. Chicago: [The Club], 1898.

Blakey, G. Robert, and Robert Kurland. "The Development of the Federal Law of Gambling." *Cornell Law Review* 63 (Aug. 1978): 923–1021.

Blaszczyk, Regina Lee. *Imagining Consumers: Design and Innovation from Wedgwood to Corning*. Baltimore: Johns Hopkins Univ. Press, 2002.

Block, Alan A. "Organized Crime: History and Historiography." In *Handbook of Organized Crime in the United States*, edited by Robert J. Kelly, Ko-Lin Chin, and Rufus Schatzberg, 39–74. Westport, CT: Greenwood Press, 1994.

Boddy, Kasia. *Boxing: A Cultural History*. London: Reaktion Books, 2008.

Boese, Kent. "Lost Washington: Benning Race Track." Greater Greater Washington, Jan. 25, 2010. https://ggwash.org/view/4055/lost-washington2--benning-race-track.

Bogue, Margaret Beattie. *Fishing the Great Lakes: An Environmental History, 1783–1933*. Madison: Univ. of Wisconsin Press, 2000.

"Bookmaking and Bookmakers." In *Encyclopedia of British Horseracing*, edited by Wray Vamplew and Joyce Kay, 51. London: Routledge, 2005.

Borzo, Greg. *Chicago's Fabulous Fountains*. Carbondale: Southern Illinois Univ. Press, 2017.

Brandt, Nat. *Chicago Death Trap: The Iroquois Theatre Fire of 1903*. Carbondale: Southern Illinois Univ. Press, 2013.

Braucher, Jean, and Barak Orbach. "Scamming: The Misunderstood Confidence Man." *Yale Journal of Law and the Humanities* 249 (2015): 249–71.

Breen, Timothy. "Horses and Gentlemen: The Cultural Significance of Gambling among the Virginia Planters." *William & Mary Quarterly* 34 (1977): 239–57.

Brown, Douglas A. "Thoroughbred Horse-Racing Receives an Imperialist Nod: The Parliamentary Debate on Legalizing Gambling in Canada, 1910." *International Journal of the History of Sport* 11 (Aug. 1994): 252–69.

Burk, Robert F. *Much More than a Game: Players, Owners, and American Baseball since 1921.* Chapel Hill: Univ. of North Carolina Press, 2001.

———. *Never Just a Game: Players, Owners, and American Baseball to 1920.* Chapel Hill: Univ. of North Carolina Press, 1994.

Campbell, Richard, Christopher R. Martin, and Bettina Fabos. *Media and Culture: An Introduction to Mass Communication.* 8th ed. Boston: Bedford/St. Martin's, 2012.

Carver, Nancy Ellery. *Making Tracks: The Untold Story of Horse Racing in St. Louis.* St. Louis: Reedy Press, 2014.

Cash, Jon David. *Before They Were Cardinals: Major League Baseball in Nineteenth-Century St. Louis.* Columbia: Univ. of Missouri Press, 2002.

Chafetz, Henry. *Play the Devil: A History of Gambling in the United States from 1492 to 1955.* New York: Clarkson N. Potter, 1960.

Chapman, Mike. *Frank Gotch: World's Greatest Wrestler.* Buffalo, NY: William S. Hein, 1990.

Clapp, Elizabeth Jane. *Mothers of All Children: Women Reformers and the Rise of Juvenile Courts in America.* University Park, Pennsylvania State Univ. Press, 1998.

Clapson, Mark. "A Bit of a Flutter." *History Today* 41 (Oct. 1991): 38–44.

Clark, Herman. *The Elegant Eighties: When Chicago Was Young.* Chicago: A. C. McClurg, 1941.

Clarke, William Addison. "American Horse-Racing." *Harper's Weekly,* Aug. 4, 1888, 575.

Cohen, Kenneth. "'The Entreaties and Perswasions of Our Acquaintance': Gambling and Networks in Early America." *Journal of the Early Republic* 31 (Winter 2011): 599–638.

Cole, Jeannine. "'Upon the Stage of Disorder': Legalized Prostitution in Memphis and Nashville, 1863–1865." *Tennessee Historical Quarterly* 68 (Spring 2009): 40–65.

Cook, Frederick F. *Bygone Days in Chicago: Recollections of the "Garden City" of the Sixties.* Chicago: A. C. McClurg, 1916.

Crapp, Elizabeth Jane. *Mothers of All Children: Women Reformers and the Rise of Juvenile Courts in America.* University Park: Pennsylvania State Univ. Press, 1998.

Cronon, William. *Nature's Metropolis: Chicago and the Great West*. New York: W. W. Norton, 1991.

Cross, Whitney R. *The Burned-Over District: The Social and Intellectual History of Enthusiastic Religion in Western New York, 1800–1850*. Ithaca, NY: Cornell Univ. Press, 1950.

Crossley, Frederic Beers, and Elbert H. Gary. *Courts and Lawyers of Illinois*. 3 vols. Chicago: American History Society, 1916.

Cunningham, Hugh. *Leisure in the Industrial Revolution*. London: Croom Helm, 1980.

Czitrom, Daniel. "Underworld and Underdogs: Big Tim Sullivan and Metropolitan Politics in New York, 1889–1913." *Journal of American History* 78 (1991): 536–58.

Dash, Mike. *Satan's Circus: Murder, Vice, Police Corruption, and New York's Trial of the Century*. New York: Crown, 2007.

Davies, Richard O., and Richard G. Abram. *Betting the Line: Sports Wagering in American Life*. Columbus: Ohio State Univ. Press, 2001.

Deas, Lynn. *Horse Racing in India: A Royal Legacy*. New Delhi: Nyogi Books, 2016.

"Death of Edward Corrigan." *Thoroughbred Record* 100 (July 12, 1924): 17.

Devereux, Edward, Jr. *Gambling and the Social Structure: A Sociological Study of Lotteries and Horse Racing in Contemporary America*. New York: Arno Press, 1980.

Diner, Steven J. *A City and Its Universities: Public Policy in Chicago, 1892–1919*. Chapel Hill: Univ. of North Carolina Press, 1980.

Dixon, David. *From Prohibition to Regulation: Bookmaking, Anti-gambling and the Law*. Oxford: Clarendon Press, 1991.

Dowling, Harry Filmore. *City Hospitals: The Undercare of the Underprivileged*. Cambridge, MA: Harvard Univ. Press, 1982.

Duis, Perry. *Challenging Chicago: Coping with Everyday Life, 1837–1920*. Urbana: Univ. of Illinois Press, 1998.

———. *The Saloon: Public Drinking in Chicago and Boston, 1880–1920*. Urbana: Univ. of Illinois Press, 1983.

Dunn, Mark T. *Chicago Politics, 1884: Fraud, Perjury, Prison & Pardon, Joseph C. Mackin and Michael C. McDonald*. Bloomington, IL: Dunn, 2009.

———. *Chicago's Greatest Sportsman: Charles E. "Parson" Davis*. Charleston, SC: Dunn, 2011.

Dutson, Judith. *Storey's Illustrated Guide to 96 Horse Breeds of North America.* North Adams, MA: Storey, 2005.

Eckley, Gene. *Maiden Tribute: A Life of W. T. Stead.* Philadelphia: Xlilbris, 2007.

Eisenberg, John. *The Great Match Race: When North Met South in America's First Sports Spectacle.* Boston: Houghton Mifflin, 2006.

Ellis, Charles Edward. *An Authentic History of the Benevolent and Protective Order of Elks.* Chicago: published by the author, 1910.

Erickson, John Edward. "Newspapers and Social Values: *Chicago Evening* Journalism, 1890–1950." PhD diss., Univ. of Illinois, 1973.

Ettinger, Brian Gary. "John Fitzpatrick and the Limits of Working-Class Politics in New Orleans, 1892–1896." *Louisiana History* 26 (Autumn 1985): 341–67.

Euchner, Charles C. *Playing the Field: Why Sports Teams Move and Cities Fight to Keep Them.* Baltimore: Johns Hopkins Univ. Press, 1993.

Fabian, Ann. *Card Sharps and Bucket Shops: Gambling in Nineteenth-Century America.* New York: Routledge, 1999.

Fenich, George S. "A History of (Legal) Gaming in the U.S." *Gaming Research & Review Journal* 3, no. 2 (1996): 65–77.

Findlay, John. *People of Chance: Gambling in American Society from Jamestown to Las Vegas.* New York: Oxford Univ. Press, 1986.

Finegold, Kenneth. *Experts and Politicians: Reform Challenges to Machine Politics in New York and Cleveland.* Princeton, NJ: Princeton Univ. Press, 1995.

Flanagan, Maureen. "Grey Wolves." In *Encyclopedia of Chicago.* http://encyclopedia.chicagohistory.org/pages/540.html.

———. *Seeing with Their Hearts: Chicago Women and the Vision of the Good City, 1871–1933.* Princeton, NJ: Princeton Univ. Press, 2002.

———. "Fred A. Busse: A Silent Mayor in Turbulent Times." In *The Mayors: The Chicago Political Tradition,* edited by Paul M. Green and Melvin L. Holli. 3rd ed, 50–60. Carbondale: Southern Illinois Univ. Press, 2005.

Foster, Gaines M. *Moral Reconstruction: Christian Lobbyists and the Federal Legislation of Morality, 1865–1920.* Chapel Hill: Univ. of North Carolina Press, 2002.

Flynn, John. "Smart Money." *Collier's* (Jan. 20, 1940): 20, 54–57.

"Fred Gondorf and Charley Gondorf Case File." [Crimerack] Beyond Crime History, June 7, 2012. http://archive.today/bTH9M.

Funigiello, Phillip J. *Florence Lathrop Page: A Biography*. Charlottesville: Univ. of Virginia Press, 1994.

Geiger, Louis G. *Joseph W. Folk of Missouri*. Columbia: Univ. of Missouri Press, 1953.

Gems, Gerald. *Boxing: A Concise History of the Sweet Science*. Lanham, MD: Rowman & Littlefield, 2014.

———. "Sport and Culture Formation in Chicago, 1880–1940." PhD diss., Univ. of Maryland, 1989.

Geti, Victoria. *The Juvenile Court and the Progressives*. Urbana: Univ. of Illinois Press, 2000.

Gilbert, James B. *Perfect Cities: Chicago's Utopias of 1893*. Chicago: Univ. of Chicago Press, 1991.

Gilfoyle, Timothy. *City of Eros: New York City, Prostitution and the Commercialization of Sex, 1790–1920*. New York: W. W. Norton, 1992.

Gill, Harold B., Jr. "A Sport Only for Gentlemen." *Colonial Williamsburg Journal* 20 (Autumn 1997): 49–53.

Ginger, Ray. *Altgeld's America: The Lincoln Ideal versus Changing Realities*. New York: New Viewpoints, 1973.

———. *Eugene V. Debs: A Biography*. New York: Collier's, 1963.

Gleaves, John. "Enhancing the Odds: Horse Racing, Gambling and the First Anti-doping Movement in Sport, 1889–1911." *Sport in History* 32 (Mar. 2012): 26–52.

Gocher, William H. *Wet Sundays*. Cleveland, OH: Winn and Judson, 1903.

Goodspeed, Weston Arthur, and Daniel D. Healy. *History of Cook County, Illinois: Being a General Survey of Cook County History*. 2 vols. Chicago: Goodspeed Historical Association, 1909.

Gorn, Elliott. *The Manly Art: Bare-Knuckle Prize Fighting in America*. Ithaca, NY: Cornell Univ. Press, 1986.

Grant, Jocelyn M., and Frederick C. Jaher. "The Chicago Business Elite, 1830–1930, a Collective Biography." *Business History Review* 50 (Autumn 1976): 288–328.

Green, Paul M. "The Chicago Democratic Party, 1840–1920: From Factionalism to Political Organization." PhD diss., Univ. of Chicago, 1975.

Griffin, Richard T. "Big Jim O'Leary: 'Gambler Boss iv th' Yards.'" *Chicago History* 5 (Winter 1977): 213–22.

Gurlace, Betsy. "Cicero." In *EC*, 166.

Gustaitis, Joseph. *Chicago's Greatest Year, 1893: The White City and the Birth of a Modern Metropolis.* Carbondale: Southern Illinois Univ. Press, 2013.

Haller, Mark H. "The Changing Structure of American Gambling in the Twentieth Century." *Journal of Social Issues* 35 (1979): 87–113.

———. "Illegal Enterprise: A Theoretical and Historical Interpretation." In *Illegal Enterprise: The Work of Historian Mark Haller*, edited by Matthew G. Yeager, 207–36. Lanham, MD: Univ. Press of America, 2013.

———. "Organized Crime in Urban Society: Chicago in the Twentieth Century." *Journal of Social History* 5 (Winter 1971–72): 210–34.

———. "Policy Gambling, Entertainment, and the Emergence of Black Politics: Chicago from 1900 to 1940." *Journal of Social History* 24 (Summer 1991): 719–39.

———. "The Rise of Urban Crime Syndicates, 1865–1905." Unpublished ms., n.d., in author's possession.

Haller, Mark H., and John V. Alviti. "Loansharking in American Cities: Historical Analysis of a Marginal Enterprise." *American Journal of Legal History* 21 (Apr. 1977): 127–56.

Halttunen, Karen. *Confidence Men and Painted Women: A Study of Middle-Class Culture in America, 1830–1870.* New Haven, CT: Yale Univ. Press, 1982.

Hamburger, Susan. "Jimmy Winkfield: The 'Black Maestro' of the Race Track." In *Out of the Shadows: A Biographical History of African American Athletes*, edited by David K. Wiggins, 6–19. Fayetteville: Univ. of Arkansas Press, 2006.

Hapgood, David. *Charles R. Crane: The Man Who Bet on People.* Hanover, NH: Institute of Current World Affairs, 2000.

Harpster, Jack. *The Railroad Tycoon Who Built Chicago: A Biography of William B. Ogden.* Carbondale: Southern Illinois Univ. Press, 2009.

Heap, Chad C. *Slumming: Sexual and Racial Encounters in American Nightlife, 1885–1940.* Chicago: Univ. of Chicago Press, 2009.

Heidler, David S., and Jeanne Heidler. *Henry Clay: The Essential American.* New York: Random House, 2010.

Henschen, Henry S. *A History of the State Bank of Chicago from 1879 to 1904.* Chicago: Lakeside Press, 1905.

Hervey, John. *Racing in America, 1665–1865.* New York: Jockey Club, 1944.

———. *Racing in America, 1922–1936.* New York: Jockey Club, 1937.

Herzig, Christine. "Germans." In *EC*, 333–36.

Hillenbrand, Laura. "The Derby." *American Heritage* 50 (May–June 1999): 98–107.

Hirsch, Eric. *Urban Revolt: Ethnic Politics in the Nineteenth-Century Chicago Labor Movement.* Berkeley: Univ. of California Press, 1990.

Hirsch, Susan E. "Economic Geography." In *EC,* 254–60.

History of the City of Chicago: Its Men and Institutions. Chicago: Inter Ocean, 1900.

Hmurovic, John. "The Horse Racing and Gambling Capital of the Midwest." Whiting-Robertsdale Historical Society, July 2019. https://www.wrhistoricalsociety.com/roby-horse-racing.

Hochfelder, David. *The Telegraph in America, 1832–1920.* Baltimore: Johns Hopkins Univ. Press, 2012.

———. "'Where the Common People Could Speculate': The Ticker, Bucket Shops, and the Origins of Popular Participation in Financial Markets, 1880–1920." *Journal of American History* 93 (Sept. 2006): 335–58.

Holbrook, Stewart H. *The Story of American Railroads: From the Iron Horse to the Diesel Locomotive.* Mineola, NY: Dover, 2015.

Hora, Roy. "El turf como arena de disputa social: Jockeys y propietarios en el hipódromo argentino de fines del siglo XIX." *Jahrbuch für Geschichte Lateinamerikas* 51 (2014): 303–28.

Hotaling, Edward. *The Great Black Jockeys: The Lives and Times of the Men Who Dominated America's First National Sport.* Rocklin, CA: Forum, 1999.

———. *They're Off: Horse Racing at Saratoga.* Syracuse, NY: Syracuse Univ. Press, 1995.

Hoyt, Homer. *One Hundred Years of Land Values in Chicago.* Chicago: Univ. of Chicago Press, 1933.

Huggins, Mike. "Culture, Class and Respectability: Middle-Class Racing in Nineteenth-Century England." In *A Sport-Loving Society: Victorian and Edwardian Middle-Class England at Play,* edited by J. A. Mangan, 219–38. London: Routledge, 2006.

———. *Flat Racing and British Society, 1790–1914.* London: Frank Cass, 2000.

"An Incorrigible Character." *Thoroughbred Record* 213 (May 20, 1981): 2225.

Jaher, Frederic Cople. *The Urban Establishment: Upper Strata in Boston, New York, Charleston, Chicago, and Los Angeles.* Urbana: Univ. of Illinois Press, 1982.

Jensen, Richard. *The Winning of the Midwest: Social and Political Conflict, 1888–1896.* Chicago: Univ. of Chicago Press, 1971.

Jensen, Trgvie. *Wooden Boats and Iron Men: History of Commercial Fishing in Northern Lake Michigan & Door County, 1850–2005*. De Pere, WI: Paisa (Alt), 2007.

Johnson, Claudius O. *Carter H. Harrison I: Political Leader*. Chicago: Univ. of Chicago Press, 1928.

Johnson, David R. *Policing the Urban Underworld: The Impact of Crime on the Development of the American Police, 1840–1887*. Philadelphia: Temple Univ. Press, 1979.

———. "Sinful Business: The Origins of Gambling Syndicates in the United States, 1840–1887." In *Police and Society*, edited by David Bayley, 17–47. Beverly Hills, CA: Sage, 1977.

Johnston, J. J., and Sean Curtin. *Chicago Boxing*. Charlestown, SC: Arcadia, 2005.

Joyce, Tony. "Canadian Sport and State Control: Toronto, 1845–1886." *International Journal of the History of Sport* 16 (Jan. 1999): 22–37.

Karamanski, Theodore. "Civil War." In *EC*, 169.

Karcheski, Walter J., Jr. *Arms and Armor in the Art Institute of Chicago*. Chicago: Art Institute of Chicago, 1995.

Kelly, Joseph B. "At the Track: Thoroughbred Racing in Maryland, 1870–1973." *Maryland Historical Magazine* 100 (2005): 506–22.

Kleber, John E., et al. *Encyclopedia of Louisville*. Lexington: Univ. Press of Kentucky.

Kleppner, Paul. *The Cross of Culture: A Social Analysis of Midwestern Politics, 1850–1900*. New York: Free Press, 1970.

Kirschner, Don S. *City and Country: Rural Responses to Urbanization in the 1920s*. Westport, CT: Greenwood, 1970.

Krout, John. *Annals of American Sport*. New Haven, CT: Yale Univ. Press, 1929.

Kupfer, Barbara Stern. "A Presidential Patron of the Sport of Kings: Andrew Jackson." *Tennessee Historical Quarterly* 29 (1970): 243–53.

Landesco, John. *Organized Crime in Chicago*. Chicago: Illinois Association for Criminal Justice, 1929.

———. *Organized Crime in Chicago: Part III of the Illinois Crime Survey, 1929*. 1929. Reprint, Chicago: Univ. of Chicago Press, 1968.

Lang, Arne K. *The Nelson-Wolgast Fight and the San Francisco Boxing Scene, 1900–1914*. Jefferson, NC: McFarland, 2012.

———. *Sports Betting and Bookmaking: An American History*. Lanham, MD: Rowman & Littlefield, 2016.

Larsen, Lawrence Harold. *Upstream Metropolis: An Urban Biography of Omaha and Council Bluffs.* Lincoln: Univ. of Nebraska Press, 2007.

Larson, Erik. *The Devil in the White City: Murder, Magic, and Madness at the Fair That Changed America.* New York: Crown, 2003.

La Touche, Royal L., and John Henry Potter. *Chicago and Its Resources Twenty Years after, 1871–1891: A Commercial Showing the Progress and Growth of Two Decades from the Great Fire to the Present Time.* Chicago: Chicago Times, 1892.

Laybourn, Keith. *Working-Class Gambling in Britain, c. 1906–1960s: The Stages of the Political Debate.* Lewiston, NY: Edwin Mellen Press, 2007.

Lears, Jackson. *Something for Nothing: Luck in America.* New York: Viking Penguin, 2003.

Levitt, Aimee. "'An Evening at the Pekin Theatre' Re-creates the Country's First Black-Owned Music Hall." *Chicago Reader,* June 15, 2017. https://www.chicagoreader.com/Bleader/archives/2017/06/15/an-evening-at-the-pekin-theatre-re-creates-the-countrys-first-black-owned-music-hall.

Levy, George. *To Die in Chicago: Confederate Prisoners at Camp Douglas, 1862–65.* Evanston, IL: Evanston, 1999.

Lindberg, Richard. *Chicago by Gaslight: A History of Chicago's Netherworld, 1880–1920.* Chicago: Academy Chicago, 1996.

———. *Chicago Ragtime: Another Look at Chicago, 1880–1920.* South Bend, IN: Icarus Press, 1985.

———. "The Evolution of an Evil Business." *Chicago History* 22 (1993): 38–53.

———. *Gambler King of Clark Street: Michael C. McDonald and the Rise of Chicago's Democratic Machine.* Carbondale: Southern Illinois Univ. Press, 2009.

———. *Gangland Chicago: Criminality and Lawlessness in the Windy City.* Lanham: MD: Rowman & Littlefield, 2016.

———. *To Serve and Collect: Chicago Politics and Police Corruption from the Lager Beer Riot to the Summerdale Scandal.* New York: Praeger, 1991.

Linder, Marc, and Lawrence S. Zacharias. *Of Cabbages and Kings County: Agriculture and the Formation of Modern Brooklyn.* Iowa City: Univ. of Iowa Press, 1999.

Lineham, Mary. "Vice Commissions." In *EC,* 854.

Link, Arthur S., and Richard L. McCormick. *Progressivism.* Wheeling, IL: Harlan Davidson, 1983.

Logan, Gabe. "Soccer." In *EC,* 760–61.

Lombardo, Robert M. *Organized Crime in Chicago: Beyond the Mafia*. Urbana: Univ. of Illinois Press, 2013.

Longrigg, Roger. *The History of Horse Racing*. New York: Stein and Day, 1972.

Longstreet, Steven. *Chicago, 1860–1919*. New York: McKay, 1973.

Lovell, Odd. *A Century of Urban Life: The Norwegians in Chicago before 1930*. Northfield, MN: Norwegian-American Historical Society, 1988.

Lowe, David. *Lost Chicago*. Chicago: Univ. of Chicago Press, 2010.

Lurie, Jonathan. *The Chicago Board of Trade, 1859–1905: The Dynamics of Self-Regulation*. Urbana: Univ. of Illinois Press, 1979.

Mahoney, Olivia. *Douglas/Grand Boulevard: A Chicago Neighborhood*. Charleston, SC: Arcadia, 2001.

Mallon, Bill. *The 1904 Olympic Games Results for All Competitors in All Events, with Commentary*. Jefferson, NC: McFarland, 1999.

Martel, Marcel. *Canada the Good: A Short History of Vice since 1500*. Waterloo: Wilfred Laurier Univ. Press, 2014.

Martin, Kevin. "Racetrack Plunger Riley Grannan, 1869–1908." *Colin's Ghost: Thoroughbred Racing History*. http://colinsghost.org/2009/06/race track-plunger-riley-grannan-1869.html.

"Martin B. Madden." In *Biographical Dictionary of the United States Congress, 1774–Present*. https://bioguideretro.congress.gov/Home/Member Details?memIndex=M000038.

Maurer, David W. *The Big Con: The Story of the Confidence Man*. Indianapolis: Bobbs-Merrill, 1940.

Mayer, Harold M., and Richard Wade. *Chicago: Making of a Metropolis*. Chicago: Univ. of Chicago Press, 1973.

McDaniels, Pellom, III. *Prince of Jockeys: The Life of Isaac Burns Murphy*. Lexington: Univ. Press of Kentucky, 2013.

McGerr, Michael E. *A Fierce Discontent: The Rise and Fall of the Progressive Movement in America, 1870–1920*. New York: Free Press, 2003.

McGirr, Lisa. *The War on Alcohol: Prohibition and the Rise of the American State*. New York: W. W. Norton, 2015.

McKibbin, Ross. "Working-Class Gambling in Britain, 1880–1939." *Past and Present* 82 (Feb. 1979): 147–78.

McReynolds, Louise. *Russia at Play: Leisure Activities at the End of the Tsarist Era*. Ithaca, NY: Cornell Univ. Press, 2003.

McSeveney, Samuel T. *The Politics of Depression: Political Behavior in the Northeast, 1893–1896*. New York: Oxford Univ. Press, 1972.

Metcalfe, Alan. *Canada Learns to Play: The Emergence of Organized Sport, 1887–1914.* Toronto: McClellan and Stewart, 1987.

Meyer, Jeff. "Henry Clay's Legacy to Horse Breeding and Racing." *Register of the Kentucky Historical Society* 100 (Autumn 2002): 473–96.

Mikkelsen, Glen. "The Sport of Kings in Victorian Canada." *Beaver* 76 (Aug.–Sept. 1996): 18–21.

Miller, Donald L. *City of the Century: The Epic of Chicago and the Making of America.* New York: Simon & Schuster, 1996.

Mitrani, Sam. *The Rise of the Chicago Police Department: Class and Conflict, 1850–1894.* Urbana: Univ. of Illinois Press, 2013.

Mooney, Katherine C. *Race Horse Men: How Slavery and Freedom Were Made at the Racetrack.* Cambridge, MA: Harvard Univ. Press, 2014.

Morrow, Don, and Kevin B. Wamsley. *Sport in Canada: A History.* Don Mills, ON: Oxford Univ. Press, 2005.

Morton, Richard A. "Edward F. Dunne, Illinois' Most Progressive Governor." *Illinois Historical Journal* 83 (Winter 1990): 218–34.

———. *Justice and Humanity: Edward F. Dunne, Illinois Progressive.* Carbondale: Southern Illinois Univ., 1999.

———. *Roger C. Sullivan and the Making of the Chicago Democratic Machine, 1881–1908.* Jefferson, NC: McFarland, 2016.

Morton, Suzanne. *At Odds: Gambling and Canadians, 1919–1969.* Toronto: Univ. of Toronto Press, 2003.

Muccigrosso, Ivan. *Celebrating the New World: Chicago's Columbian Exposition of 1893.* Chicago: I. R. Dee, 1993.

Munsell, F. Darrell. *From Redstone to Ludlow: John Cleveland Osgood's Struggle against the United Mine Workers of America.* Boulder: Univ. of Colorado Press, 2009.

Munting, Roger. *An Economic and Social History of Gambling in Britain and the USA.* Manchester: Manchester Univ. Press, 1996.

Nathan, Daniel. *Saying It's So: A Cultural History of the Black Sox Scandal.* Urbana: Univ. of Illinois Press, 2003.

Nicholson, James C. *The Kentucky Derby: How the Run for the Roses Became America's Premier Sporting Event.* Lexington: Univ. Press of Kentucky, 2012.

———. *The Notorious John Morrissey: How a Bare-Knuckle Brawler Became a Congressman and Founded Saratoga Race Course.* Lexington: Univ. Press of Kentucky, 2016.

Oberholtzer, Ellis Paxson. *Philadelphia, a History of the City and Its People: A Record of 225 Years*. Philadelphia: S. H. Clark, 1912.

O'Brien, Gillian. *Blood Runs Green: The Murder That Transfixed Gilded Age Chicago*. Chicago: Univ. of Chicago Press, 2015.

Ogden, Christopher. *Legacy: A Biography of Moses and Walter Annenberg*. Boston: Little, Brown, 1999.

O'Hara, John. *A Mug's Game: A History of Gaming and Betting in Australia*. Kensington, NSW: New South Wales Univ. Press, 1988.

O'Hare, John Richard. *The Socio-economic Aspects of Horse Racing*. Washington, DC: Catholic Univ. of America Press, 1945.

Otis, Lara. "Washington's Lost Racetracks: Horse Racing from the 1760s to the 1930s." *Washington History* 24 (2012): 137–54.

Otis, Stephen Frank. "Gambling on Horse Races." JD diss., Univ. of California, Berkeley, 1910.

Ownby, Ted. *Subduing Satan: Religion, Recreation & Manhood in the Rural South, 1865–1920*. Chapel Hill: Univ. of North Carolina Press, 1990.

Ozanian, Michael K. "Selective Accounting." *Forbes*, Dec. 14, 1998, 124–32.

Pacyga, Dominic A. *Chicago: A Biography*. Chicago: Univ. of Chicago Press, 2009.

Parmer, Charles B. *For Gold and Glory: The Story of Thoroughbred Racing in America*. New York: Carrick and Evans, 1938.

Parmet, Robert D., and Francis L. Lederer. "Competition for the World's Columbian Exposition: The New York Campaign and the Chicago Campaign." *Journal of the Illinois State Historical Society* 65 (Dec. 1972): 364–94.

Petersen, Jacqueline. "The Absorption of French-Indian Chicago." In *Ethnic Chicago: A Multi-cultural Portrait*, edited by Melvin Holli and Peter D. Jones, 25–42. 4th ed. Grand Rapids, MI: Erdman's, 1994.

Pierce, Bessie Louis. *A History of Chicago*. 3 vols. Chicago: Univ. of Chicago Press, 1937–57.

Piott, Steven L. *Holy Joe: Joseph W. Folk and the Missouri Idea*. Columbia, MO: Univ. of Missouri Press, 1997.

Rasmussen, Chris. *Carnival in the Countryside: The History of the Iowa State Fair*. Iowa City: Univ. of Iowa Press, 2105.

Raum, Green B. *History of Illinois Republicanism*. Chicago: Rollins, 1900.

Reiff, Janice L. "Chicago's Social Geography." In *Encyclopedia of Chicago*. http://www.encyclopedia.chicagohistory.org/pages/11409_em.html.

Remini, Robert. *The Life of Andrew Jackson*. New York: Perennial Classics, 2001.

Riess, Steven A. "The Business of Baseball, 1920–1956." In *Baseball in America & America in Baseball*, edited by Don Kyle and Robert Fairbanks, 88–142. College Station: Texas A&M Univ. Press, 2008.

———. *City Games: The Evolution of American Urban Society and the Rise of Sports*. Urbana: Univ. of Illinois Press, 1989.

———. "The Cyclical History of Horse Racing: The USA's Oldest and (Sometimes) Most Popular Spectator Sport." In *American National Pastimes: A History*, edited by Mark Dyreson and Jaime Schultz, 29–54. New York: Routledge, 2014.

———. "The Demise of Horse Racing and Boxing in Chicago in 1905." In *Sports in Chicago*, edited by Elliot J. Gorn, 43–61. Urbana: Univ. of Illinois Press, 2008.

———. "Horse Racing in Chicago, 1883–1894: The Interplay of Class, Politics, and Organized Crime." In *The Chicago Sports Reader: 100 Years of Sport in the Windy City*, edited by Steven A. Riess and Gerald Gems, 1–57. Urbana: Univ. of Illinois Press, 2009.

———. "In the Ring and Out: Boxing in New York, 1870–1920." In *New Perspectives on Sport History*, edited by David Spivey, 95–128. Westport, CT: Greenwood Press, 1983.

———. "Introduction: The History of Sports in Chicago." In *The Chicago Sports Reader: 100 Years of Sports in the Windy City*, edited by Steven A. Riess and Gerald Gems, 60–80. Urbana: Univ. of Illinois Press, 2009.

———. "Leisure." In *EC*, 467–75.

———. *The Sport of Kings and the Kings of Crime: Horse Racing, Politics, and Organized Crime in New York, 1865–1913*. Syracuse, NY: Syracuse Univ. Press, 2011.

———. "Sports and Machine Politics in New York City, 1890–1920." In *The Making of Urban America*, edited by Raymond A. Mohl, 99–121. Wilmington, DE: Scholarly Resources, 1988.

———. *Touching Base: Professional Baseball and American Culture in the Progressive Era*. 2nd ed. Urbana: Univ. of Illinois Press, 1999.

Rinker, Kimberly. *Chicago's Horse Racing Venues*. Charleston, SC: Arcadia, 2009.

Roberts, Paul, Isabelle Taylor, and Laurence Weatherly. "Looking Back: The Lost Tracks of the San Francisco Bay Area." *Thoroughbred Racing*

Commentary, Feb. 15, 2015. https://www.thoroughbredracing.com/articles
/looking-back-lost-tracks-san-francisco-bay-area.

Roberts, Sidney I. "The Municipal Voters' League and Chicago's Boodlers."
Journal of the Illinois State Historical Society 53 (Summer 1960): 117–40.

Robertson, William H. P. *History of Thoroughbred Racing*. Englewood Cliffs,
NJ: Prentice Hall, 1965.

Rosen, Ruth. *The Lost Sisterhood: Prostitution in America, 1900–1918*. Baltimore: Johns Hopkins Univ., 1982.

Rosentraub, Mark S. *Major League Winners: Using Sports and Cultural Centers
as Tools for Economic Development*. Boca Raton: CRC Press, 2010.

Roth, Mitchell P., and James Olson, eds. *Historical Dictionary of Law Enforcement*. Westport, CT: Greenwood Press, 2001.

Ryscavage, Paul. *Norman B. Ream: Forgotten Master of Markets*. Madison, NJ:
Fairleigh Dickinson Univ. Press, 2013.

Sammons, Jeffrey. *Beyond the Ring: The Role of Boxing in American Society*.
Urbana: Univ. of Illinois Press, 1990.

Saul, Norman E. *The Life and Times of Charles R. Crane, 1858–1939: American
Businessman, Philanthropist, and a Founder of Russian Studies in America*.
Lanham, MD: Lexington, 2013.

Schulman, Vanessa Meikle. "'Making the Magazine': Visuality, Managerial
Capitalism, and the Mass Production of Periodicals, 1865–1890." *American Periodicals* 22 (Mar. 1, 2012): 9–23.

Schults, Raymond L. *Crusader in Babylon: W. T. Stead and the Pall Mall Gazette*. Lincoln: Univ. of Nebraska Press, 1972.

Sennett, Richard. *Families against the City: Middle Class Homes of Industrial
Chicago, 1872–1890*. Cambridge, MA: Harvard Univ. Press, 1970.

Seymour, Harold. *Baseball: The Early Years*. New York: Oxford Univ. Press,
1960.

Smith, Alson J. *Syndicate City: The Chicago Crime Cartel and What to Do about
It*. Chicago: Henry Regnery, 1954.

Smith, Gary Scott. *The Search for Social Salvation: Social Christianity and
America, 1880–1925*. Lanham, MD: Lexington Books, 2000.

Smith, George D. "Gambling in Illinois." *Illinois Law Review* 16 (1921–22):
23–45.

Somers, Dale. *The Rise of Sports in New Orleans, 1850–1900*. Baton Rouge:
Louisiana State Univ. Press, 1972.

Sparks, Randy J. "Gentleman's Sport: Horse Racing in Antebellum Charleston." *South Carolina Historical Magazine* 93 (Jan. 1992): 15–30.

"St. Edward of Lexington." *Time*, May 7, 1934, 64–68.

Stoltzfus, Daniel C. S. *Freedom from Advertising: E. W. Scripp's Experiment.* Urbana: Univ. of Illinois Press, 2007.

Struna, Nancy. "The North-South Races: American Thoroughbred Racing in Transition, 1823–1850." *Journal of Sport History* 8 (Summer 1981): 28–57.

Sullivan, George E. *Harness Racing.* New York: Fleet, 1964.

Suttle, Danael. "Horse Racing during the Civil War: The Perseverance of the Sport during a Time of National Crisis." Master's thesis, Univ. of Arkansas, 2019.

Szuberla, Guy. "Review: A City Comes of Age: Chicago in the 1890s." *Journal of American History* 79 (Dec. 1992): 1097–1102.

Tarr, Joel. "J. R. Walsh of Chicago: A Case Study in Banking and Politics, 1881–1905." *Business History Review* 40 (Winter 1966): 451–66.

Taylor, Charles H. *History of the Board of Trade of the City of Chicago.* Chicago: R. O. Law, 1917.

Thale, Christopher. "Gambling." In *EC*, 323–24.

Thomas, Lately. *A Debonair Scoundrel: The Flamboyant Story of Abe Ruef and San Francisco's Infamous Era of Graft.* New York: Holt, Reinhart, and Winston, 1962.

Thorn, John, et al., eds. *Total Baseball: The Official Encyclopedia of Major League Baseball.* 6th ed. New York: Total Sports, 1990.

Tyre, William H. *Chicago's Historic Prairie Avenue.* Charleston, SC: Arcadia, 2008.

Vamplew, Wray. *The Turf: A Social History of Horse Racing.* London: Allen Lane, 1976.

Vincent, Ted. *The Rise and Fall of American Sport: Mudville's Revenge.* Lincoln: Univ. of Nebraska Press, 1994.

Vosburgh, W. S. *Racing in America, 1866–1921.* New York: Jockey Club, 1922.

Wade, Louise Carroll. *Chicago's Pride: The Stockyards, Packingtown, and Environs in the Nineteenth Century.* Urbana: Univ. of Illinois Press, 1987.

———. "Meatpacking." In *EC*, 516–17.

Wahl, Robert, and Arnold Spencer Wahl. "William C. Seipp." *American Brewers' Review* 26 (Apr. 1, 1912): 170.

Wall, Maryjean. *How Kentucky Became Southern: A Tale of Outlaws, Horse Thieves, Gamblers and Breeders.* Lexington: Univ. Press of Kentucky, 2010.

Waters, Greg. "'Operating on the Border': A History of the Commercial Promotion, Moral Suppression, and State Regulation of the Thoroughbred Racing Industry in Windsor, Ontario, 1884 to 1936." Master's thesis, Univ. of Windsor, 1982.

Weeks, Lyman Horace. *The American Turf: An Historical Account of Racing in the United States, with Biographical Sketches of Turf Celebrities.* New York: Historical, 1998.

Wendt, Lloyd, and Herman Kogan. *Bet-a-Million! The Story of John W. Gates.* New York: Bobbs-Merrill, 1948.

———. *Lords of the Levee: The Story of Bathhouse John and Hinky Dink.* Indianapolis: Bobbs-Merrill, 1943.

Werbel, Amy. *Lust on Trial: Censorship and the Rise of American Obscenity in the Age of Anthony Comstock.* New York: Columbia Univ. Press, 2018.

West, Elliott. *The Saloon on the Rocky Mountain Frontier.* Lincoln: Univ. of Nebraska Press, 1979.

West, J. Thomas. "Thoroughbred Racing." In *The Canadian Encyclopedia.* https://www.thecanadianencyclopedia.ca/en/article/thoroughbred-racing.

Whyte, James Christie. *History of the British Turf from the Earliest Period to the Present Day.* London: H Colburn, 1840.

Wiggins, David K. *Glory Bound: Black Athletes in a White America.* Syracuse, NY: Syracuse Univ. Press, 1997.

———, ed. *Out of the Shadows: A Biographical History of African American Athletes.* Fayetteville: Univ. of Arkansas Press, 2006.

Wills, Ridley I. "The Eclipse of the Thoroughbred Industry in Tennessee." *Tennessee Historical Quarterly* 46 (1987): 157–71.

Wilson, Dall. *Alice Nielsen and the Gayety of Nations: Standing Room Only.* Raleigh, NC: n.p., 2010.

Wunsch, James. "Protecting St. Louis Neighborhoods from the Encroachment of Brothels, 1870–1920." *Missouri Historical Review* 104 (July 2010): 198–212.

Index

Gravesend Racetrack, 79, 117, 149, 156, 164

Great Britain, and racing, 2, 3, 6, 9, 30, 234, 259–60, 318; *cf.* American racing, 174–77, 192, 257, 260, 318; 1906 Street Betting Act, 176–77; oral betting, 186; Strathrose dispute, 146

Grey Wolves, 104, 190, 196. *See also* Coughlin, "Bathhouse" John; Kenna, Mike "Hinky Dink"; Powers, Johnny

Gurnee, Walter S., 9

Hackenschmidt, George, 221

Haggin, James Ali Ben, 77

Haller, Mark, xiii, 17–18, 282, 291

Hamilton, Anthony, 81, 139

Hammond, Thomas, 131

Hammond (IN), 130–31, 273. *See also* Roby Racetrack

handbooks, xvi, xvii, xix, 89, 92, 117, 102, 243, 245, 249–50, 267–68, 305, 310, 311, 320; definition, 92; and Carter Harrison II, 244–45, 287–89, 294; as neighborhood services, 88, 89, 310; and raids, 244–45, 254, 278, 280, 283–84, 287, 291; and telephony, 289–90, 298; and Mont Tennes, 266, 284–86, 303, 309, 312. *See also* bookies; bookmaking; offtrack gambling

Hankins, Al, 40, 98, 100, 119

Hankins, George, 37, 38, 95, 183, 197, 271; and Garfield Park, 104, 112, 126, 142; and Mike McDonald, 90–91, 93, 198; and stable, 129, 143, 187, 271

Hankins, Jeff, 37

Harlan, John Maynard, 196–97, 254, 299

Harlem Jockey Club, 186, 188

Harlem Racetrack, 49, 103, 165–67, 202, 271–72; attendance, 200, 201, 205, 211, 213, 226; and finances 202, 271–72. *See also* Condon, "Blind John"

harness racing, xv, 1–2, 4–11, 13–16, 18–38, 44–45, 47–49, 73, 216, 313–14; and Washington Park Racetrack, 80, 85–86, 150, 182, 193. *See also* Bonner, Robert; Dexter; Trussell, George

Harper's Weekly, 83, 191–92

Harrison, Carter H., I: inaction against gambling, 68–69, 75–76, 91, 100; as mayor, 33, 39, 40, 69, 140–42, 147, 152; and Mike McDonald, 39–41, 109, 119–20, 125; and Sunday racing, 62; and wife at track, 56

Harrison, Carter H., II: as mayor, 197, 279–80; mayoral candidate, 196–97, 221, 273; opposition to boxing, 241; opposition to gambling, xix, 216, 224, 244–46, 249, 264; opposition to poolrooms, 287–88; as racing fan, 68–69; support for racing, 199–200

Haverley, J. H. "Jack," 27, 31, 335n69

Hawthorne Racetrack, 49, 64, 99–102, 129–30, 178; attendance, 110, 129–30, and American Turf Congress, 154–56; and business, 133–34; fight with Garfield Park, 110–11; and Carter Harrison I, 140–42; rivalry with Washington Park Racetrack, 149–50; serving warrants, 168. *See also* Corrigan, Edward

300–301, 305. *See also* Coughlin, "Bathhouse" John

Kentucky Derby, 38, 63, 80–81, 84, 109, 225, 306

Ketchum, William A., 191, 215

Kettering, Albert J., 211–12

Kilcourse, Leonard, 184, 195

Kipley, Joseph, 197–98, 206, 224–25, 278, 280

Kimball, C. F., 64

Lady Suffolk, 9

Lakeside Jockey Club, 227–28, 233, 235–38, 251, 254–56, 261, 264. *See also* Indiana horse racing

Lawrence, Harry, 2, 23, 27, 34

Lindberg, Richard, 39, 108

Lindsay, William L., 263

lower class, xiv–xv, 39, 53, 59, 71, 87, 89, 176, 221–23, 310; and moral reform, 71, 75, 88, 223. *See also* working class

Lynch, Daniel, J., 238–29

Madden, Martin B., 153

Madison County Fair and Racing Association, 118

Madison Turf Association, 118; and attendance 118, 167

Mann, James R., 258, 302–3

Martin, Morris, 22, 23

Martin, William, 165, 199

Martyn, Carlos, 159, 161, 169

Mathews, Claude, 184, 191

McClaughry, Robert W., 101, 122, 124–26, 142

McDonald, Mike, 13, 26, 34–35, 43–44; and Cregier, 90–91, 93–94,

99; crime boss, xvi, xvii, 18; and Garfield Park Racetrack, 104, 108–9, 112, 120, 123, 125–29; and politics, 38–42, 86, 91–94, 99, 118, 140–42, 198; and sport, 38–41; and the Store, 34, 36, 43, 136, 197; and the syndicate, 188, 279, 312, 336. *See also* Hankins, George; Harrison, Carter H., I

McGarigle, William, 39

McGinnis, Tom, 106, 246, 278–80, 284, 304, 309

McGovern, Terry, 240

McGrath, Price, 29

McHie, Sid, 76, 101, 104, 187

McKeaver, William, 1, 2

McWeeney, John, 309–10

middle class, 6, 51, apparel, 235; and baseball, 59; in Canada, 260; in Chicago, xiv, 87–88; fans, 77, 89–90, 175–76, 232; and female bettors, 276–77; and harness racing, xv; opposition to racing, 89; opposition to Sunday racing, 60. *See also* moral reformers

Miller, H. H., 260–61

Milwaukee racing, 187–88, 211–12, 272

Monmouth Park Racetrack (NJ), 83, 133–34, 158, 174

moral reformers: and gambling, 39, 106–7, 122–23, 139–40, 222–23, 257–58, 268–69, 319–20; and middle class, 246

Morris Park Racetrack (NY), 115, 133–34, 164, 165, 174, 181, 223

Municipal Voters League, 196

Murphy, Isaac, 57, 58, 65, 78, 80–81

Murphy, Tim, 306–7

Myrick, Willard F., 7, 8, 11, 14

Steven A. Riess taught the history of American sport for thirty-seven years and retired as the Bernard Brommel Distinguished Research Professor in the Department of History at Northeastern Illinois University, Chicago, after thirty-five years. He attended New York University and the University of Chicago, where he received his PhD. He wrote four monographs and edited nine books that received four citations from *Choice* for "Outstanding Academic Book." Steve received the 2015 NASSH Prize for Best Anthology for *American Sport History* (2014), and his *The Sport of Kings and the Kings of Crime: Horse Racing, Politics, and Organized Crime in New York, 1865–1913* (Syracuse University Press, 2011; audio version, 2020) was runner-up for the Best Book of Adult Nonfiction, the Society of Midland Authors. Four of his journal articles were identified as essays of the year. His scholarship has been supported by several grants from the National Endowment for the Humanities, including a Fellowship for College Teachers, and he codirected an NEH summer seminar on sport for college teachers. Steve edited the Syracuse University Press series Sport and Entertainment for twenty-five years and was the editor of the *Journal of Sport History* for eight years, consulting editor for *Encyclopedia of Chicago* (2004), and associate editor of *National American Biography* (1999).